```
void PaintRoundRect(Rect *r; int
    ovalWidth,ovalHeight);
void EraseRoundRect(Rect *r; int
    ovalWidth,ovalHeight);
void InvertRoundRect(Rect *r; int
    ovalWidth,ovalHeight);
void FillRoundRect(Rect *r; int
    ovalWidth,ovalHeight; Pattern *pat);
```

Graphic Operations on Arcs and Wedges

```
void FrameArc(Rect *r; int
    startAngle,arcAngle);
void PaintArc(Rect *r; int
    startAngle,arcAngle);
void EraseArc(Rect *r; int
    startAngle,arcAngle);
void InvertArc(Rect *r; int
    startAngle,arcAngle);
void FillArc(Rect *r; int
    startAngle,arcAngle; Pattern *pat);
```

Calculations with Regions

```
RgnHandle NewRgn();
void OpenRgn();
void CloseRgn(RgnHandle dstRgn);
void DisposeRgn(RgnHandle rgn);
void CopyRgn(RgnHandle srcRgn,dstRgn);
void SetEmptyRgn(RgnHandle rgn);
void SetRectRgn(RgnHandle rgn; int
    left,top,right,bottom);
void RectRgn(RgnHandle rgn; Rect *r);
void OffsetRgn(RgnHandle rgn; int dv,dh);
void InsetRgn(RgnHandle rgn; int dv,dh);
void SectRgn(RgnHandle
    srcRgnA,srcRgnB,dstRgn);
void UnionRgn(RgnHandle
    srcRgnA,srcRgnB,dstRgn);
void DiffRgn(RgnHandle
    srcRgnA,srcRgnB,dstRgn);
void XorRgn(RgnHandle srcRgnA,srcRgnB,dstRgn);
char PtInRgn(Point pt; RgnHandle rgn);
char EqualRgn(RgnHandle rgnA,rgnB);
char EqaualRgn(RgnHandle rgnA,rgnB);
char EmptyRgn(RgnHandle rgn);
```

Graphic Operations on Regions

```
void FrameRgn(RgnHandle rgn);
void PaintRgn(RgnHandle rgn);
void EraseRgn(RgnHandle rgn);
void InvertRgn(RgnHandle rgn);
void FillRgn(RgnHandle rgn; Pattern *pat);
```

Bit Trans

```
void S
    u
void Co
    *srcRect,*dstRect; int mode; RgnHandle
    maskRgn);
```

Pictures

```
PicHandle OpenPicture(Rect *picFrame);
void PicComment(int kind,dataSize; Handle
    dataHandle);
void ClosePicture();
void DrawPicture(PicHandle myPicture; Rect
    *dstRect);
void KillPicture(PicHandle myPicture);
```

Calculations with Polygons

```
PolyHandle OpenPoly();
void ClosePoly();
void KillPoly(PolyHandle poly);
void OffsetPoly(PolyHandle poly; int dv,dh);
```

Graphic Operations on Polygons

```
void FramePoly(PolyHandle poly);
void PaintPoly(PolyHandle poly);
void ErasePoly(PolyHandle poly);
void InvertPoly(PolyHandle poly);
void FillPoly(PolyHandle poly; Pattern *pat);
```

Calculations with Points

```
void AddPt(Point srcPt,*dstPt);
void SubPt(Point srcPt,*dstPt);
void SetPt(Point *pt; int h,v);
char EqualPt(Point pt1,pt2);
void LocalToGlobal(Point *pt);
void GlobalToLocal(Point *pt);
```

Miscellaneous Routines

```
int Random();
char GetPixel(int h,v);
void StuffHex(Ptr thingPtr;Str255 *s);
void ScalePt(Point *pt; Rect
    *srcRect,*dstRect);
void MapPt(Point *pt;Rect *srcRect,*dstRect);
void MapRect(Rect *r,*srcRect,*dstRect);
void MapRgn(RgnHandle rgn; Rect
    *srcRect,*dstRect);
void MapPoly(PolyHandle poly; Rect
    *srcRect,*dstRect);
```

USING THE
MACINTOSH
TOOLBOX WITH C

Using the
Macintosh®
Toolbox with C

Second Edition

Fred A. Huxham
David Burnard
Jim Takatsuka

 SYBEX® SAN FRANCISCO · PARIS · DÜSSELDORF · LONDON

Acquisitions Editor: Dianne King
Supervising Editor: Joanne Cuthbertson
Copy Editor: Gina Jaber
Editor (First Edition): Geta Carlson
Technical Editor: Dan Tauber
Word Processors: Scott Campbell and Chris Mockel
Book Designer & Chapter Art: Suzanne Albertson
Technical Illustrations: Jeff Giese
Screen Graphics: Sonja Schenk
Typesetters: Charles Cowens and Suzanne Albertson
Proofreader: Vanessa Miller
Indexer: Paul Geisert
Cover Designer: Thomas Ingalls + Associates
Cover Photographer: Michael Lamotte

Macintosh is a trademark licensed to Apple Computer, Inc.

MC68000 is a trademark of Motorola, Inc.

Apple, Switcher, Resource Compiler, Resource Editor, QuickDraw, Finder, Inside Macintosh, and Lisa are trademarks of Apple Computer, Inc.

Mac C is a trademark of Consulair Corporation.

MacDraw and MacPaint are trademarks of Apple Computer, Inc.

MacWrite is a trademark of Encore Systems and Apple Computer, Inc.

Think C is a trademark of Symantec Corp.

Word and Excel are trademarks of Microsoft Corp.

Jazz is a trademark of Lotus Development Corp.

MacDraft is a trademark of Leonard G. Barton.

Fedit is a trademark of John Mitchell.

SetFile 2.0 and BaseTool Desk Accessories © 1985 Fred, Sam, and Dave Software.

SYBEX is a registered trademark of SYBEX, Inc.

SYBEX is not affiliated with any manufacturer.

Every effort has been made to supply complete and accurate information. However, SYBEX assumes no responsibility for its use, nor for any infringements of patents or other rights of third parties which would result.

First Edition copyright 1986 SYBEX Inc.

Library of Congress Card Number: 89-62280
ISBN: 0-89588-572-7
Manufactured in the United States of America
10 9 8 7 6 5 4 3 2 1

To our parents:

Fred and Marjorie Huxham
Carl and Dorsey Burnard
Walter and Gail Takatsuka

Acknowledgments

Writing this book was quite an experience for the three of us and there were a lot of people who helped us through. We'd like to thank William Adams, Reese Jones, Raines Cohen, Nicole Kowalski, Don Yost, and Steve Costa for their encouragement and support throughout the course of this project. We'd also like to thank everyone who showed up at the BMUG Developers Group meetings at UC Berkeley and at our classes at Lawrence Livermore National Laboratories for keeping us on our toes by proving that even the simplest of examples can be laden with bugs.

World-famous desk accessory author Sam Roberts of Fred, Sam, and Dave Software proved to be a lot of help (and great fun) in the realization of this book. Our C guru, Peter Moore, made some valuable contributions in proofreading a lot of the example routines and sample source code. Steve Capps and Larry Kenyon provided technical assistance on some of the more esoteric workings of the file system, for which we are very grateful.

Finally, JT would like to extend a special "mahalo" to Rick Iwamoto and Robert Antonio for doing a terrific job holding down the fort while he was writing. FH also would like to thank Jennifer Iscol for being his best friend throughout the ups and downs of the book. Without all of these people, this book would never have made it out in any reasonable period of time. Once again, we would like to thank them all very much.

Fred, Dave, and Jim

Contents
at a Glance

Table
of Contents

Introduction

Using the Macintosh Toolbox with C is the first book written especially for C programmers on the Macintosh. While there have been implementations of C for the Macintosh for several years now, it is only recently that they have really caught up with the Pascal development environments which were originally created for the Mac. The latest generation of C compilers, and in particular Think C, the package which this book is based upon, are professional quality compilers which can produce complex applications every bit as good as those written under the Pascal Workshop system originally designed for Mac developers.

The difficulty in using C which is experienced by many programmers new to the Macintosh is that the Mac's extensive Toolbox was written expressly to be used with Pascal. There are many subtle differences in the ways that C and Pascal work, and these complicate the interface between a C language program and the Mac's firmware. More than this, though, the documentation for the Toolbox, the voluminous *Inside Macintosh* books, explains the Toolbox in Pascal terms. One must be quite familiar with Pascal in order to use *Inside Macintosh* to program the Mac in C.

In addition, *Inside Macintosh* is huge, running to five volumes as of this writing, and quite expensive. It's more of a reference book than a tutorial. It doesn't lend itself to simply sitting down and cranking out an application.

Programmers wishing to learn C on the Macintosh will probably be frustrated by a lack of sample source code, even though C has been extant on the Mac for several years now. There is little of it around, and what there is tends to be very specific and exotic. As with most programs released into the public domain, the source code one finds is rarely commented as well as it might be, making it less than ideal as a learning tool. Furthermore, each of the various C compilers released for the Mac have implemented the language a bit differently. Source code written for, say, Aztec C will probably present you with some subtle lexical twists if you try to use it with Think C.

Having faced all of these problems ourselves, *Using the Macintosh Toolbox with C* was created to help you learn the essentials of

Macintosh programming without bogging you down with too much information. Each chapter in this book explains the implementation of a fundamental element of the Macintosh user interface, including all the important data structures and how to use the Toolbox routines related to that aspect of the interface. Numerous examples of the Toolbox routines are provided throughout each of the chapters, as well as source code for several applications.

This book will not replace *Inside Macintosh*. You will probably eventually want to buy a copy of it. There are all sorts of subjects which are simply not within the scope of this book, and you may want to know about them one day. However, *Using the Macintosh Toolbox with C* will tell you everything you need to know about writing basic, workable Macintosh applications in much less time than it would have taken you to puzzle through *Inside Macintosh* to learn the same things.

Contemporary Mac programmers may take heart in knowing that *Inside Macintosh* is now available in relatively low cost paper bound volumes. The original books came only in a prohibitively expensive hard bound edition.

How to Use This Book

Using the Macintosh Toolbox with C is designed to be a Macintosh programmer's guide. Its chapters are meant to be read in sequence, with each chapter building upon what was previously discussed. By the time you reach the end, you will have learned all the fundamentals of programming the Macintosh user interface. The sample programs included in this book also provide a good reference to use when you begin creating your own applications.

Unlike other computers, the Macintosh does not lend itself to compiling fragments of code to see what they do. A Mac program must be a complete application which, as you'll see while you work your way through the book, is quite an elaborate thing. As such, you can't just type in the example functions and compile them though you can type in the complete applications.

Conventions Used in This Book

All the programming examples in this book are written in Think C for the Macintosh, which is a product of Symantec. They will work on most C compilers for the Macintosh, but you should be aware that no two Macintosh C implementations are exactly the same. As the developers of C compilers for the Mac have grown more proficient at optimizing their products, the divergences between the various languages have grown more noticeable.

If you are familiar with C these differences should not be too difficult to work around. If you are new both to C and to the Macintosh, we strongly recommend that you start with Think C. It's bad enough trying to find your own programming bugs; you'll find learning C a great deal easier if you're not trying to isolate compiler problems at the same time.

Throughout the book, all Macintosh Toolbox functions will be printed in boldface and in a special **program font**. This same program font, minus the boldface, will be used in all examples and sample programs, as well as for various names associated with the Toolbox. That way, anything associated with programming will clearly stand out from the rest of the text. Finally, any special terms related to the Macintosh or its user interface will be printed in *italics*.

The Macintosh Toolbox and C

As we noted previously, the Macintosh Toolbox was originally intended to be used with programs written in Pascal or in native 68000 assembly language cooked up to look like Pascal. In order to successfully write C programs in this Pascal environment, it's necessary to become more than usually familiar with the subtle distinctions between these two languages. While it's not normally essential to understand how C passes arguments to a function, for example, just to be able to program in C, having this sort of "inside information" is very helpful when using C on the Macintosh.

Before we begin our discussion of how to write an application with the Macintosh Toolbox, we must briefly cover a few important points concerning the relationship between the Toolbox and C. The first point concerns the various simple data types which C will be using and, as such, passing to the Toolbox.

The second point is that the Toolbox is very much enamored of complex data types. If you are familiar with C, you will know that under C these are called "structs". Think C defines well over a hundred specialized structs as unique Macintosh data types. An important part of mastering the use of the Toolbox, then, is in understanding how to use these data types effectively.

The third point is that Pascal is a slightly more obliging language than C tends to be, and it takes care of a lot more of the low level things that languages do. There are drawbacks to this, too, which will become clear as you proceed through this book. What is important, however, is that a C programmer must take great care in using the appropriate data types and using them correctly.

The Simple Data Types used by the Toolbox and C

Experienced users of C will be familiar with its basic data types and will probably think of them in certain fixed ways. For example, an int is usually thought of as having 16 bits.

In fact, the abstract definition of C, Kernighan and Ritchie's *The C Programming Language*, does not specify the sizes of data types. They are allowed to be whatever is natural for the environment the language is implemented for. In this case, it is convenient for the creators of Macintosh C compilers to use the same conventions as does Macintosh Pascal wherever possible, to allow for the least amount of data type conversion when a C program goes to call the Toolbox.

The basic data types for Macintosh Pascal as they relate to the Toolbox are shown in Figure I.1. Figure I.2 shows the simple data types for C and their sizes. These values are specific to Think C. For example, some Macintosh C compilers use 32 bit ints. This can cause trouble in using source code written for a different C compiler if the author of the program counted on having 32 bit ints and the compiler you're using only supports 16 bit ints.

The Think C data sizes are much the same as the data sizes used in IBM PC based C compilers, which does make porting PC code to the Macintosh a great deal easier. Note that a long integer and a pointer to a long integer are the same size. This will return to haunt you again and again.

Type	Name	Storage Size
character	CHAR	1 byte†
flag	BOOLEAN	1 byte†
integer	INTEGER	2 bytes
long integer	LongInt	4 bytes
pointer	Ptr	4 bytes

† An individual character or flag requires 2 bytes. In a packed array, each character or flag requires only 1 byte.

Figure I.1: The Basic Data Types of the Toolbox

Type	Name	Storage Size
character	char	1 byte
flag	char	1 byte
short integer	short	2 bytes
integer	int	2 bytes
long integer	long	4 bytes
pointer	char *	4 bytes
floating point	float	4 bytes
double floating point	double	10 bytes ‡

† not really a data type
‡ 12 bytes if 68881 option is on

Figure I.2: The Basic Data Types of Think C

Strings

The sizes of data types under Think C have been thoughtfully chosen, and rarely become an issue except in exotic circumstances. One of the things which does lead to innumerable difficulties in this area, however, is the difference between a string in Pascal and one in C.

Under Pascal, a string consists of some number of characters preceded by an index byte, that is, by a number which defines how long the rest of the string is. The string "Think C" is 7 bytes long, so if you wanted to define it as a Pascal style string under C you would write this:

```
"\007Think C"
```

If you passed this to a Toolbox function which expected to see a string, this would be interpreted correctly.

Under C, strings are represented as some characters followed by a terminating zero byte, or "null". When you define a string under C you do not explicitly define the null, any more than you need define the index byte under Pascal. The language puts it there for you.

If you pass a Toolbox function a C string when it expects a Pascal string, very strange things may happen. For example, the string "Think C", when passed to a Toolbox function as it stands, would be regarded by the Toolbox as being 84 bytes long. If you are wondering how 84 crept into the discussion, observe that the ASCII value of the letter "T" is 84. A Pascal function passed a C string will use the first character of the string as its index byte.

Think C gives you two very elegant ways of converting between C strings and Pascal strings. First of all, if you want to define a string which you know is to be passed to a Toolbox routine, that is, a Pascal string, you would do this:

```
"\pThink C"
```

The "\p" tells Think C to treat this as a Pascal string, and to put an index byte in front of it.

Second, there are two library functions provided by the compiler to convert existing strings between these two conventions. You can use **CtoPstr** to make a C string into a Pascal string and **PtoCstr** to make a Pascal string into a C string. It's worth noting that these functions actually change the strings which they are given as arguments, rather than copying their arguments to new strings.

It is very, very important to know which sort of string a function expects to be passed when you go to use it. Passing the wrong sort of string will at best make your program misbehave, and will frequently crash your Macintosh, necessitating a reboot. All of the Toolbox functions expect Pascal strings. All of the C functions provided by Think C, with the exception of **PtoCstr**, of course, expect C strings.

If a Toolbox function returns a string, you must convert it back to a C string before you use it with any C functions.

There is an additional catch to using strings from C with the Toolbox. Under Pascal, a string is a specific complex data type called Str255. As you might expect, this allots 255 bytes of string space for each string. Under C, a string is an array of however many chars the programmer feels like allocating. The Toolbox, which thinks it's dealing with a Pascal program, will assume that it can increase the size of a string passed to it as much as it needs to, so long as the string remains within 255 bytes.

When you define string variables in your C programs which will be passed to Toolbox routines that might change their sizes, make very sure that you have allocated enough space to allow for any contingency. When in doubt, allocate 256 bytes. This is the largest possible Pascal string plus one byte for either the Pascal index byte or the C null terminator byte, as is applicable.

Alternately, you can use one of the data types which Think C provides for Pascal compatibility. A variable of the type Str255 can be defined in your C program to behave just like an Str255 variable in Pascal.

In this book, when you see a Toolbox function specified as requiring an Str255 variable as an argument, this is a key that it requires a Pascal style string.

Toolbox Data Structures

The Macintosh utilizes over a hundred complex data types. A complex data type is a collection of simple data types bundled together into one new variable. Under most C environments this is a fairly advanced practice. However, because the Toolbox uses complex data types for even the simplest functions, it's important for Macintosh C programmers to know about them from the start.

Here's an example of how complex data structures work. The Toolbox provides us with a function which draws rectangles on the screen. It's called **FrameRect**. In order to define where a rectangle will go on the Mac's screen, we must specify four numbers. These are the number of dots down from the top for the upper horizontal line, the number of dots in from the left for the left vertical line, the number of dots down from the top for the lower horizontal line and the number of dots in from the left for the right vertical line.

The obvious way to handle this would be to pass **FrameRect** four ints. In fact, the Toolbox doesn't do things this way. Instead, it defines a new data type called Rect. A Rect is a collection of four ints called top, left, bottom and right, in that order.

Under C, if r is a variable of the type Rect, then r.top is the integer which defines the position of the top line of the rectangle. You might say r.top = 100 to assign it a specific value.

There are many more complex data types associated with the Toolbox, most of which contain combinations of differing simple data types. It's not unusual to find complex data types which contain other complex data types.

The Toolbox data types are defined in header files included with Think C. Assuming that you include the headers as the Think C manual says you should, you can always assume that these complex data types are "on tap" when you need them.

- - - - - - -

Calling the Toolbox from C

Under Think C, the Macintosh Toolbox appears to your programs just like any other library of functions. In order to call it, you simply assume that all those functions are there and the compiler does the rest.

The biggest single headache in learning to program the Macintosh C in C is getting the calls to the Toolbox right. They are very confusing at times, because C expects us to do a few things by hand which Pascal handles automatically.

In addition, the Toolbox includes a few curves of its own. This is the first and perhaps the trickiest curve. In some cases, you will pass a number to a Toolbox function expecting it to do something with the number. In other cases, the Toolbox will wish to be able to modify the number as it exists in the calling function. Under Pascal, the compiler takes care of this by knowing whether or not each Toolbox function might wish to be able to modify its arguments.

In technical terms, when we wish to simply give a number to a Toolbox function, we pass the *value* of the number. The compiler pushes the number onto the stack and calls the Toolbox function in question. The Toolbox peeks at the number on the stack to see what it is and does whatever it's supposed to do. When the Toolbox function returns, the number on the stack is thrown away by the calling function.

If the Toolbox function expects to actually modify the number it's passed, things are handled differently. In this case, we must tell the Toolbox where the number is in the original calling function so that it can go and change its contents. This is called passing by *reference*. What we actually do is push the address in memory where the number is onto the stack, rather than the number itself, before we call the Toolbox.

All sorts of terrible things will happen if a particular Toolbox function thinks it's going to be passed the address of a number and you pass it the number instead. It will interpret the number as an address and usually modify some totally unrelated memory location. If this happens to be part of your program or something else important, your Macintosh will usually crash.

You might be wondering how to tell when a Toolbox function expects to be passed an argument by value and when it expects to be passed an argument by reference. The answer is in knowing a little bit of Pascal. Under Pascal, if a function is declared as, for example,

```
Function( i : integer);
```

this is a function which expects to have i passed by value. On the other hand, if it was

```
Function( VAR i : integer);
```

this function expects to have i passed by reference.

The notation for passing arguments under C is very similar to that of Pascal. In the first case, you would call the above hypothetical Toolbox function like this to pass it an argument by value.

```
Function(i);
```

In the second case, you would do this to pass it one by reference.

```
Function(&i);
```

As you work through this book, you will have no difficulty recognizing how arguments are passed to the Toolbox for the functions discussed herein, as the notation will all be in C. If a function is described like this, it indicates passing by value.

```
Function(i)
        int i;
```

If it's described like this, its argument is being passed by reference.

```
Function(i)
        int *i;
```

However, you will want to keep this point in mind for when you start delving into uncharted territory, and using the functions described in *Inside Macintosh*.

When you are passing a complex data type to a Toolbox function, there is no choice between passing it by value and passing it by reference. Under Think C, nothing bigger than four bytes is ever passed by value. If, for example, we wanted to pass a Rect variable to **FrameRect**, we would always pass the address of the Rect, not the Rect itself. This a typical call to **FrameRect**.

```
FrameRect(&r);
```

There is an interesting exception to this. One of the commonly used complex data types which the Toolbox defines is Point, which contains two integers. This specifies the horizontal and vertical coordinates of something, such as the point at which the mouse was clicked. Now, this is a complex data type but it's only four bytes long. As such, under Think C you are expected to break the rules and pass Point variables by value, that is, without the "&" operator, unless the Point is actually going to be modified by the Toolbox function in question.

Pointers and Handles

The final area of potential confusion for C programmers on the Macintosh concerns pointers and handles. The Macintosh is especially fond of handles, a phenomenon which rarely crops up on most other common microcomputers.

The function of a pointer will be fairly obvious from its name. It tells a program where to look for something. In real terms, a pointer contains the location in memory where the first byte of the thing it points to lives.

If i is an integer and p is a pointer to an integer, then if we say p = &i, p will point to the integer i. If we subsequently say *p = 6, then i will contain the value six.

Under C, pointers are "type checked." This means that if p is declared to be a pointer to an int, for example, and you attempt to make it point to a Rect variable without telling C what you're doing, the compiler will complain. In practice, a pointer to an int and a pointer to a Rect are both four byte numbers, but C tries to keep you from making obvious mistakes by preventing you from, for example, trying to make a Rect variable equal to six.

This part is pretty simple. If it doesn't make perfectly lucid sense just yet, don't worry. You'll find that you understand it intuitively before you're even part way through this book.

A handle is a pointer to a pointer to a thing. If i is an integer, and p is a pointer to an integer and h is a handle to an integer, then we would do this to make h into a handle to i.

```
p = &i;
h = &p;
```

This doesn't take a lot of work to understand. What is a little mysterious is why anyone might want to do it.

On the Macintosh, the position of things in memory is left up to the Mac itself much of the time. If you ask the Mac to give you some memory to store data in, the Mac can't suddenly take your memory away from you later on, but it is allowed to move it around behind your back wherever it feels like doing so. It might do this if it's trying to allocate a big block of memory by combining several smaller, unused areas of memory.

When the Toolbox moves your chunk of memory around, it cannot know where in your program pointers into the memory might lie. As such, it has you deal with the memory through a handle. The handle lives in your program, and points to a pointer. The Mac knows where the pointer is. If it elects to move your memory, it will change where the pointer points to. However, your handle will know where the pointer is, and so you will still be able to find your memory.

Although it might not sound like one, this is a simple example of handles on the Macintosh.

It's very important to differentiate between handles and pointers. It's also very important not to attempt to use the pointer a handle points to as you would a pointer which you have defined, because the Macintosh might change where it points to without telling you about it.

This is discussed in detail in Chapter 6.

Additional Background Information

In addition to the background information we have already outlined, there is some further information that you will need before you begin to learn about the Toolbox in the first chapter.

Toolbox Naming Conventions

The functions, constants and data types which are used with the Toolbox follow a more or less standardized naming convention. When you write the functions which will comprise your own applications, you should attempt to either stick to this convention or devise one of your own which is equally readable. There are those Macintosh programmers who deliberately adopt a different naming style to make it easy to spot which functions are Toolbox calls and which are calls to parts of their own code.

Here's a quick summary of how Toolbox names are formed.

- First, as a general rule a Toolbox name is comprised of two or more descriptive words with the first letter of each word capitalized. For example, we have **FrameRect, MyFileFilter, FixRound** and so on (shown here in the bold faced program font we will use for functions throughout this book). In a few cases, a single word is sufficiently descriptive, such as **Create** or **Munger**. If it is not obvious from its name what **Munger** does, don't worry. The description of this function isn't much help either.

- The names of Toolbox data structures and their associated pointers and handles are named using the same conventions, such as EventRecord, WindowPtr and ControlHandle (shown here in the program font we will use for data structures, variables and the names of constants throughout this book).

- Individual field names from the Toolbox data structures begin with a lower case letter. For example, the where field of an EventRecord or the portRect of a GrafPort.

- All of these conventions can be abandoned whenever Apple feels like it. So, for example, we have TEGetText, PBEject, noErr and so on.

Pascal is not case sensitive. We could write **FRAMERECT** rather than **FrameRect** under Pascal without upsetting the compiler. C is case sensitive. **FRAMERECT** and **FrameRect** are two unique names under C. This is important to remember if you are attempting to transliterate a Pascal program to C. It's also the cause of a particularly frustrating group of compiler errors, wherein you know that a Toolbox function or data type exists but the compiler fails to recognize it. Check it again— you have probably capitalized the name incorrectly.

Other Predefined Constants

Under Pascal, there are many situations wherein things are either true or false. To pass a true argument to a function, for example, you simply pass the word TRUE. This is a predefined constant under Pascal, and its actual value is never used.

In fact, the TRUE and FALSE behave under Pascal exactly as they would under C. A value of zero is false. Everything else is true. As such, of you are told to pass a false value to a Toolbox function, pass zero. If you are told to pass a true value, pass something other than zero. A good choice is 0xff.

Under Pascal, a pointer which points to location zero is said to point to NIL, or be a "nil pointer." Under C, we would say that it points to NULL.

Suggested Reading

The best place to start to learn C is by reading the book which started it all, *The C Programming Language* by Brian W. Kernighan and Dennis M. Ritchie, published by Prentice-Hall, Inc. The second edition of this book is now available, covering all the recent and proposed changes to C. If you get through K&R and the book you're holding now you will probably be able to do without any other general purpose C books.

Sooner or later you should acquire all five volumes of *Inside Macintosh*, published by Addison-Wesley, Inc. The first three deal with the basic Macintosh, and all of the code in this book is drawn from them. The latter two volumes handle the upgrades to the newer Macintosh versions, the hierarchical file system, the Mac II and so on. If you're a bit short of cash, you can get by with the first three.

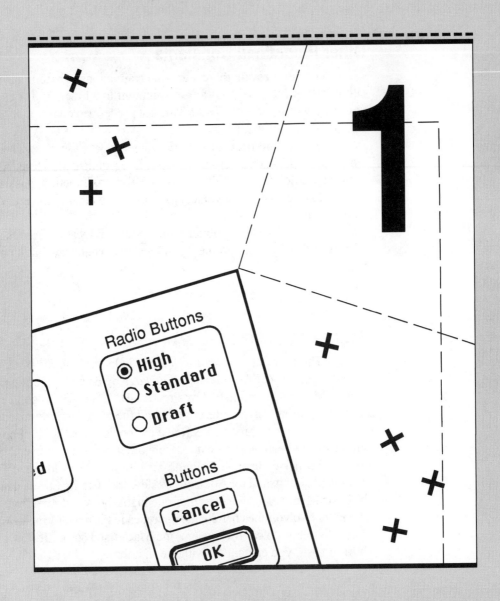

The Macintosh Toolbox and the User Interface

Using the Macintosh is very easy. There is something unique about a computer that seems to make users comfortable right away. The user's sense of control over Macintosh applications seems to develop more quickly than with applications designed for other computers.

Most users take the operation of the Macintosh for granted. They know it's an easy machine to use and they enjoy being able to learn new applications quickly. We as application programmers, however, need to be more aware of just what it is that makes a Macintosh application "Mac-like."

We know, of course, that the key to the Macintosh's uniqueness is its user interface. It is through the interface that the user interacts with the computer and the computer communicates with the user. The quality of the mediation between user and computer provided by the interface is especially important when you have, on the one hand, a computer as sophisticated as the Macintosh and its 68000 series processor and, on the other hand, users who are much more interested in getting their work done efficiently than in knowing about the inner workings of the machine or program they're using.

In this chapter, we will introduce you to the Macintosh's user interface by looking at the role and operation of its basic elements and by reviewing a few conventions that apply to each. We will begin by discussing the qualities of a user friendly, and hence of a Mac-like, application.

Characteristics of a Good Macintosh Application

The user interface that Apple created for the Macintosh represents a significant advance in user friendliness. The designers of the Macintosh wanted their machine to appeal to as wide an audience as possible. Since that meant primarily an audience of nonprogrammers, many of whom had never before used a computer, the new design had to be easy to learn and use.

You can achieve an overall effect of user friendliness in your Macintosh application by ensuring that it contains three characteristics: responsiveness, permissiveness, and consistency.

A "responsive" application should produce direct results from a user's actions. When the user selects an icon, it should become highlighted. When the user boldfaces a word in a word processor, the word should appear boldfaced on the screen. It is this kind of direct response that gives the person using the application a sense of control over what he or she is doing. It's frustrating for a user to execute a command in an application and be left wondering whether anything really happened. As much as possible, the effects of a command should be shown directly, encouraging the user to move on to the next task.

The "permissiveness" of an application refers to the ability of the user to move quickly and freely between features without having to go through a lot of intermediate steps. For example, issuing a print command in a word processor should not be too much harder than issuing a command to boldface text, and the user should be able to jump from one to the other as directly as possible. Using an application should become an intuitive process, encouraging spontaneity. The designers of the Macintosh felt that the person using the application should have to worry less about using the application than about completing the task at hand.

Finally, the Macintosh's designers felt that the most important characteristic of an application is "consistency." When users move from one application to another, they shouldn't be forced to learn an entirely new interface. Clearly, if application control does not vary greatly between programs, the time spent learning to use a new program will be minimized.

The overall intention behind giving your application these characteristics is to make the user more comfortable with the program he or she is using. It is the implementation of these characteristics that makes Macintosh applications truly Mac-like. For example, Macintosh menus eliminate the task of memorizing a great many keyboard commands. Spontaneity is encouraged because all the user's options are right there at the top of the screen—readily available but not in the way. When the user selects a menu from the menu bar, the menu responds by displaying its menu items. What is more, the operation of menus remains consistent from one Macintosh application to another. Through the use of windows, menus, controls, alerts, dialogs, and all the other familiar aspects of the interface, Apple provides the Macintosh user with a simple yet powerful environment in which to work.

The Macintosh User Interface

To ensure implementation of their user interface, Apple provided programmers with two resources. The first, *Inside Macintosh*'s "User Interface Guidelines," offers recommendations on the operation of the user interface in a Macintosh application. An outline of the operation of menus, windows, and the like is provided, as well as some general suggestions as to the appearance and flow of an application.

In general, the "User Interface Guidelines" recommend a copious use of graphics. Whenever possible, commands, features, and parameters of an application should be presented as graphics objects on the screen. The pattern palette in MacPaint, dialog boxes, icons, and menus are familiar examples of the use of graphics.

Because using the standard Macintosh interface necessarily meant doing a lot of complicated graphics, Apple provided the second resource, the Toolbox ROM. Residing in the Macintosh ROM are the fundamental routines needed for implementing the user interface. Through the use of these routines, something as vital to the user interface as displaying a window—a task that would normally require quite of bit of coding—is as simple as passing a few parameters to one of the Toolbox routines.

Technically speaking, the Macintosh ROM is divided into two sections. The *operating system* portion of the ROM contains routines for memory management, file management, handling system errors, handling external devices, and so on. The *User Interface Toolbox* contains the routines that are used to actually build the user interface. These include routines for implementing windows, menus, QuickDraw, and TextEdit. Over time, the two sections of the ROM have become collectively known simply as the *Toolbox*.

Of course, using the ROM routines to create an application is the primary topic of this book. In the subsequent chapters, we don't make a distinction between the operating system and user interface Toolbox. Although we discuss routines from each section of the ROM, we refer to all ROM routines as "Toolbox" routines.

User Interface Conventions

Because many of the broader guidelines of the user interface—single- and double-clicking, for example—are very familiar to all but the newest Macintosh users, we will not go through an exhaustive coverage of the user interface. Instead we'll look at some of the more subtle behaviors and conventions associated with each of the major user interface elements that we, as application programmers, need to be conscious of. This review will provide us with a common ground of ideas about how a Macintosh application is supposed to work and about when certain features and behaviors should be implemented.

Windows

Windows in a Macintosh application can contain a variety of things. Examples include information generated by the program (for example, status messages from a compiler) and alert and dialog messages; in the case of desk accessories, a window can even embody an entire program. By far the most common use for windows, however, is to contain application documents. Documents range in kind from text files produced on a word processor to pictures produced on a graphics program to the transcripts of a bulletin board session on a terminal program.

To accommodate the many uses of document files, the Macintosh operating system has predefined a special style of document window, familiar to anyone who has ever used MacWrite. Because this window is such an integral part of nearly every Macintosh application, it needs to be capable of a variety of behaviors. The user should be able to open or close it, move it, resize it, hide it, and put it in front of or behind other windows. The graphics features associated with these behaviors are all designed into the Macintosh's predefined document window. The behaviors themselves, however, must be programmed into the application, as we will describe. Although the following discussion pertains specifically to the document window, most of the behaviors are directly applicable to other window styles.

Opening and Closing Windows

Windows are usually opened either by a menu command or automatically by the application. As we'll see in Chapter 3, the placement of the window when it is opened is determined by the application. When the user closes a window (if in fact the application wants to allow the window to be closed), the user should have the option of clicking in the close box in the upper left-hand corner of the window. If the application doesn't support closing a window with the close box, the close box should, of course, be omitted from the window so as not to create confusion.

The Active Window

Although an application may be capable of having several windows open on the desktop, the user can only work with a single window at any given time. This window, called the active window, must always be the frontmost window and should be easily recognizable as the window with the highlighted title bar. By the same token, an *inactive window* must have the title bar unhighlighted and cannot be the frontmost window. To make an inactive window active, the user should be able to click on that window once and have the window activate itself, highlighting the title bar and bringing it to the front. Whichever window was previously active should be deactivated (that is, the title bar should be unhighlighted to avoid confusing the user).

Moving and Resizing Windows

When an application allows the creation of multiple windows, the desktop can become cluttered very quickly. To help the user keep the desktop "clean" and in order, the application should allow the user to move and resize the windows on the desktop. To allow for resizing, document windows should have a grow icon in the lower right-hand corner. The programmer can also set a maximum and minimum size for the window. This would help the user to avoid problems such as making the window too small to redraw the grow icon in the bottom-right corner or too large to completely fit on the screen. If a window cannot be resized, as is the case in some applications that allow only a single window, the size box should be omitted.

Resizing a window goes hand in hand with moving it. Since the primary purpose of both resizing and moving is desktop organization, achieving that goal would be difficult if one function were implemented and not the other. When the user clicks the mouse in the title bar and drags, the window should move. The application can specify the boundaries to which the window can be moved. Such boundaries are a helpful addition to an application because they prevent the window from being moved completely off the screen.

Scroll Bars in Windows

Document windows can also have scroll bars. Scroll bars make it easier for the user to look through a document too long to fit in a single screen. They should be implemented whenever there is a possibility of creating such a document.

As shown in Figure 1.1, scroll bars should support moving through a document in three ways. First, the user should be able to scroll smoothly in either direction by clicking in the scroll bar's arrows. Second, the user should be able to page through the document one screenful at a time by clicking in the gray area on either side of the scroll box. And finally, the user should be able to go to any portion of the document by positioning the scroll bar thumb (scroll box) directly.

Menus

Although they're not the only means of controlling an application, menus are by far the most common. There are a few conventions for menu layout and operation that you've undoubtedly seen in other applications but may not have recognized as conventions. The more important of these conventions will be described next.

Presenting Menu Commands

Menu commands can be divided into two categories: verbs and adjectives (or actions and attributes). *Verb commands*, as their classification implies, actually do something, such as print or copy. *Adjective commands*, on the other hand, describe a certain state or attribute of an object. Adjective commands can be further distinguished as either *accumulating attributes* or mutually *exclusive attributes*. An attribute is accumulating when it can be added to other attributes, as when the user can boldface *and* italicize text. Attributes are mutually exclusive when they can only exist by themselves, as when the user is invited to either show or hide a window.

As you've probably noticed in the applications you use, the menu itself can be divided into groups, indicated by a gray line spanning the width of the menu. Whenever a menu contains a large number of commands, you should use this type of grouping to create a logical subset of commands within a particular menu.

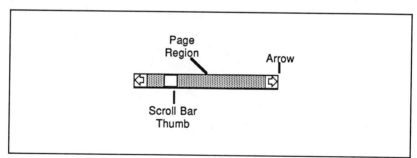

Figure 1.1:   The Operation of Scroll Bars

Another important convention for the visual organization of menus is to divide attributes—either accumulating, exclusive, or both—into respective groups in order to emphasize their relationship. Figure 1.2 shows a hypothetical menu for paragraph formatting. Notice how related attributes are grouped together. The Style menu shown later in the chapter (in Figure 1.5) is an example of an instance in which it is all right to have accumulating attributes grouped with an exclusive attribute. Often, however, grouping accumulating and exclusive attributes together will result in a confusing menu. The Style menu is a special case in that the function of each selection is clear.

The state of an attribute, in turn, can be indicated in several ways. If the grouped attributes are mutually exclusive (that is, only one option is available at a time), the command that's in effect can be preceded by a check mark (as is done in the Font menu we'll be talking about shortly). You can also use check marks to identify accumulating attributes, where any number of attributes from a particular group can be in effect at the same time. In this case, whichever attributes are selected will be marked by a check mark. If there are only two mutually exclusive choices, the command can be simply toggled. In other words, the text of the menu item will change from something like "Show Item" to something like "Hide Item."

If a menu selection will require further information when it is chosen, the command should be followed by an ellipsis (. . .). A good example is the "Print . . ." item in the File menu. When selected, this command puts up a dialog box requesting further information about

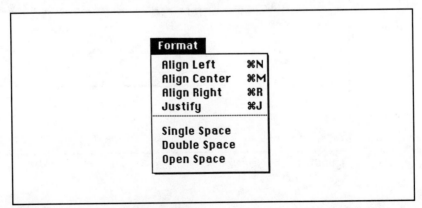

Figure 1.2:   A Paragraph Format Menu

such matters as print resolution and number of copies needed.

If an option isn't available at a certain time, the application can dim the corresponding menu command so that it cannot be selected. For example, if the user has not opened any documents, there is obviously no document to close. In that case, you should disable the Close option in your File menu.

Menu items can also have keyboard equivalents. In other words, the application can allow the user to select certain menu items from the keyboard without having to use the mouse. When a keyboard equivalent exists for a menu item, you should make sure that this is indicated in that item by displaying to the right of the item the Command key symbol (⌘) followed by the equivalent key character.

Some Standard Menus

There are three standard menus on the Macintosh that should be present in all applications that support menus. You'll find that this convention has been adhered to rather strictly by all but the most specialized programs. Some copy programs, for instance, don't use these menus because the entire application serves only a single purpose.

The Apple Menu   If your application supports desk accessories (and it should), the names of all available desk accessories should reside in the Apple menu. This should be the leftmost menu and the title should be the Apple symbol (ASCII character hex 14). If you include an "About . . ." window in your application, the command calling it out should be the first item in the Apple menu.

The File Menu   This menu should contain all the commands dealing with general file management, including actions such as opening, closing, saving, and quitting. A typical File menu is pictured in Figure 1.3. As you can see from this figure, if your application allows printing, those commands also go into the File menu.

The Edit Menu   Probably the single most important factor in maintaining consistency from application to application is represented by the Edit menu. If an application is going to support desk accessories, the edit menu must appear exactly as shown in Figure 1.4. Since the Undo, Cut, Copy, and Paste commands are passed to desk accessories by the system according to relative position in the menu and not according to the command itself, following the conventional Edit menu format will ensure compatibility with any desk accessory that needs to make use of these commands. The keyboard equivalents for these commands also need to be exactly as shown in Figure 1.4, again to ensure compatibility with all desk accessories.

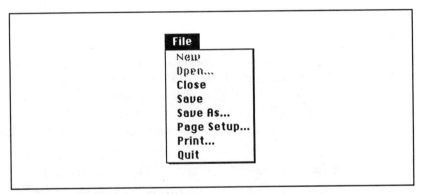

Figure 1.3:   File Menu from MacWrite

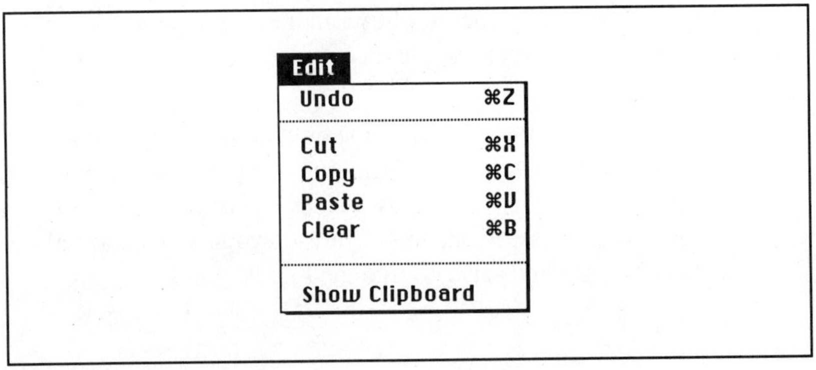

Figure 1.4:   The Edit Menu

Font-Related Menus

There are a few other menus that are applicable only to word processors and other applications that allow the user to change text fonts and alter font appearance. With the increasing availability of mass storage devices for the Macintosh, the feasibility of listing all the available fonts in a single menu is diminishing since now there is the possibility of having a dozen or more fonts installed in the system. If you decide not to use these menus for displaying fonts and font options, try to come up with a method that's as intuitive as possible. In other words, use an interface feature that is familiar to Macintosh users (a dialog box, perhaps). Remember that the whole idea behind the user interface is to make applications as easy to use as possible. In this case, you want to add flexibility without sacrificing ease of use.

The Font Menu   A Font menu should always list the fonts that are currently available to the user. It is from this menu that the user will select which font he or she wants to use. A check or other mark should be used to indicate which selection is the active one.

The Style Menu   The Style menu should contain the commands shown in Figure 1.5. All the commands except Plain Text are accumulating attributes and should be marked when active. When selected, the Plain Text command should override any other option.

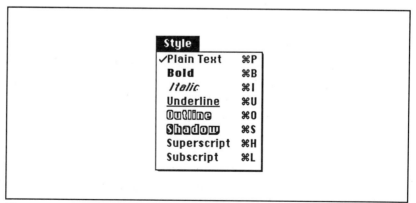

Figure 1.5: The Style Menu

Keyboard equivalents for the style enhancements are optional. If you do decide to use keyboard equivalents, however, convention dictates that they be the same keyboard equivalent characters as those used in Figure 1.5.

The FontSize Menu   The FontSize menu should list the possible sizes of the active font. The sizes that are currently installed in the system should be listed in outline letters as shown in Figure 1.6.

Although the font may be scaled to a size that is not installed in the system, it will not look as good as one of the installed sizes since the computer will need to improvise a bit in displaying and printing it. If there is limited room in the menu bar, the name of this menu can be shortened to simply "Size" or else the contents of the FontSize menu can be appended to the Font or Style menu.

Controls

Controls are graphics objects that can be manipulated by the mouse. Resembling the control dials on household appliances, controls in a Macintosh application provide an additional method of issuing commands. Examples of the four basic types of controls—buttons, check boxes, radio buttons, and dials—are shown in Figure 1.7. Let's take a look at each of these four basic types.

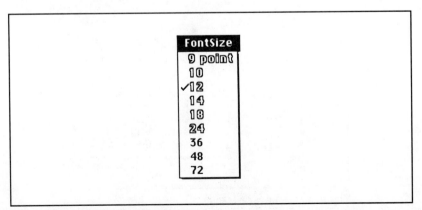

Figure 1.6:   A Typical FontSize Menu

Buttons

Although buttons can be any shape you wish to make them, they are usually small boxes or rectangles labeled with text. Appearing for the most part inside dialog and alert boxes, their function is usually to allow the user to confirm an option or to initiate an action. Thus in many dialog boxes, buttons indicate to the computer both that the user is ready to move on and in which direction. For example, when a dialog box comes up in MacPaint asking whether the user wants to save changes, three buttons are present: Yes, No, and Cancel. The user must select one of these choices before moving on.

Check Boxes and Radio Buttons

Check boxes and radio buttons differ from the buttons we have just described in that they act more like simple switches, either turning an option on or off. Check boxes allow the user to select between accumulating attributes: any number of check boxes grouped together can be on or off at a given time. Radio buttons, on the other hand, are for selecting mutually exclusive attributes. They function just like the channel select buttons on a car radio: only one radio button in a group can be

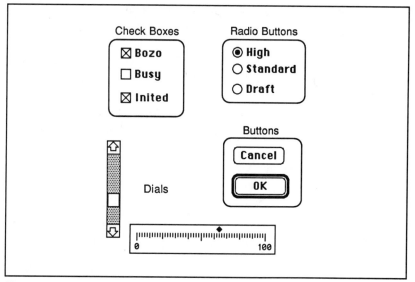

Figure 1.7: Sample Controls

"on" at a time, and selecting one radio button automatically turns "off" any other button that is on.

Dials

Dials are used to indicate the value, level, or magnitude of something. They usually display their values graphically in an analog fashion, much like the dials on equipment and appliances. Some dials also allow the user to change their values by dragging or clicking with the mouse. A common example of a dial used by many Macintosh programs is the scroll bar. In a RAM disk program, for example, the scroll bar can serve as the size indicator of the disk, with the scroll bar thumb showing the current amount of RAM allocated to the disk. The user can then change the amount of memory allocated to the RAM disk by moving the scroll bar thumb with the mouse.

Dialog Boxes

When menu commands require more information before they can be executed, the application should use dialog boxes to prompt the user for further input. Dialog boxes contain check boxes, radio buttons, and text fields through which the application can gather the information it requires.

Dialog boxes fall into two classes. A *modal dialog box* forces the user to acknowledge it before he or she can move on. No other part of the application can be accessed while the modal dialog box is displayed. *Modeless dialog boxes*, the other category of dialog boxes, allow the user to perform other operations in the application without having to close the dialog box. Figure 1.8 shows two familiar dialog boxes—one modal, the other modeless.

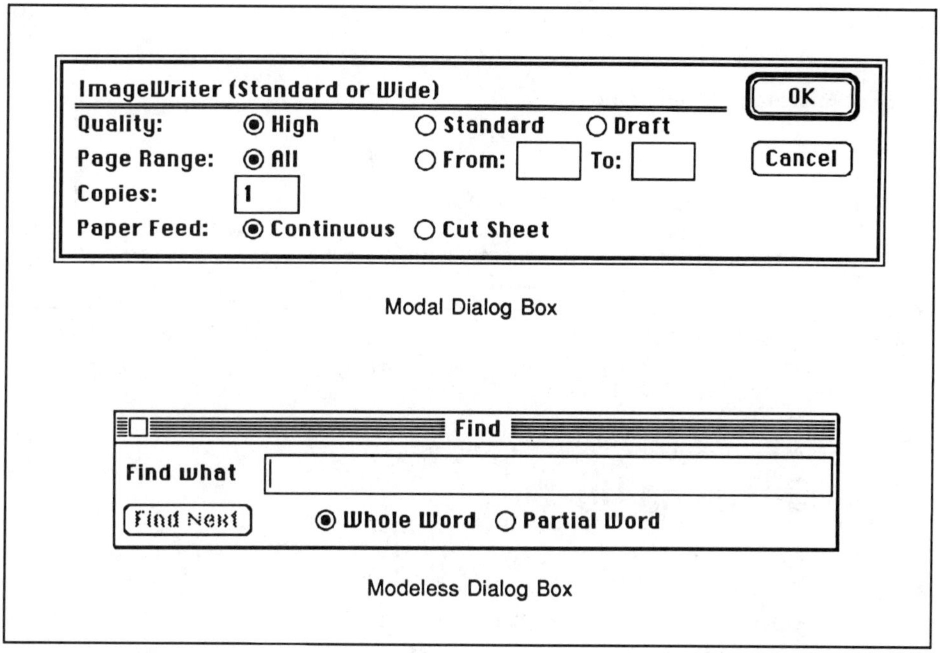

Figure 1.8: Modal and Modeless Dialog Boxes

Alerts

Alerts are messages from the application to the user. Although these messages are generally error messages, they are also often used to caution users when they are about to do something drastic, such as erasing a disk. They provide a consistent and informative way to warn the user that something is wrong.

The simplest form of alerts is a beep. Beeps are used when a minor and relatively obvious error occurs. Clicking the mouse outside of a modal dialog box is an example of such an error. Alert boxes, on the other hand, are very similar to modal dialog boxes and serve to actually stop users from proceeding until they have read and responded to the message contained in the alert box. The only way for users to proceed is by clicking in one of the buttons that are always a part of the alert box. Figure 1.9 shows a sample alert box.

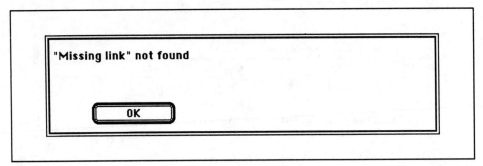

Figure 1.9:   A Sample Alert Box

Summing Up

This about wraps up our overview of the user interface. In the subsequent chapters, you will learn how to manipulate the various aspects of the interface we have discussed here and how to tie them all together to create your own application. As you think about this application, keep in mind that you shouldn't feel compelled to limit yourself to existing Mac features. It never hurts the appeal of an application to have a clever new feature as part of its interface.

All the same, it's important that you try to make every feature of your application as Mac-like in style as possible. In particular, you should be sure that features shared by all applications, such as menus and windows, work the same way as they do in well-known Macintosh applications so as not to confuse the user. The rule of thumb is that if you're going to use a feature that's already a part of the user interface, do it exactly as it's done in other programs.

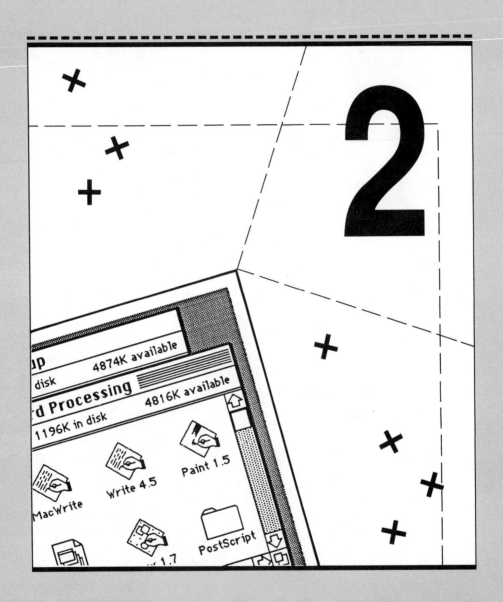

Using the
Event Manager

Now that we've discussed the Macintosh user interface, and have gotten a general idea of what's in the Toolbox ROM, we are ready to examine some of the Toolbox procedures and functions in detail. The first section of the Toolbox we will examine is the Event Manager.

A thorough understanding of events is essential to writing Macintosh applications because events are the backbone or guiding force behind a Macintosh application program. Unlike applications that run on other microcomputers and that are typically sequential in nature, with the program code going from point A to point B, a Macintosh application is constantly responding to various types of events. It is for this reason that the Macintosh is said to be an *event-driven computer*. Events are generated by the user, by the other Toolbox managers (which we will discuss in subsequent chapters), by device drivers, and even by the application itself.

A typical Mac application has a main event loop that repeatedly checks for events that need to be processed. Each time through the loop, the application, using Event Manager routines, analyzes the events awaiting processing, and then responds accordingly. A sample main event loop is given at the end of the chapter.

In this chapter we will first learn about the various types of events and how or why they are generated. Then we will take an in-depth look at an event record, the information each of its fields contains, and how and why our application uses this data structure. We will study the event queue, the priority of different events, and event masks. Finally, we will examine each of the different Event Manager routines to see how they work and how our application can use them.

Types of Events

It's always good to know what you're looking for before you go searching for something. For this reason, it's important to know what types of events our application may need to respond to. Figure 2.1 shows all the different event types. In the sections that follow are descriptions of the 16 event types and the manner in which each is generated. Twelve of them are predefined, while the other four are left for each application to define and use in any manner it chooses.

Null Events

An application will continuously poll the Event Manager for events to respond to. If there are no events to process, the Event Manager will return to the application a *null event*.

Mouse-Down and Mouse-Up Events

Mouse events are very simple. When you press the mouse button, a *mouse-down event* is generated. Releasing the button creates a *mouse-up event*.

Event type	Event Code	
Null	nullEvent	= 0
Mouse-down	mouseDown	= 1
Mouse-up	mouseUp	= 2
Key-down	keyDown	= 3
Key-up	keyUp	= 4
Auto-key	autoKey	= 5
Update	updateEvt	= 6
Disk-inserted	diskEvt	= 7
Activate	activateEvt	= 8
Network	networkEvt	= 9
Device driver	driverEvt	= 10
Application defined	app1Evt	= 11
Application defined	app2Evt	= 12
Application defined	app3Evt	= 13
Application defined	app4Evt	= 14

Figure 2.1: Event Types and Event Codes

Key-Down, Auto-Key, and Key-Up Events

Pressing a character key on the keyboard or on the keypad generates a *key-down event*; releasing the key generates a *key-up event*; and holding the key down creates *auto-key events*. The character keys consist of all the keys on the Macintosh keyboard or keypad except for the *modifier keys*: Shift, Caps Lock, Command, and Option. Modifier keys do not generate a character; instead, they modify the character generated when it is held down in conjunction with a character key. For example, striking the s key generates a lowercase "s," while striking the s key with the Shift key held down generates a capital "S." (In order for an application to detect if one of the modifier keys is being held down, it will need to examine the modifiers field of the event record. We will discuss event records in a moment.)

After each key-down event occurs, the application takes into consideration two auto-key time variables: the *auto-key threshold* and the *auto-key rate*. The auto-key threshold indicates how long in ticks (sixtieths of a second) a character key must be held down in order to generate an auto-key event. After the first auto-key event, if the key continues to be held down for the number of ticks specified by the auto-key rate, another auto-key event is generated. The initial values for the auto-key threshold and the auto-key rate are 16 ticks and 4 ticks, respectively. These values are easily changed using the Control Panel desk accessory.

Disk-Inserted Events

Inserting a disk into the internal or external drive generates a *disk-inserted event*. One other source of disk-inserted events is hard disk software. Hard disk drives are often divided into several smaller partitions called volumes. Each volume is treated like a separate floppy disk. Mounting a hard disk volume is analogous to inserting a floppy disk into one of the drives. When the hard disk user mounts a hard disk volume, the mounting software will generate a disk-inserted event and send it to the Event Manager.

The next two event types, activate and update, are generated by the Window Manager.

Activate and Update Events

It is a very common situation on the Macintosh to have multiple overlapping windows on the screen at once. Most activate and update events stem from this multiple window situation. Anytime the user moves any of the windows, we can count on activate and update events being generated.

Activate events are generated by the Window Manager whenever an inactive window becomes active or an active window becomes inactive. *Update events* are also generated by the Window Manager whenever any part of a window's contents region needs to be drawn or redrawn.

Since we haven't studied windows yet, it may not be clear what an active or inactive window is, or what a window's content region is. We'll learn about these aspects of windows in Chapter 3 and in Chapter 7. Until then, look at Figure 2.2 for a pictorial explanation of activate and update events.

Device Driver Events

The serial ports, disk drives, and printers all have device drivers that can generate *device driver events*. For example, if our application uses the serial drivers, it can request the driver to post a device driver event whenever the driver detects a change in the hardware handshake status or whenever a break occurs. Our application could then, upon detecting the device driver event, put up an error message or perform some other appropriate action.

Network Events

A network event may be generated by the AppleTalk Manager. Network events are a highly specialized topic. For more information, refer to the AppleTalk Manager documentation in *Inside Macintosh*.

Application-Defined Events

An application may define four event types of its own. The application will generate these events itself, and then send them to the Event Manager with the routine **PostEvent**. The routine **PostEvent** will be described later in this chapter.

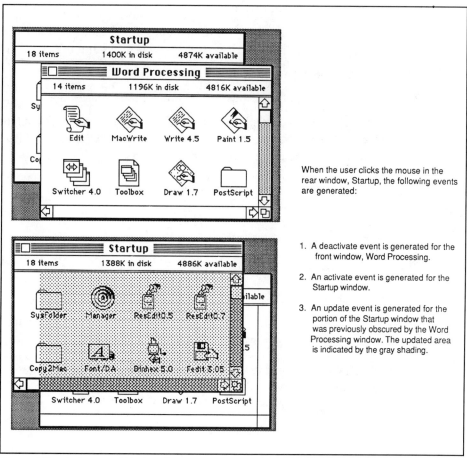

When the user clicks the mouse in the rear window, Startup, the following events are generated:

1. A deactivate event is generated for the front window, Word Processing.

2. An activate event is generated for the Startup window.

3. An update event is generated for the portion of the Startup window that was previously obscured by the Word Processing window. The updated area is indicated by the gray shading.

Figure 2.2: Activate and Update Events

Event Records

Each time an event occurs, information particular to the event is placed by the Event Manager into an event record. The information stored in an event record consists of

1. The type of event that occurred (for example, mouse-down, key-up, disk-inserted, and so on).

2. A message about the event explaining, for example, which key was pressed, or which drive the disk was inserted into.

3. When the event took place.

4. The location of the mouse at the time of the event.

5. Information regarding the status of the modifier keys, the status of the mouse button, and for activate events, whether the window involved is being activated or deactivated.

Let's examine the structure of an event record:

```
struct ER {
    short what;
    long message;
    long when;
    Point where;
    short modifiers;
};

#define EventRecord struct ER
```

The five fields of the event record contain the five pieces of information we have just listed. We will now examine each of the five fields in depth, beginning with the what field.

The what Field

The what field contains an event code identifying the type of event. (For a list of all the event codes see Figure 2.1.) These event code constants are normally predefined in header files supplied with your compiler.

Besides being the first field of an event record, it is typically the first field an application examines when it is processing events. The contents of the what field have a direct effect on the application's next action. For example, if an application detects a disk-inserted event, its next move might be to find out which drive the disk was inserted into, whereas if the same application detects a mouse-down event, its next move would probably be to figure out the location of the mouse-down event.

The message Field

Once an application has determined the type of event that occurred by examining the what field, it can examine the message field to gain more information about the event. The information stored in the event message field changes depending on the event code for that particular event record (see Figure 2.3).

Event Message for Null, Mouse-Down, and Mouse-Up Events

For null, mouse-down, and mouse-up events, the event message contains no information.

Event type	Contents of the event message
Null	Not Used
Mouse-down	Not Used
Mouse-up	Not Used
Key-down	ASCII character code and key code in low order word
Key-up	ASCII character code and key code in low order word
Auto-key	ASCII character code and key code in low order word
Update	Pointer to the window that needs to be updated
Disk-inserted	Drive number in the lower 16 bits, MountVol resut code in the upper 16 bits
Activate	Pointer to window that needs to be activated or deactivated
Network	See the AppleTalk documentation
Device driver	See the particular driver's documentation
Application defined	Anything the programmer wants
Application defined	Anything the programmer wants
Application defined	Anything the programmer wants
Application defined	Anything the programmer wants

Figure 2.3:   Event Message Contents

Event Message for Keyboard Events

For keyboard events, the lower eight bits (0-7) of the event message contain the integer ASCII *character code* of the key (or modifier/key combination) that was pressed or released. The next eight bits of the message (8-15) contain the integer *key code* of the key or combination that was pressed or released (see Figure 2.4).

In most cases, the upper 16 bits of the message are not used. However, the Macintosh II has a facility which allows it to be connected to multiple keyboards. In this case, the third eight bits of the message (16-23) contain information which allows an application to determine which of several keyboards a particular character has come from. This can usually be ignored.

The character code returned in the event message is the ASCII code that is generated internally by the key or combination of keys pressed. See Appendix C for a complete table of the ASCII character codes. The key code returned is an integer that represents which physical key that was struck. See Figure 2.5 for the key code values of the standard U.S. keyboard and keypad.

To get an idea of how character codes and key codes differ, let's consider the event message for two different key-down events, the first for pressing the e key and the second for pressing Shift-e. For the first event, the event message would contain the character code for "e" and a key code value of 14 (decimal). For the second event, the event message would contain the character code for "E" and the same key code value of 14 (decimal). Observe that for the two key-down events,

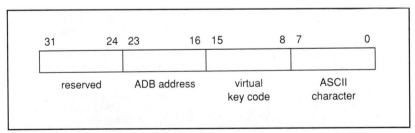

Figure 2.4: Event Message for Keyboard Events

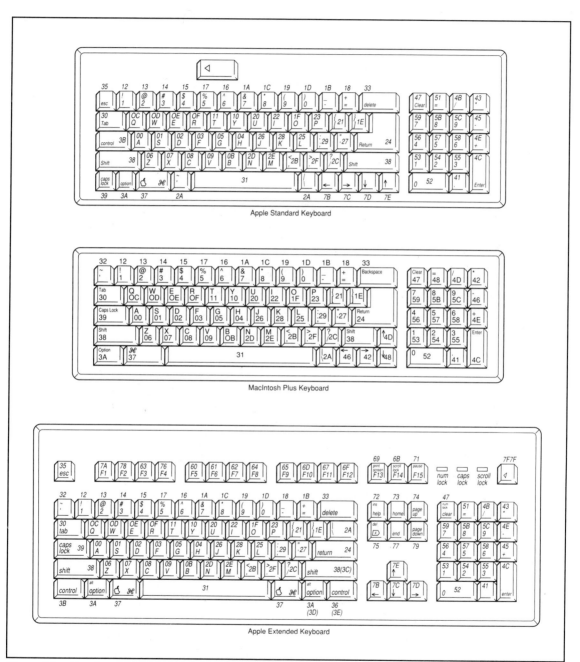

Figure 2.5:   Key Code Values for U.S. Standard Keyboard and Keypad

while the character codes were different, the key code values remained the same. The character code is linked to the character generated, which for the first event was "e" and for the second event "E." The key code is linked to the actual key on the keyboard that is struck, which for both events was the fourth key over on the second row from the top of the keyboard, or 14 (decimal). If an application is placing text from the keyboard onto the screen, it will use the character code value from the event message. If an application uses the keyboard for something other than inputting text—for example, as a music keyboard—and is only concerned with the actual key that is struck, it will examine and use the key code value. In short, just remember that when any of the modifier keys—the Shift, Caps Lock, or Option key—is held down with a character key, the character code changes, but the key code always remains the same.

To make it easier for us to get at the character code and key code values, we can use the following constant masks, which are provided by Think C.

```
#define charCodeMask 0x000000FF
#define keyCodeMask 0x0000FF00
```

We can use these constant masks in the following manner:

```
theASCIICode = theEvent.message & charCodeMask;
theKeyCode = theEvent.message & keyCodeMask;
```

Event Message for Update and Activate Events

For update and activate events, the event message contains a pointer to the window that needs to be updated. The application passes the window pointer to update or activate handling routines. (These routines are discussed in Chapter 7, the chapter on multiple windows.)

Event Message for Disk-Inserted Events

For disk-inserted events, the event message contains two pieces of information. The lower 16 bits (0-15) contain the drive number, indicating which disk drive the disk-inserted event took place in. The internal drive is equal to 1 and the external drive is equal to 2. The upper

16 bits (16-31) contain the File Manager result code from **MountVol** (see Figure 2.6).

If the drive number returned is greater than 2, the disk-inserted event took place on a disk drive connected to either the modem or printer port. Whenever a disk-inserted event takes place, the system immediately tries to mount the volume by calling the File Manager function **MountVol**, which returns the value stored in the upper 16 bits of the event message. The value indicates whether or not the volume was successfully mounted. Our application should check the result code and display some sort of error message if the value returned is anything other than zero. See Figure 2.7 for the possible result codes returned by **MountVol**.

We can define our own constant masks to simplify the task of getting at the drive number and **MountVol** result code.

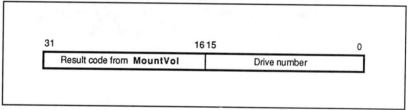

Figure 2.6:   Event Message for Disk-Inserted Events

Result Code	Meaning
0 = noErr	No error.
-60 = badMDBErr	The disk's master directory is bad. The volume must be reinitialized.
-58 = extFSErr	The file system identifier is nonzero, or the path reference number is greater than 1024.
-36 = ioErr	Disk input/output error.
-41 = mFullErr	The system heap (memory) is full.
-57 = noMacDskErr	Not a Macintosh volume; the disk does not have a Macintosh format directory.
-56 = nsDrvErr	The indicated drive number does not match any in the drive queue.
-50 = paramErr	Bad drive number; parameters do not specify an existing volume, and there is no default volume.
-55 = volOnLinErr	The specified volume is already mounted and on line.

Figure 2.7:   Possible Results from the File Manager Function MountVol

```
#define drvNumMask 0x0000FFFF
#define resultCodeMask 0xFFFF0000
```

We can use these masks in the following manner:

```
theDrive = theEvent.message & drvNumMask;
theResult = theEvent.message & resultCodeMask;
```

The when **Field**

Each time an event is generated, the number of ticks (sixtieths of a second) since the system was started up is placed in the when field. If our application implements a stopwatch feature, it could simply check for mouse-down events in the start button and the stop button of the stopwatch. The elapsed time for the application to display would equal the difference between the values stored in the when fields of each event record.

The where **Field**

The location of the mouse, in global coordinates, is placed in the where field of the event record each time an event is generated. The location of the mouse is very important to an application when handling mouse-down events. The location determines the next course of action an application will take. If the mouse is clicked in a window, the application should, using Window Manager routines, determine where in the desktop the mouse was clicked (these are covered in Chapter 3). If it is clicked in a menu, control should be passed to menu routines (covered in Chapter 4). If it is clicked in a control, alert or dialog box, control should be passed to control, alert and dialog handling routines (the topics of Chapters 10 and 11).

The modifiers Field

For certain types of events, simply knowing the event code is not enough information for an application to respond accurately. By examining the modifiers field, an application can determine the status of the modifier keys and the status of the mouse button; and in the case of an activate event, the modifiers field indicates whether the window involved is being activated or deactivated. Let's take a look at some examples of when and why an application would have to examine the modifiers field.

One of the features of the Macintosh is that an application may have keyboard equivalents for its various menu items. Basically, a keyboard equivalent is a combination of keys, usually the Command key and a character key, that when struck simultaneously, execute the particular menu item they are assigned to. As an example, it is customary for the menu item "Paste" to have a keyboard equivalent of Command-v. An application, by examining the what and message fields of an event record, may know that a key-down event has occurred and, for example, that the key struck was the v key. But the application also needs to know if the Command key was held down or not. This is one thing the application can find out by examining the modifiers field. If the Command key was held down, the application should execute a Paste command; otherwise, it should respond to a simple v keystroke.

For mouse-down events, the application needs to know whether or not the shift key is being held down. Shift-clicking often indicates something quite different from a simple mouse click. Once again, the application could obtain this additional information by examining the modifiers field of the event record. A diagram of the modifiers field is shown in Figure 2.8.

To simplify the process of reading the modifiers field, we can use the masks shown in Figure 2.9. For the modifier key flags (bits 8-11), a value of 1 indicates that the key is down. As we saw earlier, if our program uses menus and it detects a key-down event, it should check to see if the user is also holding down the Command key. A Command and character-key event generally indicates that the user is selecting a menu item by hitting its keyboard equivalent.

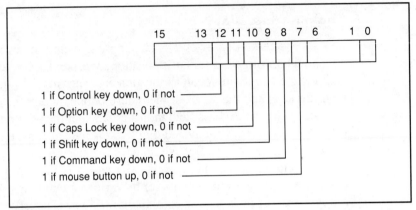

Figure 2.8: Diagram of Modifiers Field

Figure 2.9: Modifiers Field Masks and Their Values

The following code block shows how our application might respond to key-down events:

```
char charhit;
case keyDown:
    /* assign the ASCII character code of the key hit to charhit*/
    charhit = theEvent.message & charCodeMask;
    /* determine whether or not the command key
       was also held down */
    if (theEvent.modifiers & cmdkey) {
        /* respond to a command-character key event....
           pass the information to menu handling routines */
    } else {
    }
```

Note that it is not necessary for the status of the Shift, Caps Lock or Option keys to be checked when an application responds to a key-down event. When any of these three keys is held down along with a character key, the character code is appropriately changed. For key-down events, it is usually only necessary to check the status of the Command key.

The control key bit of the modifiers field only applies to the Apple Extended and Macintosh II keyboards, as these are the only keyboards with control keys. Your application will probably want to ignore the possible existence of a control key since it cannot be assumed to be available on all Macs.

When any type of event occurs, our application can check the status of the mouse button by examining bit 7 of the modifiers field. For the mouse button (bit 7), a value of 0 (zero) indicates the mouse button is down.

When an activate event is generated, an application would look to the message field for a pointer to the window affected, and then it would look to bit 0 of the modifiers field to see whether the window is being activated or deactivated. A value of 1 in bit 0 indicates the window is being activated. When our application begins dealing with multiple windows in Chapter 7, the importance of activate events will become more evident.

The Event Queue

Whenever an event is generated, information about the event is placed in an event record. Once the information is placed in the event record, the Event Manager places the event record into the *event queue*. The event queue is part of the Event Manager. The application doesn't have to do anything to set it up or prepare it for events. The first events placed in the queue are generally the first events returned when an application polls the queue for events to process.

Let's take a closer look at how events are returned from the event queue.

Priority of Events

When an application retrieves events from the event queue, they are generally returned in the order they were generated. Because some events have a higher priority than others, however, they disrupt the standard first-in first-out action of the event queue. When the Event Manager is polled, it will return the highest priority event available according to the order shown in Figure 2.10.

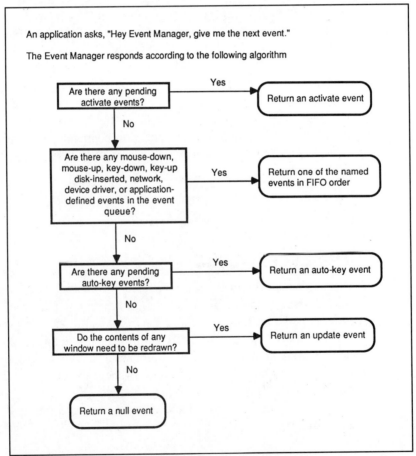

Figure 2.10: Priority of Events Returned by the Event Manager

Activate and update events are not actually placed in the event queue. When an application polls the Event Manager, the Event Manager checks for any pending activate events before going to look in the event queue. For update events, if no higher priority event is available, the Event Manager will examine, from front to rear, all windows to see if any of their content regions need to be redrawn. If such a window is found, an update event is generated and returned to the application. The application can then pass information about the update event to the update handling routines covered in Chapter 7.

Event Masks

Many Event Manager routines have an event mask parameter. The *event mask* indicates to the function or procedure which different event types the routine applies to. An event mask is a 16-bit integer with one bit for each event type (see Figure 2.11). If a bit is set to 1, the event type for that bit is active, and the routine applies to it.

For each individual event type, there is a constant event mask defined (see Figure 2.12). To specify multiple event types, we can simply add event masks together. For example, passing an event mask of (mDownMask + autoKeyMask + driverMask) to a function or procedure would indicate to the particular routine to only act upon mouse-down, auto-key, and device driver events.

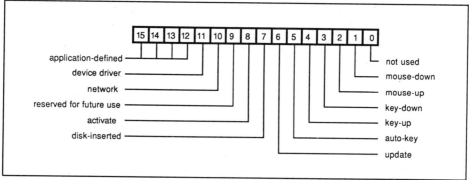

Figure 2.11: Event Mask Diagram

Event Type	Event Mask & Value	
all event types	everyEvent	= -1
mouse-down	mDownMask	= 2
mouse-up	mUpMask	= 4
key-down	keyDownMask	= 8
key-up	keyUpMask	= 16
auto-key	autoKeyMask	= 32
update	updateMask	= 64
disk-inserted	diskMask	= 128
activate	activMask	= 256
network	networkMask	= 1024
device driver	driverMask	= 2048
application-defined	app1Mask	= 4096
application-defined	app2Mask	= 8192
application-defined	app3Mask	= 16384
application-defined	app4Mask	= -32768

Figure 2.12: Event Mask Values

Using the Event Manager Routines

The Event Manager has routines to manipulate event records and to read the mouse location and its button status, and a routine to see how long the system has been running. In the following sections, we will examine each of these routines in order to see how they work and how they might fit into a Macintosh application.

Manipulating Event Records

A Macintosh application must constantly poll the Event Manager for events to respond to. To do this, most applications have a main event loop containing a **GetNextEvent** call (see the end of the chapter for a sample main event loop). According to the priority of events and the eventMask specified, **GetNextEvent** returns, in theEvent parameter, an event record of the next available event.

```
char GetNextEvent (eventMask, theEvent)
    int eventMask;
    EventRecord *theEvent;
```

If the event is stored in the event queue, it is removed. Events that are not specified in the eventMask but that are present in the event queue are left there. The function value returned by **GetNextEvent** is true if an event is returned in theEvent, and false if a null event is returned. The function also returns a false value when the system wants to intercept and respond to theEvent. The system will intercept activate, update, and keyboard events when they correspond to desk accessories and when the desk accessory is able to handle the event.

If our application has a need to see what events are waiting to be processed, but doesn't want to alter the contents of the event queue, we can use the function **EventAvail**.

```
char EventAvail(eventMask, theEvent)
   int eventMask;
   EventRecord *theEvent;
```

EventAvail works exactly like **GetNextEvent** except that if the event is stored in the event queue, it is not removed.

If our application uses its own particular event type, it will need to post the event to the event queue using the function **PostEvent**.

```
short PostEvent(eventCode, eventMsg)
   int eventCode;
   long eventMsg;
```

The eventCode and the eventMsg parameters indicate the event type and event message of the event being posted to the queue. The other fields of the event record (when, where, and modifiers) are filled in automatically by the Event Manager with the current time, mouse location, and modifiers field information.

To get rid of events as opposed to posting them, our application can call the procedure **FlushEvents**.

```
FlushEvents(eventMask, stopMask);
   int eventMask;
   int stopMask;
```

FlushEvents removes all the events from the event queue that are specified in the eventMask. It removes all the events indicated up to the first event specified in the stopMask. For example, if we called **Flush-**

Events with an eventMask of mDownMask and a stopMask of keyDownMask, all of the mouse-down events up to the first key-down event would be removed from the queue. If we specified a stopMask value of 0 instead, all the mouse-down events would be removed.

Note: Apple has, in its technical documentation, defined **Flush-Events** twice, with each definition having a different number of arguments. Think C uses the more common definition, as illustrated above. Some development systems call **FlushEvents** in a different manner. Instead of passing two int arguments, an application will pass a long with the event-Mask in the low order word and stopMask in the high order word. Keep this in mind if you use source code which originates with a different version of C.

Before your application enters the main event loop for the first time, its a good idea for the program to call **FlushEvents** with an eventMask of everyEvent and a stopMask of 0. This will clear the event queue of any stray mouse-downs or keystrokes that were clicked or typed to the Finder.

Mouse Routines

If we are interested in the location of the mouse at any particular time, even when an event has not occurred, we can call the procedure **GetMouse**.

```
GetMouse(mouseLoc)
    Point *mouseLoc;
```

After calling **GetMouse**, the variable mouseLoc will contain the position of the mouse in the coordinate system of the current grafPort. (We will learn about grafPorts in Chapter 5. For now, you can think of a grafPort as the current window.)

To check and see whether the mouse button is currently up or down, we can use the functions **Button** or **StillDown**.

```
char Button();
```

The function **Button** returns a true value if the mouse button is down, and a false value if the button is up.

The function **StillDown** is generally called after a mouse-down event.

```
char StillDown();
```

It returns the same values as **Button**, but under the following circumstances. If the mouse button is currently down and there are no pending mouse events in the queue, a true value is returned. Under any other circumstances, a false value will be returned. The advantage of **StillDown** is that it indicates whether or not the button is still down from its original pressing. The result of **StillDown** is used in conjunction with a number of window handling routines that we will look at in the next chapter.

Time Routines

It is possible to find out how long it has been since the system was started up by calling **TickCount**.

```
long TickCount();
```

The long integer returned by **TickCount** is the number of ticks (sixtieths of a second) that have occurred since the system was started up. If our application implemented a clock or timer—as in a game for example—it might have a **TickCount** call somewhere in its main event loop. This call would allow the application to update the clock every time through the loop.

Escape from the Main Event Loop

One last thing we'll need to know is how to get out of the main eventloop, in other words, how to let the user exit from an application. The toolbox provides the procedure **ExitToShell** specifically for this purpose.

```
ExitToShell();
```

The procedure **ExitToShell** quits the current application and returns to the Finder.

The other way to do this is to simply allow the loop to cease looping. The program will then fall through to the end of itself and re-start the Finder. You may prefer to exit this way for a number of reasons. If the value which the eventloop tests is a global variable, you can signal the end of the program from multiple locations within your code by simply setting this global variable false.

A commonly used name for this variable is alive. When alive is no longer true, your program will no longer be alive.

A Sample Main Event Loop Program

The following is a sample main event loop. The loop has switch statements for each possible event type, except for application defined events. In practice, your application's main event loop will typically not have switch statements for every event type, but rather only those that your application wants to respond to. Inside of each case, you would insert the appropriate routines to respond to the event detected.

It's time to move on to another essential feature of Macintosh applications—namely, windows.

```
EventRecord    event;

while (TRUE){
    if (GetNextEvent(everyEvent,&event)) {
        switch (event.what) {

            case mouseDown:                      /* mouse-down event */
                break;

            case mouseUp:                         /* mouse-up event */
                break;

            case keyDown:                         /* key-down event */
                break;

            case keyUp:                            /* key-up event */
                break;

            case autoKey:                         /* auto-key event */
                break;

            case updateEvt:                        /* update event */
                break;

            case diskEvt:                    /* disk-inserted event */
                break;

            case activateEvt:                    /* activate event */
                break;

            case networkEvt:                      /* network event */
                break;

            case driverEvt:                 /* device driver event */
                break;

            case nullEvent:              /* no events are pending */

        }
    }
}
```

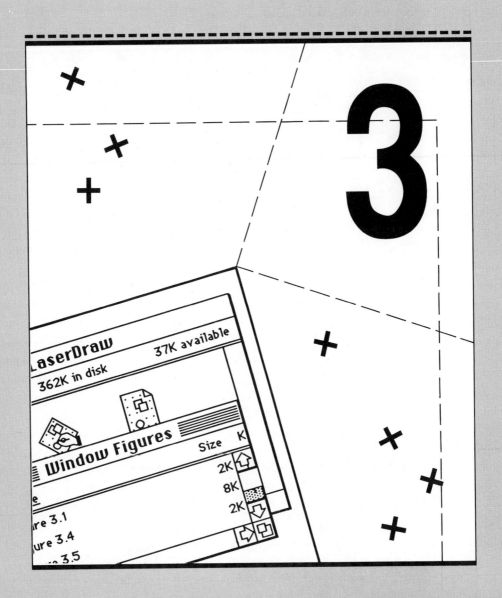

An Introduction to the Window Manager

Windows like those shown in Figure 3.1 are perhaps the single most striking feature of the Macintosh. Windows serve primarily as a means for organizing the display of information on the desktop, allowing the program user to rapidly access information organized in a natural extension to an office desk environment. It is important that we begin the topic of windows early, to emphasize their fundamental importance in the Toolbox. Now that we understand how the Macintosh uses events to react to the world around it, an examination of windows will provide a convenient setting for our first elementary programming examples.

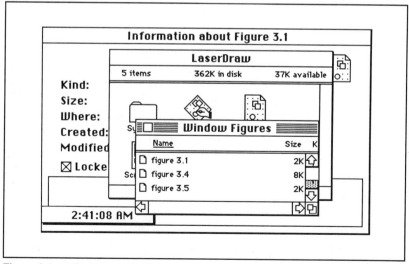

Figure 3.1: Windows on the Desktop

We begin our discussion of windows with an introduction to the Toolbox procedures used to perform basic window operations. The Window Manager contains commands for creating, manipulating, and destroying windows. In this chapter we will not attempt a complete discussion of the Window Manager but will instead offer a description of the features needed to construct a program using a single window. For many types of applications—namely games and utilities—a single window is sufficient. Including desk accessories or dialog windows in an application is a more complex process because it involves overlapping windows. At this time, however, it is important to concentrate our efforts on the processes involved in creating, disposing, moving, and resizing a single window. In Chapter 7 we will return to the Window Manager to discuss the more difficult subject of manipulating multiple windows.

When the MultiFinder is running, even a single application such as the one described in this chapter, may have to contend with multiple windows. The other windows belong to different applications that are running concurrently. The methods of responding to this are beyond the scope of this book.

Types of Windows

Before we can begin to discuss how an application interacts with the Window Manager, we must first discuss windows themselves. The Toolbox contains the definitions for six types of windows; in addition, you may choose to define your own custom window styles. These predefined window types are shown in Figure 3.2. The window types are actually constants that are defined in the Window Manager header file included with your development system. Figure 3.3 lists, for each predefined window style, the type name and the window definition ID, along with its assigned value. The names of the standard window types suggest the usual ways in which these types are used, as document windows and dialog and alert boxes.

The two types of document windows, documentProc and noGrow-DocProc, are nearly identical, the only difference being that the former can be resized, while the latter cannot. The rounded document window, rDocProc, is often used for desk accessories; the radii of curvature can be varied by adding a constant, from 1 to 7, to the definition ID (see Figure 3.4). The remaining windows types are commonly used for dialogs and alerts.

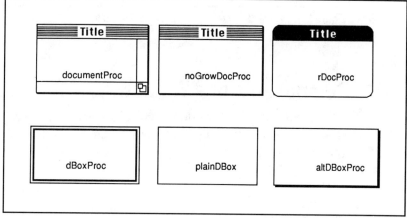

Figure 3.2:   Predefined Window Styles

Window Type	window ID	
Document window	documentProc	= 0
Dialog box	dBoxProc	= 1
Plain dialog box	plainDBox	= 2
Alternative dialog box	altDBoxProc	= 3
Fixed size document window	noGrowDocProc	= 4
Rounded document window	rDocProc	= 16

Figure 3.3:   Window Types and Definition IDs

windowID	radii
rDocProc	16,16
rDocProc + 1	4,4
rDocProc + 2	6,6
rDocProc + 3	8,8
rDocProc + 4	10,10
rDocProc + 5	12,12
rDocProc + 6	20,20
rDocProc + 7	24,24

Figure 3.4:   Radii of Curvature for rDocProc Windows

Components of a Window

An individual window can be divided into distinct regions. These regions are illustrated in Figure 3.5 and are described in the following sections.

Title Bar (Drag Region)

The frame containing the window's title, if there is one, is known as the *title bar*. This area is used for dragging the window with the mouse. Dialog and alert boxes have no title bar and thus cannot be moved like document windows. To conform with the "User Interface Guidelines," the title bar of the active, or frontmost, window should always be highlighted, while for inactive windows the title bar should remain unhighlighted.

Close Box (Go-Away Region)

The *close box* is the small square in the upper left-hand corner of document windows. The close box, which is optional, can be used to notify the application that the user is finished with a window and that it should be put away. Alerts and many dialogs do not contain close boxes since they are not designed to be put away by the user.

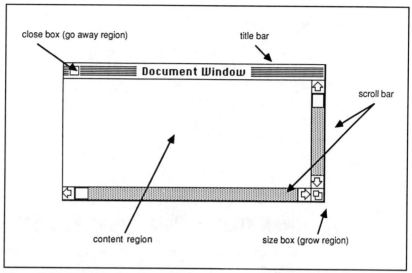

Figure 3.5:   Parts of a Document Window

Size Box (Grow Region)

The small icon in the lower right hand corner of many document windows is the *size box*. The presence of such a grow region
indicates that the size of the window may be adjusted with the mouse,
although as we shall see later in this chapter, the size box need not be
visible to resize a window.

Content Region

The *content region* is the interior of the window where text or
graphics will be drawn. For inactive windows, the grow region becomes
part of the content region. Under normal circumstances when a mouse-
down event occurs in the content region of an inactive window, the
application should instruct the Window Manager to make it become
the active window.

Structure Region

The *structure region* is defined by the sum of all the parts of a window we have just discussed. The role of the structure region is to indicate the total size of the window on the desktop. When an application moves overlapping windows, the structure regions of the frontmost windows are used by the Window Manager to determine which portions of the underlying windows must be redrawn.

Window Manager Data Types and Structures

As is the case for nearly all of the sections within the Toolbox, the Window Manager has its own internal types of variables and data structures. Associated with each and every window in the system is a structure known as a WindowRecord, which contains information unique to the window. The box entitled "Window Manager Data Structures" contains the definitions of the data type WindowRecord and several associated data types, which can be found in the header files of your development system.

The storage for a WindowRecord must be nonrelocatable and can easily be allocated by the application itself as a local variable. In addition, the Window Manager can obtain the necessary memory. The contents of a nonrelocatable object, like a WindowRecord, can be accessed through a pointer, in this case a variable of type WindowPeek. To refer to a window as an entity on the desktop, use the variable type WindowPtr.

Most of the fields in a WindowRecord used by the operating system are rarely directly manipulated by the application. The refCon field, however, is designed for use by the application and can contain any 32-bit value the application decides to associate with a particular window (a pointer or handle to a related data structure might be kept here). The updateRgn field is also read by many applications, as it contains a handle to the region describing which portions of a window need to be redrawn. The uses of the updateRgn will be discussed when we return to the Window Manager in Chapter 7.

Window Manager Data Structures

```
struct  WR  {
        GrafPort           port;               /* grafPort for window */
        int                windowKind;         /* creator of window */
        char               visible;            /* TRUE if visible */
        char               hilited;            /* TRUE if hilighted */
        char               goAwayFlag;         /* TRUE if has go-away region */
        char               spareFlag;          /* system use */
        RgnHandle          strucRgn;           /* handle to structure region */
        RgnHandle          contRgn;            /* handle to content region */
        RgnHandle          updateRgn;          /* handle to update region */
        Handle             windowDefProc;      /* window definition function */
        Handle             dataHandle;         /* data for definition function */
        Handle             titleHandle;        /* handle to title string */
        int                titleWidth;         /* width of title in pixels */
        Handle             controlList;        /* control list for window */
        struct WR          *nextWindow;        /* next window in window list */
        PicHandle          windowPic;          /* picture for drawing window */
        long               refCon;             /* reference value for application */
};

#define            WindowRecord struct WR
typedef            WindowRecord *WindowPeek;
typedef            GrafPtr   WindowPtr;     /*a GrafPtr is a QuickDraw data type*/
```

Windows and GrafPorts

When drawing text or graphics in a window, an application must inform the Toolbox where to draw by referring to the window as a *grafPort*, a type of graphics device. Choosing a particular *grafPort* is similar to sending a printer file to one of several printers and plotters connected to a computer. Since the Macintosh can support multiple windows on the screen, the Toolbox must know which window the upcoming drawing commands should be carried out in. It is not necessary for the window you wish to modify to be the active window on the desktop, indeed, the window may not even be visible while you are drawing into it. We will discuss *grafPorts* further in Chapter 5, when we focus on QuickDraw.

To inform the Macintosh Toolbox which window it should begin drawing into, use the procedure

```
SetPort(gp)
     GrafPtr gp;
```

The parameter passed to **SetPort** is a pointer to the data contained in the grafPort that is assigned to the window that the Toolbox should begin drawing in. If you study the structure of a WindowRecord, you will see that the WindowPtr is in fact the GrafPtr of the window.

The procedure **GetPort** returns in its parameter a pointer to the current grafPort, which is the same as the WindowPtr of the window where a drawing command last took place.

```
GetPort(gp)
     GrafPtr *gp;
```

The following is a short example that uses **GetPort** to obtain a copy of the current grafPort.

```
/* locally defined variables - GrafPtr for current grafPort */

GrafPtr currentGrafPtr;

/* get current GrafPtr - pass location of currentGrafPtr */

GetPort(&currentGrafPtr);
```

We will make use of this example in Chapter 7 when dealing with multiple windows.

Using the Window Manager

Before you can use any of the Window Manager's routines, it must be initialized with the procedure

```
InitWindows();
```

which draws the desktop and an empty menu bar. **InitWindows** also reserves storage for the desktop (a variable of type GrafPort) and makes the desktop the current grafPort. If you wish to draw on the desktop or alter any of the default settings such as background pattern, refer to Chapter 5 where the actual contents of a GrafPort are discussed.

Creating a New Window

As you'll see in many of the following chapters, there are two ways to create most of the things on the Macintosh which involve significant amounts of static storage. The most obvious way to create a new window is to define it with Toolbox calls from your program. The less obvious way is to define it as a program resource.

Chapter 9 of this book includes a complete description of how to create and utilize resources. We'll touch on the process here, however, as it pertains to the Window Manager.

Let's begin with the easy way to create a window, a Toolbox call from your program. To create a new window on the desktop, call the function

```
WindowPtr NewWindow(wStorage,boundsRect, title, visible, procID,
    behind, goAwayFlag, refCon)
        WindowPeek    wStorage;
        Rect          *boundsRect;
        Str255        *title;
        char          visible;
        int           procID;
        WindowPtr     behind;
        char          goAwayFlag;
        long          refCon;
```

Let's examine each of the parameters of **NewWindow** in detail.

wStorage **Parameter**

When the window is created, the Window Manager will place the WindowRecord at the location pointed to by the wStorage parameter. If the value NULL is passed, **NewWindow** will request space from the Memory Manager instead. In most cases the application should supply storage directly, by setting wStorage to the address of a WindowRecord declared in the application. We will see in Chapters 6 and 7 how to request this space directly from the Memory Manager. A good rule of thumb is to allow **NewWindow** to allocate the storage for windows that appear only briefly, such as dialogs or alerts.

boundsRect **Parameter**

The boundsRect parameter points to a variable of type Rect containing the bounding rectangle, in global coordinates (see boxed discussion of global coordinates). The coordinates are global and as such specify not only the size of the window but also its position on the desktop. The area enclosed by the boundsRect becomes the content region of the window. For rounded or plain document windows, the bounding rectangle does not include the region occupied by the title bar. One must consider the additional area occupied by the title bar when drawing windows, especially when placing them near the menu bar (the height of the menu bar is 20 pixels).

title **Parameter**

The title for the window, pointed to by title, is passed as a Pascal string. The title parameter may also be specified as a C string, but it must first be converted to a Pascal string before being passed to **NewWindow**. It is important to recall from our earlier discussion of C to Pascal string

---

Macintosh Global Coordinates

The coordinates used on the Macintosh desktop are referred to as global coordinates. In this Cartesian system the top left corner of the screen is the origin, the point (0,0), while the lower right hand corner of the screen, on a standard Macintosh, is the point (512,342). Any point on the desktop, even though it may not fit on the current screen, can be expressed in this system of coordinates as a horizontal and vertical offset from the origin at (0,0). To define a rectangle, one needs two points corresponding to the top-left and bottom-right corners of the rectangle. Coordinate systems, points and rectangles are discussed in greater detail in Chapter 5, the QuickDraw chapter.

conversion that if the string will be reused (for example to recreate the title if the window has been closed), you must make certain to reconvert the string to C format. **NewWindow** requests the Memory Manager to make a private relocatable copy of the string and places a handle to it in the titleHandle field of the WindowRecord. The title parameter will be ignored for windows that cannot have titles.

If you simply want to pass a fixed string for this argument, you can define it by using the special Think C Pascal string notation, like this:

```
"\pUntitled"
```

Note that even if your window is not a type which has a title, you must have an argument here. It should be an empty string, but it should be an empty *Pascal* string. This would be written as "\p".

visible **Parameter**

The visible parameter is a Boolean value that determines whether the window should appear on the desktop or remain hidden. Windows are often created in an invisible state, so that the contents can be drawn before the window appears on the desktop. Pass a true value here to make the window visible.

procID **Parameter**

The type of window to draw is specified by the procID parameter. Pass one of the window definition IDs shown in Figure 3.2.

behind **Parameter**

To place the new window underneath an existing window on the desktop, set the behind parameter to the WindowPtr of the existing window. Alternatively, the new window can be placed either in front of or behind all other windows by passing a value of (WindowPtr)−1L or (WindowPtr)0L, respectively. Note that casting the values to type WindowPtr is mandatory in C, since the internal representation of an integer may not be the same as that for a pointer.

goAwayFlag **Parameter**

The parameter goAwayFlag determines whether the window
will be drawn with a close box. You must pass a true - nonzero - value
if the window should contain a close box, or a false value if it should
not. This parameter will be ignored if the window style does not include a close box.

refCon **Parameter**

As we mentioned earlier, each WindowRecord contains a 32-bit
value, the refCon field, for use by the application program. This value
may be initialized by passing the desired value as the refCon parameter in
a call to **NewWindow**. Subsequent chapters will provide examples of possible ways in which an application can use the refCon field.

An Example: Creating a New Window from C

The following function entitled MakeAWindow creates a new window on the desktop and makes it the current grafPort. Before creating the
window, the routine must create a bounding rectangle for the window
and convert the title string to the (Pascal) format used by the Toolbox.

```
WindowPtr MakeAWindow()/* MakeAWindow() */
{
        /* locally defined variables */

        Rect     myBoundsRect;
        char     *myTitle;

        /* initialize bounding rectangle
        - use SetRect from QuickDraw
        - SetRect(&myBoundsRect, left, top, right, bottom);

          */

        SetRect(&myBoundsRect, 50, 60, 150, 260);

        /* initialize pointer with C string constant */
        myTitle = "My Window Title";

        /* create myWindow
```

```
          - convert title with CtoPstr()
          - window ID = rDocProc (rounded document window)
          - visible & in front of all other windows
          - with go-away region
          - use global WindowRecord myWindowRec
          - allocate storage locally */

     myWindowPtr = NewWindow(&myWindowRec, &myBoundsRect,
              CtoPstr(myTitle), 0xff, rDocProc, (WindowPtr) -1L,
              0xff, 0L);

     PtoCStr(myTitle);          /* reconvert to C string */

     SetPort(myWindowPtr);   /* set current port to myWindow */
     return myWindowPtr;
}
```

Notice that the routine has assumed the WindowRecord is a global variable. For now this is acceptable, but in a real application it would be better to keep this and other Toolbox structures in a separate block of memory requested explicitly from the Memory Manager. We will see just how to do this in Chapter 6.

Creating a New Window as a Resource

Think C comes with a program called *RMaker*. This is a resource compiler. In effect, it is a special language for writing data definitions in. Because the Macintosh uses so many kinds of complex data, having a streamlined way of defining them is important to writing efficient programs.

Under Think C, the compiler will automatically link a compiled resource file with the same name as your program. If your program is called *MyProgram.C*, Think C will look for a file called *MyProgram. Rsrc* and include it in the compilation process if it's found. The complete details of this procedure can be found in Chapter 9.

In order to create a window as a resource, you must write a resource file which contains the window definition in RMaker's language, transfer to RMaker, compile the resource file, transfer back to Think C and then compile your program. Again, a more complete explanation of this process can be found in Chapter 9.

Despite the obvious complexity of using resources rather than using C language calls, (for those circumstances where you have a choice) using resources is preferable when you get into writing large applications. It gives the Macintosh a lot more flexibility in managing its memory.

In addition, resources can be modified after your program has been compiled. The *ResEdit* program, which also comes with Think C, allows you to extract any resource, make changes to it, and return it to your program. An advanced technique along these lines allows applications to modify their own resources, for example, to allow users to configure the size and placement of windows to their liking. At various places in *Inside Macintosh*, Apple hints at this not being a very good idea, but it's widely used in professional application development just the same.

This is the RMaker definition for a window:

```
TYPE WIND
        ,128
Untitled
100 120 200 450
Visible GoAway
0
0
```

Let's see what each of these lines does.

The *TYPE* Field

The first line tells RMaker what sort of resource this is. There is a list of the common resource types in Appendix D of the Think C user's manual. RMaker will deal with the rest of the fields in this resource in a way which is appropriate to the *TYPE* field. All resource types are exactly four characters long.

The *Reference Number*

This is the number which your program will use to call this window. It can be any integer you want. It is allowable to have multiple resources in the same file with the same numbers so long as you don't have multiple resources of the same type and the same number. Later on in this resource file you might define a *MENU* resource numbered 128.

The *title*

This is the title which will appear in the window, assuming that the window you are defining is of a type which supports a title. Even if it is not, you must put some text on this line. You can alter the title from within your program later on by using the **SetWTitle** and **GetWTitle** Toolbox functions.

RMaker automatically generates this title as a Pascal style string.

The *Bounding Rectangle*

This defines where the window will appear on your screen, in global coordinates. These numbers appear in the order top, left, bottom, right.

The *Visible* Field

This tells the window manager that the window is to be visible and that it is to have a GoAway box.

The *Window Type*

This defines which of the six basic window types this is to be. The zero on this line means that this will be a document window with a size box. Consult Figures 3.2 and 3.3 for the other window types and their appropriate numbers.

The refCon

This is the same as the refCon argument in **NewWindow** above.

Calling a Window Resource from C

If the definition of a window resource seems complicated, it is at least partially offset by the C language call for a window resource, which is much simpler.

```
WindowPtr GetNewWindow(windowID,   wStorage, behind)
      int    windowID;
      WindowPeek      wStorage;
      WindowPtr       behind;
```

The windowID in this example would be 128. In order to make the window appear in front of all the other windows on the screen, which is usually what you will want to do, pass −1L for the behind argument.

Disposing of Windows

Windows should be disposed of as soon as they are no longer needed by the application. Disposing of a window decreases the amount of overhead the operating system incurs while manipulating multiple windows; in addition, any memory requested from the Memory Manager will be released.

Two Toolbox functions exist for disposing of windows:

```
DisposeWindow(theWindow)
      WindowPtr       theWindow;
```

```
CloseWindow(theWindow);
      WindowPtr       theWindow;
```

DisposeWindow should be used if **NewWindow** requested space from the Memory Manager so that the memory can be released. In the case where storage for the WindowRecord is handled entirely by the application, use **CloseWindow**, which does not attempt to release the memory occupied by the WindowRecord. Attempting to release the storage occupied by a variable declared in the application will result in a system error.

Window Display Routines

The Window Manager includes procedures to alter the appearance and front-to-back ordering of windows on the Desktop. Several of these routines are designed to be called by other Window Manager routines and are rarely used directly by the application. We will exclude many of these nonessential routines here. Refer to *Inside Macintosh* for a complete description of these routines.

The Order of Windows on the DeskTop

It is often necessary for an application to determine which window is active. The function **FrontWindow** returns the WindowPtr of the active window, or NULL if there is no active window.

```
WindowPtr FrontWindow()
```

The following example uses **FrontWindow** to determine whether a mouse-down event has occurred in an active or inactive window. The example assumes that the Event Manager has returned a mouse-down event for the window theMouseWindow:

```
/* given the non-NULL WindowPtr theMouseWindow */

if( FrontWindow() == theMouseWindow) {
        /* mouse-down in active window */
} else {
        /* mouse-down in inactive window */
}
```

Such a test should always be performed for mouse-down events. If the event occurred in an inactive window, it will need to be activated. (An exception to this rule is discussed later in this chapter in the section on moving windows.)

To change the active window when more than one window is present, as when a mouse-down event occurs in the content region of an inactive window, call the **SelectWindow** procedure, as follows:

```
SelectWindow(theWindow)

        WindowPtr theWindow;
```

This procedure first unhighlights the previously active window, moves the specified window in front of all other windows, and then highlights it. **SelectWindow** also generates activate events for the appropriate windows.

For windows that are created as invisible or are subsequently made invisible, call **ShowWindow**:

```
ShowWindow(theWindow)
        WindowPtr
        theWindow;
```

This procedure makes the window visible. Conversely, to make a visible window invisible, call **HideWindow**:

```
HideWindow(theWindow)
        WindowPtr        theWindow;
```

Calling **HideWindow** for the active window will make the frontmost remaining window active. A subsequent call to **ShowWindow** will make the window visible again, but will not bring it to the front. If no other windows are present on the desktop, **ShowWindow** will make the window active.

The Window Title

The title of a window may be changed by using the procedure **SetWTitle**, where the title parameter is a pointer to a Pascal string:

```
SetWTitle(theWindow, title)
        WindowPtr        theWindow;
        Str255           *title;
```

When converting a C string for use in **SetWTitle**, remember to reconvert to a C string before reusing the string. Alternatively, the string pointer can be declared as a global and the string converted to Pascal format one time only at the beginning of the application. The following example shows how to change the title of an existing window. The new title is in C string format:

```
/* locally defined variables */

WindowPtr      theWindow;
Str255         *newTitle;

/* initialize the pointer with a C string constant */

newTitle = "A Different Title";

/* set the new title */
```

```
SetWTitle(theWindow, CtoPstr(newTitle));

/* restore string to C format - so newTitle string
   can be reused */

PtoCstr(newTitle);
```

At times it may be useful to directly manipulate the title string of a window. **GetWTitle** returns a pointer to the title string of the window specified by theWindow.

```
GetWTitle(theWindow, title)
        WindowPtr       theWindow;
        Str255          *title;
```

It is important to recall from our earlier discussion of a Window-Record that the title string is stored in a relocatable block. Since **GetWTitle** returns a pointer to the string, any operations on the title should be performed immediately in case the string is relocated. The Memory Manager contains several procedures that permit safe access to the string in this situation (see Chapter 6).

The Size Box

If the size of a window can be adjusted, then it should have a size box. While the operation of enlarging or shrinking the window is handled by the window definition in the operating system, the need to highlight and unhighlight the size box must be handled by the application.

The procedure **DrawGrowIcon** should be called when the Event Manager reports an activate or update event for a window with a size box.

```
DrawGrowIcon(theWindow)
        WindowPtr       theWindow;
```

Of the predefined window types, only document windows can be resized. For active document windows **DrawGrowIcon** redraws the size box, and the outlines of the scroll bars. If the window is inactive **Draw-GrowIcon** redraws the outlines of the scroll bar and size box and removes the size box icon to indicate that the window cannot be resized.

More complete use of the window's content region can be made by not displaying the size box. This can be especially important when using many small windows. If the size box is not displayed, however, the user may not realize that the window can be resized.

Manipulating Windows with the Mouse

The Macintosh mouse is the primary tool for manipulating windows on the desktop. The mouse can be used to activate, move, resize, and close windows. When the Event Manager function **GetNextEvent** reports a mouse-down event, the application must first determine where the event occurred. A mouse-down event could occur in a window, in the menu bar, or in several other places. For mouse-down events in windows, the response of the application will depend on where in the window the event took place.

Determining the Location of a Mouse-Down Event

Given the global coordinates of the mouse-down event, the routine **FindWindow** will return the WindowPtr of the window, if any, in which the event occurred.

```
int FindWindow(thePt, whichWindow)
     Point          thePt;
     WindowPtr      *whichWindow;
```

Recall that under Think C, Points are passed by value rather than by reference much of the time. The whichWindow parameter is actually the address of the WindowPtr being passed. If w is a WindowPtr, you would use &w here.

FindWindow also returns one of the predefined constants, listed in Figure 3.6, to indicate the location of the mouse-down. These values should be defined in the header file for the Window Manager. After calling **FindWindow**, the parameter whichWindow will point to the WindowPtr of the window that the mouse event occurred in. If the mouse event did not occur in a window, the pointer will be set to NULL. The application can use the value returned by **FindWindow** to call routines to handle the different contexts in which a mouse-down event can occur.

Location of mouse-down	windowCode	
none of the following	inDesk	= 0
in menu bar	inMenuBar	= 1
in system window - usually a desk accessory	inSysWindow	= 2
in content region	inContent	= 3
in drag region	inDrag	= 4
in grow region - active windows only	inGrow	= 5
in go-away region - active windows only	inGoAway	= 6

Figure 3.6: Constants Returned by FindWindow

The following example demonstrates the general method for separating mouse-down events:

```
/* locally defined variables */

WindowPtr      whichWindow;
EventRecord    theEvent;
short          windowCode;

        /* This example is from a portion of the
        - application's main event loop
        - we begin at part of the switch on the event type
        - returned by GetNextEvent */

case mouseDown:

/* pass location of where field in EventRecord theEvent
- returns WindowPtr in whichWindow */

        windowCode = FindWindow(theEvent.where,
                                &whichWindow);
        switch(windowCode) { /* where did event occur? */

            case inDesk:
              /* actions appropriate for the Desktop */
              break;
            case inMenuBar:
              /* actions appropriate for the menu bar */
              break;
            case inSysWindow:
              /* actions appropriate for a system window */
              break;
```

```
case inContent:
    /* actions appropriate for content region */
    break;
case inDrag:
    /* actions appropriate for the drag region */
    break;
case inGrow:
    /* actions appropriate for the grow region */
    break;
case inGoAway:
    /* actions appropriate for
        the go-away region */
    break;
}
```

Every application that uses the mouse will include a section of code similar to this example. In upcoming chapters we will discuss how to handle mouse-down events that occur in the menu bar (Chapter 4), in the content region of a window (Chapter 7), and in system windows (Chapter 13). Mouse-down events that occur on the desktop are generally ignored (the finder is one exception to this rule, as it places icons on the desktop). In the remainder of this chapter we discuss the routines that are used to handle the parts of a window where a mouse-down event can occur.

Using the Go-Away Region

If **FindWindow** reports that the event occurred in the go-away region, the user is probably trying to close the window. However, the window should not be closed until the mouse button has been released. If the mouse was still in the go-away region when the button was released, the window should be closed. The function **TrackGoAway** simplifies this process

```
char TrackGoAway(theWindow, thePt)
    WindowPtr       theWindow;
    Point           thePt;
```

Pass **TrackGoAway** the WindowPtr of the window in question and the global coordinates of the mouse-down event. **TrackGoAway** takes control until the mouse button is released and will highlight or unhighlight the go-away region depending on the mouse location. The value returned by **TrackGoAway** will be true if the mouse button was released in the go-away region and false otherwise.

The following demonstrates the use of **TrackGoAway**:

```
/* locally defined variables */

WindowPtr       theWindow;
EventRecord     theEvent;
char            stillInGoAway;

/* portion of switch statement following FindWindow()
- is the user trying to close the window? */

case inGoAway:
        stillInGoAway = TrackGoAway(theWindow, &theEvent.where);
        if(stillInGoAway) {
                /* Do housekeeping and close/dispose of window */
        }
        break;
```

Depending on the nature of the application, closing a window may signify additional actions, such as saving the contents of the window to a disk file. The "User Interface Guidelines" provide information about the actions appropriate to various types of applications.

Dragging a Window with the Mouse

When **FindWindow** returns the constant inDrag, the user is attempting to move the window designated by the whichWindow parameter. To allow the window to move, the application should call the following procedure:

```
DragWindow(theWindow, startPt, boundsRect)
        WindowPtr theWindow;
        Point startPt;
        Rect *boundsRect;
```

Here WindowPtr is the pointer to the window to be moved and startPt is the location of the mouse-down event in global coordinates. The bounds-Rect parameter contains a pointer to a rectangle specifying a delimiting region on the desktop, outside of which the window (actually, the mouse) cannot be moved during a call to **DragWindow**. The bounding rectangle prevents the window from being dragged off the desktop or under the menu bar where the user cannot recover it.

DragWindow takes control and waits for the mouse button to be released. During this time a gray outline of the window follows the movement of the mouse. Once the button is released, **DragWindow** calls the procedure **MoveWindow** to place the window at the new location. Unless the window is already active or the Command key is being held down, **DragWindow** activates the window by passing a true value as the front parameter to **MoveWindow**. Activation takes place after the window is moved to the new location.

To actually move the window and its contents, **DragWindow** calls the procedure **MoveWindow**. The application can move a window without using the mouse by calling **MoveWindow** itself. The parameters are the WindowPtr for the window to be moved, the new location of the upper left hand corner of the content region (in global coordinates), and whether or not the window should become the active window once the move is completed.

```
MoveWindow(theWindow, hGlobal, vGlobal, front)
      WindowPtr theWindow;
      int       hGlobal, vGlobal;
      char      front;
```

The following example illustrates the use of **DragWindow**. The bounding rectangle in this example is determined from the actual size of the screen stored in a Toolbox global variable. This enables the example to work properly on the differing screen sizes of the Macintosh and the Macintosh II (as well as on future models of the Macintosh).

```
/* Toolbox global variable: pointer to QuickDraw globals
 - global if InitGraf called in this program file
 - screen size is contained in QuickDraw globals*/
external struct QDVar *QD;

/* locally defined variables */

WindowPtr    theWindow;
EventRecord  theEvent;
Rect         dragBoundsRect;

/* initialize dragBoundsRect
```

```
        - typically inset four pixels from menubar, sides
        - and bottom of screen
        - SetRect(&dragBoundsRect, limLeft, limTop, limRight, limBottom);
        - InitGraf returns QD, pointer to QuickDraw globals
        - QD->screenBits.bounds is bounding Rect for screen */

    /* Set drag bounding rectangle to screen size -4 pixels, allow 20
    pixels for menubar */

    SetRect(&dragBoundsRect,
            QD->screenBits.bounds.left +4,
            QD->screenBits.bounds.top +24,
            QD->screenBits.bounds.right -4,
            QD->screenBits.bounds.bottom -4);

    /* portion of switch statement following FindWindow() */

    case inDrag:
            DragWindow(whichWindow, theEvent.where, &dragBoundsRect);
            break;
```

Remember, if the mouse-down occurs in the title bar of an inactive window, the application must not activate the window itself. **DragWindow** will take care of highlighting if necessary, depending on the current state of the window and, for inactive windows, the state of the Command key.

Resizing Windows: Using the Mouse to Determine the New Size

When **FindWindow** reports a mouse-down in the size box of the active window, the user is attempting to resize the window. The application can use the function **GrowWindow** to obtain the new window size. Pass the appropriate WindowPtr indicated by **FindWindow**, the global coordinates of the mouse-down event, and a pointer to a rectangle describing the limiting sizes of the window. This limiting rectangle is constructed as follows: the maximum (minimum) vertical extent is contained in the top (bottom) field, and the maximum (minimum) horizontal extent is contained in the left (right) field.

```
long GrowWindow(theWindow, startPt, sizeRect)
        WindowPtr    theWindow;
        Point        startPt;
        Rect         *sizeRect;
```

GrowWindow takes control and waits for the mouse button to be released. While the mouse button is held down, a gray outline (the "grow" image) of the window expands and contracts to follow the movement of the mouse. When the mouse button is released, **GrowWindow** returns as its value the new size determined from the position of the mouse. The size is returned as two short (16-bit) integers packed into a single long (32-bit) integer (see Figure 3.7).

The high-order word of the value returned by **GrowWindow** contains the vertical size in pixels (the low-order word contains the horizontal size). If the size selected by the user is the same as the current size of the window, a value of NULL will be returned. Figure 3.8 shows the appearance of a window being resized during a call to **GrowWindow**.

The Toolbox provides two functions to extract the short integers from the long value returned by **GrowWindow**: **HiWord** and **LoWord**. These

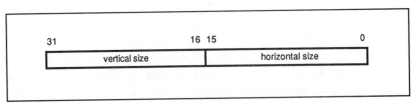

Figure 3.7: The Window Size Returned by GrowWindow

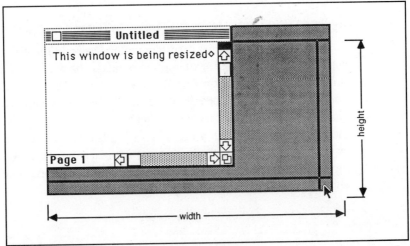

Figure 3.8: Resizing a Window Using GrowWindow

functions take the long (32-bit) value as a parameter and return the appropriate int (16-bit) values.

```
int HiWord(x)
        long x;

int LoWord(x)
        long x;
```

Resizing Windows: Redrawing the Window at the New Size

To change the size of the window to the dimensions specified by **GrowWindow**, the application should call the **SizeWindow** procedure:

```
SizeWindow(theWindow, width, height, fUpdate)
        WindowPtr    theWindow;
        int          w, h;
        char         fUpdate;
```

The calling parameters are the WindowPtr of the window to be resized, the desired width and height, in pixels, of the window's content region, and a flag to indicate whether **SizeWindow** should accumulate any new area into the update region for the window. If both width and height of the new size are zero, as would be the case if **GrowWindow** previously returned a value of NULL, the size of the window is not changed. Setting fUpdate to a true value instructs **SizeWindow** to automatically modify the window's update region, which is what is normally done. In some cases it is convenient for the application itself to maintain the update region, for instance if the window contains a QuickDraw picture (this is covered briefly in Chapter 7).

Here is an example using **GrowWindow** and **SizeWindow** in conjunction to modify the size of a window:

```
/* locally defined variables */

WindowPtr      theWindow;
EventRecord    theEvent;
Rect           limitRect;
long           newSize;

/* initialize limitRect
```

```
- determines max and min window dimensions
- typically based on screen size or other
- program constraint
- SetRect(&limitRect, minHoriz, minVert, maxHoriz, maxVert);*/

SetRect(&limitRect, 80, 40, 500, 300);

/* portion of switch statement following FindWindow */

case inGrow:
        newSize = GrowWindow(whichWindow, theEvent.where,
                             &limitRect);
        SizeWindow(whichWindow, LoWord(newSize),
               HiWord(newSize), 0xff);
        break;
```

The maximum size of a window can be based either on the actual size of the screen or on a constraint imposed by the application itself. It is best not to make any assumptions about the size of the screen since it's of a different size on the Macintosh II, and will probably undergo further changes in future Macs.

▬▬▬▬▬

A Sample Program: Using Events and Windows

This concludes our discussion of the routines comprising the Toolbox Window Manager for the time being. We will resume the discussion of windows in Chapter 7, which covers more advanced aspects of using the Window Manager: handling update and activate events, maintaining the update region, using the refCon field of the WindowRecord, and other miscellaneous items.

The first complete program we are presenting begins on the following page. It includes nearly everything we have learned in this and the previous chapter, and as such will serve as an excellent chance to review the Event and Window Managers. The program consists of a single procedure, main. The first part of main initializes the Toolbox, changes the cursor shape from the watch to the familiar arrow, empties the event queue, and sets up the rectangles used to limit window movement and window size.

The second part of the procedure main is the event loop which begins with the **GetNextEvent** function. The example uses key-down events in conjunction with the Command key to create a window, close the window, make the window visible or invisible, change the window's title, and return to the Finder. Mouse-down events are screened to determine where they occurred, and if appropriate are used to unhighlight the window, highlight the window, drag the window, resize the window, and close the window using the go-away region. All other types of events are ignored.

In order to make this sample program complete, we have had to borrow a few routines from QuickDraw and the Memory Manager, which are the topics of Chapters 5 and 6. Portions of the program that use routines from these chapters include comments that indicate we are anticipating material we have not yet covered.

```c
/* Window & Event Manager Sample Program */

#include <EventMgr.h>
#include <WindowMgr.h>
#include <Pascal.h>                          /* string conversion utilities */
#include <stdio.h>
/* Program begins here */

main()      /* main() */
{
   /* declare local variables */

   EventRecord     theEvent;
   WindowRecord    theWindowRec;
   WindowPtr       theWindow, whichWindow;
   RgnHandle       contRgnHnd;
   Rect            myBoundsRect, dragBoundsRect, limitRect;
   Rect            tempRect;                        /* Not listed in Book! */
   short           windowCode, stillInGoAway, wType;
   static char     *myTitle, *newTitle;
   char            c;
   long            newSize;
```

```
      InitGraf(&thePort);                    /* Initialize QuickDraw        */
      InitFonts();
      InitWindows();                         /* Initialize the Window Manager */
      InitCursor();                          /* Set cursor to arrow style
                                                otherwise will remain watch */

      FlushEvents(everyEvent, 0);            /* Empty event queue of
                                                stray or leftover events */

      SetRect(&myBoundsRect,50,50,300,150);  /* initialize myBoundsRect */


   /* initialize dragBoundsRect - limits movement of window
         - for use with Mac & MacXL
         - InitGraf returns QD (thePort), pointer to QuickDraw globals
         - QD->screenBits.bounds is bounding Rect for screen */

   SetRect(&dragBoundsRect,
      screenBits.bounds.left +4,
      screenBits.bounds.top +24,
      screenBits.bounds.right -4,
      screenBits.bounds.bottom -4);

   /* initialize limitRect - limits size of window */

   SetRect(&limitRect, 60, 40,
      screenBits.bounds.right  - screenBits.bounds.left -4,
      screenBits.bounds.bottom - screenBits.bounds.top  -24);

theWindow = NULL;

/* Begin event loop */

while (1) {
   if (GetNextEvent(everyEvent, &theEvent)) {
      switch (theEvent.what) {

         case keyDown:

            if(!(theEvent.modifiers & cmdKey)) break; /* if Command-key not down
                                                          ignore key-down */
            c = theEvent.message & charCodeMask;      /* char code in lower 8 bits */

            if( c == 'q' || c =='Q')
                  ExitToShell();                       /* quit program, return to Finder */

            if (theWindow == NULL) {                  /* if no window, look for 'M'
                                                          and create new window */

               if(c == 'm' || c == 'M') {

               /* create theWindow - use local storage for WindowRecord */

               myTitle = "\pMy Window Title";        /* static string myTitle */

                  wType = documentProc + 8;
```

```
            theWindow = NewWindow(&theWindowRec, &myBoundsRect,
                         myTitle, 0xff, wType,
                         (WindowPtr) -1, 0xff, 0);

          DrawGrowIcon(theWindow);          /* draw size box and
                                               scroll bar outlines */
        } else SysBeep(1);

    } else {

      /* a window already exists, try various window commands */

      switch(c) {

        case 'x':
        case 'X':                           /* Close theWindow
                                               don't dispose of storage */
          CloseWindow(theWindow);
          theWindow = NULL;
          break;

        case 's':
        case 'S':                           /* make theWindow visible */

          ShowWindow(theWindow);
          DrawGrowIcon(theWindow);        /* draw size box and */
          break;                          /* scroll bar outlines */

        case 'h':
        case 'H':                           /* make theWindow invisible */

          HideWindow(theWindow);
          break;

        case 't':
        case 'T':                           /* change the title of theWindow */

          newTitle = "\pA Different Title";   /* Pascal static string */

          SetWTitle(theWindow, newTitle);     /* set the new title */

          break;

        default:
          break;
      }
    }
    break;

case mouseDown: {
```

```
     /* where did mouse-down occur? */
windowCode=FindWindow(theEvent.where, &whichWindow);
switch (windowCode) {

    case inDesk:                              /* on the desktop */

        if(theWindow != NULL) {               /* if theWindow exists... */
            HiliteWindow(theWindow,0);        /* unhilight window */
                DrawGrowIcon(theWindow);         /* hide the size box */
        }
            break;

    case inMenuBar:                          /* do nothing */
        SysBeep(1);
        break;

        case inSysWindow:                        /* do nothing */
            SysBeep(1);
            break;

        case inContent:                          /* hilight window */

            HiliteWindow(whichWindow, 0xff);

        DrawGrowIcon(theWindow);              /* draw size box and */
        break;                                /* scroll bar outlines */

    case inDrag:                             /* drag window */

        DragWindow(whichWindow,theEvent.where,&dragBoundsRect);
                              /* can you see why this is needed */
        DrawGrowIcon(theWindow);                 /* draw size box and */
        break;                                   /* scroll bar outlines */

    case inGrow:                             /* resize window */

        newSize = GrowWindow(whichWindow,theEvent.where,
                        &limitRect);     /* get new size from user */

        SizeWindow(whichWindow, LoWord(newSize),
HiWord(newSize), 0);            /* redraw window to newSize */

            /* Erase inside of window and
                  - redraw size box and scroll bar outlines
                  - try commenting out this section to see what happens

                  - refer to QuickDraw for definition of a -Region- */

    contRgnHnd = theWindowRec.contRgn;   /* get handle to content
                                              region of theWindow */
```

```
                  tempRect = (*contRgnHnd)->rgnBBox;
                                    /* Memory Manager - copy rect as
                                       EraseRect may compact heap */
                                    /* More efficient than lock/unlock */
                  EraseRect(&tempRect);   /* erase window, parameter is
                                       bounding Rect of content */
                  DrawGrowIcon(theWindow); /* draw size box and */
                  break;                  /* scroll bar outlines */

              case inGoAway:              /* in close box */
                  stillInGoAway = TrackGoAway(whichWindow,theEvent.where);
                                          /* is mouse still in close box? */
                  if(stillInGoAway) {
                      CloseWindow(whichWindow);  /* Yes, close window */
                      theWindow = NULL;
                  }
                  break;

                  /* Treat ZoomBox: Erase inside of window and
                        - redraw size box and scroll bar outlines
                        - Note the alternate way to erase content
                        - (GrafPorts portRect)
                        - refer to QuickDraw for definition of a -GrafPort- */

                  case inZoomIn:
                  case inZoomOut:
                     if(TrackBox(whichWindow,theEvent.where, windowCode)) {
                     GrafPtr curPort;

                     contRgnHnd = theWindowRec.contRgn;
                        tempRect = (*contRgnHnd)->rgnBBox;
                        EraseRect(&tempRect);

                         GetPort(&curPort);
                         SetPort(whichWindow);
                        ZoomWindow(whichWindow, windowCode, 0);
                        DrawGrowIcon(theWindow);
                         SetPort(curPort);
                     }
                     break;
                  }
               break;
            }

         default:
            break;
         }
      }
   }
}    /* end of procedure main() */
```

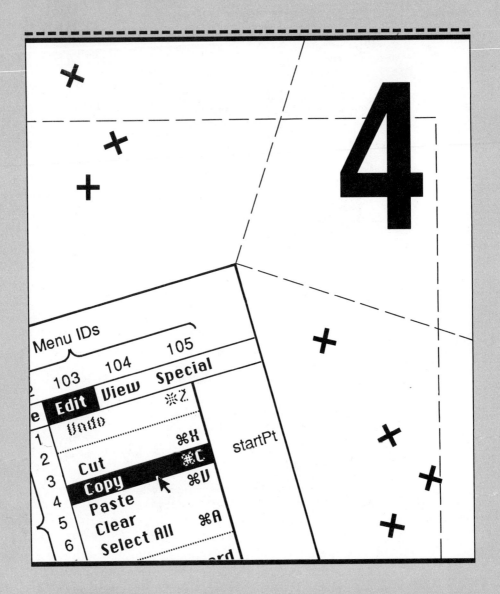

Using the Menu Manager

After events and windows, the next most fundamental element of a Macintosh application is the use of menus. Menus are the central control element of nearly all Macintosh applications and one of the more distinctive elements of the Macintosh user interface. To use menus effectively in an application, we'll first need to be able to create them. That means defining their titles and contents and deciding on the appearance of each menu item. Next we'll need to insert the menus into the application—that is, actually make them show up on the top of the screen. Finally we'll need to know how to tell the rest of the program which menu item (if any) was selected and what to do as a result.

Anatomy of Menus

Before we examine the functions provided by the Menu Manager we should take some time to go over the nomenclature of menus (see Figure 4.1). At the top of the Macintosh screen in all menu-driven applications (which comprise the majority of Macintosh applications) is the thin white strip called the *menu bar*. The menu bar measures 20 pixels high and is bordered on the bottom by a thin black line. Up to 16 menus may reside in the menu bar at any given time but with titles of average length, 10 to 12 menus are usually the most that will fit. Text in the menu bar is always in the system font and the system font size.

Menus themselves consist of a vertical list of *menu items* inside a shadowed rectangle. The text of the menu items, like that of the title in the menu bar, is always in the system font and system font size. Despite

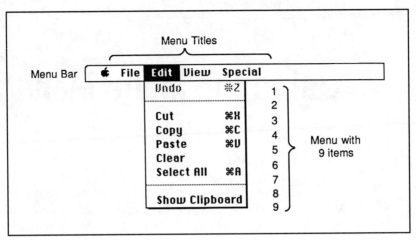

Figure 4.1: Menu Parts

the font limitations, however, you do have the flexibility to vary the appearance of menu items. Besides the standard type style enhancements (boldface, italics, and so on), an icon can be added to the left side of the item and a check mark or other symbol can be used to indicate that an item has been selected. Each menu item can also show a keyboard equivalent at the right, indicated by the Command key symbol (⌘) together with the appropriate keyboard character. A maximum of 20 items will fit in a menu. Because of the size of icons, menu items with icons count as two items.

Menu Manager Types and Structures

All the information required by the system about a particular menu is stored in a *menu record*. A menu record is defined as data type MenuInfo and is referred to by an application through a *menu handle*. Because the Menu Manager takes care of all the manipulation within menu records, it isn't necessary to be familiar with the exact field names. However, knowing the structure of a menu record, as shown in the box "Menu Manager Data Structures," helps in understanding the Menu Manager.

Menu Manager Data Structures

```
struct MenuRecord
{
        int            menuID;              /* menu ID */
        int            menuWidth;           /* menu width in pixels */
        int            menuHeight;          /* menu height in pixels */
        Handle         menuProc;            /* Handle to menu definition procedure */
        long           enableFlags;         /* tells if menu items are enabled or not */
        Str255         menuData;            /* menu title (and other stuff) */
};

#define         MenuInfo            struct MenuRecord
typedef         MenuRecord          * MenuPtr;
typedef         MenuPtr             * MenuHandle;
```

The first field of the menu record is filled by a unique menuID that identifies the menu to the Menu Manager. The menuID is assigned by the programmer and can be any positive integer, as long as the ID is unique within the program. Negative menuIDs are reserved for the system.

The next two fields hold the menu's width and height measured in pixels. These fields are set and used by the Menu Manager and the programmer never has to worry about their contents.

The menuProc field contains a handle to the menu definition procedure, which defines the appearance of the menu as well as the location of its menu items and how they react to being selected. This field defaults to the standard menu definition procedure, which is the procedure that defines the menus you're accustomed to seeing. A good example of a custom menu is the fill-pattern menu in MacDraw. Since custom menus are beyond the scope of this discussion, you need not worry about the menuProc field.

The enableFlags field contains a long word whose bits correlate to the items of the menu in question. Beginning at bit 1, each bit corresponds to a menu item. If a bit is set, then the corresponding item is enabled; if it's clear, the item is disabled. Bit 0 toggles the status of the entire menu.

Finally, the menuData field consists of a variable length data string which contains information about the menu's text. The menu title, as well as the text and other parts of the individual menu items are stored here.

The other important pool of information on which the Menu Manager draws is the *menu list*. The menu list contains the handles, in order, to all the menus that will appear in the menu bar. Space for the menu list is automatically allocated by the Menu Manager upon initialization. The data structure for the menu list is not really important. The thing to remember about the menu list is that its contents determine the contents of the menu bar.

Creating Menus

Before using the Menu Manager, we need to initialize Quick-Draw (**InitGraf**), the Font Manager (**InitFonts**),the Window Manager (**InitWindows**), and of course the Menu Manager (**InitMenus**). The conceptual outline for creating menus in your application, as well as the accompanying code, is very simple. For each menu, you need to create a new menu record, fill in the menu items along with the desired enhancements, and add them to the menu list. After all the menus are set up, they are put into the application by drawing the menu bar.

We will first look at creating a menu through C calls, then as a resource file.

Creating a New Menu Record from C

For every new menu you want to create, a call needs to be made to **NewMenu** as follows:

```
MenuHandle NewMenu(menuID, menuTitle)
        int      menuID;
        Str255   *menuTitle;
```

When passed a menuID and menuTitle, this function creates an empty menu record and returns a handle to it. Henceforth, whenever the Menu Manager refers to this menu, it is actually referring to the associated menu record. The new menu record is not yet added to the menu list.

Filling the Menus with Items

Next, the menus need to be filled with items. This can be done in two ways. The first, **AppendMenu**, adds the items indicated by a data string to the menu designated by theMenu, as follows:

```
AppendMenu(theMenu, data)
        MenuHandle  theMenu;
        Str255      *data;
```

The data string passed to **AppendMenu** consists of the actual menu items separated by a semicolon or carriage return. A left parenthesis preceding an item disables it. One or more spaces can be used to indicate a blank item, while a hyphen (-) used as an item instructs the Menu Manager to draw a dividing line across the width of the menu. It is a good policy to always disable the dividing line; that way a user won't get confused when trying to select it.

The data string can also specify any enhancements to particular menu items. Through the use of *metacharacters*, the programmer can tell the Menu Manager exactly how to modify each menu item. The metacharacters themselves do not appear in the menu. Figure 4.2 lists the recognized metacharacters.

Meta-Character	Meaning
; or Return	Separates Items
^	When followed by an icon number, adds that icon to the item
!	When followed by a character, marks the item with that character
<	When followed by B, I, U, O, or S, sets the character style of that item
/	When followed by a character, sets that character as the item's keyboard equivalent
(	When precedes an item, disables that item

Figure 4.2: Metacharacters

For example, the code

```
NewMenu(myMenu,"\pMy Menu");
AppendMenu(myMenu,"\p&LTBFirst;Second/J;&LTUThird;(-;Fifth");
```

will create a menu that looks like the one shown in Figure 4.3. Remember that the disabled dividing line counts as an item.

The other way to fill items into a menu is with the procedure **AddResMenu**.

```
AddResMenu(theMenu, theType)
        MenuHandle        theMenu;
        ResType     theType;
```

This procedure searches all open resource files for the resource type specfied by theType (see Chapter 9 for more on resources). It then appends the names of all resources found to the menu indicated by theMenu. The resource names found appear in the menu as enabled items, without icons or marks and in the normal character style. **AddResMenu** will not add any resources whose names begin with a period (.) or a percent sign (%). In our sample program at the end of this chapter, we use **AddResMenu** to set up the desk accessory menu.

```
DeskMenu=NewMenu(DeskID, "\p\024");
AddResMenu(DeskMenu, 'DRVR');
```

The "\024" above is the octal code for the Apple character in the system font and serves as the title of the menu.

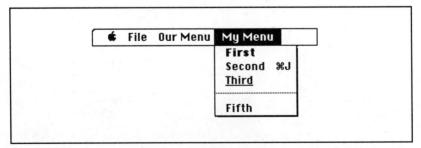

Figure 4.3: Sample Menu Using **AppendMenu**

The Menu Manager also allows you to add a resource type to the middle of a menu with the procedure **InsertResMenu**:

```
InsertResMenu(theMenu, theType, afterItem)
        MenuHandle        theMenu;
        ResType           theType;
        int     afterItem;
```

InsertResMenu works in the same way as **AddResMenu** except that it adds the resource names after the item specified by the afterItem parameter. If afterItem is zero, the names are inserted before the first menu item. If it's greater than the number of menu items, the resource names are added to the end of the menu.

Note that **AddResMenu** and **InsertResMenu**, unlike **AppendMenu**, cannot make use of metacharacters. Because of this, the Menu Manager provides functions that perform enhancements equivalent to those done by the metacharacters. Since it's not really practical to recreate an **AppendMenu** data string every time you want to change the appearance of a menu item, these functions can also be used during the course of a program to alter the appearance of a menu item.

Changing Menu Items and Their Appearance

Menu items can be dynamically changed by the program with the **SetItem** function as follows:

```
SetItem(theMenu, item, itemString)
        MenuHandle        theMenu;
        int               item;
        Str255            *itemString;
```

SetItem replaces the menu item whose item number is item to the string given by itemString. This is handy when you want to switch between two choices like "Show clipboard" and "Hide clipboard."

Enabling and Disabling Menus and Items

Menus and their items can also be enabled and disabled by the application. **EnableItem** and **DisableItem** both take the same parameters and allow the programmer to prevent the user from making inappropriate menu choices from the application. The item parameter indicates which menu item to enable or disable. If item is zero, the entire menu is enabled or disabled.

```
EnableItem (theMenu, item)
        MenuHandle        theMenu;
        int      item;

DisableItem (theMenu, item);
        MenuHandle        theMenu;
        int      item;
```

A good example of using the enable/disable toggle is when an application doesn't have any documents open. Since there are no documents open, it doesn't make much sense to select Close from the File menu. To remind the user of this, we can disable the Close command until a document is opened. Then we can call **EnableItem** to enable the Close command, allowing it to be selected.

Marking Menu Items

For menus that contain accumulating attributes, it's usually a good idea to mark items with a check mark when they are selected. To accomplish this, the Menu Manager provides this procedure:

```
CheckItem(theMenu, item, checked)
        MenuHandle      theMenu;
        int      item;
        char      checked;
```

The checked field determines whether the item indicated by the menu handle and item number should be checked or not. If a true value is passed, **CheckItem** will mark the item. If checked is false, the item will be unmarked.

You aren't limited to using a check mark as the marking character. The procedure **SetItemMark** will allow you to specify exactly which character you wish to use to mark the menu item.

```
SetItemMark(theMenu, item, markChar)
        MenuHandle      theMenu;
```

```
int          item;
int          markChar;
```

This procedure will mark the indicated menu item with whichever character is specified by markChar, allowing you to use any character from the system font. All you need to do is pass the code for the character to **SetItemMark** in the markChar parameter (a code chart for the system font is provided in Appendix C). Some of the more unique characters of the system font and their character codes are shown in Figure 4.4.

To determine which character is being used to mark a menu item, the procedure **GetItemMark** returns in its markChar parameter the ASCII code for the marking character.

```
GetItemMark(theMenu, item, markChar)
       MenuHandle    theMenu;
       int           item;
       char          *markChar;
```

If there is no marking character, markChar will be equal to zero (the ASCII code for the NULL character). This procedure can also be used to determine which way to toggle the mark next to a menu item. For instance, whenever the Bold option for text enhancement is selected from the Style menu of your application, you'll need to determine whether the item was previously marked or not and then do the opposite. In the example program at the end of this chapter, we use **GetItemMark** for this purpose. After calling the procedure, we check to see if markChar is nonzero. If it is, we know the menu was already marked and we need to un-mark it. Of course, the method used to determine whether an item is marked or not is entirely up to

Character	ASCII Value
noMark	0
commandMark	$11
checkMark	$12
diamondMark	$13
appleMark	$14

Figure 4.4:   Special Mark Characters

the programmer and is usually very dependent upon what the application is doing.

Changing the Typestyle of Menu Item

The Menu Manager also allows you to change the text style of menu items as the application proceeds. **SetItemStyle** takes the menu item indicated by the menu handle and item number passed to it and changes the character style of the item's text to that indicated by chStyle.

```
SetItemStyle (theMenu, item, chStyle)
        MenuHandle        theMenu;
        int     item;
        Style   chStyle;
```

In Think C, the variable type Style is already defined for you in the QuickDraw.h header file. You might want to look into this header file to see how the various typeface effects are named. For example, bold typeface is indicated by the variable bold (see Figure 4.5). Thus, in code **SetItemStyle** would look like this:

```
SetItemStyle(theMenu, item, bold);
```

Variable	Value
bold	1
italic	2
underline	4
outline	8
shadow	16
condense	32
extend	64

Figure 4.5: Sample Style Variables

Adding Menus to the Menu Bar

When all the menus have been set up, they need to be added to the menu list. This is done through the function **InsertMenu**.

```
InsertMenu(theMenu, beforeID)
        MenuHandle    theMenu;
        int           beforeID;
```

InsertMenu will add the menu specified by theMenu to the menu list and put it before (to the left of) the menu whose ID is specified by the beforeID parameter. If the beforeID is zero, **InsertMenu** just adds the given menu to the end of the menu list. If theMenu already exists in the menu list or the menu list is full, **InsertMenu** will do nothing. It doesn't make a difference if you insert each menu as you define it or define all your menus and then insert them. The important thing to note is that **Insert-Menu** needs to be called for each menu. If you define a menu but don't insert it, it won't show up in the menu bar.

Removing Menus from the Menu List

The reciprocal function of **InsertMenu** is **DeleteMenu**. This procedure will remove the menu specified by menuID from the menu list but will not deallocate the memory it occupies.

```
DeleteMenu (menuID)
        int      menuID;
```

If you are through using a particular menu and wish to free the memory occupied by its menu record, you need to call **DisposeMenu**:

```
DisposeMenu(theMenu)
        MenuHandle    theMenu;
```

It's important to remember to call **DeleteMenu** before disposing of its menu record and to be careful not to use the menu handle of the disposed menu.

Creating a New Menu Record as a Resource

As you saw in the Window Manager, resource definitions involve a lot less work than do creating things from C. You do have to employ RMaker to use them, of course.

This is a menu definition as written into an RMaker file. All of the preceding metacharacters and other menu phenomena can be used in a menu defined as a resource.

```
TYPE MENU
        ,128
File
Open
Close
Save As...
Save
(-
Printer setup
Print
(-
Transfer
Quit
```

The first line tells RMaker what type of resource this is. In this case, it's a *MENU* resource. Note that resource names are case sensitive. The resource *MENU* is different from the resource *Menu*.

The next line is the resource number, 128 in this case.

The line after that is the name of the menu. This is the text which will appear on the menu bar.

The rest of this definition contains the various menu items. The syntax of these is the same as they would be had you created this menu using calls to **AppendMenu**, except that rather than separating the menu items with semicolons we put each on its own line.

The definition for this menu extends down to the first blank line in the resource file.

One of the things you might have noticed in the discussion about metacharacters, particularly in Figure 4.2, was the reference to including an icon in menus. This is something which is only practical to do using a resource file. As you will see in greater detail in Chapter 9, you can define an icon as a resource. If that icon's resource number is between 257 and 265, you can make it appear in a menu right next to the item.

You can create a menu item with reference to an icon with **AppendMenu,** but not the icon itself.

This is a menu with an icon in it.

```
TYPE MENU
        ,129
Edit
Undo
(-
Cut
Copy
Paste
Clear
(-
^1Options
```

The Options item will have icon 257 beside it, assuming that there is a resource definition for this icon. The number of the icon specified with the "^" metacharacters is 256 plus the number after the metacharacters. The number after the metacharacter can be 1 through 9.

Using Resource Menus

Having defined some menus in a resource file, you must still tell your program to use them. The Menu Manager provides this function to do this:

```
MenuHandle GetMenu(number)
        int number;
```

For example, to get a handle to the above menu, you would do this:

```
handle = GetMenu(129);
```

With a handle to each of your menus, usually stored in an array of MenuHandles, you would use **InsertMenu** to add them to the menu bar.

Drawing the Menu Bar

The last step in setting up your menus is to draw the menu bar. Not surprisingly, this is done through the command **DrawMenuBar**.

```
DrawMenuBar()
```

No parameters are required. **DrawMenuBar** simply redraws the menu bar, displaying all menus that were in the menu list. A call needs to be made to **DrawMenuBar** whenever any menus are added or deleted from the menu list; otherwise, any changes the application made to the menu bar won't show up.

Choosing from Menus

Once the menu bar has been drawn, the application is ready to deal with menu selection. Thanks to the Menu Manager, this is an extremely simple task. When **GetNextEvent** detects a mouse-down event in the menu bar, all that's required is a call to **MenuSelect**.

```
long MenuSelect(startPt)
       Point   startPt;
```

Once it has been passed the point of the mouse-down event, **MenuSelect** takes control of the application, tracking the mouse, pulling down menus, and highlighting enabled menu items under the cursor until it encounters a mouse-up event. When the mouse button is released over a highlighted menu item, **MenuSelect** returns menuResult, a long word containing in its high-order word the menuID of the selected menu and in its low-order word the item number within that menu. It also highlights (that is inverts the text of) the menu title. If no choice is made, **MenuSelect** returns zero in the high-order word and the low-order word is undefined.

Handling the keyboard equivalents of menu items is no more difficult than handling regular menu selections. When there is a key-down event modified by the Command key, pass the key character to the function **MenuKey**. **MenuKey** will then determine whether that particular key is the equivalent of any active menu item. If so, it returns the same long word result as **MenuSelect** and highlights the menu title. If the key doesn't correspond to any menu items, the menu result is the same as a nonselection from **MenuSelect** (see Figure 4.6).

So what do we do now that the menu and the item have been selected? The easiest thing to do is pass the menu result to a function that switches first on the menu ID, and then on the item number to determine what task to carry out. For example, we can have a function that would look something like this:

```
doMenu(menuResult)
        long menuResult;
{
        short menuID, itemNumber;
        menuID=HiWord(menuResult);
        itemNumber= menuResult;
        switch (menuID) { /* which menu was selected? */
                case theRightID:
                        switch (itemNumber) {
                        /* which item in the menu was selected?*/
                                case theRightItem:
                                        DoSomething();
```

Our function would first decipher which menu was selected, then which item was selected, and then tell the application to go and do whatever it's supposed to.

After a selection is made with either **MenuSelect** or **MenuKey**, the menu's title is highlighted. The menu title will remain that way until the application tells the Menu Manager to return the text to its original form. To do this, the application needs to call

```
HiliteMenu(menuID)
        short   menuID;
```

with a menuID of zero. **HiliteMenu** highlights the title of the menu indicated by the given menu ID. If that title is already highlighted, this

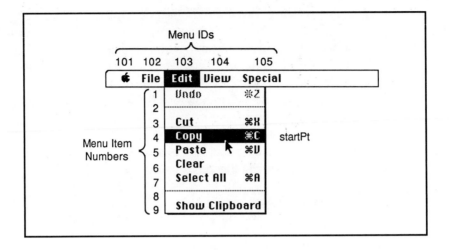

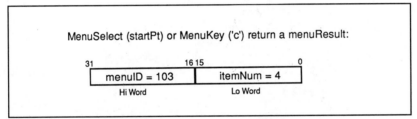

Figure 4.6: MenuSelect and MenuKey (above) and MenuResult (below)

procedure won't do anything. Because only one menu title can be highlighted at a time, **HiliteMenu** will unhighlight any menu previously highlighted. If the menu ID doesn't exist in the menu bar, **HiliteMenu** simply unhighlights whichever menu is highlighted. Thus, since by convention a menu ID cannot be zero, the call

```
HiliteMenu(0);
```

will unhighlight any highlighted menu title.

When menu items are added to a menu using either **AddResMenu** or **InsertResMenu**, the rest of your program has no way of knowing exactly how many items will be added. More importantly, your application won't know the identity of each menu item simply by its item number.

Thus, using **MenuSelect** will not work correctly. In this case, you need to use the procedure **GetItem**.

```
GetItem(theMenu, item, itemString)
       MenuHandle   theMenu;
       int          item;
       Str255       *itemString;
```

This procedure will return the text of the item given by the menu handle and item number. A word of caution is in order here. This is one of those sticky places where C and Pascal strings can get mixed up if you're not careful. **GetItem** returns a Pascal string.

At this point, we don't really know how to do anything with a text string returned from a menu selection. We'll look in depth at dealing with desk accessory menus in Chapter 13.

A Sample Program for Windows and Menus

Now we get to take a look at what we've learned to do with menus. You'll notice that we've written a couple of new procedures. The first, SetUpMenus, does exactly that; it creates new menu records and appends items to each of the menus we create. The second, doMenu, takes the result of a mouse down event in the menu bar, decides which menu item was selected, and carries it out. Aside from these two procedures, the code is essentially the same as the code we saw in Chapter 3. As far as this example program goes, nearly everything we need for dealing with menus is in these two procedures.

One other point to notice is in the case of a key down event. If the key was pressed along with the Command key, we pass the character associated with the key to **MenuKey** and then pass the **MenuKey** result to our new procedure doMenu.

That about wraps up our introduction to menus. We now know how to create and implement menus in our code. As we mentioned earlier, we'll discuss desk accessory menus in Chapter 13.

It's time to draw pictures—on to QuickDraw.

```
/* Include Header Files - contains Toolbox data types & constants */

#include <EventMgr.h>
#include <WindowMgr.h>
#include <MenuMgr.h>
#include <Pascal.h>
#include <stdio.h>


/*  Menu Stuff  */
#define   Desk_ID              100
#define   File_ID              101
#define   Our_ID               102
#define   BMUG_ID              103
#define   My_ID                104


MenuHandle          DeskMenu;
MenuHandle          FileMenu;
MenuHandle          OurMenu;
MenuHandle          BMUGMenu;
MenuHandle          MyMenu;


EventRecord          theEvent;
WindowRecord         theWindowRec;          /* Don't Fragment the Heap */
WindowPtr  theWindow,whichWindow;
Rect                      windowR,legalR,limitR;
short               windowcode,still_InGoAway;
char                      c;
long                      markChar;
long                      newSize;


/* Procedure to set up menus and add them to the menu list */

SetUpMenus()
{
/*  Desk Accessory Menu  */
DeskMenu = NewMenu (Desk_ID,"\p\24");
AddResMenu (DeskMenu, 'DRVR');
InsertMenu (DeskMenu, 0);


/*  File Menu  */
FileMenu = NewMenu (File_ID,"\pFile");
AppendMenu (FileMenu,"\pOpen Window/M;Close Window/X;Quit/Q");
InsertMenu (FileMenu,0);
DisableItem (FileMenu, 2);


/*  Our Menu  */
OurMenu = NewMenu (Our_ID, "\pOur Menu");
AppendMenu (OurMenu, "\pHide Window/H;Show Window/S;
New Window Title;(-;Show BMUG;Hide BMUG");
InsertMenu (OurMenu, 0);
DisableItem (OurMenu, 6);
```

```
/*   BMUG Menu   */
BMUGMenu = NewMenu (BMUG_ID, "\pBMUG");
AppendMenu (BMUGMenu, "\pDevelopers Group");

/* Sample Menu */
MyMenu = NewMenu (My_ID, "\pMy Menu");
AppendMenu (MyMenu, "\p<BFirst;Second/J;<UThird;(-;Fifth");
InsertMenu (MyMenu,0);

DrawMenuBar();
}

/* Program begins here */

main()                                              /* main() */
{
   InitGraf(&thePort);                    /* Initialize QuickDraw */   •
   InitFonts();
   InitWindows();
   InitCursor();

   FlushEvents(everyEvent, 0);
   InitMenus();
   SetUpMenus();
   theWindow = NULL;
   SetRect(&windowR,50,50,300,150);
   SetRect(&legalR,5,5,505,335);
   SetRect(&limitR, 50,10,500,330);


while (1) {
    if (GetNextEvent(everyEvent,&theEvent))  {
          switch (theEvent.what)  {

              case keyDown:
                    c = theEvent.message & charCodeMask;
                    if (theEvent.modifiers & cmdKey)  {
                        doMenu( MenuKey (c) );
                          HiliteMenu(0);
                    }
                    break;

              case mouseDown:
                    windowcode=FindWindow(theEvent.where,&whichWindow);
                    switch (windowcode) {
                          case inDesk:
                                  if((whichWindow = FrontWindow()) != 0)
        HiliteWindow(whichWindow, 0);
    break;
```

```
            case inMenuBar:
                doMenu(MenuSelect(theEvent.where));
                break;

            case inSysWindow:
                SysBeep(1);
                break;

            case inContent:
                HiliteWindow(whichWindow, 0xff);
                break;

            case inDrag:
                DragWindow(whichWindow,theEvent.where,&legalR);
                break;

            case inGrow:
                newSize = GrowWindow(whichWindow,theEvent.where,
                        &limitR);
                SizeWindow(whichWindow,LoWord(newSize),
                        HiWord(newSize),0);
                        /* newSize is split into short
                                    ints for width and height   */
                break;

            case inGoAway:
                still_InGoAway = TrackGoAway(whichWindow,
                        theEvent.where);
                if(still_InGoAway) {
                    CloseWindow(whichWindow);
                     theWindow = NULL;
                     EnableItem(FileMenu,1);
                     DisableItem(FileMenu, 2);
                }
                break;
        case inZoomIn:
        case inZoomOut:
                if(TrackBox(whichWindow,theEvent.where, windowcode)) {
                    GrafPtr curPort;
                GetPort(&curPort);
                SetPort(whichWindow);
                ZoomWindow(whichWindow, windowcode,0);
                SetPort(curPort);
            }
            break;
    }
break;
                default:
                        break;
                }
            }
        }
    }
```

```
doMenu(menuResult)
    long           menuResult;
{
    short          menuID, itemNumber, wType;
    menuID = HiWord (menuResult);
    itemNumber = LoWord (menuResult);

    switch (menuID)
        {
        case File_ID:
            switch (itemNumber)
                {
                case 1:
                    wType = documentProc + 8;
                    theWindow = NewWindow (&theWindowRec,&windowR,"\pHi Mom!",
                                  0xff,wType, (WindowPtr) -1,0xff,0);
                    DisableItem (FileMenu, 1);
                    EnableItem (FileMenu, 2);
                    break;

                case 2:
                    CloseWindow (theWindow);
                    theWindow = NULL;
                    DisableItem (FileMenu, 2);
                    EnableItem (FileMenu, 1);
                    break;

                case 3:
                    ExitToShell();
                    break;
                }
            break;

        case Our_ID:
            switch (itemNumber) {
                case 1:
                    if (theWindow) HideWindow (theWindow);
                    break;

                case 2:
                    if (theWindow) ShowWindow (theWindow);
                    break;

                case 3:
                    if (theWindow) SetWTitle (theWindow,"\pA New Title");
                    break;

                case 5:
                    InsertMenu (BMUGMenu, 0);
                    EnableItem (OurMenu, 6);
                    DisableItem (OurMenu, 5);
```

```
                            DrawMenuBar();
                            break;

                    case 6:
                            DeleteMenu (BMUG_ID);
                            EnableItem (OurMenu, 5);
                            DisableItem (OurMenu, 6);
                            DrawMenuBar();
                            break;
                }
                break;

        case Desk_ID:
                            break;

        case My_ID:
                GetItemMark(MyMenu,itemNumber,&markChar);
                if (markChar) CheckItem(MyMenu,itemNumber,0);
                else CheckItem(MyMenu,itemNumber,0);
                break;

        }
        HiliteMenu(0);

}
```

Some more text

Drawing with QuickDraw

Quickdraw is responsible for everything we see on a Macintosh screen. We can use it to draw and manipulate lines, shapes such as rectangles, ovals and rounded-corner rectangles, and more complicated structures such as polygons, regions, and pictures. QuickDraw also provides our means of displaying text, specifying the state and shape of the cursor, and defining patterns that are used to paint areas of the screen. Figure 5.1 shows some examples of the things QuickDraw is capable of drawing.

In addition to being used directly by an application, QuickDraw is also called by many of the other Toolbox Managers. The Window Manager calls it to draw windows, the Menu Manager calls it to draw menus, the Control Manager calls it to draw controls, and so on (see Figure 5.2).

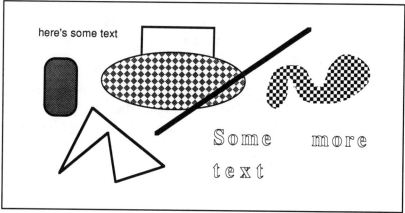

Figure 5.1:   Lines, Shapes, and Text Drawn by QuickDraw

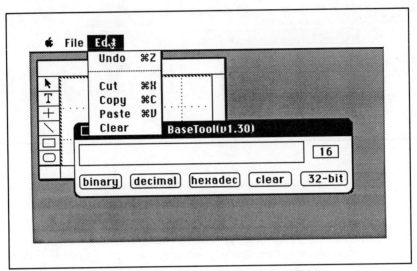

Figure 5.2:   Windows, Menus, and Controls Drawn by QuickDraw

We're studying QuickDraw at this point of the book for a number of reasons. In the previous four chapters, we've learned how to create a very simple Macintosh application complete with menus and a single window. If we were interested in programming an arcade-type game, what we've already learned, combined with the information discussed in this chapter, is probably sufficient to get the game up and running. The information in this chapter is also a helpful prerequisite for many parts of the chapters yet to come. What we will cover in this chapter about grafports, which are the basis of the Mac's multiple-window interface, will be helpful not only when dealing with QuickDraw, but also when we get to Chapter 7, which shows us how to implement multiple windows. This chapter will also cover fonts and their characteristics, which will be helpful when we get to Chapter 8—Text Editing with the Toolbox. In general, knowing what QuickDraw does and how it does it is helpful when studying any of the Macintosh ROM Managers that draw on the screen.

QuickDraw Basics—The Coordinate Plane, Points, and Rectangles

Before we can effectively discuss or use the any of the Quick-Draw routines, there are a few underlying concepts and data structures that we must know about. The coordinate plane, the place where things are drawn, as well as points and rectangles—locations and areas we specify in the plane to draw at or in—are all discussed here as a prerequisite to what we will learn in the rest of the chapter.

The Coordinate Plane

When using various QuickDraw routines, an application will have to specify a location to place or draw an object, or a distance to move it. The application specifies these locations or distances with regard to the coordinate plane. The coordinate plane is similar to the real-number plane you learned about in high school geometry. There are however, three important dissimilarities:

1. All coordinates in the plane are integers.

2. The horizontal and vertical coordinates range from −32768 to +32767.

3. Horizontal values increase from left to right while vertical values increase from top to bottom, as shown in Figure 5.3.

It is very important to remember that vertical coordinates increase downward, unlike the traditional number plane. On the Macintosh, if we want something to move downward, we must increase its vertical coordinate. As is shown in Figure 5.3, the origin (0,0), is in the middle of the coordinate plane.

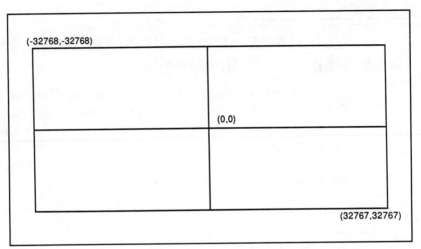

Figure 5.3: The Coordinate Plane

Defining and Manipulating Points

The most basic way to indicate a location in the coordinate plane is by specifying a horizontal and a vertical coordinate—that is, a point—in the plane. We refer to a point as (h,v)—that is, horizontal coordinate, vertical coordinate—just as we would specify (x,y) in the real number plane. There is a data structure of type Point defined in QuickDraw that applications will use to indicate locations in the plane.

```
struct pt {
        int v;
        int h;
};
typedef struct pt Point;
```

Each pixel on the screen can be thought of as a Point. Since there are 65,536 vertical lines and 65,536 horizontal lines in the drawing plane, there are 65,536 times 65,536, or 4,294,967,296 unique points. On a normal, monochrome Macintosh screen, however, there are only 512 vertical lines and 342 horizontal lines, or 175,104 pixels. The Mac's screen is actually a small window into a very large coordinate plane. We will see that it is possible, even easy, to move the plane around behind the Mac screen to view different portions of the plane. Figure 5.4 shows this relationship of the large plane to the small screen.

Our drawing is not limited to the Mac screen. It is very easy to draw off screen and is sometimes very advantageous to do so. An application might, for example, want to draw pictures off screen ahead of when they are needed so that when the time comes for one to be displayed, there will be no noticeable hesitation in the program. The drawing will be displayed instantly since it has already been calculated and drawn.

Defining Points

To assign horizontal and vertical coordinates to a variable of type Point, we use the procedure **SetPt**:

```
SetPt(pt,h,v)
        Point *pt;
        int h,v;
```

The integers h and v specify the horizontal and vertical coordinates to be assigned to the Point pt. For example, the call

```
Point samplePoint;
SetPt(&samplePoint,20,25);
```

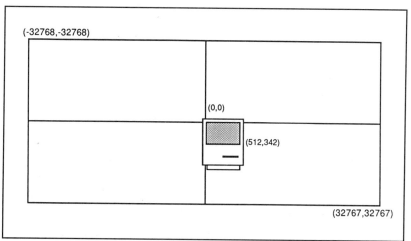

Figure 5.4: The Mac Screen in the Coordinate Plane

would assign the location (20,25) to the Point samplePoint.

Manipulating Points

To determine if two Points are equal, we use the Boolean function **EqualPt**:

```
char EqualPt(ptA,ptB)
        Point    ptA, ptB;
```

The function returns a true value if the points ptA and ptB are the same or a false one if they are not.

To add or subtract points, an application can use the procedures **AddPt** or **SubPt**.

```
AddPt(srcPt,dstPt)
        Point    srcPt,*dstPt;
SubPt(srcPt,dstPt)
        Point    srcPt,*dstPt;
```

AddPt adds srcPt to dstPt, and the result is placed in dstPt. **SubPt** subtracts srcPt from dstPt and places the result in dstPt. For example, if srcPt were (10,10) and dstPt were (90,60) and we made the call

```
AddPt(srcPt,&dstPt)
```

dstPt would now equal (100,70). If we were then to call

```
SubPt(srcPt,&dstPt)
```

dstPt would once again equal (90,60). The value stored in srcPt is never affected.

Notice that the destination points in these calls are passed by reference but the source points are not.

Changing a Point's Coordinate System

A point's coordinates are always expressed in terms of its coordinate plane. It is possible for an application to have a number of coordinate planes. QuickDraw, when dealing with multiple coordinate planes, or grafPorts, always keeps track of two. It keeps track of the active or local coordinate system, the one that is currently being drawn into, as well as the global coordinate system, the one that has its origin (0,0) at the top-left corner of the Mac screen.

An application can convert a point from its local coordinate system to the global coordinate system and then back again with the two routines **LocalToGlobal** and **GlobalToLocal**. The routine **LocalToGlobal** takes a point expressed in the active coordinate system and converts its coordinates to the global coordinate system.

```
LocalToGlobal(pt)
        Point   *pt;
```

The routine **GlobalToLocal** converts points in the opposite direction. **GlobalToLocal** takes a point expressed in the global coordinate system and converts its coordinates to the local coordinate system.

```
GlobalToLocal(pt)
        Point   *pt;
```

Many of the other Toolbox Managers have routines that require a point parameter to be expressed in local coordinates, while others require it to be expressed in global coordinates. As a result, the two routines **LocalToGlobal** and **GlobalToLocal** are used quite often, even if an application isn't using QuickDraw routines.

Defining and Manipulating Rectangles

Rectangles are another important basic part of QuickDraw and of the other Toolbox Managers that draw anything on the screen. In QuickDraw, Rectangles are the underlying structure used to draw rectangles themselves, as well as rounded-corner rectangles and ovals. Rectangles are also used, as was shown in Chapter 3, to indicate a window's size and location on the screen. We will see in future chapters how rectangles are used to specify the size and location of controls and alert and dialog boxes.

An application specifies a rectangular area of the coordinate plane with two Points, or four coordinates. The two Points or four coordinates indicate the top-left and bottom-right corners of the rectangle (see Figure 5.5).

Rectangles have an associated data structure of type Rect defined as follows:

```
union rect {
        struct {
                Point TopLeft, BottomRight;
        };
        struct {
                int top, left, bottom, right;
        };
};
typedef union rect Rect;
```

Note once again that the Rect can be defined as either two values of type Point—TopLeft and BottomRight—or as four individual coordinates: top, left, bottom, and right.

Defining Rectangles

To define a Rect we can use the procedure **SetRect**:

```
SetRect(r, left, top, right, bottom)
        Rect    *r;
        int     left,top,right,bottom;
```

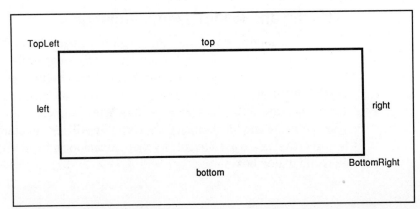

Figure 5.5: Diagram of a Rect

SetRect assigns to the Rect r the coordinates left, top, bottom, and right. This is best shown with an example. The call

```
Rect sampleRect;
SetRect(&sampleRect, 10, 20, 80, 100);
```

defines sampleRect to be a rectangle with a top left coordinate of (10,20) and bottom-right coordinate of (80,100).

We can also define a rectangle as the intersection of two rectangles. If we have two rectangles, and we want to know if and where they intersect, we can call the function **SectRect**:

```
char SectRect(srcRectA, srcRectB, dstRect)
     Rect    *srcRectA,*srcRectB,*dstRect;
```

If the two rectangles, srcRectA and srcRectB intersect, the function returns a true value, and the rectangle that is the intersection of the two is placed in dstRect. If the rectangles do not intersect, the function returns a false value, and the Rect dstRect is set to (0,0,0,0). Rectangles that intersect in only a line or a point are not considered intersecting because their intersection encloses no bits. Also, if we have two rectangles A and B, we can determine their intersection and then set rectangle A to the rectangle that is A and B's intersection—we just call **SectRect** with rectangle A as both a source and destination Rect.

A third way to define a rectangle is to indicate it as the rectangle that is the union of two specified rectangles. If we have two rectangles and would like to find a Rect that encloses them, we can call the procedure **UnionRect**.

```
UnionRect(srcRectA, srcRectB, dstRect)
Rect      *srcRectA,*srcRectB,*dstRect;
```

The smallest rectangle that encloses srcRectA and srcRectB is returned in destRect. Also, if we have two rectangles A and B we can determine their bounding rectangle and set rectangle A to be the bounding rectangle—we just call **UnionRect** with rectangle A as both a source and destination Rect.

The last way we can define a rectangle is by specifying two Points. If we have two Points, and wish to find the smallest rectangle that encloses them, our application can use the procedure **Pt2Rect**.

```
Pt2Rect(ptA, ptB, destRect)
      Point    ptA, ptB;
      Rect     *destRect;
```

If ptA was (10,20) and ptB was (90,50) and we made the call

```
Pt2Rect(ptA,ptB,&resultRect);
```

resultRect would be set to the rectangle with coordinates (10,20,90,50).

Moving Rectangles

To move the rectangle around in the coordinate plane, we can use the procedure **OffsetRect**.

```
OffsetRect(r,dh,dv)
      Rect     *r;
      int      dh,dv;
```

The rectangle r will be moved dh coordinates horizontally and dv coordinates vertically. Calling **OffsetRect** with the following values:

```
OffsetRect(&sampleRect,30,-60);
```

would move sampleRect 30 coordinates to the right and 60 coordinates up. The rectangle itself would not be affected by this call. The procedure also has no effect on the screen. The rectangle is moved, but not redrawn. We will see how to draw or redraw a rectangle later, in the section Drawing Rectangles.

Resizing Rectangles

The procedure **InsetRect** shrinks or expands the specified rectangle

```
InsetRect(r,dh,dv)
      Rect     *r;
      int      dh,dv;
```

If the values for dh and dv are positive, the rectangle is shrunk; if they are negative, the rectangle will expand.

The following piece of code demonstrates **InsetRect**:

```
Rect sampleRect;
SetRect(&sampleRect,50,60,110,150);
InsetRect(&sampleRect,10,-20);
```

After the previous code segment executes, sampleRect would have coordinates (60,40,100,170). Note that each coordinate is inset or expanded the distance specified by dh or dv. Also, if after a call to **Inset-Rect** the rectangle's height or width is less than 1, its coordinates are set to (0,0,0,0)—that is, it is made an empty rectangle.

Determining if Points are enclosed in Rectangles

Given a Point and a Rect, we can determine with the function **PtInRect** whether the point is enclosed by the rectangle

```
char PtInRect(pt,r)
        Point   pt;
        Rect    *r;
```

If the Point pt is enclosed by rectangle r, then the function returns true; otherwise it returns false. As an example of one of the many uses of the **PtInRect** procedure, suppose we have detected a mouse-down event and need to determine if the mouse was clicked in a rectangle we have defined on the screen. The code block below shows one way an application could deal with the situation.

```
switch(theEvent.what)
        case mouseDown:
                if(PtInRect(&theEvent.where,&ourRect))
                        /* respond to a mouseDown in ourRect */
                else
                        /* otherwise do something else */
                break;
```

Comparing Rectangles

If we have two rectangles and wish to determine if they are equal, we can use the procedure **EqualRect**.

```
char EqualRect(rectA,rectB)
      Rect    *rectA,*rectB;
```

If the two rectangles have exactly the same boundary coordinates, the function returns true; otherwise it returns false.

Given a rectangle, we can determine whether it is empty or not with the function **EmptyRect**.

```
char EmptyRect(r)
      Rect    *r;
```

The function returns true if the rectangle r is empty and false otherwise. A rectangle is considered empty if the left coordinate is greater than or equal to the right or the top coordinate is greater than or equal to the bottom.

- - - - -

GrafPorts—Drawing Environments for QuickDraw

Everything that an application draws with QuickDraw is drawn into a grafPort. Each grafPort has its own characteristics that determine how the drawing commands will work. The characteristics include, among other things, the grafPort's own coordinate plane, pen characteristics, text characteristics, and patterns. An application may have multiple grafPorts, each having its own set of characteristics.

In this section, we will study the various data types that make up a grafPort. In preparation for the next section of this chapter which examines the grafPort data structure in detail, we will examine and explain transfer modes, patterns, the QuickDraw pen, and text characteristics.

Transfer Modes

When lines, text, or shapes are drawn, a transfer mode determines how they are to appear. For example, if we are drawing a rectangle to the screen, and the screen already has something drawn on it, a transfer mode will determine whether the rectangle is drawn *opaque*—covering over all the other drawing, or *transparent*—allowing some of the drawing underneath to show through. There are eight different ways the rectangle could be drawn or "transferred" to the screen. In the example, above the rectangle would be referred to as the source, and the screen would be referred to as the destination.

The types of transfer modes are broken into two categories: *pattern transfer modes*, referred to as pat, that are used when drawing lines or shapes, and *source transfer modes*, referred to as src, that are used when drawing text.

For each type of transfer mode, there are four operations: Copy, Or, Xor, and Bic. Copy simply overwrites the bits in the destination with the bits from the source. It doesn't matter what the destination bits are, they are simply replaced.

Or, Xor, and Bic all leave the destination pixels under the white source pixels unchanged. The three operations differ in the way that they affect the destination pixels that lie under black source pixels. Or sets those destination pixels to black. Bic erases the destination pixels under the black source pixels to white, while Xor inverts the destination pixels.

For each of these four operations, there is also a not version in which all the bits in the source are inverted before the transfer mode operation is performed. Figure 5.6, with a sample source and destination, shows how each of the transfer modes works.

The constant names for all the transfer modes, given in Figure 5.7, should be predefined in one of your header files, QuickDraw.h.

Patterns

A pattern in QuickDraw is an 8-by-8 square bit image, as shown in Figure 5.8. Each of the 64 individual bits is set to 1 (black) or 0 (white) to create designs such as bricks or tones such as dark gray.

When you are using MacPaint, all the designs along the bottom of the screen are examples of QuickDraw patterns. Patterns have an associated data structure of type Pattern.

```
struct P {
        char s[8];
};
#define     Pattern     struct P
typedef     Pattern     *PatPtr;
typedef     PatPtr      *PatHandle;
```

Once we have a pattern, we can use it to draw lines or to fill in or draw shapes on the screen. In fact, most of the time that we draw something on the screen, a pattern comes into play one way or another.

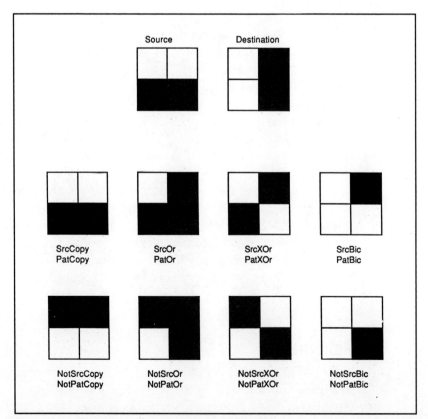

Figure 5.6: Examples of How the Transfer Modes Work

Whenever a pattern is drawn, each 8-by-8-bit image is automatically aligned with the next so that the overall design or tone is continuous and even.

In QuickDraw, there are five predefined patterns (see Figure 5.9) for us to use: white, ltGray, gray, dkGray, and black.

We can use any of the standard patterns, or we can create and use our own. One way of creating a pattern is to use the procedure

Transfer Mode	Value
srcCopy	= 0
srcOr	= 1
srcXor	= 2
srcBic	= 3
notSrcCopy	= 4
notSrcOr	= 5
notSrcXor	= 6
notSrcBic	= 7
patCopy	= 8
patOr	= 9
patXor	= 10
patBic	= 11
notPatCopy	= 12
notPatOr	= 13
notPatXor	= 14
notPatBic	= 15

Figure 5.7:   The 16 Transfer Modes and Their Values

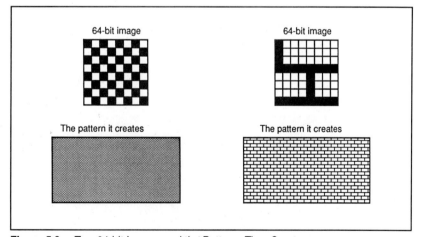

Figure 5.8:   Two 64-bit Images and the Patterns They Create

StuffHex (There is an easier way to do this by using the application RMaker, which we will discuss in Chapter 9 on Resources.)

```
StuffHex(thingPtr,s)
       Ptr      thingPtr;
       Str255   *s;
```

StuffHex allows us to assign a string of hexadecimal digits to any data structure. The following code segment shows how to set the variable our-Pattern to be a pattern with a brick design.

```
Pattern *ourPattern
StuffHex(ourPattern, "\p808080FF080808FF");
```

We must be extra careful when using **StuffHex**. No variable checking is done to make sure there is enough room in the destination variable for the hex string specified. If a hex string is given that is larger than the data structure it is being stuffed into, other things in memory may be destroyed.

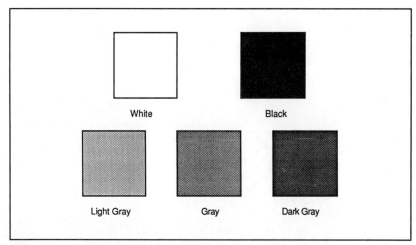

Figure 5.9: The Standard Patterns

Pen Characteristics

A QuickDraw pen has 5 characteristics: its location, size, transfer mode, pattern, and a flag indicating whether it is visible or not. These characteristics are stored in the pnLoc, pnSize, pnMode, pnPat, and pnVis fields of a grafPort. The pen of the grafPort we are drawing into is used whenever we draw lines, shapes, or text.

The pnLoc Field

The pnLoc is a point that indicates the location of the pen in the grafPort's coordinate plane. The pen's actual location is not restricted to the screen; it can lie anywhere in the coordinate plane. We can find out the pen's current location by calling the procedure **GetPen**.

```
GetPen(pt)
        Point     *pt;
```

GetPen will return in the variable pt, the location of the pen, expressed in terms of the current grafPort's coordinate system.

The pnSize Field

The pnSize is another variable of type Point, but instead of representing a location in the coordinate plane, it represents the pen's horizontal and vertical dimensions. The default size of the pen is a 1-by-1-bit square, but it can be defined to be any size from (0,0) to (32,767,32,767). An application changes the pen's size with the procedure **PenSize**.

```
PenSize(width,height)
        int      width,height;
```

When you draw with the pen, the upper left-hand corner of the pen is lined up with the Point that is the pnLoc. The rest of the pen hangs below and to the right of the pnLoc (see Figure 5.10).

The pnMode Field

The pnMode is a variable of type int that specifies which transfer mode to use when doing any pen drawing. The mode may be any one of the eight pattern transfer modes. The pnMode value is easily changed with the routine **PenMode**.

```
PenMode (mode)
        int   mode;
```

The pnMode is initially set to the patCopy transfer mode. If the mode is set to any of the source transfer modes or negative, no drawing will take place.

The pnPat **Field**

The pnPat is a Pattern data type. It indicates the tone or design to be used whenever any line drawing occurs. If the pnPat is black, the pen will draw in black, if the pnPat is gray, pen drawing will be done with gray, and so on. We set the pnPat with the procedure **PenPat**.

```
PenPat (pat)
        Pattern *pat;
```

The initial value of the pnPat is black.

The pnVis **Field**

The pnVis is a variable of data type int. It determines whether or not the pen will be visible on the screen or not. If the pnVis is negative, the pen will be invisible; zero or a positive value will make the pen visible. We can

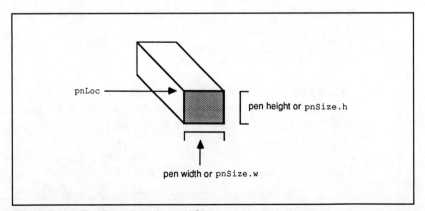

Figure 5.10: The Pen's Location and Size

alter the pnVis field with the two routines, **HidePen** and **ShowPen**. **HidePen** decrements the pnVis field; **ShowPen** increments the field.

```
HidePen();
ShowPen();
```

If the pnVis field is zero and we call **HidePen** three times in succession, it will be necessary to call **ShowPen** three times to make it visible again.

Restoring the Pen's Default Fields

A call to the procedure **PenNormal** restores the initial values of the pnSize, pnMode, and pnPat fields of the current pen.

```
PenNormal();
```

Figure 5.11 lists the pen's initial values.

Moving the Pen

To change the location of the pen without drawing anything, we have two routines, **MoveTo** and **Move**. **MoveTo** moves the pen to absolute location (h,v) in the current grafPort.

```
MoveTo(h,v)
        int     h,v;
```

The procedure **Move** offsets the pen a distance of dh horizontally and dv vertically from its current position pnLoc.

```
Move(dh,dv)
        int     dh,dv;
```

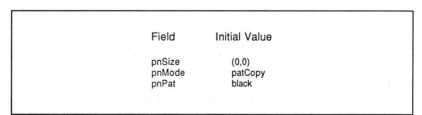

Field	Initial Value
pnSize	(0,0)
pnMode	patCopy
pnPat	black

Figure 5.11: The Pen's Initial Values

Drawing Lines with the Pen

There are two similar routines for line drawing: **LineTo** and **Line**. **LineTo** draws a line from the pen's current location pnLoc to the absolute point (h,v).

```
LineTo(h,v)
        int     h,v;
```

Line draws a line a distance of (dh,dv) relative to the current value in pnLoc.

```
Line(dh,dv)
        int     dh,dv;
```

Preserving a Pen's Characteristics

Often, an application will have the pen's characteristics all set, but will then want to change some of the characteristics for just a short time—for example, when a particular procedure is called. When the application finishes calling the routine, it will want the pen's characteristics restored to their original state. A program can accomplish this with the two routines **GetPenState** and **SetPenState**.

GetPenState saves the pen's location, size, pattern, and transfer mode into the storage variable pnState, which can later be passed to the routine **SetPenState**.

```
GetPenState(pnState)
        PenState        *pnState;
```

The pen's characteristics can be restored to the values stored in the pnState variable with the routine **SetPenState**.

```
SetPenState(pnState)
        PenState        *pnState;
```

The PenState data type is not useful for anything except saving and resetting the pen's location, size, pattern, and transfer mode with **GetPenState** and **SetPenState**.

Text Characteristics

Text has five characteristics which determine: the character font it will be displayed in, its style, its transfer mode, its size, and some spacing information for fully justified text. The characteristics are stored in the txFont, txFace, txMode, txSize, and spExtra fields of a grafPort.

The txFont Field

The txFont is an int data type, a font number that specifies the character font, or typeface, to use when displaying text in the current grafPort. Figure 5.12 lists the font names and numbers of the standard Macintosh fonts. You will probably have other fonts in your system, and, as you'll see in chapter 9, it is possible to add special fonts to a resource file to make them available to your application.

To change the character font being used, an application uses the procedure **TextFont**.

```
TextFont(font)
        int     font;
```

The parameter font is simply the font number of the font we wish to change to. Its initial value is zero which specifies the system font.

Font Name	Value	
System Font	systemFont	= 0
Application Font	applFont	= 1
New York	newYork	= 2
Geneva	geneva	= 3
Monaco	monaco	= 4
Venice	venice	= 5
London	london	= 6
Athens	athens	= 7
San Francisco	sanFran	= 8
Toronto	toronto	= 9

Figure 5.12:   Font Names and Their Font Numbers

The txFace **Field**

The txFace field determines the style of the font specified by txFont. There are eight different font styles: plain, bold, italic, underline, outline, shadow, condense, and extend. Figure 5.13 lists the eight different font styles and their constant equivalents.

The styles can be used alone or in any combination. We turn on and off the various type styles with the procedure **TextFace**.

```
TextFace(face)
      Style    face;
```

The face parameter passed to **TextFace** is a Style data type, which is simply an int data type. The integer passed in face indicates the style or combination of styles that the txFont is to be displayed in. The following line shows how to set the font style to be bold, italic, and underline.

```
TextFace(boldStyle + italicStyle + underlineStyle);
```

The txMode **Field**

The txMode field is similar to the pnMode field of the pen. It contains a transfer mode that determines how a character will be drawn on the screen. We can change its value with the procedure **TextMode**.

```
TextMode(mode)
      int      mode;
```

Style	Value
plain	= 0
bold	= 1
italic	= 2
underline	= 3
outline	= 4
shadow	= 5
condense	= 6
extend	= 7

Figure 5.13:   Font Styles and Their Values

Only three of the transfer modes should be used for text drawing: srcOr, srcXor, or srcBic. The initial value of txMode is srcOr.

The txSize **Field**

The txSize field specifies the size that the characters are to be displayed in. The size of the text is specified in points (1/72 inch, not the data type Point). An application changes the text's size with the procedure **TextSize**.

```
TextSize(size)
        int      size;
```

Any size font may be specified. The size we specify and the sizes the font exists in affect the way the font will appear. Specifying a size that the Font Manager has will result in the best looking fonts. The next degree of quality is obtained when we specify a font size to display that is an even multiple of an existing one. Requesting a 27 point font when only a 9 point size is defined will cause the 9 point font to be scaled evenly up to the 27 point font. The worst appearance occurs when an application asks to display a point size that the Font Manager doesn't have and that isn't an even multiple of a size that the manager has. If zero is specified as the size, the Font Manager will display the font in the size closest to the system font size (12-point, usually).

The spExtra **Field**

The last text characteristic is the spExtra field. It is used whenever text needs to be fully justified, that is, aligned with both left and right margins. The value in spExtra is the number of pixels by which each space character needs to be widened to fill out the line of text. An application sets the spExtra field with the routine **SpaceExtra**.

```
SpaceExtra(extra)
        int extra;
```

The initial value of the spExtra field is zero.

Text Drawing Routines

At this point, we're ready to begin talking about actual text drawing routines. When text drawing occurs, each character is placed to the right of the current pen location pnLoc. The left edge of a character's baseline is aligned with the pnLoc. After a character is drawn, the pnLoc is moved to the right side of the character just drawn.

Drawing Characters, Strings, and Text buffers

There are three routines for drawing text: **DrawChar**, **DrawString**, and **DrawText**. **DrawChar** draws a single character, **DrawString** draws a specified string, and **DrawText** draws characters taken from a specified buffer.

The procedure **DrawChar** places the specified character ch to the right of the pen location pnLoc, and moves the pen to the right side of ch. If the character isn't defined in the font, then QuickDraw will draw the missing symbol.

```
DrawChar(ch)
       int     ch;
```

DrawString calls **DrawChar** for each character in the string s. After the procedure, the pnLoc will be at the right side of the last character in the string s.

```
DrawString(s)
       Str255  *s;
```

DrawText draws the text stored in the buffer textBuf. The arguments firstByte and byteCount indicate the number of bytes into the structure to begin and the number of bytes to draw. As usual, the text begins to the right of the current pen.

```
DrawText(textBuf,firstByte,byteCount)
       char    *textBuf;
       int     firstByte,byteCount;
```

Determining the Width of a Character, String, or Text in a Buffer

There are three similar routines for determining the width of a character or string: **CharWidth**, **StringWidth**, and **TextWidth**.

CharWidth returns the width of the character ch specified. Any style enhancements such as bold, italic, and so on are taken into consideration when the width is calculated. The spExtra field is added to the width if ch is a space character. The width returned is the number of coordinates the pnLoc will be moved to the right after the character ch is drawn.

```
int CharWidth(ch)
      int     ch;
```

Both **StringWidth** and **TextWidth** call **CharWidth** to determine the width of the strings specified. For **StringWidth** the specified string is the string s, and for **TextWidth** the specified string is the string **byteCounts** long, beginning at **firstByte** in the buffer **textBuf.**

```
int StringWidth(s)
      Str255  *s;
int TextWidth(textBuf,firstByte,byteCount)
      char    *textBuf;
      int     firstByte,byteCount;
```

Determining a Font's Ascent, Descent, Width, and Leading

With the Toolbox it is possible to have more that one font size and style in the same line of text. This can lead to problems with line spacing when an application must display multiple lines of text containing a number of different font sizes and styles. There is, however, a solution. Using the routine **GetFontInfo**, an application can determine a font's ascent, descent, maximum character width, and leading (the distance between the descent line and the ascent line below it). It can then use this information to accurately change the line spacing so that everything is displayed correctly. In the sample code of Chapter 8, Text Editing with the Toolbox, there is an example of how **GetFontInfo** can be used.

```
GetFontInfo(info)
      FontInfo       *info;
```

The FontInfo data type is a structure of four shorts as is shown below. **Get-FontInfo** returns values expressed in pixels, in each field of the FontInfo structure.

```
typedef struct {
        int     ascent;
        int     descent;
        int     widMax;
        int     leading;
} FontInfo;
```

Figure 5.14 shows the ascent, descent, and width characteristics of a character.

The GrafPort **Data Structure and Routines**

Now that we have enough background knowledge, it is time for us to study the structure of a grafPort data type, its fields, and the routines that will allow our application to take full control of how drawing will occur.

The grafPort **Data Structure**

The grafPort data structure, shown in the box titled "grafPort Data Structure," consists of a number of fields, some of which we discussed in the last section and others that we will cover now.

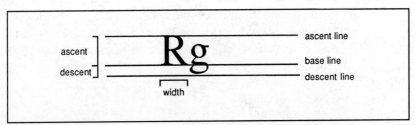

Figure 5.14: The Ascent, Descent, and Width Characteristics of a Character

```
Grafport Data Structure

struct GP
{
        int             device;
        BitMap          portBits;
        Rect            portRect;
        RgnHandle       visRgn;
        RgnHandle       clipRgn;
        Pattern         bkPat;
        Pattern         fillPat;
        Point           pnLoc;
        Point           pnSize;
        int             pnMode;
        Pattern         pnPat;
        int             pnVis;
        int             txFont;
        Style           txFace;
        int             txMode;
        int             txSize;
        long            spExtra;
        long            fgColor;
        long            bkColor;
        int             colrBit;
        int             patStretch;
        Handle          picSave;
        Handle          rgnSave;
        Handle          polySave;
        QDProcsPtr      grafProcs;
};

#define     GrafPort        struct GP
typedef     GrafPort        *GrafPtr;
```

The device **Field**

The device field, an int, indicates the output device the grafPort will be using. The default device number is 0, representing the Macintosh screen.

The portBits **Field**

The portBits field is the bitMap that is used by the grafPort. A bitMap points to a bit image, which is simply a rectilinear collection of bits in memory. All drawing that is done in a grafPort will take place in the portBit's bit image. The default bit image is set to be the entire Macintosh screen.

The portRect **Field**

The portRect field is a rectangle that defines the portion of the portBits that will be used for the grafPort. Whenever an application draws something, it will occur inside of the portRect rectangle. Recall from Chapter 3, that a window pointer is the same thing as a grafPtr. A window's content region is a grafPort's portRect.

The visRgn **Field**

The visRgn field is used primarily by the Window Manager and is rarely changed by the programmer. It indicates the region of a grafPort that is visible on the screen. Normally the visRgn is set to be the same size as the portRect. When a window (a grafPort), has an object moved in front of it, the area of the window obscured by the object is removed from the window's visRgn. Then, if drawing occurs in the window, the drawing is clipped to the visRgn so that no drawing occurs on the obscuring object.

The clipRgn **Field**

The clipRgn is a programmer-definable region that an application can use to limit drawing in specific areas of the portRect. The clipRgn is initially set to be very large so that no drawing to the portRect is obscured by it. If, for example, an application wanted items to be drawn only in the upper half of a grafPort, the clipRgn could be set to be the upper half. The sample program at the end of Chapter 10 changes the clipRgn often and is a practical example of why an application might want to limit drawing.

The bkPat **and** fillPat **Fields**

The bkPat and fillPat fields are both patterns that are used by the grafPort and QuickDraw routines. The bkPat, or background pattern, is used in areas on the screen that are "erased" or have bits scrolled out of them by various QuickDraw routines. The fillPat, or fill pattern, is used to fill in areas of the screen that are specified by QuickDraw's Fill routines. Filling and erasing routines will be discussed in the section on QuickDraw drawing verbs.

The pnLoc, pnSize, pnMode, pnPat, **and** pnVis **Fields**

The pnLoc, pnSize, pnMode, pnPat, and pnVis fields—covered in detail earlier in this chapter—all have to do with a grafPort's pen characteristics. The pnLoc and pnSize fields indicate the location and size of the grafPort's pen. The pnMode and pnPat fields indicate the pen's transfer mode and pattern to be used when drawing. Finally, the pnVis field determines whether the pen is visible or not.

The txFont, txFace, txMode, txSize, **and** spExtra **Fields**

The txFont, txFace, txMode, txSize, and spExtra fields—also covered in detail above—all have to do with a grafPort's text. The txFont and txFace fields determine the font and style to be used when displaying text. The txMode and txSize fields indicate the transfer mode and size for the text of the grafPort. Finally, the spExtra field is used when an application wants to display fully justified text.

The fgColor, bkColor, **and** colrBit **Fields**

The fgColor, bkColor, and colrBit fields of a grafPort are used with color QuickDraw. This is an extension of the basic QuickDraw package which is used on the Macintosh II. There is, in fact, a lot of color with QuickDraw which is not covered in this book, as it's beyond the scope of this text. You will need *Inside Macintosh* if you want to write programs which draw in color.

The patStretch **Field**

The patStretch field is sometimes used by QuickDraw when it is printing a pattern to a printer. An application should not change this field's value and has no use for its contents.

The picSave, rgnSave, **and** polySave **Fields**

The picSave, rgnSave, and polySave fields of a grafPort reflect the status of picture, region, or polygon definition. For example, to define a picture, region, or polygon, an application calls a routine to open it, then the application executes the drawing commands to draw it, and finally calls a routine to close it. If a picture, region, or polygon is open, the picSave, rgnSave, or polySave field will contain a handle to the open picture, region, or polygon.

The grafProcs **Field**

The grafProcs field may contain a pointer to a customized Quick-Draw data structure that an application might use. If the field is set to NULL, QuickDraw will respond in the normal manner. Customized QuickDraw routines are beyond the scope of this book, so we won't be discussing the grafProcs field.

GrafPort **Routines**

A lot of routines that could be classified as grafPort routines have already been discussed under different headings. The routines that change a grafPort's pen and text characteristics, for example, were discussed in the earlier sections on Pen Characteristics and Text Characteristics. The routines we will discuss here deal mainly with the first five fields of a grafPort.

Initialization

The first routine, **InitGraf**, should be called at the beginning of a program to initialize QuickDraw. It initializes the QuickDraw global variables listed in Figure 5.15.

```
InitGraf(globalPtr)
        char    *globalPtr;
```

Creating and Disposing of GrafPorts

Before using any grafPort, an application needs to create it by calling the routine **OpenPort**. Given a pointer gp, created with the routine **NewPtr**, **OpenPort** creates a new grafPort gp, initializes the grafPort's fields as listed in Figure 5.16, allocates memory for the grafPort's visRgn and clip-Rgn, and makes the port gp the current port. The current port is the port where all drawing commands will be directed.

```
OpenPort(gp)
        GrafPtr gp;
```

To reinitialize a currently open grafPort, an application calls the routine **InitPort**. **InitPort** initializes the fields of the specified port to the values listed in Figure 5.16, and makes gp the current port.

```
InitPort(gp)
        GrafPtr gp;
```

When an application is through with a grafPort, it should dispose of the grafPort with the routine **ClosePort**. **ClosePort** releases the memory occupied by the specified grafPort's visRgn and clipRgn. After an application calls **ClosePort**, it should dispose of the grafPtr gp with a call to the Memory Manager routine **DisposPtr**.

```
ClosePort(gp)
        GrafPtr gp;
```

Variable	Type	Initial Setting
thePort	GrafPtr	NIL
white	Pattern	all-white pattern
black	Pattern	all-black pattern
gray	Pattern	50% gray pattern
ltGray	Pattern	25% gray pattern
dkGray	Pattern	75% gray pattern
arrow	Cursor	pointing arror cursor
screenBits	BitMap	Macintosh Screen (0,0,512,342)
randSeed	LongInt	1

Figure 5.15:   QuickDraw's Global Variables

Keeping Track of GrafPorts

When an application uses multiple grafPorts, it will have to use the two routines **GetPort** and **SetPort** to switch between them. The routine **SetPort** is used to set the specified grafPort gp to be the current port. This will cause all future drawing commands to be directed to the grafPort gp until the application does a **SetPort** to another port.

```
SetPort(gp)
        GrafPtr gp;
```

Before each call to **SetPort**, however, an application should save the current grafPort (so that it can later be reset to the current port), by calling the routine **GetPort**. **GetPort** saves a pointer to the current grafPort in the specified variable gp. For example, when an application wants to create a new grafPort with the routine **OpenPort**, it should first execute a

Field	Type	Initial Setting
device	short	0 (Macintosh Screen)
protBits	BitMap	screenBits
protRect	Rect	screenBits.bounds (0,0,512,342)
visRgn	Rgnhandle	handle to (0,0,512,342)
cliprgn	RgnHandle	handle to (-30000,-30000,30000,30000)
bkPat	Pattern	white
fillPat	Pattern	black
pnLoc	Point	(0,0)
pnSize	Point	(1,1)
pnMode	short	patCopy
pnPat	Pattern	black
pnVis	short	0 (visible)
txfont	short	0 (System Font)
txFace	Style	normal
txMode	short	srcOr
txSize	short	0 (Font Manager Decides)
spExtra	short	0
fgColor	long	blackColor
bkColor	long	whiteColor
colrBit	short	0
patStretch	short	0
picSave	QDHandle	NIL
rgnSave	QDHandle	NIL
polySave	QDHandle	NIL
grafProcs	QDProcsPtr	NIL

Figure 5.16: The Initial Values of a GrafPort

GetPort to save the current port away, then call **OpenPort** to create a new grafPort, and finally call **SetPort** to restore the previous grafPort to be the current one.

```
GetPort(gp)
        GrafPtr *gp;
```

Moving a GrafPort's Coordinate System

To move a grafPort's coordinate system, an application uses the procedure **SetOrigin**. **SetOrigin** moves the current origin of the coordinate plane to the new coordinates specified by the parameters h and v. An application will often want to move the coordinate plane around after it performs a scrolling operation. The sample program at the end of Chapter 10 shows one way an application might use the **SetOrigin** procedure. **SetOrigin** also offsets the coordinates of a grafPort's portBits, portRect, and visRgn. The application, however, must manually move the clipRgn with a call to **OffsetRgn**.

```
SetOrigin(h, v)
        int     h,v;
```

Manipulating a GrafPort's clipRect

We can alter the clipRect of the current grafPort with the three routines **GetClip**, **SetClip**, and **ClipRect**. **GetClip** changes the specified region rgn to be a region equivalent to the current grafPort's clipRgn.

```
GetClip(rgn)
        RgnHandle        rgn;
```

The routine **SetClip** does just the opposite of what **GetClip** does. **SetClip** sets the clipRgn field of a grafPort to be a region equivalent to the specified region rgn.

```
SetClip(rgn)
        RgnHandle        rgn;
```

Our final clipRect manipulating routine is **ClipRect**. **ClipRect** allows an application to set the clipRect field of the current grafPort to the specified rectangle r. **ClipRect** is used in the sample program at the end of Chapter 10.

```
ClipRect(r)
        Rect      *r;
```

Changing a GrafPort's Background Pattern

To change the background pattern of the current grafPort, an application can call the routine **BackPat**. **BackPat** changes the bkPat field of the current grafPort to the specified pattern pat.

```
BackPat(pat)
        Pattern *pat;
```

▬ ▬ ▬ ▬ ▬

The QuickDraw Drawing Verbs

To draw a number of the shapes in QuickDraw, an application will specify a procedure that consists of a drawing verb combined with the shape or structure the verb is to act upon. The procedure will look like **VerbShape**. In this section we will study the five drawing verbs and the shapes or structures that they act upon, in preparation for the next six sections of the chapter, which discuss the individual routines.

There are five drawing verbs in QuickDraw: **Frame, Paint, Erase, Invert,** and **Fill.**

- **Frame** is used to draw the shape's outline.

- **Paint** is used to paint the shape with the pen pattern of the current grafPort.

- **Erase** is used to paint the shape with the current grafPort's background pattern.

- **Invert** is used to change the shape's black pixels to white and white to black.

- Fill is used to fill the shape with a specified pattern.

These five drawing verbs operate on six different QuickDraw shapes or structures, for a total of 30 routines. The shapes are

- Rectangles
- Ovals
- Rounded-corner rectangles
- Arcs and wedges
- Polygons
- Regions

Each verb works the same way with each shape or structure, with one exception that we will discuss in the section on polygons.

Drawing Rectangles

FrameRect outlines the rectangle specified, just inside of its coordinates. The line is drawn using the current grafPort pen's pattern pnPat, transfer mode pnMode, and size pnSize.

```
FrameRect (r)
        Rect     *r;
```

PaintRect paints the specified rectangle r with the current grafPort's pen pattern pnPat, using the pnMode transfer mode.

```
PaintRect (r)
        Rect     *r;
```

EraseRect works exactly like **PaintRect** except that it paints the Rect r using the background pattern bkPat and transfer mode patCopy.

```
EraseRect (r)
        Rect     *r;
```

InvertRect simply inverts all the pixels within the rectangle r. All the white pixels are changed to black, and all the black pixels are changed to white.

```
InvertRect(r)
      Rect      *r;
```

FillRect, unlike the other four rectangle displaying routines, requires two arguments: a rectangle r and a pattern pat. The rectangle r is painted with the specified pattern pat using the patCopy transfer mode.

```
FillRect(r,pat)
      Rect      *r;
      Pattern *pat;
```

Drawing Ovals

The data type Rect is also used when drawing ovals. All ovals are drawn inside rectangles, as shown in Figure 5.17. To draw a circle, we just specify a square rectangle. The following five routines work exactly like the corresponding rectangle-drawing routines:

```
FrameOval(r)
      Rect      *r;
PaintOval(r)
      Rect      *r;
EraseOval(r)
      Rect      *r;
InvertOval(r)
      Rect      *r;
FillOval(r,pat)
      Rect      *r;
      Pattern *pat;
```

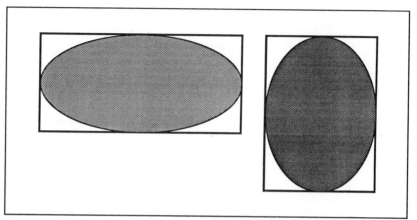

Figure 5.17: Ovals Drawn Inside Rectangles

Drawing Rounded-Corner Rectangles

We also use Rects for drawing rounded-corner rectangles. As with rectangles and ovals, there are five display operations: **Frame**, **Paint**, **Erase**, **Invert**, and **Fill**. With rounded-corner rectangles, however, each routine requires two additional arguments: ovalWidth and ovalHeight. The two integers ovalWidth and ovalHeight are used to indicate the diameters of curvature for the rounded corners of the rectangle, as shown in Figure 5.18. Apart from the two additional arguments, the drawing routines work exactly as they did with rectangles.

```
FrameRoundRect(r, ovalWidth, ovalHeight)
        Rect    *r
        int     ovalWidth,ovalHeight;
PaintRoundRect(r, ovalWidth, ovalHeight)
        Rect    *r
        int     ovalWidth,ovalHeight;
EraseRoundRect(r, ovalWidth, ovalHeight)
        Rect    *r
        int     ovalWidth,ovalHeight;
InvertRoundRect(r, ovalWidth, ovalHeight)
        Rect    *r
        int     ovalWidth,ovalHeight;
```

```
FillRoundRect (r, ovalWidth, ovalHeight, pat)
        Rect    *r
        int     ovalWidth, ovalHeight;
        Pattern *pat;
```

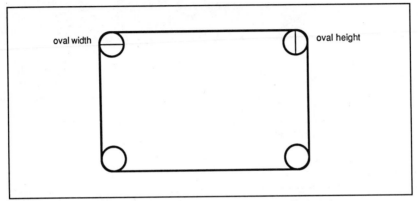

Figure 5.18:   Corner Measurement of a Rounded-Corner Rectangle

▄▄▄▄▄
‾‾‾‾‾‾‾‾‾‾‾‾

Defining and Drawing Angles, Arcs, and Wedges

In QuickDraw there are six routines that deal with angles, arcs, and wedges. One of the routines, **PtToAngle**, is used to measure angles, while the other five are the standard display routines **Frame**, **Paint**, **Erase**, **Invert**, and **Fill**. In all of the following six routines, angles are measured with respect to the rectangle r that we are dealing with, as shown in Figure 5.19. Zero degrees is a vertical line from the center of the rectangle upward; 90 degrees is a horizontal line from the center of the rect to the right; 180 degrees is a vertical line downward from the center; and 270 degrees is a horizontal line from the center to the left. An angle of 45 degrees is a line from the center of the rectangle, through its top-right corner. Similarly, a line through the rectangle's bottom-left corner would measure 225 degrees. These measurements hold true for every rectangle, no matter what its size or shape.

Defining an Angle

To define an angle, an application uses the routine **PtToAngle**. **PtToAngle** measures a clockwise angle from a line straight up from the center of the specified rectangle r to another line drawn from the center of the rectangle to the point pt. The integer degree value is returned in the variable angle, always measured with respect to the rectangle r, as was discussed in the previous section.

```
PtToAngle(r, pt, angle)
        Rect    *r;
        Point   pt;
        int     *angle;
```

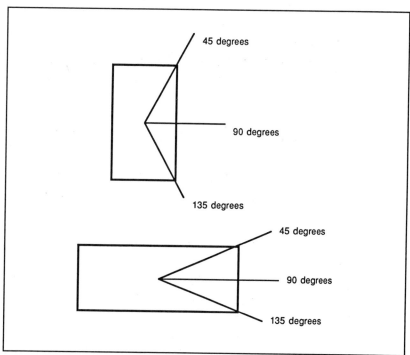

Figure 5.19:   How Angles are Drawn with Respect to Rectangles

Drawing Angles

The five standard display routines work for angles just as they did with rectangles, except that each routine requires two additional integer arguments: **startAngle** and **arcAngle**. The integer startAngle indicates where the arc is to begin, while **arcAngle** indicates how many degrees the arc should span. If the **arcAngle** is positive, the arc is drawn clockwise from the **startAngle**; if the **arcAngle** is negative, the line is drawn counterclockwise.

```
FrameArc(r, startAngle, arcAngle)
        Rect    *r;
        int     startAngle,arcAngle;
PaintArc(r, startAngle, arcAngle)
        Rect    *r;
        int     startAngle,arcAngle;
EraseArc(r, startAngle, arcAngle)
        Rect    *r;
        int     startAngle,arcAngle;
InvertArc(r, startAngle, arcAngle)
        Rect    *r;
        int     startAngle,arcAngle;
FillArc(r, startAngle, arcAngle, pat)
        Rect    *r;
        int     startAngle,arcAngle;
        Pattern *pat;
```

Defining and Drawing Polygons

QuickDraw gives us the ability to draw and manipulate polygons. A polygon is a closed figure made of any number of connected lines. Some sample polygons are shown in Figure 5.20.

To define a polygon we use the two routines **OpenPoly** and **Close-Poly**. We call **OpenPoly** to begin the definition and **ClosePoly** to end it. Any line drawing routines called between **OpenPoly** and **ClosePoly** are added to the polygon's definition. The data structure of a polygon is as follows:

```
struct PY {
        int     polySize;
```

```
            Rect        polyBBox;
            Point       polyPoints[1];
    };
    #define     Polygon     struct PY
    typedef     Polygon     *PolyPtr;
    typedef     PolyPtr     *PolyHandle;
```

The polySize field contains the size of the polygon in bytes. The polyBBox field is the smallest rectangle that encloses the entire polygon. The poly-Points array stores all the points of the polygon. This array of points is what really defines the polygon. When an application draws a polygon, lines are simply drawn between each point in the polyPoints array.

Defining and Disposing Polygons

To begin our polygon definition, we call the function **OpenPoly**.

```
PolyHandle OpenPoly();
```

OpenPoly returns a PolyHandle to a new polygon and tells QuickDraw to save all **Line** and **LineTo** calls as part of the polygon definition. Only the end points of the lines are stored in the polyPoints array. Also, none of the pen characteristics are taken into consideration. **HidePen** is called so that no drawing occurs on the screen while the polygon is being defined.

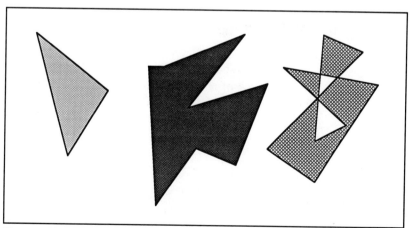

Figure 5.20: Pictures of Polygons

To end the polygon definition, we call **ClosePoly**.

```
ClosePoly();
```

ClosePoly tells QuickDraw to stop saving all the **Line** and **LineTo** calls as the definition of the polygon. The polygon's polyBBox is calculated, and **ShowPen** is called to balance the **HidePen** called by **OpenPoly**. Here's an example of how we would define a triangular polygon:

```
PolyHandle triPoly;
triPoly = OpenPoly();
MoveTo(300,100);
LineTo(400,200);
LineTo(200,200);
LineTo(300,100);
ClosePoly();
```

To deallocate the memory occupied by the polygon we call the procedure **KillPoly**.

```
KillPoly(poly)
        PolyHandle      poly;
```

We should only call **KillPoly** when we are completely through with the polygon poly.

- - - - - - - -

Moving Polygons

We can move a polygon in the same manner that we are able to move a rectangle. When an application calls **OffsetPoly**, the polygon poly is offset a distance of dh horizontally and dv vertically. **OffsetPoly** does not affect the screen or the polygon's shape or size.

```
OffsetPoly(poly,dh,dv)
        PolyHandle    poly;
        int           dh,dv;
```

Drawing Polygons

To display a polygon, we can use any of the five standard drawing verbs: **Frame**, **Paint**, **Erase**, **Invert**, or **Fill**. The polygon-displaying routines work the same as the corresponding rectangle-displaying routines, except for **FramePoly**. **FramePoly** re-executes the **Line** and **LineTo** calls of the polygon's definition with the current pnSize, pnMode, and pnPat pen characteristics. As a result, the framed polygon does not fit inside its polyBBox. The pen extends beyond the bottom and right sides of the polyBBox by the pen height and width.

```
FramePoly(poly)
        PolyHandle      poly;
PaintPoly(poly)
        PolyHandle      poly;
ErasePoly(poly)
        PolyHandle      poly;
InvertPoly(poly)
        PolyHandle      poly;
FillPoly(poly,pat)
        PolyHandle      poly;
        Pattern         *pat;
```

Defining, Manipulating, and Drawing Regions

A region is a complex object that can consist of any combination of lines, shapes such as ovals and rectangles, and even other regions. In a region, you may have one or more disjointed shapes. Because a region can be nearly any shape or set of shapes, its data structure is of variable size. The structure consists of two fixed fields followed by a variable-length data field.

```
struct RG {
        int       rgnSize;       /* = 10 if region is rectangular */
        Rect      rgnBBox;
/* plus byte codes for region content */
};
```

```
#define       Region        struct RG
typedef       Region        *RgnPtr;
typedef       RgnPtr        *RgnHandle;
```

The rgnSize field contains the size, in bytes, of the region, and the rgnBBox is the smallest rectangle that completely encloses the region. The rest of the data structure contains a compressed version of the drawing commands that define the region.

Defining Regions

To define a region, we use three routines: **NewRgn**, **OpenRgn**, and **CloseRgn**. The function **NewRgn** allocates space for and returns a handle to a new region. Once we have a region handle and we want to start defining the region, we call the procedure **OpenRgn**. **OpenRgn** tells QuickDraw to start saving all calls to the line drawing routines **Line** and **LineTo** and to the procedures that draw framed shapes (except for **Frame-Arc**) as the definition of a region.

As is the case with polygons, the pen characteristics are not taken into consideration in the definition of a region. **HidePen** is called so that no drawing appears on the screen during the definition of a region. The outline of the region is defined, and the portBit bitMap is split into two groups: those bits that are within the region and those that are not. Each call to one of the **Frame** routines forms another closed loop. Any simple lines drawn must connect with another line or a closed loop.

```
RgnHandle NewRgn();
          OpenRgn();
```

When we are through defining our region, a call should be made to **CloseRegion**. **CloseRegion** combines the lines and framed shapes as the definition of a region and assigns this region to dstRgn. Once a region is defined, we will always access it through its rgnHandle.

```
CloseRgn(dstRgn)
          RgnHandle      dstRgn;
```

Here's an example of how to define a barbell shaped region:

```
rgnHandle    barbell;
Rect         tempRect;
barbell = NewRgn();
OpenRgn();
SetRect(&tempRect,20,20,30,50);
FrameOval(&tempRect);
SetRect(&tempRect,30,30,80,40);
FrameRect(&tempRect);
SetRect(&tempRect,80,20,90,50);
FrameRect(&tempRect);
CloseRgn(barbell);
```

Manipulating Regions

Once our region is defined, there are all sorts of things we can do with it. Many of the routines are very similar to the rectangle manipulating routines. A call to any of the routines has no effect on the screen whatsoever.

The OffsetRgn Procedure

OffsetRgn moves the region rgn a distance of dh horizontally and dv vertically.

```
OffsetRgn(rgn, dh, dv)
       RgnHandle    rgn;
       int          dh,dv;
```

The InsetRgn Procedure

InsetRgn moves each point on the boundary of the specified region inward a distance of dh horizontally and dv vertically. Positive values for dh and dv cause the region to be shrunk; negative values cause it to expand.

```
InsetRgn(rgn, dh, dv)
       RgnHandle    rgn;
       int          dh,dv;
```

The SectRgn Procedure

SectRgn calculates the intersection of srcRgnA and srcRgnB and places the result in dstRgn. The RgnHandle dstRgn must have been previously created with **NewRgn**; **SectRgn** does not create it. Either of the source regions may also serve as the dstRgn.

```
SectRgn(srcRgnA, srcRgnB, dstRgn)
     RgnHandle        srcRgnA,srcRgnB,dstRgn;
```

The UnionRgn Procedure

UnionRgn calculates the union of srcRgnA and srcRgnB and places the result in dstRgn. The RgnHandle dstRgn must have been previously created with **NewRgn**. Either of the source regions may also serve as the dstRgn.

```
UnionRgn(srcRgnA, srcRgnB, dstRgn)
     RgnHandle        srcRgnA,srcRgnB,dstRgn;
```

The DiffRgn Procedure

DiffRgn subtracts srcRgnB from srcRgnA and places the result in dstRgn. It does not create the dstRgn; we must create it with **NewRgn**. Either of the source regions may also serve as the dstRgn.

```
DiffRgn(srcRgnA, srcRgnB, dstRgn)
     RgnHandle        srcRgnA,srcRgnB,dstRgn;
```

The XorRgn Procedure

XorRgn calculates the difference between the union and the intersection of srcRgnA and srcRgnB and places the result into dstRgn. It does not create the dstRgn; we must create it with **NewRgn**. Either of the source regions may also serve as the dstRgn.

```
XorRgn(srcRgnA, srcRgnB, dstRgn)
     RgnHandle        srcRgnA,srcRgnB,dstRgn;
```

The PtInRgn Function

PtInRgn returns a true value if the pixel below and to the right of the Point pt is enclosed by the specified region rgn. The function returns false if pt is not enclosed.

```
char PtInRgn(pt, rgn)
        Point       pt;
        RgnHandle   rgn;
```

The RectInRgn Function

RectInRgn returns true if any bits of the Rect r are enclosed by the region rgn. The function returns false if no bits are enclosed.

```
char RectInRgn(r, rgn)
        Rect        *r;
        RgnHandle   rgn;
```

The EqualRgn Function

EqualRgn returns true if the two regions rgnA and rgnB have exactly the same size, shape, and location. Otherwise, it returns false.

```
char EqualRgn(rgnA, rgnB)
        RgnHandle       rgnA,rgnB;
```

The EmptyRgn Function

EmptyRgn returns true if rgn is an empty region and false if the region contains something.

```
char EmptyRgn(rgn)
        RgnHandle       rgn;
```

Drawing Regions

To draw a region on the screen, we have the same five standard drawing commands: **Frame, Paint, Erase, Invert,** and **Fill**. These routines work exactly the same way they do with rectangles.

```
FrameRgn(rgn)
        RgnHandle        rgn;
PaintRgn(rgn)
        RgnHandle        rgn;
EraseRgn(rgn)
        RgnHandle        rgn;
InvertRgn(rgn)
        RgnHandle        rgn;
FillRgn(rgn, pat)
        RgnHandle        rgn;
        Pattern          *pat;
```

Defining and Drawing Pictures

A picture in QuickDraw is defined much in the same way as a polygon. Just as a polygon is a series of line drawing routines, a picture is a series of any QuickDraw procedures and functions. We call **Open-Picture** to begin the picture's definition and **ClosePicture** to end it. Any QuickDraw routines called between **OpenPicture** and **ClosePicture** are saved as the definition of the picture. When we begin our picture definition, we specify an enclosing rectangle, called the picture frame, for our picture. Later, when we go to draw the picture, we specify a destination rectangle for our picture. The picture is scaled up or down so that the border of the picture frame is the same size as the destination rectangle.

```
struct PI {
        int      picSize;
        Rect     *picFrame;
/* plus byte codes for picture content */
};
#define    Picture      struct PI
typedef    Picture      *PicPtr;
typedef    PicPtr       *PicHandle;
```

The picSize field contains the size of the picture in bytes. The picFrame is the rectangle that encloses or frames the picture.

The rest of the structure contains a compact representation of the drawing commands that draw the picture. The data structure is variably sized—the last field can be any size depending on the complexity of the picture.

Defining Pictures

To begin our picture definition, we call the function **OpenPicture**. **OpenPicture** returns a PicHandle to a new picture with the specified picFrame and tells QuickDraw to begin saving all drawing routines as part of the picture definition. **HidePen** is called so that no drawing occurs on the screen while the picture is being defined.

```
PicHandle OpenPicture(picFrame)
       Rect    *picFrame;
```

To end the picture definition, we call **ClosePicture**. **ClosePicture** tells QuickDraw to stop saving drawing commands as the definition of the picture. **ShowPen** is called to balance the **HidePen** called by **OpenPicture**.

```
ClosePicture();
```

Disposing of Pictures

To deallocate the memory used by a picture, we call the procedure **KillPicture**. An application should only call **KillPicture** when we are completely through with the picture myPicture.

```
KillPicture(myPicture)
       PicHandle       myPicture;
```

Drawing Pictures

To draw a picture on the screen, we call the procedure **Draw-Picture**. The PicHandle myPicture identifies the picture to draw, scaled to fit in the dstRect.

```
DrawPicture(myPicture, dstRect)
        PicHandle    myPicture;
        Rect         *dstRect;
```

Adding to a Previously Defined Picture

Once an application calls **ClosePicture**, the picture cannot be reopened and added to. An application can however, in a rather tricky manner, add to a picture that has already been defined. We simply open a new picture with the routine **OpenPicture** and then draw the old picture into the new picture. Now we can add anything we want to the old picture since it is now the new picture. When we are through adding things to the picture, we call **ClosePicture**, as usual.

Bit Transfer Operations

The two routines in this section allow an application to scroll or copy a specified set of bits. The first routine, **ScrollRect**, scrolls the bits inside the specified rectangle that intersect with visRgn, clipRgn, portRect, and portBits.bounds.

```
ScrollRect(r, dh, dv, updateRgn)
        Rect         *r;
        int          dh, dv;
        RgnHandle    updateRgn
```

The bits inside the specified rectangle r, are shifted a distance of dh horizontally, and dv vertically. After the procedure, the updateRgn will be the region that the bits were scrolled out of. This region will be filled with the background pattern of the current grafPort. Before calling **Scroll-**

Rect, create the updateRgn with **NewRgn.** The sample program at the end of Chapter 10 uses the routine **ScrollRect** to scroll bits around a window.

The second routine, **CopyBits,** allows an application to copy a set of bits from one bitMap to another.

```
CopyBits(srcBits, dstBits, srcRect, dstRect, mode, maskRgn)
        BitMap        srcBits, dstBits;
        Rect          *srcRect, *dstRect;
        int           mode;
        RgnHandle     maskRgn;
```

CopyBits copies the bits enclosed by srcRect in the bitMap srcBits to the rectangle dstRect in the bitMap dstBits. The srcRect is scaled to fit the dstRect. The srcRect must be specified in the coordinates of the source bitMap, while the dstRect is in the coordinates of the destination bitMap. The mode parameter indicates which of the eight source transfer modes is to be used when the bits are copied. The bits that are copied may be clipped by specifying a maskRgn parameter. If the maskRgn is NULL or 0L, no clipping will be performed.

Cursors

When you move the Mac's mouse around on a table, an image (the cursor) moves around on the screen in a similar manner. The standard cursor is an arrow pointing upward and to the left. It is possible, however, to change the cursor to any shape that we choose. A good example of this is when the cursor changes to a wristwatch to indicate a lengthy operation is taking place.

The cursor is a 16-by-16-bit square, defined as a 256-bit image. A structure of type Cursor consists of three fields: a 16-word data field which contains the cursor's image, a 16-word mask field which contains the cursor's mask image, and a hotSpot of type Point which aligns the cursor to the position of the mouse.

```
typedef struct {
        short s[16];
} Bits16;
```

```
struct C {
        Bits16 data;
        Bits16 mask;
        Point hotSpot;
};
#define     Cursor      struct C
typedef     Cursor      *CursPtr;
typedef     CursPtr      *CursHandle;
```

The data and mask fields determine how the cursor will appear on the screen in accordance with the chart in Figure 5.21.

If all the mask bits are set to 1, then the cursor is opaque, and none of the bits underneath it show through. If all the mask bits are set to 0, then the cursor will appear "transparent"—pixels under the white parts of the cursor will remain the same, while any pixels under the black part will be inverted.

The hotSpot is a Point in the cursor's 16-by-16-bit image that aligns the cursor with the position of the mouse. Whenever the mouse is moved, some low-level routines (handled by the system, not you), align the cursor's hotSpot with the new position of the mouse. The hotSpot also indicates exactly where the mouse button is clicked down. The pixel on the screen that is aligned with the hotSpot of the cursor is the Point that is placed in the where field of the event record whenever an event takes place. For the standard arrow cursor, the hotSpot is at Point (0,0). Figure 5.22 shows the relationship between the cursor and its hotSpot for the standard arrow cursor.

The InitCursor Routine

One of the first procedures we need to call in any application is **InitCursor**. It sets the cursor to the standard arrow cursor and makes the

Data	Mask	Resulting Pixel on Screen
0	1	White
1	1	Black
0	0	Same as pixel under cursor
1	0	Inverse of pixel under cursor

Figure 5.21:   Cursor Appearance Chart

cursor visible by setting the cursor level to 0. (A cursor level of 0 indicates that the cursor is to be visible; a negative number indicates that it is to be invisible.) The cursor level is changed via the procedures **Hide-Cursor** and **ShowCursor**, to be discussed shortly.

```
InitCursor();
```

The importance of calling **InitCursor** or, as we will see in a moment, **Set-Cursor**, is that when an application is double-clicked to start it up, the cursor is changed to a wristwatch. The wristwatch cursor tells the user "wait a moment" while the program is loaded from disk. When the program finally begins, unless we change the cursor to something else, it will remain a wristwatch, and the user may sit there for quite a while before realizing that there is no longer a need to "wait a moment."

The SetCursor Routine

In some applications, a cursor shaped differently than the standard arrow is advantageous. We can set the cursor to any shape we want with the procedure **SetCursor**. **SetCursor** changes the cursor to the one stored in crsr. No change, however, is made to the cursor level. If the cursor was currently invisible, it will remain that way. When the cursor is made visible, or if it already was visible, it will change to its new image.

```
SetCursor(crsr)
       Cursor  crsr;
```

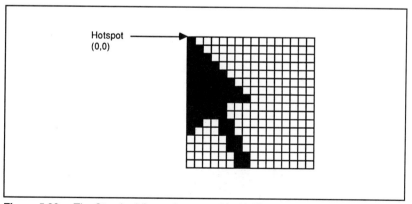

Figure 5.22:   The Standard Arrow Cursor and its HotSpot

It is customary for the cursor to be changed to a wristwatch whenever a lengthy operation must take place. A good example is disk I/O. Whenever an application begins any substantial disk I/O, it should change the cursor to a wristwatch. When the operation is completed, the cursor should be restored to another appropriate shape.

The GetCursor Routine

In the standard Macintosh System File, there are four predefined cursor shapes. A handle to any one of the four shapes, shown in Figure 5.23, can be obtained using the **GetCursor** routine. An application simply passes the number of the cursor it wants to **GetCursor**, and a handle to it is returned as the function value. The handle to the cursor can then be used with the previously discussed routine **SetCursor**.

```
CursHandle GetCursor(cursorID)
        int      cursorID;
```

The HideCursor and ShowCursor Routines

To change the cursor level, making the cursor visible or invisible, we use the routines **HideCursor** and **ShowCursor**. Each time we call **HideCursor**, the cursor is made invisible and the cursor level is decremented. Each time we call **ShowCursor**, the cursor level is incremented.

Figure 5.23: The Standard System Cursors

If the cursor level becomes 0, the cursor will become visible. Each call to **HideCursor** should be balanced by a call to **ShowCursor**. If we call **Hide-Cursor** twice, **ShowCursor** will have to be called twice to make the cursor visible again. The converse is not true. **ShowCursor** will not increment the cursor level beyond 0, so multiple calls to **ShowCursor** will not re-quire multiple calls to **HideCursor** to make the cursor invisible again. One call to **HideCursor** will always suffice to hide the cursor.

```
HideCursor();
ShowCursor();
```

The ObscureCursor Routine

There is one other way to make the cursor invisible, and that is with a call to **ObscureCursor**. **ObscureCursor** makes the cursor invisible until the next time it is moved. This can add a very nice touch to your applications. In a word processing program for example, a user typing in some text may find it annoying to have the cursor obscuring part of the text on the screen. If **ObscureCursor** is used, the cursor will be in-visible when text is being typed. It isn't until the user attempts to do something with the mouse that the cursor becomes visible again. The Toolbox sort of tucks it away for us until we need to use it again.

```
ObscureCursor();
```

A Sample Program for QuickDraw

The application that follows demonstrates many of the routines that we have discussed in the chapter. In addition, many of the other sample applications in this book use QuickDraw routines.

```
/*****************************************************************/
/*    Sample Application for Chapter 5: Drawing with QuickDraw   */
/*                                                               */
/*    This application demonstrates several of the QuickDraw     */
/*    routines discussed in the chapter. It allows you to        */
/*    clear the screen, and perform the 5 drawing verbs on       */
/*    rectangles and ovals. The application can also switch      */
/*    the cursor to any of the 4 standard system cursors.        */
/*    The application also performs simple animation,            */
/*    defines the fills a polygon, and draws a picture that is   */
/*    stored in the resource fork of the application.            */
/*                                                               */
/*****************************************************************/

/* Include Mac header files */
#include <QuickDraw.h>
#include <EventMgr.h>
#include <WindowMgr.h>
#include <MenuMgr.h>
#include <ToolboxUtil.h>
#include <stdio.h>

/*  Menu Constants   */
#define   Desk_ID          100
#define   Shape_ID         101
#define   Cursor_ID        102
#define   Special_ID       103

/* SetUpMenus simply sets up each menu
    and puts it in the menu bar */
SetUpMenus()
{
      MenuHandle    DeskMenu;
      MenuHandle    shapeMenu;
      MenuHandle    cursorMenu;
      MenuHandle    SpecialMenu;
      long  items, i;

      /*  Desk Accessory Menu - with disabled items until Ch. 13 */
      DeskMenu = NewMenu (Desk_ID,"\p\24");
      AddResMenu (DeskMenu, 'DRVR');
      items = CountMItems (DeskMenu);
            for(i=1;i<=items;i++) DisableItem(DeskMenu,i);
      InsertMenu (DeskMenu, 0);

      /*  shape menu   */
      shapeMenu = NewMenu (Shape_ID, "\pShapes");
      AppendMenu (shapeMenu, "\pClear Screen;(-;Frame Rect;Paint Rect");
      AppendMenu (shapeMenu, "\pErase Rect;Invert Rect;Fill Rect");
      AppendMenu (shapeMenu, "\p(-;Frame Oval;Paint Oval;Erase Oval");
```

```
        AppendMenu (shapeMenu, "\pInvert Oval;Fill Oval;(-;Quit");
        DisableItem(shapeMenu,2);
        DisableItem(shapeMenu,8);
        DisableItem(shapeMenu,14);
        InsertMenu(shapeMenu, 0);

        /*  Cursors Menu  */
        cursorMenu = NewMenu (Cursor_ID, "\pCursors");
        AppendMenu (cursorMenu, "\pI-Beam;Cross;Plus;Watch;Arrow");
        InsertMenu (cursorMenu, 0);

        /*  Special Menu  */
        SpecialMenu = NewMenu (Special_ID, "\pSpecial");
        AppendMenu (SpecialMenu, "\pDraw Picture;Draw Polygon;Animation");
        InsertMenu (SpecialMenu, 0);

        DrawMenuBar();
}

/* main event loop */
main()
{
        EventRecord theEvent;
        WindowPtr    whichWindow;
        short                           windowcode;

        InitGraf(&thePort);
        InitFonts();
        InitWindows();
        InitMenus();
        InitCursor();

        FlushEvents(everyEvent, NULL);

        SetUpMenus();
        while (1) {
          if (GetNextEvent(everyEvent,&theEvent)) {
             switch (theEvent.what) {
                case mouseDown:
                   windowcode=FindWindow(theEvent.where,&whichWindow);
                   switch (windowcode) {
                      case inMenuBar:
                         DoWhatTheMenuSays(MenuSelect(theEvent.where));
                         break;
                   }
                 break;
              }
          }
       }
} /* end of main() */
```

```
/* DoWhatTheMenuSays responds to each menu event */
DoWhatTheMenuSays(menuResult)
   long   menuResult;
{
   short       menuID, itemNumber,i;
   CursHandle  theCursor;
   PicHandle   thePicture;
   PolyHandle  thePolygon;
   Handle      saucer1;
   Rect        screen,theRect,icon1;
   Pattern     brickPat;

   SetRect(&theRect,150,100,362,242);
   SetRect(&screen,
       screenBits.bounds.left,
       screenBits.bounds.top + 20,
       screenBits.bounds.right,
       screenBits.bounds.bottom);

   menuID = HiWord (menuResult);
   itemNumber = LoWord (menuResult);

   switch (menuID) {
       case Shape_ID:
           switch (itemNumber) {
               case 1:
                   EraseRect(&screen);
                   break;

               case 3:
                   FrameRect(&theRect);
                   break;

               case 4:
                   PaintRect(&theRect);
                   break;

               case 5:
                   EraseRect(&theRect);
                   break;

               case 6:
                   InvertRect(&theRect);
                   break;

               case 7:
                   FillRect(&theRect,dkGray);
                   break;

               case 9:
                   FrameOval(&theRect);
                   break;
```

```
                case 10:
                    PaintOval(&theRect);
                    break;

                case 11:
                    EraseOval(&theRect);
                    break;

                case 12:
                    InvertOval(&theRect);
                    break;

                case 13:
                    FillOval(&theRect,ltGray);
                    break;

                case 15:
                    ExitToShell();
                    break;

        }
        break;

    /* each of the cursor selections pulls in
        a cursor from the system resource fork
        and makes it the current cursor */
case Cursor_ID:
    switch (itemNumber) {
        case 1:
            theCursor = GetCursor(1);
            SetCursor(*theCursor);
            break;

        case 2:
            theCursor = GetCursor(2);
            SetCursor(*theCursor);
            break;

        case 3:
            theCursor = GetCursor(3);
            SetCursor(*theCursor);
            break;

        case 4:
            theCursor = GetCursor(4);
            SetCursor(*theCursor);
            break;

        case 5:
            InitCursor();
            break;
```

```
        }
    break;

case Special_ID:
    switch (itemNumber) {

        /* The first case prints a picture on the screen that is
           stored in the resource fork of the application.
           To create a PICT resource, cut or copy a picture
           into the scrapbook, then with the Resource Editor,
           go in and cut or copy the PICT resource out of the
           scrapbook file and paste it into your application.  */
        case 1:
            thePicture = GetPicture(1);
            HLock(thePicture);
            DrawPicture(thePicture,&((**thePicture).picFrame));
            HUnlock(thePicture);
            break;

        /* This case creates a brick pattern, and then a
           triangular shaped polygon.  The polygon is filled
           with the brick pattern */
        case 2:
            StuffHex(&brickPat,"\p808080FF080808FF");
            thePolygon = OpenPoly();
                MoveTo(300,100);
                LineTo(400,200);
                LineTo(200,200);
                LineTo(300,100);
            ClosePoly();
                FillPoly(thePolygon, &brickPat);
                FramePoly(thePolygon);
                KillPoly(thePolygon);
                break;

        /* The last case performs some simple animation.
           The reason the icon does not have to be erased
           is that its left edge has a couple columns of
           white space that overwrite the previous drawing
           on the screen.  This reduces the flicker on the
           screen. */
        case 3:
            HideCursor();
            EraseRect(&screen);
            SetRect(&icon1,-33,50,-1,82);
            saucer1 = GetIcon(1);
            PlotIcon(&icon1,saucer1);
            for(i=0;i<screen.right+32;i++) {
                OffsetRect(&icon1,1,0);
                PlotIcon(&icon1,saucer1);
```

```
                }
                ShowCursor();
                break;

            }
        }
    HiliteMenu(0);
}


*    Source code for Chapter 5 sample Application Resources
*
*    Use the Apple Resource Compiler - RMaker

Chapt5.rsrc

Type ICON

    ,1
00000000
00000000
00000000
00000000
00000000
00000000
00000000
00000000
00000000
00000000
00000000
00000000
00000000
00000000
00000000
00000000
00000000
00000000
00000000
00006000
0000F000
00010800
000E0700
0011F880
00240240
002D9B40
07E0007E
0C0D9B03
0C000003
07FFFFFE
00000000
```

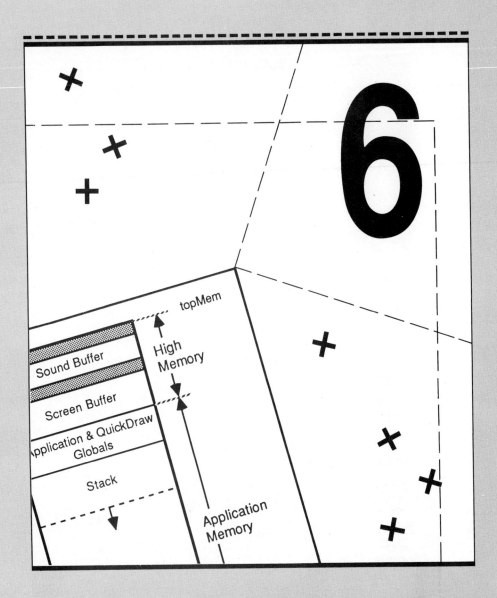

Memory Management

In the previous three chapters we discussed how to create and use windows and menus, and introduced the graphics capabilities of QuickDraw. These are very important tools to have at our disposal as we design the user interface for our application, but now it is time to move on to some of the more advanced capabilities of the Toolbox, and in particular one that lies at the heart of every program written for the Macintosh.

Up to this point we have said very little about how the memory of the Macintosh is organized or how it can best be used by an application program. The sample programs we have presented so far already make extensive use of the Macintosh Memory Manager, yet there has been no need to stop and explain how things actually happen. For the most part, in fact, the Memory Manager operates automatically, without any action required on the part of the programmer. Most of the activity handled by the Memory Manager is generated by other parts of the Toolbox rather than coming directly from the application. The Menu Manager function **NewMenu**, for example, directs the Memory Manager to set aside a section of memory to contain all of the information about an item in the menu bar, without any conscious effort on the part of the programmer.

This is an essential feature of the Macintosh Toolbox. The power and versatility of memory management are available to the application programmer, but for the most part the application and the programmer are insulated from the inner workings of the Memory Manager.

In this chapter we will look first at the overall layout of the memory of the Macintosh, with special focus on which portions of memory are used by the operating system and which portions are available for the application program. Next, we will examine some of the frequently used routines of the Memory Manager for allocating and releasing blocks of memory. Along the way we will discuss some of the pitfalls that programmers can avoid and offer some guidelines for safe and effective use of the Memory Manager.

The Macintosh Memory Map

The memory of the Macintosh can be divided into three distinct regions: *low memory*, *high memory*, and *application memory* (see Figure 6.1).

Low memory contains global variables belonging to the Toolbox and operating system, the *system heap*, and the ROM (or RAM)

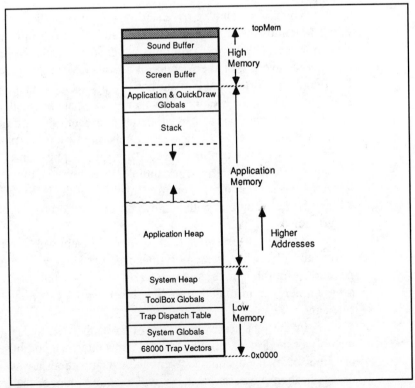

Figure 6.1: Macintosh Memory Map

locations of the Toolbox routines. *High memory* contains the screen and sound buffers. Occasionally an application will need to know the value of one of the system or Toolbox globals (for instance, the double-click time) that is not accessible through any of the Toolbox routines. In Appendix C we have listed the locations of the system and Toolbox global variables in low memory.

Application memory contains the application heap, the stack, system global variables associated with QuickDraw, and the application's own global variables. Throughout this book we will deal almost entirely with application memory. Let's take a closer look at the stack and the application heap now.

The Stack

The *stack*, which is located at the top of application memory, is a dynamic structure. As more space is needed, the stack grows from higher addresses to lower ones—that is, toward the application heap. The upper end of the stack begins at a fixed address which depends only on the amount of memory installed in your Macintosh. Space on the stack is allocated on a last-in first-out, or LIFO, basis. In other words, recently allocated items must be released from the stack before attempting to release an older item from the stack. Whenever a procedure or function is called, additional space is allocated on the stack. As a routine begins to execute, space for its local variables will be allocated on the stack. This space will be released as the routine is exited. In addition, roughly half of the routines in the Toolbox as well as several development systems expect their calling parameters to be passed on the stack. (The alternative is to pass parameters in the registers of the 68000.)

One of the advantages of using a high-level language like Pascal or C is that manipulation of the stack is handled entirely by the compiler. Typically the programmer does not need to worry about the contents of the stack. There are occasions, however, when it becomes necessary to manipulate the stack. An example of this can be seen in Chapter 10, in the implementation of a scroll bar.

The Heap

The *heap* is best described as a memory pool that is divided into many chunks or blocks of varying sizes. Three types of blocks can be found in the heap: *relocatable* blocks, *nonrelocatable* blocks, and *free* or unallocated blocks. Every memory location in the heap will be a part of only one such block. Figure 6.2 shows how these three types of blocks might be distributed in a generic heap configuration.

You will have noted in our earlier discussion of the memory map that there are actually two heaps: the system heap and the application heap. In fact, the Macintosh operating system is capable of handling multiple *heap zones*, of which the system and application heaps are but two examples. Throughout the remainder of this book, we will consider only applications that utilize a single application heap zone.

A major difference between the application heap and the system heap is that each time an application is launched, the application heap is initialized (that is, erased and set back to the default size); thus any information from the previous application will be lost. The system heap, on the other hand, remains intact across the launching of different applications.

The application heap is important for several reasons. First of all, the application code itself is stored in the application heap. In addition, any memory allocated directly by the application through

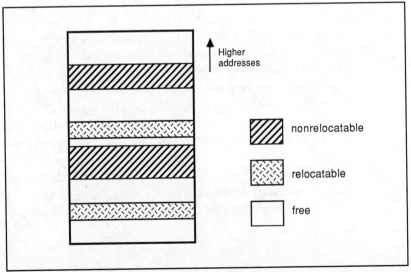

Figure 6.2: Blocks of Memory in a Generic Heap

the Memory Manager, or indirectly through the Toolbox, is located in the application heap.

The Macintosh operating system uses the system heap to store its own data, independent of the current application. It is possible for an application to place objects in the system heap, although doing so takes up precious space in the system heap and therefore cannot be recommended. In this book, we will only discuss manipulation of the application heap, and we will refer to it generically as "the heap."

Relocatable and Nonrelocatable Blocks

As we learned a moment ago, the heap is divided into three types of blocks: relocatable, nonrelocatable, and free. A free block consists of a range of memory not currently allocated; the block may have been free since the current application was launched or it may have been released back to the Memory Manager after the application no longer needed its contents. In contrast, relocatable and nonrelocatable blocks are portions of memory set aside by the Memory Manager for use by the application.

A nonrelocatable block will be found at a fixed location throughout its lifetime on the heap. An application refers to the contents of a nonrelocatable block through the use of a *pointer* to the block. A pointer is a variable containing the fixed address in memory of the beginning of the data contained in the block (see Figure 6.3).

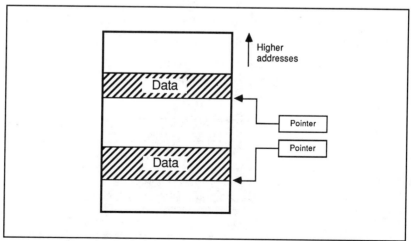

Figure 6.3: Pointers and Nonrelocatable Blocks

When an application requests space for a nonrelocatable block, the Memory Manager will attempt to situate the block near the bottom (toward lower addresses) of the heap to avoid the possibility of fragmenting the heap (we will discuss this in a moment). Whenever possible, nonrelocatable blocks should be allocated early in the application program to ensure their placement near the bottom of the heap.

Relocatable blocks may be moved at the discretion of the Memory Manager. Whenever an application releases a block of memory from the heap—either directly through the Memory Manager, or indirectly through the Toolbox—this relocation can occur. The Memory Manager will rearrange the heap while attempting to gather space for an object that is larger than any of the available free blocks. This process is known as *heap compaction*. When compaction occurs, the memory address of data contained in a relocatable block will change. To access the data in a relocatable block, the application must use a handle to the data. As we discussed briefly in the introduction to this book, a handle is a variable that contains the location of a pointer to the data (a handle is essentially a pointer to a pointer). The Memory Manager uses a special type of pointer called a *master pointer* in conjunction with handles (see Figure 6.4). Master pointers are kept by the operating system in

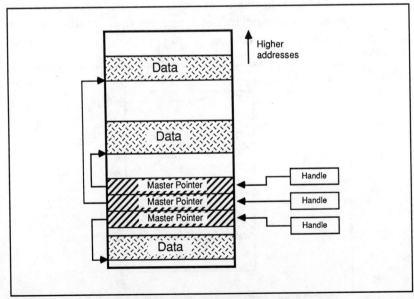

Figure 6.4: Handles, Master Pointers, and Relocatable Blocks

nonrelocatable blocks in the heap. When a relocatable block is moved, the Memory Manager updates the appropriate master pointer to reflect the new location of the block.

Heap Compaction and Fragmentation

As we just learned, the Memory Manager merges free blocks scattered throughout the heap in a process known as heap compaction. During a compaction, relocatable blocks are moved towards the bottom of the heap (to lower addresses) in an attempt to merge free space at the top of the heap. This process begins with the relocatable blocks near the bottom of the heap. If there were no nonrelocatable blocks in the heap, the Memory Manager would be able to merge all of the free space into a single contiguous block at the top of the heap. However, the Memory Manager cannot move a relocatable block around or over a nonrelocatable one. Thus the presence of nonrelocatable blocks interferes with the attempt to move the relocatable blocks downward.

Fragmentation of the heap occurs whenever nonrelocatable or locked relocatable blocks subdivide the heap into two or more pieces (locked relocatable blocks will be discussed later in the chapter). Fragmentation prevents the Memory Manager from merging free blocks to form larger ones. In almost any imaginable situation the heap will be partially fragmented since it is impossible to allocate all of the nonrelocatable blocks side by side at the bottom of the heap. The seriousness of fragmentation depends on how severely the heap is divided by nonrelocatable blocks. In a badly fragmented heap, the Memory Manager will be unable to merge the scattered free blocks, even though the total amount of available space may be large. Figure 6.5 illustrates the appearance of the heap before and after compaction in the case where the heap is only slightly fragmented. Notice the free block stranded between the two nonrelocatable blocks near the bottom of the heap. This block can only be used if the Memory Manager needs a block of exactly its size or smaller.

Figure 6.6 shows the same heap configuration as Figure 6.5, except that we have added a nonrelocatable block near the middle of the heap. In this more seriously fragmented case, the Memory Manager can no longer merge together the majority of the free space in the heap.

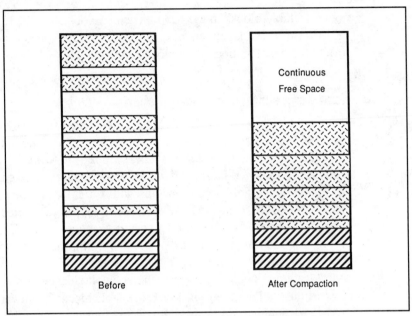

Figure 6.5: The Unfragmented Heap Before and After Compaction

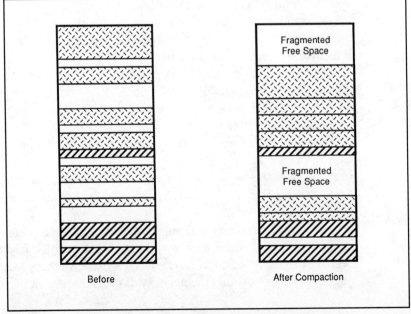

Figure 6.6: The Fragmented Heap Before and After Compaction

Using the Memory Manager

Many simple application programs will not notice the operation of the Memory Manager. Heap compaction and memory allocation take place with little or no direction from the application. In more complex applications, however, the need will arise to allocate memory for an array or structure that is not part of the Macintosh operating system. In addition, when accessing the contents of relocatable blocks, it often becomes necessary to communicate directly with the Memory Manager (this topic is discussed later in this chapter under the heading "Dereferencing"). For these reasons some knowledge of the routines in the Memory Manager is essential. We will limit our discussion to only the most frequently used routines.

Dereferencing: Using Pointers and Handles to Access Data

To access a variable, structure, or structure field from its handle or pointer, the application must *dereference* the handle or pointer; that is, the application must follow the pointer or handle into memory to find the actual memory location of the data of interest. Suppose that we have defined a structure named Thing, and that we have declared variables corresponding to a pointer and handle to a variable of type Thing, as follows:

```
struct Thing {
        int        theInt;
        char       theChar;
        long       theLong;
};
#define    Thing       struct Thing
typedef    Thing       *ThingPtr;
typedef    ThingPtr    *ThingHandle;
```

Given this definition for the Thing structure and its contents, we can construct the following, rather nonsensical, example in which we demonstrate various methods of using handles and pointers to a data structure.

```
/* declare a local variable of type Thing and create a handle and
pointer to the variable */
Thing          aThing;
ThingPtr       aThingPtr;
ThingHandle    aThingHandle;
/* Pass location of structure to a procedure */
aProcedure (&aThing);           /* use address operator (&)*/
aProcedure (aThingPtr);
aProcedure (*aThingHandle)      /* use indirection operator (*) */
/* Access individual field of the structure*/
theLongPart = aThing.theLong;          /* use dot operator (.) */
theLongPart = aThingPtr->theLong;    /* use arrow operator (->) */
theLongPart = (*aThingPtr).theLong; /* or dereference pointer */
theLongPart = (*aThingHandle)->theLong;/* deference and
                                                  use arrow */
theLongPart = (**aThingHandle).theLong; /* deference twice and
                                                  use dot */
```

The parentheses used when dereferencing handles and pointers are required, since in C the structure operators dot (.) and arrow (->) take precedence over the indirection operator (*).

Allocating, Disposing and Resizing of Nonrelocatable Blocks

To allocate a nonrelocatable block on the application heap, use the function **NewPtr**:

```
Ptr NewPtr(logicalSize)
        long    logicalSize;
```

The parameter logicalSize specifies the size in bytes of the desired block. **NewPtr** returns as its value a pointer to the new block if it was successfully allocated, or NULL if it was not. The function **NewPtr** attempts to position the nonrelocatable block as close to the bottom of the heap as possible by moving relocatable blocks toward the top of the heap. Remember to cast the generic pointer to the appropriate structure pointer before passing it to a Toolbox routine or attempting to dereference the pointer to access the contents of the block.

To release the memory occupied by a nonrelocatable block, call **DisposPtr** with a pointer to the block as the parameter:

```
DisposPtr(aPointer)
        Ptr     aPointer;
```

Releasing the block allows the Memory Manager to reclaim the space occupied by the block.

The size of an existing nonrelocatable block can be obtained from the function **GetPtrSize** by passing a pointer to the desired block:

```
long GetPtrSize(aPointer)
        Ptr     aPointer;
```

GetPtrSize returns the size of the block unless an error occurs, in which case it returns NULL. The most common error involves passing a pointer that does not point to any of the existing nonrelocatable blocks.

The size of an existing nonrelocatable block may be altered with the procedure **SetPtrSize**. Pass a pointer to the block and the desired size of the block, as follows:

```
SetPtrSize(aPointer, newSize)
        Ptr     aPointer;
        long    newSize;
```

This allows an application to expand, or shrink, the amount of memory used to store its data. In C, the only universal way to determine if **SetPtrSize** succeeded in changing the size of the block (see the box entitled "Determining if a Memory Manager Error Has Occurred") is to follow up with a call to **GetPtrSize**.

Determining if a Memory Manager Error Has Occurred

Many of the routines in the Memory Manager place a result or error code into the D0 register of the 68000 upon completion. For many of the routines in the Memory Manager, it is necessary to inspect this value to determine if the operation was carried out successfully. Under Think C, the return value of any function is placed in the D0 register just prior to the conclusion of the function. As such, no special manipulation is required to read the result or error codes from Memory Manager routines. You can simply treat them as return values.

A listing of the appropriate error codes for the routines of the Memory Manager may be found in Appendix B.

Allocating, Disposing and Resizing of Relocatable Blocks

The Memory Manager also contains routines for use with relocatable blocks. These routines are similar to the ones used with non-relocatable blocks.

To allocate a relocatable block on the application heap, use the function **NewHandle**, as follows:

```
Handle NewHandle(logicalSize)
        long    logicalSize;
```

The parameter logicalSize once again specifies the size in bytes of the desired block. **NewHandle** returns as its value a handle (equivalent to a char**) to the new block if it was successfully allocated, or NULL if it was not. **NewHandle** will position the relocatable block near the top of the heap and will, if necessary, compact the heap to merge sufficient free space for the new block. Before using the generic handle returned by **NewHandle** in a Toolbox routine, or to access the contents of the relocatable block, remember to cast the handle to a specific structure handle.

To release the memory occupied by a relocatable block back to the Memory Manager, call **DisposHandle** with a handle to the block as the parameter:

```
DisposHandle(aHandle)
        Handle   aHandle;
```

The size of an existing relocatable block can be obtained from the function **GetHandleSize** by passing a handle to the desired block:

```
long GetHandleSize(aHandle)
        Handle   aHandle;
```

GetHandleSize returns the size of the block, or NULL if an error occurs. The most common error again involves passing a handle that does not correspond to any existing relocatable block.

The size of an existing relocatable block may be increased or decreased with the procedure **SetHandleSize**. Pass a handle to the block and the desired final size of the block as the parameters:

```
SetHandleSize(aHandle, newSize)
        Handle   aHandle;
        long     newSize;
```

Properties of Relocatable Blocks

A relocatable block can be temporarily locked to prevent its movement during a memory compaction. It is often necessary to lock a relocatable block when a Toolbox routine will access some part of its contents. Furthermore, in time-critical portions of an application, it may be desirable to access the contents of a block through a pointer instead of a handle, since using a pointer rather than the handle removes one level of indirection and results in faster execution. Whenever a pointer is being used to access the contents of a relocatable block, the block must be locked in case memory is compacted. Be certain to unlock the block after the relevant portion of the application has been completed to allow memory compaction to occur properly.

To lock or unlock the block with the handle aHandle, use the following procedures:

```
HLock (aHandle)
        Handle   aHandle;
HUnlock (aHandle)
        Handle   aHandle;
```

By default, the Memory Manager creates unlocked relocatable blocks.

In memory critical situations that occur when you are trying to fit a large application into a small amount of memory, it may be convenient to allow the Memory Manager to purge the contents of a relocatable block. A block should be marked as *purgeable* only if the contents of the block can be easily reconstructed and then only when the application is nearly out of memory. The Memory Manager will only reclaim the space occupied by a purgeable block if it has exhausted all other means of obtaining free space.

To mark a relocatable block as either purgeable or *unpurgeable* (relocatable blocks are created as unpurgeable), use the procedures:

```
HPurge (aHandle)
        Handle   aHandle;
HNoPurge (aHandle)
        Handle   aHandle;
```

If a block has been marked as purgeable, you must determine if it has actually been purged before attempting to access its contents. The Memory Manager will place the value NULL into the block's master pointer before purging the block. Thus if the handle points to a NULL master pointer, the block has been purged. Attempting to access the contents of a block whose master pointer has the value NULL will produce unpredictable results. Interpreting NULL as a pointer leads to address zero at the bottom of system memory. This is where system global variables are stored. Therefore, if you write to it, the system will probably crash. If the block has been purged, the application should instead reallocate the block and reconstruct its contents before proceeding. Since the block's master pointer is not released when the block is purged, the application should always reallocate the block using the existing master pointer, instead of creating a new block with **NewHandle**. Use the procedure

```
ReallocHandle(aHandle, logicalSize)
        Handle  aHandle;
        long    logicalSize;
```

to reallocate space using the existing master pointer for the relocatable block that has been purged.

The Dangers of Dangling Pointers

One of the most common errors made when working with memory management involves creating and dereferencing a *dangling pointer*. The danger of a dangling pointer exists whenever the application dereferences a handle to a relocatable block and then passes the resulting pointer or absolute memory location to a Toolbox routine, or worse yet makes a local copy of the dereferenced handle. If the Memory Manager compacts the heap and relocates the block, the pointer created by the application will be left dangling; in other words, the pointer will no longer point correctly to the data in the block. Figure 6.7 illustrates this situation. Before compaction, both the master pointer and the application's copy correctly point to the data in the relocatable block. After the compaction, the master pointer has been updated by the Memory Manager to reflect the new position of the relocatable block while the application's copy still reflects the old position of the block.

Most often dangling pointers are created when the application is passing a pointer to a structure, which is located in a relocatable block, to a Toolbox routine. If the Toolbox routine causes a memory compaction before it finishes with the structure, the pointer passed to the routine may become invalid. To avoid dangling pointers, the application should lock the relocatable block in memory before calling a Toolbox routine with a dereferenced handle. It is important to remember to unlock the block as soon as the application has finished calling the routine or routines that require a dereferenced handle—and may cause a heap compaction—since the locked block may fragment the heap.

Let's take a look at two examples leading to the creation of dangling pointers, along with the appropriate remedies. The first example illustrates the more obvious case where the application itself uses the dangling pointer.

```
/* EXAMPLE 1:
- using local copy of master pointer */
/* dereference handle to get a pointer to the data */
localThingPtr = *aThingHandle;
/* call a procedure which may cause a heap compaction */
RiskyProcedure();
/* if RiskyProcedure caused a memory compaction
- localThingPtr becomes a dangling pointer
- the next operation using it will be bogus */
theLongPart = localThingPtr->theLong;
/**/
/* Solution A: Don't make a copy of the dereferenced handle!  */
someThing = (*aThingHandle)->theInt;
RiskyProcedure( );
theLongPart = (*aThingHandle)->theLong; /* dereference here
   again! */
/* Solution B: If you must copy the master
   pointer—lock the handle */
HLock(aThingHandle);
localThingPtr = *aThingHandle;
```

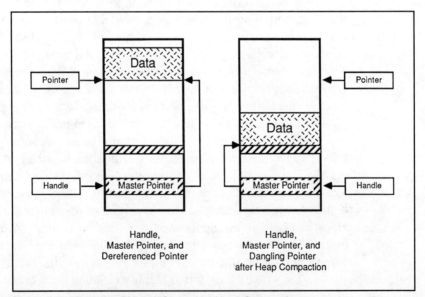

Figure 6.7: Dangling Pointers Caused by Heap Compaction

```
RiskyProcedure( );
theLongPart = (aThingHandle)->theLong;
HUnlock(aThingHandle);
```

The second example passes a pointer to a structure, which is contained within a relocatable block, to a Toolbox routine that may cause a heap compaction. This is the most common way of inadvertently creating a dangling pointer. In this case the error is likely to occur within the Toolbox routine itself. This example should be a familiar one, as it first appeared in the sample program used in Chapter 3.

```
/* EXAMPLE 2:
- passing structure pointer to a Toolbox routine */
/* Erase the window content, pass boundsRect to EraseRect
- the boundsRect is contained in the relocatable
- block used to store the content region */
/* get handle to content region first */
contRgnHnd = theWindowRec.contRgn;
/* pass pointer to boundsRect
- note that handle is dereferenced in the process */
EraseRect (&(*contRgnHnd)->rgnBBox);
/* even an innocuous routine like EraseRect can cause
a heap compaction. If this occurs, the pointer
to the boundsRect becomes invalid */
/**/
/* Solution: lock relocatable block before dereferencing */
contRgnHnd = theWindowRec.contRgn;
HLock(contRgnHnd);
EraseRect (&(*contRgnHnd)->rgnBBox);
HUnlock(contRgnHnd);
```

Miscellaneous Routines

The Memory Manager also contains several routines designed to report on the available space in the heap, or to explicitly compact the heap.

To determine the total amount of free space in the application heap, call the function **FreeMem**:

```
long FreeMem()
```

Note that allocating a block equivalent to the total amount of free space in the heap is not usually possible because of the fragmentation caused by nonrelocatable and locked relocatable blocks.

The size of the largest block that can be allocated after memory compaction can be determined with the function MaxHeap:

```
long MaxHeap()
```

The application can perform a memory compaction explicitly (as opposed to the compactions performed indirectly by the Memory Manager as it gathers free space) with the function **CompactMem**:

```
long CompactMem(cbNeeded)
      long    cbNeeded;
```

Here the parameter cbNeeded specifies the amount of free space that the Memory Manager should attempt to gather in one place. **CompactMem** moves relocatable blocks downward in the attempt to gather free space near the top of the heap. The result returned from **CompactMem** is the size of the largest free block available after the compaction.

If the application contains a relocatable block that will be locked for long periods of time, the block should be placed near the bottom of the heap. In contrast to **CompactMem**, the procedure **ReservMem** moves relocatable blocks upward in an attempt to gather free space near the bottom of the heap:

```
ReservMem(cbNeeded)
      long    cbNeeded;
```

If necessary, **ReservMem** will purge blocks from the heap in order to free the specified amount of memory. Following **ReservMem** with a call to **NewHandle** results in locating the block near the bottom of the heap. Recall that a locked relocatable block acts just like a nonrelocatable block in fragmenting the heap. Locating the block near the bottom of the heap with the nonrelocatable blocks, however, minimizes the extent to which a locked block can cause fragmentation.

The final Memory Manager routine we will discuss is a general purpose utility for copying an arbitrary portion of memory. **BlockMove** copies a specified number of bytes from one memory location to another.

```
BlockMove(sourcePtr, destPtr, byteCount)
        Ptr       sourcePtr, destPtr;
        long      byteCount;
```

Here the parameter sourcePtr specifies the starting location in memory of the source of data to be copied, while destPtr is the starting location for the destination, and byteCount is the number of bytes to be copied. You can use **BlockMove** whenever the application needs to copy a data structure, and thus avoid having to copy each field separately.

Here is an example of copying the contents of one structure variable into a block allocated on the heap:

```
/* locally defined variables */

WindowRecord    theWindowRec;
WindowPeek      copyOfTheWR;

/* allocate a nonrelocatable block of the right size
- remember to cast generic pointer */

copyOfTheWR = (WindowPeek) NewPtr(sizeof(WindowRecord));

/* make a copy of theWindowRec */

BlockMove(&theWindowRec, copyOfTheWR, sizeof(WindowRecord));
```

C Language Equivalents

If you leaf through the Think C Standard Libraries Reference book, you will discover that the storage library offers some functions which seem to do much the same things as the Memory Manager functions do. In some cases, it might not be obvious which to use for a particular application.

In fact, these functions call the Memory Manager directly. Thus, for example, the **malloc** function, which allocates memory under any C language environment, is equivalent to the **NewPtr** function of the Mac's Memory Manager. The C language functions are provided with Think C to make it easier to port source code from other computers to the Mac, and to subsequently recompile it with a minimum of changes.

Good arguments can be constructed for using the C language storage functions rather than the direct Memory Manager calls whenever possible. A program which uses **malloc** rather than **NewPtr**, for example, will be easier for a C programmer not familiar with the Macintosh to read at some future time. It will also be a lot easier to port out of the Mac, if you want to run it on a different machine.

In practice, the C language storage functions don't provide equivalents for most of the useful functions of the Memory Manager in any case, and their use doesn't come up that often. They can't allocate relocatable blocks, for example. On the other hand, C provides a function called **calloc** which will allocate a non-relocateable buffer to hold an array of structs and clear it, all with one call. Since this is something which comes up a lot in C programs, it's a useful thing to know about.

C also provides you with memory movers. The **movmem** function, in the unix library of Think C, is equivalent to the Memory Manager's **BlockMove** function. Again, it's useful principally for reasons of portability.

There's a trap in porting code from other machines to the Macintosh involving this function. The equivalent to **movmem** under many IBM PC C language compilers is **memcpy**, and it's an easy procedure to simply replace one with the other, or to use a *#define* statement to have the compiler do the work for you. However, most implementations of **memcpy** copy in the opposite direction to **movmem**, that is, the source and destination arguments are reversed. Watch for this.

No Example

In contrast to our usual procedure, we will not wrap up our discussion of memory with an example demonstrating the Memory Manager *per se*. It would be difficult to present a very meaningful example without the surrounding context of a sample application. Instead, in the upcoming chapters the programming examples will be sprinkled with routines from the Memory Manager. Pay particular attention to the way in which these routines are used in conjunction with other Toolbox routines. Mastering the use of the Memory Manager will be an important step in writing any application.

Now that we have a little more of the fundamentals of the Toolbox under our belts, we are ready to move on to a more challenging topic—the use of multiple windows.

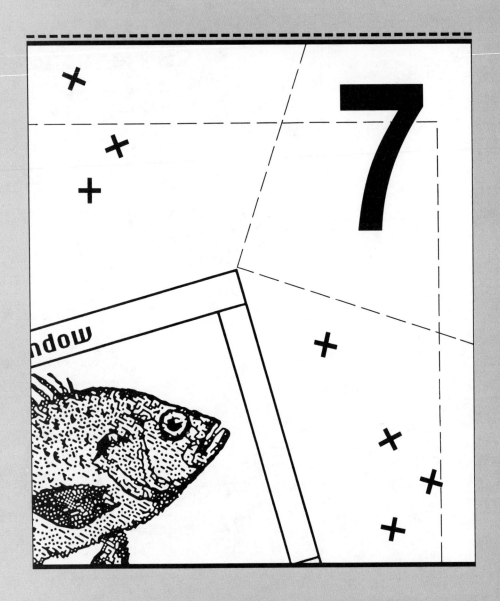

Using Multiple Windows

In Chapter 3 we learned the basics skills required to manipulate a single window on the desktop. This chapter concludes our discussion of the Window Manager by covering the slightly more complicated situations that can arise when multiple windows are present on the desktop. Reading this chapter will enable you to write an application that has one or more windows, in addition to dialogs, alerts, and desk accessories.

The interaction between multiple windows produces the two types of events we discussed briefly in Chapter 2: namely, activate and update events. Activate events result from changes in the front-to-back ordering of the windows. Update events indicate that a previously obscured portion of a window has become visible and must now be redrawn. In this chapter we will describe in detail and also provide examples of the ways in which an application should respond to activate and update events.

In addition to discussing activate and update events, this chapter will include information on manipulating update regions from within the application. Several miscellaneous topics—for example, determining the size and type of a window, manipulating the refCon field, and the use of double-clicks in the title bar to resize a window (a feature found, for instance, in Microsoft Word and Excel)—are covered at the end of this chapter.

Activate Events

When multiple windows are present on the desktop, the frontmost window is referred to as the *active window*, while any remaining windows are called *inactive windows*. The active window is set apart by highlighting the title bar (if indeed the window contains a title bar). In addition, a window may contain controls (scroll bars, buttons, check boxes, and so on) or other features (for example, a flashing text insertion point) whose appearance should change as the window changes between its active and inactive states.

In Chapter 3, we learned to bring a window to the front of the desktop with **SelectWindow** when a mouse-down event occurs in the content region of an inactive window. The Window Manager will automatically highlight the title bar of the newly activated window, then determine which window should be deactivated, automatically unhighlighting its title bar. Other operations necessary to transform the appearance of a window from the active state to the inactive state, or vice versa, must be performed explicitly by the application. All of the routines of the Window Manager that affect the order of windows on the desktop will generate and post the appropriate activate events to the Macintosh's event queue automatically. Figure 7.1 shows what happens when two windows containing text, scroll bars, and other controls change their front-to-back order on the desktop. The process occurs in two stages, beginning with the original desktop as shown in Figure 7.1a. In the first step, the application calls **SelectWindow**, which highlights or unhighlights the title bars of the windows (see Figure 7.1b) and posts the activate events to the event queue. The process is completed when the application receives and processes the activate events generated by **SelectWindow**, taking actions appropriate to the contents of the individual windows, as shown in Figure 7.1c.

Information concerning which windows have been activated or deactivated is passed to the application in the form of an activate event. In Chapter 2 we learned that when the Event Manager function **GetNext-Event** returns an activate event, the message field of the EventRecord will contain a pointer to the window to be activated. Bit zero, the least significant bit, of the modifiers field will have a true value if the window should be activated, or a false value if it should be deactivated.

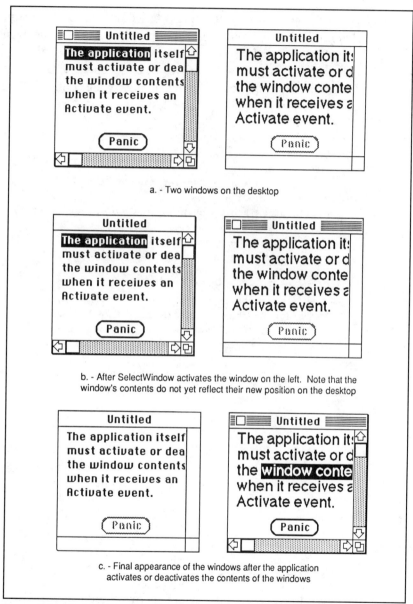

a. - Two windows on the desktop

b. - After SelectWindow activates the window on the left. Note that the window's contents do not yet reflect their new position on the desktop

c. - Final appearance of the windows after the application activates or deactivates the contents of the windows

Figure 7.1:   Activate Events and the Appearance of the Desktop

The following example is based on a portion of the main event loop of a typical application. Upon receiving an activate event, the application first determines which window will be affected and then whether the window will be activated or deactivated. Once this has been determined, the application can then modify the contents of the window to reflect its new position on the desktop.

```
/* locally defined variables */
EventRecord            theEvent;
WindowPtr actWindow;
/* constant from Window Manager header file
activeFlag = 0x0001 */
/* portion of switch on event type from GetNextEvent */
case activateEvt:
        /* determine windowPtr for window,
           set as current grafPort */
        actWindow = theEvent.message;
        SetPort(actWindow);
        /* activate or deactivate the window? */
        if(theEvent.modifiers & activeFlag) {
                /* activate window controls, text items, etc.
                - redraw size box if appropriate */
        } else {
                /* deactivate window controls, test items, etc.
                - redraw size box if appropriate */
        }
        break;
```

In Chapters 8 and 9, where we will discuss TextEdit and controls, we will see examples of activating and deactivating windows containing text items, scroll bars, and buttons.

Update Events

In addition to the need to activate and deactivate windows, applications using multiple windows entail the need to redraw the contents of a window when its position changes relative to the other windows on the desktop. When the application brings a partially obscured window to the front of the desktop, in effect, it must redraw the previously obscured region, in addition to performing the actions required to activate the window.

This whole situation is clearer if we isolate the update process from that of activation. In Figure 7.2 we show two overlapping windows before, during, and after the lower window is moved. While moving the lower window in this way does not disturb the front-to-back ordering of the windows, it does require that a part of the lower window be redrawn. The Window Manager routine used by the application to change the relative position of the windows will post the appropriate update events to the event queue. Figure 7.2a shows the desktop just prior to the movement of the window. In Figure 7.2b we see the appearance of the desktop after the window has been moved but before the application has redrawn the necessary portion of the window (the region that needs to be redrawn is known as the *update region*). Finally, in Figure 7.2c we see the desktop after the application has received the update event and has redrawn the contents of the lower window.

As is the case for activate events, when the function **GetNextEvent** reports an update event, the WindowPtr for the appropriate window can be found in the message field of the EventRecord. The Window Manager keeps track of exactly which portion of each window needs to be redrawn in the window's update region, which is stored in the updateRgn field of the window's WindowRecord. Typically it is easier for the application to redraw the entire window, instead of just the update region, because of the complications involved in determining how to redraw only the contents of the update region. However, in certain situations you can easily specify that the application redraw only the necessary portions of the window and thereby speed up the update process significantly.

Update events are not posted to the event queue in the same way that other types of events are posted. Instead, the operating system periodically examines all of the visible windows on the desktop to determine if any of the windows require updating. If one or more of the windows contain a nonempty update region, the operating system will report, through the next **GetNextEvent** call, an update event. Update events are reported in the front-to-back order of the windows if multiple windows need to be updated. The application will thus be asked to redraw the frontmost windows first, since they contain the most visible information.

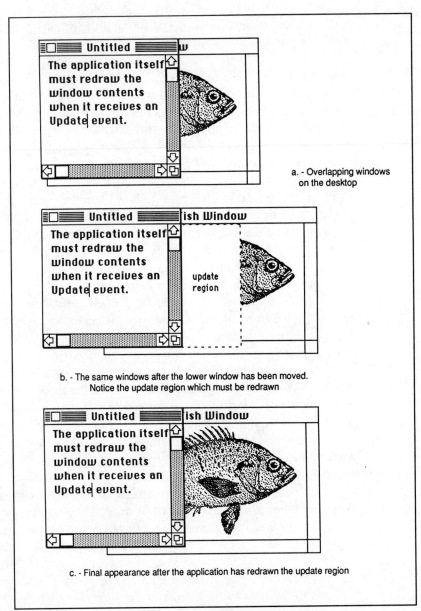

a. - Overlapping windows
on the desktop

b. - The same windows after the lower window has been moved.
Notice the update region which must be redrawn

c. - Final appearance after the application has redrawn the update region

Figure 7.2: Update Events and the Appearance of the Desktop

Redrawing the Window

Before we discuss the details of redrawing a window, you should note that we will often be drawing in an inactive window. In order to draw in an inactive window, the application must first make the window to be updated the current grafPort, since drawing can only take place in the current grafPort. After the drawing is completed, the grafPort should be restored to its previous value so that the application can continue to work in the active window.

The Window Manager provides procedures for informing the operating system that the application has begun and completed the update for a particular window. The procedure **BeginUpdate**, as the name implies, should be called to begin the update process:

```
BeginUpdate(theWindow)
        WindowPtr        theWindow;
```

BeginUpdate replaces the region describing the visible portion of the window, the visRgn, with the intersection of the visible region and the update region, and then sets the update region to zero. The application can redraw the visible region of the window, which now contains the visible portion of the update region. Setting the updateRgn to zero prevents the update event from being reported again.

When the application completes the update process, call **EndUpdate** to restore the visible region of the window to its usual value:

```
EndUpdate(theWindow)
        WindowPtr        theWindow;
```

The following example was taken from the portion of the event loop responsible for handling update events. The application saves the current grafPort before changing the grafPort to the update window. The actual commands used to redraw the window are placed between the **BeginUpdate** and **EndUpdate** calls. Afterwards, the current grafPort is restored to its previous value.

```
/* locally defined variables */
EventRecord          theEvent;
WindowPtr updateWindow;
GrafPort  theCurrentPort;
```

```
/* portion of switch on event type from GetNextEvent */
case updateEvt:
        /* save current port */
        GetPort(&theCurrentPort);
        /* get WindowPtr to be updated, set as current port */
        updateWindow = theEvent.message;
        SetPort(updateWindow);
        /* begin update process */
        BeginUpdate(updateWindow);
        /* redraw contents of updateWindow */
        EndUpdate(updateWindow);
        /* restore current port */
        SetPort(theCurrentPort);
        break;
```

Manipulating the Update Region

The update region of each window on the desktop is maintained automatically by the Window Manager. Since the Window Manager has no way to determine the exact contents of each window on the desktop, it may be necessary for the application to modify the automatically determined update region.

A simple example involves a document window containing a size box and scroll bars. Since the scroll bars and size box are an optional part of a document window, the Window Manager will not consider their possible presence when determining the update region. Figure 7.3 illustrates both the problem that occurs when such a window is resized, and the appropriate solution.

In this example the application must add the area formerly occupied by the scroll bars and size box to the update region for the window. If instead the window were made smaller, the area to be occupied by the new scroll bars and size box would have to be added to the update region. Whether the window is made larger or smaller, once the new scroll bars and size box have been redrawn, the area they occupy should be removed from the update region. If you choose to have your application redraw the entire window in response to an update event, then erasing the content region of the window prior to redrawing will provide the desired result. Note that this is basically the same technique we used to resize the window in the program sample at the end of Chapter 3.

The Window Manager provides four procedures for modifying the update region of a grafPort. Rectangles or regions, specified in local coordinates, may be accumulated or removed from the update region of the current grafPort. To add to the update region, use either **InvalRect** to add the rectangle specified by the parameter badRect or **InvalRgn** to add

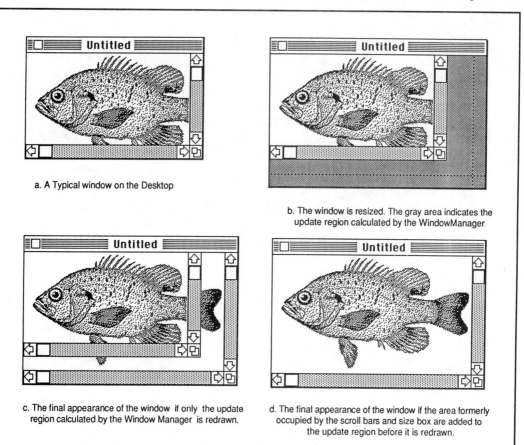

a. A Typical window on the Desktop

b. The window is resized. The gray area indicates the update region calculated by the WindowManager

c. The final appearance of the window if only the update region calculated by the Window Manager is redrawn.

d. The final appearance of the window if the area formerly occupied by the scroll bars and size box are added to the update region before it is redrawn.

Figure 7.3: Manipulating the Update Region

the area specified by badRgn:

```
InvalRect(badRect)
        Rect     *badRect;
InvalRgn(badRgn)
        RgnHandle        badRgn;
```

To subtract from the update region, use either **ValidRect** to subtract the rectangle specified by goodRect or **ValidRgn** to subtract the area specified by goodRgn:

```
ValidRect(goodRect)
        Rect     *goodRect;
ValidRgn(goodRgn)
        RgnHandle        goodRgn;
```

In a situation like that shown in Figure 7.3, the application should remove the area occupied by the new scroll bars and size box from the update region to avoid either having to redraw or overwriting this area. Remember that these routines can only modify the update region of the current grafPort. The application will have to change the current grafPort to the window whose update region it needs to modify.

Programming Techniques

In this section we present a series of short topics related to using multiple windows in an application. These topics, which at first glance may seem unrelated, are an important part of building our knowledge of the Toolbox into an application program. Many of these ideas will appear in the program examples in the upcoming chapters.

Obtaining the Size of a Window

To perform many of the calculations involved in manipulating windows, it is necessary to know both the size of the content region of a window and also its position on the desktop. To make a local copy of the bounding rectangle of the content region found in the WindowRecord for the window, we can make use of the **BlockMove** procedure discussed in Chapter 6. The following procedures will copy the dimensions of a window into the rectangle pointed to by the parameter theSize. LocWindowSize returns the dimensions in the local coordinates of the window itself, while GlobWindowSize returns them in the global coordinates of the desktop.

```
LocWindowSize(tempWindow, theSize)
        WindowPtr      tempWindow;
        Rect           *theSize;
/* Procedure to copy size of a window's content region in LOCAL
   coordinates of window*/
{
        /* copy window's portRect from its GrafPort */
        BlockMove(&tempWindow->portRect, theSize, sizeof(Rect));
}
GlobWindowSize(tempWindow, theSize)
        WindowPtr      tempWindow;
        Rect           *theSize;
/* Procedure to copy size of a window's content region in GLOBAL
   coordinates */
{
        GrafPtr theCurrentPort;
        LocWindowSize(tempWindow, theSize);
        /* change grafPort to tempWindow */
        GetPort(&theCurrentPort);
        SetPort(tempWindow);
        /* convert Rect to global coordinates - as two Points */
        LocalToGlobal(&theSize->topLeft);
        LocalToGlobal(&theSize->botRight);
        /* restore grafPort */
        SetPort(theCurrentPort);
}
```

These procedures will be used in the examples throughout the remainder of this chapter as well as in upcoming chapters.

Determining the Type or Creator of a Window

In an application that includes desk accessories, dialogs, and alerts in addition to the usual types of application windows, it may be useful to determine to which of these categories the active window belongs. The WindowRecord for each window contains a windowKind field that contains a constant value describing the type or creator of the window. Possible values of the windowKind field are listed in Figure 7.4.

As an example, suppose that at some point an application needs to determine what type of window is at the front of the desktop. The application could use the following skeleton example to determine the type of a window.

```
/* excerpt used to determine windowKind of front window */

/* locally declared variables */
WindowPtr       theFrontOne;
short   theFrontKind;

/* Get WindowPtr of front window */
theFrontOne = FrontWindow();

/* Get the windowKind - cast WindowPtr as WindowPeek to access
   WindowRecord */
theFrontKind = ((WindowPeek) theFrontOne)->windowKind;

/* do something depending on what the windowKind is */
switch(theFrontKind) {
        case dialogKind:
        /* a dialog or alert window */
                break;
        case userKind:
```

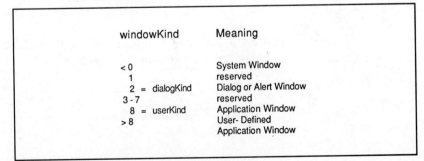

windowKind		Meaning
< 0		System Window
1		reserved
2	= dialogKind	Dialog or Alert Window
3 - 7		reserved
8	= userKind	Application Window
> 8		User- Defined Application Window

Figure 7.4:   The Meaning of windowKind Values

```
                    /* an ordinary window created by our application */
                            break;
                default:
                            if(theFrontKind < 0 ) {
                                    /* a desk accessory */
                            } else if(theFrontKind > 8) {
                                    /* a custom window type belonging to our
           application */
                            } else {
                                    /* oops, somebody used a reserved type!
           */
                            }
                            break;
        }
```

Using the Window refCon Field

The WindowRecord of every window contains a 32-bit field designed to be used by the application for keeping track of some quantity associated with the window. For instance, you may want to associate a string of characters or other data to each window in an application. If you place a pointer or handle to this data in the refCon field, the application can easily retrieve the data associated with each window.

To store the value to be associated with a particular window into the refCon field, use the function **SetWRefCon**, as follows:

```
SetWRefCon(theWindow, data)
        WindowPtr       theWindow;
        long    data;
```

To retrieve the value associated with a window, call the function **Get-WRefCon**, as follows:

```
long GetWRefCon(theWindow)
        WindowPtr       theWindow;
```

The example at the end of this chapter demonstrates the use of these routines. In the more ambitious sample application program of Chapter 8, we use the refCon field to store a handle to a structure containing information about each of several windows.

Windows Containing QuickDraw Pictures

The Window Manager allows the contents of any window to be either explicitly drawn by the application or specified by a QuickDraw picture. If the contents of a window do not change and can be drawn with a series of QuickDraw commands, the commands can be grouped together as a QuickDraw picture. (Refer to Chapter 5 for a complete discussion of the data type Picture.) The process of updating the contents of a window specified as a picture is quite different from the process used for ordinary windows. Instead of generating an update event for the portion of the window that needs to be redrawn, the Window Manager can immediately redraw the window contents by calling the QuickDraw procedure **DrawPicture**.

In order to inform the Window Manager that the contents of a window are described by a QuickDraw picture, the application should call the procedure **SetWindowPic** with the appropriate PicHandle, as follows:

```
SetWindowPic(theWindow, pic)
        WindowPtr        theWindow;
        PicHandle        pic;
```

SetWindowPic stores the picture handle in the windowPic field of the WindowRecord. If the contents of the window are subsequently drawn, the Window Manager will redraw the picture instead of generating an update event. To obtain a handle to the picture describing the contents of such a window, call the function **GetWindowPic**:

```
PicHandle GetWindowPic(theWindow)
        WindowPtr        theWindow;
```

Using the Toolbox Window List

The Window Manager keeps track of all of the windows on the desktop in a linked list of WindowRecords called the *window list*. In addition to the information about the window, each WindowRecord in the list contains a pointer to the next WindowRecord in the list. The order of the windows in the list is the same as the front-to-back order of the windows as they appear on the desktop (note that one or more of the windows in the list may be invisible to the user). The last item in the list—the window furthest back on the desktop—contains a NULL pointer to the next window. A pointer to the first window in the list is stored in a system global variable named windowList.

In the course of debugging an application, or in the interest of safety, you may wish to verify that a WindowPtr returned from a function or procedure is a valid one. The function **IsValidWindow** searches through the window list to find the particular window and returns a true value if theWindow is contained in the list.

```
char IsValidWindow(tempWindow)
        WindowPtr        tempWindow;
/* determines if tempWindow is a valid window by searching
   through the window list */
{
        WindowPeek       aWindow, testWindow;
        /* define windowList to be the WindowPeek
           in system global - at location 0x09D6 */
        #define windowList *((WindowPeek *)0x09D6)
        /* cast tempWindow to WindowPeek */
        testWindow = (WindowPeek) tempWindow;
        /* start at beginning of list */
        aWindow = windowList;
        /* if we are not at end of list
        - is this tempWindow ?
        - if not then skip to the next window in list */
        while( aWindow != NULL ) {
                if( aWindow == testWindow) {
                        return 1;
                } else {
                        aWindow = aWindow->nextWindow;
                }
        }
        return 0; /* can't find tempWindow */
}
```

▬ ▬ ▬ ▬ ▬

A Programming Example: Using Double-Clicks to Resize Windows

Up to this point, the only thing we have learned how to put in a window is a QuickDraw picture. Windows that contain QuickDraw pictures, however, do not call for the use of update events since the Window Manager causes these windows to be updated immediately. Only when we have learned how to use TextEdit in a window will update events become necessary.

For this reason we will postpone presenting activate and update events in the setting of a complete program until we discuss TextEdit in Chapter 8. In the place of a complete application program, we will present the essential components (consisting of several procedures and some slightly modified portions of the familiar main event loop) of a convenient method for instantly resizing a window to the full size of the desktop or shrinking the window back to its previous size. Ordinarily the user must move or resize a window by dragging the size box or title bar with the mouse. When using multiple windows, it is convenient to be able to *zoom* (that is, to expand) a small window up to the full size of the desktop to examine its contents, and then to shrink it back to its previous size and location in order to view the other windows.

This zooming technique is used in several Microsoft products, including Word and Excel, and it is a natural extension of the Macintosh "User Interface Guidelines." In this example we will use a double-click in the title bar (we could just as well have chosen the size box) of a window to signal that the window should be zoomed to one size or the other. In the application program of Chapter 8, we generalize this method to include a menu item named "Zoom."

The definition of a double-click is a mouse-up event followed by a mouse-down event that occurs within a certain time interval known as the *double-click* time. The double-click time can be changed with the Control Panel desk accessory and is accessible through the function **Get-DblTime** or as a system global variable.

If the double-click time is set to its maximum value, in addition to measuring the time interval the application should also check that the mouse location has not changed by more than a small amount between the two events.

In the following example, detecting the double-click is a little tricky since usually a mouse-down in the title bar of a window indicates that the user wants to move the window around on the desktop. Before proceeding to drag the window, the application must first wait a reasonable amount of time (for example, the double-click time) to see if a mouse-up event occurs. If indeed a mouse-up event does occur, the application must wait an additional double-click time and then check for the second mouse-down.

In this example, when a user double-clicks in the title bar of the window, one of two things will happen: if the window does not fill the desktop the window will be expanded until it does, or if the window already fills the desktop, it will be resized to the most recent size and location determined in the usual way with the mouse. The application will need to keep a private copy of the window's size and location that it updates only when the window is moved or resized using the title bar or the size box. The size rectangle should be specified in global coordinates to indicate not only the dimensions of the window, but also the position of the window on the desktop.

The application can store the rectangle containing the old window coordinates in a relocatable block along with other information relevant to the window. A handle to the relocatable block can be kept in the refCon field of the window.

The following section of code initializes several variables of interest, including the full-size rectangle and the size rectangles of each of several windows. The relocatable blocks associated with each window are also allocated in this section.

```
#define         howMany 5        /* howMany windows */
/* global variables */
Rect fullSize;
WindowPtr       someWindows[howMany];    /* an array of
   WindowPtrs */
Rect someRects[howMany];        /* an array of Rects */
char *someTitles[howMany];      /* an array of Pascal Titles */
/* definition of user defined type, WindowStuff */
struct WStuff 2
        . . .
        Rect oldSize;
        . . .
```

```
#define       WindowStuff       struct WStuff
typedef       WindowStuff       *WStuffPtr;
typedef       WStuffPtr         *WSHandle;
/* locally defined variables */
WindowPeek    wRecPtr;
WSHandle      tempWS;
short         i;
/* set fullSize Rect to some pleasing size and location, don't
        assume the screen size to be 512 x342. Use QD, the
        pointer to QuickDraw globals returned by InitGraf */
SetRect(&fullSize,
        QDglob->screenBits.bounds.left +2,
        QDglob->screenBits.bounds.top +20 +20,
        QDglob->screenBits.bounds.right -2,
        QDglob->screenBits.bounds.bottom -2);
/* Open howMany windows using nonrelocatable blocks for their
    WindowRecords.
  Create a relocatable block for each window to hold a
    WindowStuff containing among other things the oldSize
    rectangle used for zooming.
  Initialize the oldSize's with the global coordinates of the
    window's content region */
/* loop over the number of windows */
for(i=0; i < howMany; i++) {
        /* allocate non-relocatable block for WindowRecord */
        if(IsValidWindow(someWindows[i]) {
                /* this window has already been created */
        } else {
                /* open a new window */
                wRecPtr = (WindowPeek)
                        NewPtr(sizeof(WindowRecord));
                someWindows[i] = NewWindow(wRecPtr,
                                someRects[i], someTitles[i],
                                0xff, 0, -1, 0xff, 0);
        }
        tempWS = (WShandle) GetWRefCon(someWindows[i]);
        if(tempWS == NULL) {
                /* allocate relocatable block for WindowStuff -
                put handle into window's refCon */
                tempWS = (WSHandle)
        NewHandle(sizeof(WindowStuff));
                SetWRefCon(someWindows[i], tempWS);
        } else {
                /* the window already has a relocatable block
                assigned to it */
        }
```

```
/* lock down WindowStuff and copy global size of window
   into the oldSize Rect */
HLock(tempWS);
GlobWindowSize(someWindows[i], &(*tempWS)->oldSize);
HUnlock(tempWS);
}
```

Next we will present the section of the main event loop responsible for mouse-down events in the size box of a window. Here the application must update the copy of the window size when the user resizes the window. Note that this example will not update the variable containing the old size of the window if **GrowWindow** returns a value of NULL, thus indicating that the window size was not changed.

```
/* Extracted from main event loop - resizing windows */
/* locally defined variables */
long          newSize;
WindowPtr     whichWindow;
EventRecord   theEvent;
WSHandle      tempWS;
Rect          limitRect;
case inGrow:
      newSize = GrowWindow(whichWindow, theEvent.where,
                          &limitRect);
      SizeWindow(whichWindow, LoWord(newSize),
               HiWord(newSize), 0xff);
      /* if size was changed update the oldSize Rect -
         handle to WindowStuff is in window's refCon */
      if(newSize != 0) {
            tempWS = (WSHandle) GetWRefCon(tempWindow);
            HLock(tempWS);
            GlobWindowSize(tempWindow, &(*tempWS)->oldSize);
            HUnlock(tempWS);
      }
      break;
```

Next is a section of code removed from the portion of the event loop for handling mouse-down events that occur in the title bars of active windows. To look for a double-click, the application must first compute at what time it can stop waiting for a mouse-up event (which signals that the user may be attempting a double-click). Adding the double-click time to the value of the when field of the first mouse-down event yields an appropriate time.

Once the double-click interval has elapsed, the application calls **GetNextEvent** to determine if a mouse-up event is waiting to be read from queue. If **GetNextEvent** does not find a mouse-up event, the user is probably trying to drag the window. The application should check to see if the mouse button is still down and if it is, it should call **DragWindow** as usual to move the window. If the user moves the window, the application should update the variable containing the old window size to reflect the new position.

On the other hand, if the a mouse-up event does occur, then the application must once again wait, this time to see if a second mouse-down will occur. During this wait, the application constructs a rectangle that is 16 pixels on a side and that is centered on the position of the first mouse-down in order to be certain that the mouse position has not strayed too far from the mouse-up. After completing this task, the application completes the wait for a second mouse-down event. If **GetNextEvent** reports a second mouse-down event, the application should check the position to see if it occurred within the allowable rectangle before zooming the window.

```
/* Extracted from event loop - dragging windows */
/* locally defined variables */
long          upTime, clickTime;
short         vert, horiz;
Rect          clickRect, screenRect;
EventRecord   *theEvent
EventRecord   upEvent, downEvent;
WindowPtr     mouseWindow;
WSHandle      tempWS;
case inDrag:
        /* Delay to wait for mouse-up */
        upTime = theEvent->when + GetDblTime();
        while( TickCount() < upTime );
        /* has a mouse-up occurred? */
        if( GetNextEvent(mUpMask, &upEvent) ) {
                /* Delay to wait for mouse-down */
                clickTime = upEvent.when + GetDblTime();
                /* set up rectangle to check stray clicks */
                vert = upEvent.where.v;
                horiz = upEvent.where.h;
                SetRect(&clickRect, horiz-8, vert-8,
                        horiz+8, vert+8);
                /* finish wait until clickTime */
```

```
                        while( TickCount() < clickTime );
                        /* did the second click occur? */
                        if( GetNextEvent(mDownMask, &downEvent) ) {
                                /* did second click happen
                                   inside clickRect? */
                                if(PtInRect(downEvent.where, &clickRect))
                                {
                                        /* doubleclick in dragRegion */
                                        ZoomWindow(mouseWindow);
                                        break;
                                }
                        }
                } else {
                        /* drag the window as usual */
                        if(StillDown()) {
                                DragWindow(mouseWindow, theEvent->where,
                                        &dragBoundsRect);
                                /* update the old window size */
                                tempWS = (WSHandle)
                                        GetWRefCon(mouseWindow);
                                HLock(tempWS);
                                GlobWindowSize(mouseWindow,
                                        &(*tempWS)->oldSize);
                                HUnlock(tempWS);
                        }
                        break;
                }
        break;  /* end of inDrag case */
```

Finally we have the procedure ZoomWindow, which performs the actual resizing. This routine tests to see if the window dimensions correspond to some predetermined full-sized rectangle, which is kept in the global variable fullSize. If the window is not currently at full size, the application will resize the window to these dimensions. If the window is already full-sized, it will be resized to the old-sized rectangle contained in the relocatable block pointed to by the refCon field of the window. To add a little excitement to this process, ZoomWindow calls the procedure ZoomRect to draw a series of expanding or contracting rectangles to indicate the new window size. The sample application at the end of Chapter 8 contains the source code to one such routine.

```
ZoomWindow(tempWindow)/* ZoomWindow() */
        WindowPtr          tempWindow;
/* This routine will zoom a window between the size/location
```

specified by the global Rect fullSize, and that specified by the
rectangle contained in the oldSize Rect in the relocatable
WindowStuff kept in the window's refCon field */

```
{
        Rect theStart, theFinal;
        WSHandle        tempWS;
/* Get a copy of the window coordinates in startRect and compare
with the fullSize rectangle */
        GlobWindowSize(tempWindow, &theStart);
        if(EqualRect(&theStart, &fullSizeRect)) {
/* the window is currently full size - copy oldSize into
finalRect and do animation */
                tempWS = (WSHandle) GetWRefCon(tempWindow);
                BlockMove(&(*tempWS)->oldSize, &theFinal,
                        sizeof(Rect));
                ZoomRect(&theStart, &theFinal);
                /* erase contents of the window to wipe out
                    scroll bars */
                LocWindowSize(tempWindow, &theStart);
                EraseRect(&theStart);
                /* since window is becoming smaller resize
                    before moving the window */
                SizeWindow(tempWindow,
                        theFinal.right - theFinal.left,
                        theFinal.bottom - theFinal.top, 0xff);
                MoveWindow(tempWindow, theFinal.left,
                        theFinal.top, 0);
        } else {
                /* the window is not currently full size -
                copy fullSize into finalRect and do animation */
                BlockMove(&fullSize, &theFinal, sizeof(Rect));
                ZoomRect(&theStart, &theFinal);
                /* erase contents of the window to wipe out
                    scroll bars */
                LocWindowSize(tempWindow, &theStart);
                EraseRect(&theStart);
                /* since window is becoming larger move
                    the window before resizing it */
                MoveWindow(tempWindow, theFinal.left,
                        theFinal.top, 0);
                SizeWindow(tempWindow,
                        theFinal.right - theFinal.left,
                        theFinal.bottom - theFinal.top, 0xff);
        }
        /* erase the contents of the final window force an
            update event for the entire content region */
```

```
LocWindowSize(tempWindow, &theFinal);
EraseRect(&theFinal);
InvalRect(&theFinal);
}
```

This rather lengthy example is incorporated into the sample text editing application listed at the end of Chapter 8. The various components shown here will be modified slightly in Chapter 8 to reflect the particular type of application presented there, although their function will remain unchanged.

8

Text Editing with the Toolbox

Nearly every Macintosh application uses routines from Text-Edit, the portion of the Toolbox devoted to text editing. There are two main reasons for including the capabilities of TextEdit in the Toolbox. The obvious reason is that it greatly simplifies the work of any programmer trying to include some of the available text editing features in an application; otherwise, the routines would have to be developed from scratch. The second and perhaps most important reason relates to the fact that text editing is such a common requirement used in every type of application, not just in word processing. TextEdit helps to maintain consistency between the widely varying situations in which the user enters or edits text. In fact, on the Macintosh many of the features associated with sophisticated word processing applications are available when the user performs a simple action like entering a file name. As we mentioned in Chapter 1, the consistency and predictability that exist among diverse situations like these are essential features of the "User Interface Guidelines."

TextEdit provides most of the familiar operations that can be performed during text editing. These features include inserting and deleting text, using the mouse to specify a range of text for cut and paste operations, scrolling the text of a large document in a window, word wrap at the right edge of a document, and many others. Nevertheless, TextEdit does not contain all of the features found in a word processing application like MacWrite or Microsoft Word. The major features missing from TextEdit are full justification (flush right and left margins), individual paragraph formatting, and multiple fonts, sizes, or styles of text in a single document. However, word processing applications that do not make use of TextEdit are still required to conform to the

"User Interface Guidelines" to avoid confusing the user.

Despite these restrictions, there are a great variety of uses for TextEdit. Aside from word processing, any type of data entry—for example, entering data into a database or typing into a communications program—could be handled with TextEdit. In fact, any application using the keyboard probably also uses TextEdit either directly or indirectly through another part of the Toolbox. Several indirect uses of TextEdit common to every Macintosh application are desk accessories like the Notepad or the dialog and alert boxes used to request information from the user or to notify the user when something important is about to happen.

Our discussion will first focus on the methods used by TextEdit for keeping track of text and on how the text is drawn on the Macintosh screen. The section covering how to use TextEdit from an application begins with a discussion of creating and disposing of text items and goes on to explain the various editing routines responsible for actions like Cut, Copy, and Paste. Next we discuss the interaction required between the application and the Toolbox to maintain the insertion point and selection range. Our discussion of using TextEdit concludes by explaining how the application can alter the font and layout of the text used on the screen. Throughout this section, we will provide information and examples outlining how and where the various routines fit within a typical application.

The last portion of the chapter is devoted to several advanced topics that are used to build a nearly complete application. At the end of this chapter we have included a detailed sample application encompassing nearly everything we have discussed in the book so far.

━ ━ ━ ━ ━

The Appearance of Text on the Screen

TextEdit keeps track of text strings and the formatting information associated with them in a data structure called an *edit record*. Such a text string might consist of the entire contents of a file created by a text editor, or it could be as small as a one- or two-character item used to select the desired page number when printing a single page of a document. When the Toolbox draws the text associated with an edit record in a window on the desktop, there are several parameters that control the actual appearance of the text.

TextEdit arranges for the text to be drawn within the confines of a rectangle known as the *destination rectangle*. The destination rectangle defines an imaginary "page" on which TextEdit places the text. The top of the destination rectangle determines the position of the first line of the text. Within the destination rectangle, the text can be either right-, left- or center-justified. TextEdit uses the left and right sides of the destination rectangle to determine the width of the area in which the text will be drawn. When an individual line of text (the end of a line is usually signalled by a carriage return character) exceeds the width of the destination rectangle, the text will normally be wrapped onto the next line at a convenient word boundary. Word wrap can be suppressed, however, in which case the rest of the line will simply extend over one or both edges of the page and become invisible. The bottom of the destination rectangle has no real significance; as the number of lines of text exceeds the number that will fit in the destination rectangle, text continues to be drawn beyond the bottom.

The destination rectangle containing the text is viewed by the user through the *view rectangle*. Text outside the view rectangle is not visible on the desktop. In most applications the view rectangle will not be as large as the destination rectangle, in which case the user will only be able to see a portion of the text at any given time. The remainder of the text can be made visible by *scrolling* the text, which simply changes the relative positions of the view and destination rectangles and allows other portions of the text to become visible. Figure 8.1 shows the effect of different relative sizes of the destination and view rectangles.

TextEdit is capable of formatting the text with either right-, left- or center-justification within the destination rectangle. In addition to these three styles of justification, word wrap is also available. As the length of a line exceeds the width of the destination rectangle, the text is broken at a boundary between words and moved to the next line. If the application chooses not to word wrap text, a new line of text will begin only after a carriage return has been typed. Word wrap is essential to most word processing applications but becomes quite a nuisance when you are writing source code in a programming language. Figure 8.2 illustrates the effect of word wrap on different types of text.

As the user enters text from the keyboard, the characters are inserted into the existing text at the location of the *insertion point*. The

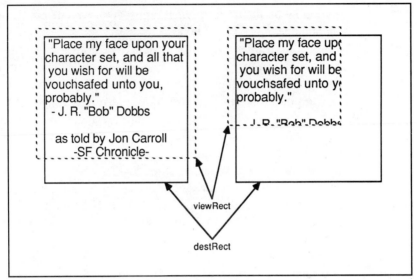

Figure 8.1: The View and Destination Rectangles

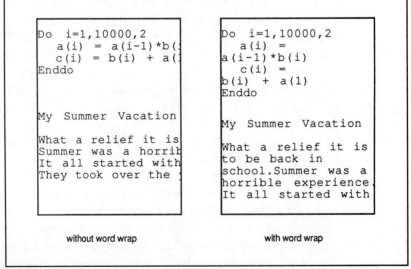

Figure 8.2: The Effects of Word Wrap

location of the insertion point is indicated on the Macintosh screen by a flashing vertical bar. The insertion point may be moved, in order to enter text in another location on the screen, by clicking the mouse at the desired location.

The insertion point may also take the form of a range of text known as the *selection range*. The selection range will be highlighted (normally with inverse video) on the screen. The selection range serves to mark a range of text to be either removed or replaced through the use of Cut and Paste commands or by typing characters from the keyboard. The user can choose the selection range by holding down the mouse button and then dragging the mouse from one location to another. The current selection range can be shortened or lengthened if the user holds down the Shift key while dragging the mouse.

TextEdit Data Structures

Nearly all of the routines in TextEdit operate on a data structure called an *edit record*, which is actually a structure of type TERec (we will use the terms edit record and TERec interchangeably). The TERec stores all of the information about a particular item of text, including all of the on-screen formatting information. The complete description of an edit record and the associated pointer and handle are shown in the box "TextEdit Data Structures." Many of the fields of a TERec can be manipulated directly or indirectly through the routines contained in TextEdit. Several of the fields are used internally by TextEdit and should not be manipulated by the application.

Before we discuss the various kinds of information contained in an edit record, we should first understand how TextEdit stores the text and how it references the individual characters. The character data is stored in a variable-sized array of bytes that is located in a relocatable block separate from the edit record itself. The first character in the array is located at position 0, with subsequent characters located at positions 1 to teLength. Planning the character mapping so that the *character index*, which is used to specify the start and end of a selection range, actually falls between characters allows the Toolbox to give a unique interpretation as to which characters should be included in the selection range.

Figure 8.3 illustrates how the character index used to specify the selection range corresponds to the actual character data.

Fields within an Edit Record

It is important to briefly discuss several of the fields contained in an edit record because, unlike most of the Toolbox data structures we

---

TextEdit Data Structures

```
struct TE {
        Rect            destRect;       /* destination rectangle */
        Rect            viewRect;       /* view rectangle */
        Rect            selRect;        /* current selection rect */
        int             lineHeight;     /* line spacing in pixels */
        int             fontAscent;     /* caret/highlighting height */
        Point           selPoint;       /* mouse-down location */
        unsigned int    selStart;       /* start of selection range */
        unsigned int    selEnd;         /* end of selection range */
        int             active;         /* non-zero if active */
        Ptr             wordBreak;      /* points WordBreak routine */
        Ptr             clikLoop;       /* points ClikLoop routine */
        long            clickTime;      /* ticks of 1st click */
        int             clickLoc;       /* char location of click */
        long            caretTime;      /* time for next caret blink */
        int             caretState;     /* on or off */
        int             just;           /* current justification */
        int             teLength;       /* number of chars in text */
        Handle          hText;          /* handle to chars */
        int             recalBack;      /* internal use */
        int             recalLines;     /* internal use */
        int             clikStuff;      /* internal use */
        int             crOnly;         /* <0 for no word wrap */
        int             txFont;         /* text font */
        Style           txFace;         /* text style */
        int             txMode;         /* drawing mode for text */
        int             txSize;         /* text size */
        GrafPtr         inPort;         /* in which grafPort */
        Ptr             highHook;       /* points to highlight routine */
        Ptr             caretHook;      /* points to caret routine */
        int             nLines;         /* number of lines of text */
        unsigned int    lineStarts[1];  /* positions of line starts */
};

#define   TERec     struct TE
typedef   TERec     *TEPtr;
typedef   TEPtr     *TEHandle;
```

have seen so far, the application will often need to directly manipulate these fields. Since an edit record is a relocatable object in memory, this also means that you must watch out for circumstances that might lead to a dangling pointer.

Destination and View Rectangles

The destination and view rectangles used by TextEdit to format the text are contained in the destRect and viewRect fields. They are specified in the local coordinates of the window in which the text appears. To insure that the text remains readable, you should inset the destination rectangle at least four pixels from the edges of the window in which the text appears. This will keep the text from running into the edge of the window and also allows space for the overhang of italic characters. Allow an additional 16 pixels on the right or bottom if a scroll bar will be present.

Line Spacing

The lineHeight determines the spacing between the lines of text, while the fontAscent measures the height of the character in the font

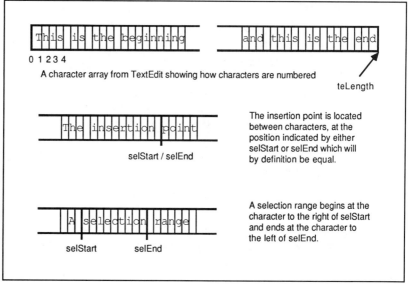

Figure 8.3:   Character Numbering in TextEdit

(without including characters like "g", which descend below the baseline). TextEdit uses the fontAscent field to correctly position the insertion point or selection range. In order to change the line spacing of the text, you should change both fields by the same amount; otherwise, the position of the insertion point and selection range may not be correct. Both the lineHeight and fontAscent fields are measured in pixels. At the end of this chapter, we will explain how to change these fields to reflect the spacing appropriate for a specific font and size.

Selection Range and Insertion Point

The position of the insertion point or extent of the selection range is specified by the selStart and selEnd fields. When an insertion point is present, both fields will contain the same value. If the user has chosen a selection range, however, these fields will contain the beginning and ending points of the selection range. Note that in order to include the nth character in a selection range, the application must specify selStart = n and selEnd = n+1. This is because the selection range starts at the character after the selStart position and ends at the character just before the selEnd position.

Justification

The current setting for text justification is contained in the just field. The three possible types of justification are indicated by the following predefined constants.

```
#define       teJustLeft      0
#define       teJustCenter    1
#define       teJustRight    -1
```

Character Data

The number of characters in the text is stored in the teLength field. The hText field contains a handle to the relocatable block containing the text itself. One can rapidly replace the text in an existing edit record with new text by changing the hText and teLength fields.

Word Wrap

Word wrap is controlled by the crOnly field of the edit record. A non-negative value of crOnly indicates that the text should be word wrapped according to the width of the destination rectangle. A negative value indicates that a new line should only be started after a return character has been entered.

Font Characteristics

The text contained in the edit record is drawn with the font, style, pen mode, and size specified in the txFont, txFace, txMode, and txSize fields. Since TextEdit cannot handle multiple fonts, sizes, and styles, these fields determine the text appearance throughout the edit record.

grafPort

The grafPort of the window in which the text appears is kept in the inPort field. When an edit record is first allocated and initialized, it is by default assigned to the current grafPort.

Dividing the Text into Lines

The nLines field contains the number of lines of text in the TERec. For the same character data, the value of nLines will depend on whether word wrap has been selected or not. The character positions of the beginning of each line are stored in the dynamically allocated array lineStarts.

The remaining fields of the edit record are only used in advanced applications or are used internally by TextEdit.

Using TextEdit

The routines which make up TextEdit fall into several functional categories: allocating and disposing of text edit records, manipulating the contents of an edit record, editing functions, handling the insertion point and selection range, using the TextEdit scrap and the Clipboard and other miscellaneous routines.

Initializing TextEdit

Before using any of the routines in TextEdit, the application must call **TEInit** to allocate a handle to TextEdit's private scrap. In fact, even if the application does not explicitly use any of the routines within TextEdit, it must still call **TEInit** to insure that dialogs, alerts, and desk accessories, which may use routines from TextEdit, will operate properly. Since Text-Edit itself calls upon other portions of the Toolbox, the application should initialize QuickDraw, the Font Manager, and the Window Manager before initializing TextEdit.

```
TEInit()
```

The private scrap allocated by **TEInit** is used to hold the text selected in copy and cut operations and provides the text for paste operations. The data contained in the TextEdit scrap must be transferred to and from the Clipboard (or desk scrap), which is maintained by the Scrap Manager, in order to allow cutting and pasting between applications and/or desk accessories. The Macintosh Pascal Workshop contains several routines that are not part of the Toolbox (these routines are known as Toolbox extension routines) to enable the application to transfer text between the TextEdit scrap and the desk scrap. We will discuss this process and present C versions of the necessary routines at the end of this chapter.

Allocating and Disposing of Edit Records

The function **TENew** allocates an edit record on the heap, incorporating the drawing environment of the current grafPort, and returns as its value a handle to the new edit record. The parameters destRect and viewRect specify, in the local coordinates of the current grafPort, the destination and view rectangles in which the text will be drawn.

```
TEHandle TENew(destRect, viewRect)
        Rect    *destRect;
        Rect    *viewRect;
```

The edit record is initialized as single-spaced and left-justified with the insertion point at character position zero. The insertion point will not become visible until the edit record is explicitly activated with a call to **TEActivate**, which will be discussed later in the chapter.

An application containing multiple text windows must determine which edit records belong to a specified window. The edit record contains a pointer to the window (actually a GrafPtr) in which the text will appear. The process of determining which edit records belong to which windows is made easier if each window keeps track separately of which edit records are associated with it. In the simplest case of one edit record per window, it will suffice to store the TEHandle, returned by **TENew**, in the refCon field of the WindowRecord of the window. In advanced applications, as we learned in Chapter 7, one can use the refCon field to store a handle to a custom data structure containing a list of handles to the edit records, plus any other information.

To dispose of an edit record once it is no longer needed by the application, call the procedure **TEDispose**:

```
TEDispose (hTE)
        TEHandle        hTE;
```

TEDispose deallocates the edit record indicated by the hTE parameter and releases the block occupied by the text itself.

To have the application place text into an edit record when it is first created, or to substitute new text for the existing text, use the procedure **TESetText**:

```
TESetText (text, length, hTE)
        char    *text;
        long    length;
        TEHandle        hTE;
```

The parameter text should be a pointer to the text to be placed into the edit record, with length indicating the number of characters to be used. **TESetText** makes a copy of the specified text in a relocatable block and places a handle to the text in the hText field of the edit record which is pointed to by hTE. When the application calls **TESetText**, the relocatable block that contains the original text from the edit record will not automatically be released from memory. The application should explicitly dispose of this block, if the data it contains is no longer needed, in order to return the space to the Memory Manager.

If the application needs a copy of the handle to the text of an edit record, it can call the routine **TEGetText**:

```
Handle TEGetText(hTE)
        TEHandle         hTE;
```

Under Think C, the type Handle is equivalent to a char **, which allows direct access to the character data. Alternatively, the application can copy the value of the hText field of the edit record.

The following example shows how to allocate an edit record and place the TEHandle in the refCon field of the window. The example then calls **TESetText** to place a text string into the edit record, which will appear when the edit record is first drawn.

```
/* locally defined variables */
WindowPtr theWindow;
TEHandle  theText;
Rect      destRect, viewRect;
Handle    oldCharHandle;
char      *startUpStr;

startUpStr = "Don't Panic - Enter text here";

/* set up the destRect and viewRect
- use LocWindowSize() from Chapter 7
- allow for scroll bars on right, bottom
- indent destRect 4 pixels for readability */

LocWindowSize(theWindow, &viewRect);

viewRect.right -= 16;
viewRect.bottom -= 16;

/* copy viewRect into destRect */
BlockMove(&viewRect, &destRect, sizeof(Rect));
InsetRect(&destRect, 4, 4);

/* allocate a new TERec for theWindow
- theWindow must be the current grafPort */
SetPort(theWindow);
theText = TENew(&destRect, &viewRect);

/* store TEHandle into refCon of the window */
SetWRefCon(theWindow, theText);
```

```
/* Substitute start-up text into edit record
- get copy of text handle in theText
- substitute text
- dispose of old handle to release storage */

oldCharHandle = TEGetText(theText);

TESetText(startUpStr, strlen(startUpStr), theText);

DisposHandle(oldCharHandle);
```

Active and Inactive Edit Records

In analogy to the case of multiple windows, an edit record can exist in either an active or inactive state. In order to direct input from the keyboard unambiguously, there can be only one active edit record at a given moment. The active edit record must always be located in the active window. The application uses activate events, which indicate a change in the front-to-back ordering of the windows on the desktop, to signal the application that the edit record in a window should become either active or inactive. In the inactive state the insertion point will not be shown, or the selection range will not be highlighted; whereas in the active state the insertion point will blink or the selection range will be highlighted.

Figure 8.4 illustrates the difference between the active and inactive states of an edit record. When an edit record is first created, it will be inactive until the application calls **TEActivate** to activate the edit record. In the first part of this section, we will discuss how the application should respond to an activate event for a window containing one or more edit records.

In an active edit record, the flashing insertion point indicates to the user the location at which new data will be added to the text on the screen. The application is partly responsible for maintaining the insertion point. TextEdit provides a routine, which must be called periodically by the application, to blink the insertion point at a constant rate.

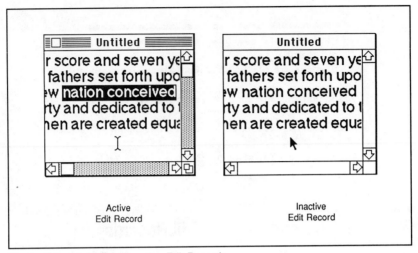

Figure 8.4: Active and Inactive Edit Records

Activating and Deactivating Edit Records

The procedures **TEActivate** and **TEDeactivate** are used to switch an edit record between the active and inactive states.

```
TEActivate(hTE)
        TEHandle        hTE;

TEDeactivate(hTE)
        TEHandle        hTE;
```

In the simplest case where each window on the desktop contains only a single edit record, the application can simply activate or deactivate the edit records as the windows containing them are activated or deactivated. The following example shows how activating edit records can be included into the portion of an application's main event loop responsible for activating windows.

```
/* Based on example from Chapter 7
- portion of main event loop to activate/deactivate windows
- assume the TEHandle of the window is kept in the refCon
- global variables:

theWindow    the current active window
theText      the current active edit record */
```

```
/* locally defined variables */
EventRecord         theEvent;
WindowPtr           actWindow;
TEHandle            actEditRecord;

/* constant from Window Manager header file
   activeFlag = 0x0001 */

case activateEvt:
        /* determine windowPtr for window, set as current
           grafPort */
        actWindow = theEvent.message;
        SetPort(actWindow);

        /* get copy of TEHandle from refCon of window - if any */
        actEditRecord = (TEHandle) GetWRefCon(actWindow);

        /* activate or deactivate? */
        if(theEvent.modifiers & activeFlag) {

                /* other activate stuff - controls,
                   size box, etc.
                 - then activate edit record - if any */

                if(actEditRecord) TEActivate(actEditRecord);
                theText = actEditRecord;

        } else {

                /* other deactivate stuff - controls,
                   size box, etc.
                 - then deactivate edit record - if any */

                if(actEditRecord) TEDeactivate(actEditRecord);
                theText = NULL;

        }
        break;
```

In the case where a window can contain more than one edit record, the application should activate the most recently active edit record as the window moves to the front. Whenever the user clicks the mouse in the content region of the window, the application should check to see if the corresponding event returned by **GetNextEvent** occurred inside the view rectangle of one of the edit records. If so, the application can activate the edit record selected by the user and deactivate the previously active edit record. We will not discuss any further the case of multiple edit records in a single window, although in Chapter 11 we will see that dialogs frequently contain several edit records.

Blinking the Insertion Point

The routine **TEIdle** does the necessary drawing to blink the insertion point.

```
TEIdle(hTE)
        TEHandle        hTE;
```

The application should call **TEIdle** as often as possible (once each time through the event loop is usually sufficient) to insure that the insertion point is updated regularly. The insertion point will not blink any faster than the rate set by the Control Panel desk accessory no matter how frequently the application calls **TEIdle**.

Editing Routines

The editing routines from TextEdit allow the user to enter text from the keyboard, and also include the familiar cut, copy, and paste operations. The application will be notified by **GetNextEvent** in the main event loop if the user enters text from the keyboard. On the other hand, the Cut, Copy, and Paste commands are usually chosen through menu selection (see Chapter 4). All of the routines in this section will automatically redraw the text on the screen when it becomes necessary.

Text that is entered from the keyboard is added to the edit record by the function **TEKey**. When a key-down event is returned by **GetNextEvent** in the main event loop of an application, the application must first make certain that the key is not part of a Command key combination used for a menu selection. If the Command key was not held down during the key-down, then the application should call **TEKey**, passing both the ASCII character code from the low-order byte of the message field of the EventRecord and the TEHandle of the edit record to which the text should be added.

```
TEKey(c, hTE)
        char      c;
        TEHandle          hTE;
```

The new character will be inserted after the insertion point or will replace the current selection range. Afterwards the insertion point will be placed to the right of the new character. If a backspace character is passed to **TEKey**, the selection range will be deleted and replaced with the insertion point; if no selection range is present, the character to the left of the insertion point will be removed.

Use the procedure **TECut** to remove the text contained in the current selection range:

```
TECut (hTE)
        TEHandle          hTE;
```

Pass **TECut** a handle to the currently active edit record. **TECut** places the text it removes into the TextEdit scrap for use in subsequent paste operations. If the selection range is empty when **TECut** is called, the scrap will be emptied.

The procedure **TECopy** makes a copy of the current selection range without deleting it from the document.

```
TECopy (hTE)
        TEHandle          hTE;
```

Like **TECut**, **TECopy** places a copy of the text into the TextEdit scrap; if the selection range is empty, the scrap will be emptied.

To paste a copy of the text in the scrap after the current insertion point, call the procedure **TEPaste**.

```
TEPaste(hTE)
        TEHandle          hTE;
```

TEPaste will replace the contents of the current selection range with the contents of the scrap by first deleting the selection range and then copying the text after the insertion point. After the text from the scrap has been added, the insertion point is placed just beyond the right end of the new text.

TextEdit also contains a procedure named **TEDelete**, which in contrast to **TECut**, removes the text contained in the selection range without disturbing the contents of the scrap.

```
TEDelete(hTE)
        TEHandle        hTE;
```

A common use of the **TEDelete** procedure is in implementing the Clear command of the standard edit menu.

Another procedure, **TEInsert**, allows the application to insert an arbitrary text string just before the current insertion point or selection range.

```
TEInsert(text, length, hTE)
        char        *text;
        long        length;
        TEHandle    hTE;
```

The text parameter points to the first character of a string of characters (not a Pascal string) whose length is denoted by the length parameter. **TEInsert** does not alter the position of the insertion point or selection range relative to the text of the edit record.

It is possible to implement an Undo command, allowing the user to backup one step, by using suitable combinations of the editing routines of TextEdit. The simplest form of an Undo command that might appear in an application would only allow the user to undo the last Cut or Paste command. For simplicity, this version of Undo would not allow the user to undo the last command once the selection range or the insertion point is moved or once a key is typed on the keyboard.

In this situation, the application must record—in a global variable named undoType, for instance—the last operation selected by the user that can be undone. In order to undo a Paste command, the application must also keep a copy of the text in the selection range at the time the Paste command is issued, as well as a count of the number of characters pasted into the edit record. Then, whenever the user types a key or moves the insertion point, the variable undoType can be cleared. Now when the user selects Undo from the Edit menu, the application can look at the contents of undoType and act accordingly.

For instance, to undo a Cut command, the application would call **TEPaste**. To undo a Paste command, the application must first call **TESetSelect** (discussed in the next section) and **TEDelete** to remove the characters inserted by the Paste command, and then call **TEInsert** followed by **TESetSelect** to restore the former text and insertion point or selection range.

Changing the Selection Range and the Insertion Point

The application may need to change the selection range or move the insertion point in two different situations. First, when the user attempts to move either the selection range or the insertion point, the application will receive a mouse-down event inside the view rectangle of the active edit record and must respond. Second, in certain circumstances it may be convenient for the application to change the selection range independent of any action on the part of the user.

Responding to Mouse-Down Events

After determining that a mouse-down event has occurred in the content region of an active window, the application should check to see if the coordinates of the point also fall within the view rectangle of the active edit record. If this is the case, the application must call

```
TEClick(pt, extend, hTE)
        Point   pt;
        char    extend;
        TEHandle        hTE;
```

where pt specifies the local coordinates of the mouse-down event, extend is a flag indicating whether the Shift key was held down in order to extend an existing selection range, and hTE is the TEHandle of the edit record in which the event occurred. TEClick controls the position of the insertion point as well as the position and highlighting of the selection range. To be specific, **TEClick** expands or shrinks the selection range according to the current mouse position, until the mouse button is released. If **TEClick** determines that the mouse-down was part of a double-click, the *word* (which can be defined as a blank delimited sequence of characters with no embedded control characters) nearest the mouse location becomes the selection range. The combination of a double-click and drag will expand or contract the selection range in word-sized chunks.

The following example illustrates how **TEClick** should be called from within the portion of the main event loop responsible for mouse-down events. This example covers only the situation in which the mouse-down occurs within the content region of a window belonging to the application. Notice that the position of the mouse-down returned by **GetNextEvent** must be converted to the local coordinates of the window before being passed to **TEClick**.

```
/* based on an example from Chapter 4
- global variables:
theWindow      the current active window
theText        the current active edit record */

/* locally defined variables */

WindowPtr      whichWindow;
EventRecord    theEvent;
int            windowCode;

/* portion of switch on event type returned by GetNextEvent */
case mouseDown:

        /* pass location of where field in EventRecord theEvent
        - returns WindowPtr in whichWindow */
        windowCode = FindWindow(theEvent.where, &whichWindow);

        switch(windowCode) {
                case . . .

                case inContent:
                /* if not active window, activate */
                        if((FrontWindow() != whichWindow) &&
                                (whichWindow != NULL)) {
                                SelectWindow(whichWindow);
                                break;
                        }
                        /* switch to local coordinates for
                           TEClick, etc. */
```

```
                              GlobalToLocal(&theEvent.where);

                              /* If there is an active edit record
                              it is in this (active) window,
                              - did mouse-down occur in its viewRect? */
                              if(theText) {
                                        if(PtInRect(theEvent.where,
                                           &(*theText)->viewRect))
                                                TEClick(theEvent.where,
                                                (theEvent.modifiers &
                                                shiftKey),
                                                theText);
                              } else {
                                        /* mouse-down occurred
                                           somewhere else . . .
                                        - controls or inactive edit
    records? */
                              }
                   break;
}
```

At the end of this chapter we include a description of two of the internal functions of **TEClick** which may be redefined by advanced programmers: 1) the algorithm used by TextEdit to determine word boundaries; and 2) scrolling the text of an edit record while changing the selection range.

Directly Changing the Selection Range

Frequently the application will need to change the position of the insertion point or the selection range independent of what the user does with the mouse. The application might need to do this, for instance, to implement cursor keys or a Select All or Find command. TextEdit provides the function **TESetSelect** for this purpose:

```
TESetSelect(selStart, selEnd, hTE)
        long      selStart, selEnd;
        TEHandle        hTE;
```

Here selStart and selEnd are the character positions for the start and end of the new selection range. Specifying the same position for both parameters will result in moving the insertion point to that position. To select from a given location to the end of the edit record, the application can either obtain the value of the teLength field from the edit record or use the integer 32767 (the maximum number of characters in an edit record) to specify the end position of the selection range.

Redrawing the Text in Response to Update Events

When the Toolbox Event Manager reports an update event for a window containing one or more edit records, call the procedure **TEUpdate** to redraw the contents of the edit records.

```
TEUpdate(rUpdate, hTE)
        Rect      *rUpdate;
        TEHandle          hTE;
```

TEUpdate will redraw the text that belongs to the edit record that is specified by hTE and that falls inside the rectangle rUpdate. The update rectangle, rUpdate, should be specified in the local coordinates of the edit record's grafPort. The application will usually pass the view rectangle of the edit record as the update rectangle, which will result in some unnecessary drawing. Typically **TEUpdate** will be called between the **BeginUpdate** and **EndUpdate** calls in the update portion of the main event loop, as shown in the following example. Be certain to erase the contents of the update rectangle before calling **TEUpdate** to redraw the text.

```
/* based on an example from Chapter 7 */

/* locally defined variables */
EventRecord    theEvent;
WindowPtr      updateWindow;
GrafPort       theCurrentPort;
TEHandle         updateTEH;

/* portion of switch on event type from GetNextEvent */
case updateEvt:
        /* save current port */
        GetPort(&theCurrentPort);

        /* get WindowPtr to be updated, set as current port */
        updateWindow = theEvent.message;
        SetPort(updateWindow);
```

```
/* begin update process */
BeginUpdate(updateWindow);

/* redraw contents of updateWindow */

/* redraw any edit records in window (assume one only)
   - get TEHandle from refCon of updateWindow
   - redraw entire viewRect for simplicity */
updateTEH = (TEHandle) GetWRefCon(updateWindow);
HLock(updateTEH); /* don't let &viewRect dangle */

/* erase viewRect and redraw text */
EraseRect(&(*updateTEH)->viewRect);
TEUpdate(&(*updateTEH)->viewRect, updateTEH);

HUnlock(updateTEH);

EndUpdate(updateWindow);

/* restore current port */
SetPort(theCurrentPort);

break;
```

TEUpdate should also be called any time the appearance (for example, the font style) or the contents of the edit record are changed. Only the editing routines (**TEPaste**) redraw the text automatically.

The Appearance of Text on the Screen

The on-screen appearance of the text of an edit record can be changed in several ways. The most obvious changes are those involving the font or character size and style used to draw the text. Other changes involve the justification of the text or the use of word wrap.

When the application directly alters the fields of an edit record that affect the appearance of the text (i.e. the destination rectangle, font or font size, or word wrap), the position of the beginning of each line of text may need to be recalculated before the text is redrawn. (These positions are kept in the lineStarts array, as you will recall from our earlier discussion of the fields of an edit record.) In this situation, the application should call the procedure

```
TECalText (hTE)
        TEHandle        hTE;
```

before calling **TEUpdate** to redraw the text.

Changing the Font Characteristics

There are no Toolbox routines designed to alter the font, size, style, or word wrap used in an edit record; instead, the application must alter the fields of the edit record directly and then redraw the text to reflect whatever changes have been made. Be certain to recalculate the lineStarts array as we just described if either the font type or size has been changed.

In addition, when the application changes the font or size used in an edit record, the lineHeight and fontAscent fields of the edit record must be recalculated to insure proper line spacing and highlighting. Use the QuickDraw routine **GetFontInfo** to determine the vertical spacing and character size of the font in the current grafPort. The following routine, SetLineHeight, first determines the spacing characteristics of the font used in the edit record and then recalculates the lineHeight and fontAscent fields, including in its calculation the possibility of double-spacing and one-and-a-half spacing of the text.

```
SetLineHeight (spacing, hTE)/* SetLineHeight () */
        int     spacing;        /* line spacing */
        TEHandle        hTE; /* the edit record */

#define         singleSp        0
#define         oneandhalfSp    1
#define         doubleSp        2

/* this routine changes the lineHeight and fontAscent of
        the edit record hTE to reflect its font and size. The
        line spacing can be either single 1 1/2 or double */
{
        GrafPtr     theCurrentPort;
        FontInfo    fontStuff;
        short       extra;

        /* set current port to window containing hTE */
        GetPort (&theCurrentPort);
```

```
SetPort((*hTE)->inPort);
/* set font and size of grafPort to same as hTE */
TextFont((*hTE)->txFont);
TextSize((*hTE)->txSize);

/* get font information */
GetFontInfo(&fontStuff);

/* set up for single space */
(*hTE)->fontAscent = fontStuff.ascent;
(*hTE)->lineHeight = fontStuff.ascent +
                        fontStuff.descent +
                        fontStuff.leading;

/* modify for other spacings */
if(spacing == singleSP) return;
else if(spacing == oneandhalfSP)
        extra = (*hTE)->lineHeight/2;
else if(spacing == doubleSP)
        extra = (*hTE)->lineHeight;

(*hTE)->lineHeight += extra;
(*hTE)->fontAscent += extra;

return;
}
```

The application at the end of the chapter uses this method whenever the user selects a new font or size for an edit record.

Justification and Word Wrap

When the user wants to change the justification of an edit record, the application should respond by calling the routine **TESetJust**:

```
TESetJust(just, hTE)
        int        just;
        TEHandle   hTE;
```

Depending on the value of the parameter just, this routine changes the justification to either right, left, or center. Earlier in this chapter we listed the predefined constants used to specify the desired justification. **TESetJust** does not redraw the text with the new justification; for this, the application must call **TEUpdate**.

To change whether the edit record uses word wrap or not, the application must change the value of the crOnly field of the edit record. The following procedure changes the setting of the word wrap field, recalculates the lineStarts array, and finally redraws the text.

```
doWordWrap(whichTE, flag)
        TEHandle        whichTE;  /* Handle to Edit record to
                                     change */
        char    flag;    /* true (yes) or false (no) word wrap */
/* this procedure turns on or off word wrap for the edit
        record specified by whichTE. Could be more efficient
        by checking if whichTE is already set the desired way */
{
        /* local variables */
        GrafPtr         oldPort, whichPort;

        /* Lock the TERec, get copy of which Port
           it is drawn in */
        HLock(whichTE);
        whichPort = (*whichTE)->inPort;

        /* set value of crOnly */
        if(flag) {
                (*whichTE)->crOnly = +1; /* turn on word wrap */
        } else {
                (*whichTE)->crOnly = -1; /* turn off word wrap */
        }

        /* change grafPort to one containing whichTE */
        GetPort(&oldPort);
        SetPort(whichPort);

        /* recalculate lines
        - erase and redraw window contents */
        TECalText(whichTE);
        EraseRect(&(*whichTE)->viewRect);
        TEUpdate(&(*whichTE)->viewRect);

        /* restore grafPort */
        SetPort(oldPort);

        /* unlock the TERec */
        HUnlock(whichTE);

}
```

Miscellaneous Routines

To change the portion of the text that is visible on the desktop, the application can scroll the text within the view rectangle of the edit record (when the user manipulates a scroll bar, for instance) with the routine

```
TEScroll(dh, dv, hTE)
        int         dh, dv;
        TEHandle    hTE;
```

where dh and dv specify the number of pixels to move the text right and down, respectively (see Figure 8.5). The edit record is scrolled by off-setting the destination rectangle with respect to the view rectangle by the amount specified and redrawing the text. Two of the advanced techniques included at the end of the chapter make use of **TEScroll** to scroll the text under the view rectangle.

TextEdit also contains a routine that draws uneditable text. This routine can be used to place static text in any sort of window. The difference between this routine, **TextBox**, and the text drawing routines found

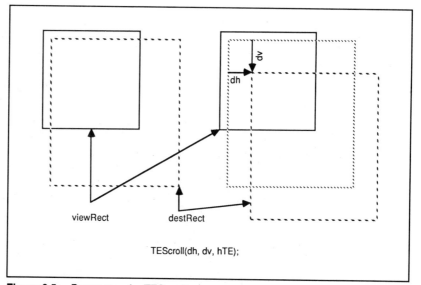

Figure 8.5: Parameters for **TEScroll**

in QuickDraw—**DrawString** and **DrawText**—is that **TextBox** draws the text justified and word-wrapped within the specified destination rectangle.

```
TextBox(text, length, box, just)
        char    *text;
        long    length;
        Rect    *box;
        int     just;
```

The application at the end of the chapter uses **TextBox** to draw an information window when the user selects the About . . . command from the Apple menu.

Advanced Techniques

In this section we present several programming examples that either enhance the basic features of TextEdit or are used to complete the requirements of the "User Interface Guidelines." The individual examples include such topics as changing the appearance of the cursor, resizing an edit record, using the TextEdit scrap, and scrolling the text of an edit record. Two of the more advanced examples require the use of in-line assembly language in order to interface correctly with the Toolbox. At the end of the chapter we combine these ideas with the basic material from TextEdit and the preceding chapters to make a nearly complete text editing application.

Changing Cursor to the I-Beam Over an Active Edit Record

The "User Interface Guidelines" specify that when the cursor is located over an active, editable text region, the cursor should change to the familiar I-beam shape. Once the cursor leaves the text region, it should return to the usual upward left-pointing arrow (see Figure 8.6). In order to accomplish this task, the application must periodically check the mouse location against the position of the active edit record, if any.

The following code fragment should be placed in the main event loop of the application to insure that the insertion point blinks at the appropriate rate and that the cursor changes to the I-beam over an active edit record.

```
/* global variables */

TEHandle    theText;        /* the active edit record */

if(theText != NULL) {
        TEIdle(theText);
        ChangeMouse(theText);
}
```

The procedure ChangeMouse first verifies that the edit record it received belongs to the frontmost window on the desktop (recall that an active edit record must be part of the active window). If the current cursor position is within the view rectangle of the edit record, ChangeMouse changes the cursor to the I-beam shape. If not, the cursor is returned to the arrow shape. The cursor shapes are retrieved from the Toolbox, the arrow shape from the QuickDraw globals, and the I-beam shape from the system file with the function **GetCursor** which was discussed in Chapter 5.

```
ChangeMouse(activeTEH)   /* ChangeMouse() */
        TEHandle        activeTEH;
```

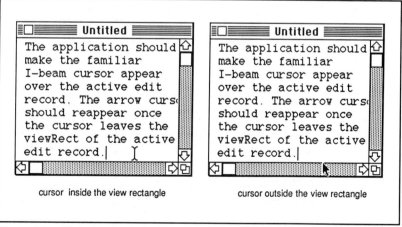

cursor inside the view rectangle   cursor outside the view rectangle

Figure 8.6:   Changing the Cursor Shape over an Active Edit Record

```
/* this routine compares the current mouse location with the
        view rectangle of the edit record activeTEH and changes
        the cursor to the I-beam, or arrow as appropriate

        - assumes QD is the pointer to the QuickDraw globals
        returned by InitGraf */

#define         iBeamCursor 1          /* from header files */


{

        PointmousePt;
        CursHandle      iBeam;

        /* Does the front window contain activeTEH ?
        - if not something is wrong! */
        if( FrontWindow() == (WindowPtr) (*activeTEH)->inPort ) {

                /* get the current mouse (local coordinates) */
                GetMouse(&mousePt);

                /* is the mouse in the viewRect
                   of the edit record? */
                if( PtInRect(mousePt,&(*activeTEH)->viewRect) ) {
                        /* Yes, get I-Beam from system and
                           change cursor */
                        iBeam = GetCursor(iBeamCursor)
                        SetCursor(*iBeam);

                } else {
                        /* No, return cursor to arrow
                           (a QuickDraw global) */
                        SetCursor(&QD->arrow);
                }
        }
}
```

This method is used in the sample application at the end of the chapter. The application should also set the cursor to the arrow shape when deactivating an edit record in order to insure that the cursor changes when there is no active edit record.

Resizing View and Destination Rectangles

When an application resizes a window, it will probably also need to adjust the view rectangles, and possibly the destination rectangles, of the edit records contained in the window. In most word processing applications, the view rectangle will closely follow the size of the window, while the destination rectangle depends only on the page size and the right and left margins. In other applications, the destination rectangle may depend on the window size. On the other hand, drafting and graphic design programs (MacDraw II, for instance) allow many edit records to be placed in a single window. In this case, the user changes the view and destination rectangles by resizing the item with the mouse.

The sample program at the end of the chapter allows the user to resize the windows containing text edit records. For the purpose of demonstration both the destination and view rectangles are controlled by the size of the window. The following procedure, ReSizeTE, changes the view and destination rectangles of the edit record associated with a window to the maximum size that will fit in the window.

```
ReSizeTE(tempWindow)/* ReSizeTE() */
        WindowPtr        tempWindow;
/* this routine resizes the view and destination rectangles
        of the edit record associated with tempWindow, to the
        maximum size that will fit in the window
        - assumes the TEHandle is located in a WindowStuff
        (whose handle is in the refCon of the window)

struct WStuff {
        TEHandle theTE; (handle to TE for window)
};
typedef         struct WStuff  WindowStuff;

*/

{
        /* declare local variables */
        Rect            aRect;
        TEHandle        tempText;
        WindowStuff     **theWSHandle;

        /* Get a copy of the WindowStuff handle */
        theWSHandle = (WindowStuff **) GetWRefCon(tempWindow);
```

```
            if(theWSHandle == NULL) return; /* in case its empty */
            /* get the TEHandle */
            tempText = (*theWSHandle)->theTE;

            /* make a copy of the window size (local coordinates) */
            LocWindowSize(tempWindow, &aRect); /* from Chapter 7 */

            /* Make room for scrollbars in viewRect and resize */
            aRect.right -= 16;
            aRect.bottom -= 16;
            BlockMove(&aRect, &(*tempText)->viewRect, sizeof(Rect));

            /* Indent a bit for destRect and resize */
            aRect.right -= 4;
            aRect.top += 4;
            aRect.left += 4;
            aRect.bottom -= 4;
            BlockMove(&aRect, &(*tempText)->destRect, sizeof(Rect));

            /* Recalculate lineStarts array for new destRect */
            TECalText(tempText);
}
```

With a few additions, this function appears in the sample application at the end of the chapter.

TextEdit and the Clipboard

As we mentioned in the beginning of the chapter, TextEdit supports cut, copy, and paste operations between edit records in a single application. A powerful feature also provided by the Macintosh Toolbox is the ability to cut and paste text and pictures between applications and between desk accessories and applications. This unique feature is embodied in the Clipboard or desk scrap, which is discussed in the Scrap Manager chapter in *Inside Macintosh*. To allow text to be copied into or pasted from the Clipboard, several routines exist which add to the capabilities of the Toolbox by making it possible to move text between the private TextEdit scrap and Clipboard. We have included source code for C versions of these routines to allow our applications to use the Clipboard (see the box entitled "Routines for Using TextEdit with the Clipboard").

```
Routines for Using TextEdit with the Clipboard

/****************************************************************/
/*                                                              */
/*              TEScrap Toolbox Extension Routines              */
/*                                                              */
/****************************************************************/

#include "MacTypes.h"
#include "MemoryMgr.h"

/* Toolbox globals */

#define          TEScrpLength    *((short *) 0x0AB0)
#define          TEScrpHandle    *((Handle *)0x0AB4)


Handle TEScrapHandle()                        /* TEScrapHandle() */
{
       return TEScrpHandle;
}

long TEGetScrapLen()                          /* TEGetScrapLen() */
{
       return TEScrpLength;
}


TESetScrapLen(length)                         /* TESetScrapLen() */
       long      length;
{
       TEScrpLength = (short) length;
}


OSErr TEFromScrap()                           /* TEFromScrap() */
{
       long offset,length;

       length = GetScrap(TEScrapHandle(), 'TEXT', &offset);

       if(length > 0) {
              TESetScrapLen(length);
       }
       return length;
}


OSErr TEToScrap()                             /* TEToScrap() */
```

```
{
        Ptr *TEScrapH;
        long length;

        HLock(TEScrapH = TEScrapHandle());
        ZeroScrap();            /* not included in Lisa Pascal Version */
        length = PutScrap(TEGetScrapLen(), TEXT, *TEScrapH);
        HUnlock(TEScrapH);

        if(length >= 0) {
                length = 0;
        }
        return length;
}
```

The TextEdit Scrap Routines

To copy the contents of the TextEdit scrap to the Clipboard, use the routine **TEToScrap**, which returns zero if the operation was completed successfully, or a 16-bit error code if an error occurred (the values of the Macintosh Operating System error codes are listed in Appendix B.)

OSErr TEToScrap()

The version of **TEToScrap** we will present has the Toolbox function **Zero-Scrap** built in, unlike the Lisa Pascal version. (Ordinarily **ZeroScrap** must be called before **TEToScrap**; we have simply included the call to **Zero-Scrap** in our version.)

To copy the contents of the Clipboard to the TextEdit scrap, use the routine **TEFromScrap**.

OSErr TEFromScrap()

This routine returns an error code if the text was not copied, or zero if the text was copied successfully. Note that this routine will not copy the contents of the Clipboard into the TextEdit scrap unless the data on the Clipboard resembles text (for example, a MacPaint picture will not be copied into the TextEdit scrap).

There are three other TextEdit scrap routines used primarily in implementing the routines **TEToScrap** and **TEFromScrap**. These routines allow the application to obtain a handle to the scrap (**TEScrapHandle**), determine the number of bytes in the scrap (**TEGetScrapLen**), and set the length of the scrap (**TESetScrapLen**).

```
Handle TEScrapHandle()

long TEGetScrapLen()

TESetScrapLen(length)
```

Using the TextEdit Scrap Routines in an Application

There are two different interactions we must consider when using the TextEdit scrap and the Clipboard. The simplest situation involves copying the contents of the Clipboard into the TextEdit scrap at the start of the application and copying from the scrap into the Clipboard as the application finishes. This will insure that the user can transfer text from one application to another in the usual fashion. To accomplish this, the application need only call **TEFromScrap** before entering the event loop, and then call **TEToScrap** just prior to returning to the Finder.

The other situation is somewhat more complicated and involves desk accessories and other applications. Whenever either the application or a desk accessory becomes the active window the application must insure that the Clipboard and TextEdit scrap both contain the text from the most recent cut or copy operation. To allow pasting text from an application to a desk accessory, the contents of the TextEdit scrap should be copied into the Clipboard after every operation that changes the scrap (using **TECut** and **TECopy**). An alternative approach would be to copy the scrap to the Clipboard whenever either the application opens a desk accessory or **FindWindow** reports that a mouse-down has occurred in a system window (see Chapter 3).

It is a bit trickier to allow pasting text in the opposite direction, from a desk accessory to the application. The Scrap Manager maintains a counter that changes every time the contents of the Clipboard are changed. The application can periodically check this counter and, if the value has changed, copy the Clipboard into the TextEdit scrap. The counter is located in low memory and can be retrieved with the following function:

```
#define scrapCount *((short *) 0x0968)

short GetScrapCount()
{
        return scrapCount;
}
```

It would also be sufficient for the application to transfer the Clipboard to the scrap whenever it receives an activate event for one of its windows (which would happen when deactivating a desk accessory to return to the application). The techniques we have just described are used in the sample program at the end of the chapter to allow pasting between desk accessories and other applications. We will not actually discuss desk accessories until Chapter 13, although if you can't wait any longer you can skip ahead and read that section, as we have by now covered all of the necessary background information.

Scrolling an Edit Record

When the text of an edit record overflows the view rectangle, the application can scroll the text either horizontally or vertically to allow the user to view different parts of the text. Scroll bars are the usual way to allow the user to select which portion of the text will be visible. This subject will have to wait until Chapter 10, where we discuss controls. For now, we can consider the problem of what to do when the insertion point moves outside the visible portion of the edit record, as will happen when the number of lines, or the line length, exceeds the dimensions of the view rectangle.

One method involves computing the position of the insertion point each time a character is inserted into the edit record with **TEKey**. We can first determine which line of the text contains the insertion point, and then determine the vertical coordinate using the line number and the line spacing. Once we have determined which line contains the insertion point, we can determine the horizontal coordinate by computing the width of the string of characters starting at the beginning of the line and ending at the insertion point. Since the Macintosh uses proportionally spaced fonts, the application must use the QuickDraw function **TextWidth** to determine the width of a string in an arbitrary font. This method works quite well, but because of the overhead incurred on each keystroke it may noticeably slow the application when used by an extremely fast typist. The sample program at the end of the chapter uses this technique to scroll vertically, but not horizontally, as the insertion point moves out of the view rectangle.

Scrolling While Selecting Text

Using the mouse to create a selection range may also require scrolling if the text extends outside of the view rectangle. The routine **TEClick** provides a way to scroll the text during a selection if text extends beyond the boundaries of the current view rectangle. As long as the mouse button is held down, **TEClick** will periodically call the function whose pointer is installed in the ClikLoop field of the active edit record. The application-defined ClikLoop routine should check the location of the mouse and, if it lies outside the view rectangle, scroll the text in the appropriate direction (see Figure 8.7).

You can also include other operations in the ClikLoop routine that should be performed during a mouse-down event in an active edit record. The Toolbox calls the ClikLoop routine directly and expects to find its result in the D0 register of the 68000. In addition, the Toolbox expects that the contents of the D2 register will not be disturbed. Think C allows the use of in-line assembly language statements, which can be used in this and other similar situations, to write a small *glue routine* that places the parameters where the compiler would normally place them, converts the function result if necessary, and restores the appropriate 68000 registers. The box entitled "The ClikLoop Routine" contains such a glue routine written for the Think C compiler.

To allow the ClikLoop routine to function properly, the application should contain a global variable that maintains a handle to the active edit record. The following routine, CClikLoop, will scroll the text either horizontally or vertically as necessary, depending on the location

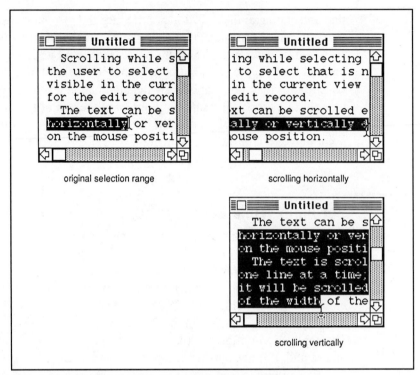

Figure 8.7: Horizontal and Vertical Scrolling During TEClick

The ClikLoop Routine

```
ClikLoop()                              /* ClikLoop() */

/* This routine interfaces TEClick to the
        routine CClikLoop. The routine has no parameters, but
        must preserve the D2 register.

        The result is returned in the D0 register and has the
        following values:

        1 - continue (the normal action)
        0 - ABORT the current mouse-down

        The C routine looks like:

        char CClikLoop();
```

```
*/
asm {
        MOVEM.L         D1-D7/A0-A6, -(SP)          ; Save registers
        JSR             CClikLoop                   ; Call C routine
        MOVEM.L         (SP)+, D1-D7/A0-A6          ; Restore registers
        MOVEQ.L         #1,D0                       ; keep mouse-down enabled
        RTS
}
```

of the mouse. We will use this routine in the sample program at the end of the chapter.

```
CClikLoop()     /* CClikLoop() */

/* This routine scrolls the text belonging to the edit
        record pointed to by the global variable theText.
        It is not very smart about what to do if the window
        needs to be scrolled in two directions at once */

{
        /*global variable: the active edit record */
        extern TEHandle theText;
        /* local variables */

        Rect        *viewR, *destR;
        Point       mousePt;
        int         viewWidth, lineHeight, destBottom;
        TEPtr       theTEPtr;

        /* lock and dereference TERec for speed */
        HLock(theText);
        theTEPtr = *theText;

        /* get pointers to view and dest rects
        - get lineheight and width of view rectangle */
        viewR = &theTEPtr->viewRect;
        destR = &theTEPtr->destRect;
        lineHeight = theTEPtr->lineHeight;
        viewWidth = viewR->right - viewR->left;
```

```
/* get current mouse location and test against viewRect */
GetMouse(&mousePt);
if(!PtInRect(mousePt, viewR)) {

        /* if mouse is below viewRect and some text
                is below, scroll up one line */
        if(mousePt.v > viewR->bottom) {
                /* where is the bottom line? */
                destBottom = destR->top +
                (theTEPtr->nLines)*lineHeight;
                if(viewR->bottom < destBottom) {
                        TEScroll(0, -lineHeight,
                                        theText);
                }
                /* if mouse is to left of viewRect and
                some text is there, scroll right a bit */
        } else if((mousePt.h < viewR->left) &&
                (viewR->left > destR->left)) {
                TEScroll(viewWidth/10, 0, theText);

                /* if mouse is to right of viewRect and
                some text is there, scroll left a bit */
        } else if((mousePt.h > viewR->right) &&
                (viewR->right < destR->right)) {

                TEScroll(-viewWidth/10, 0, theText);
                /* if mouse is above viewRect and some
                text is there, scroll down one line */
        } else if((mousePt.v < viewR->top) &&
                (viewR->top > destR->top)) {

                TEScroll(0, lineHeight, theText);
        }
}
/* unlock TERec before returning */
HUnlock(theText);
}
```

Changing TextEdit's Definition of a Word

In order to split up long lines of text with word wrap or to use a
double-click to select a word, TextEdit has to be able to determine how

to break up a text string into a series of words. As we saw earlier, the default definition used by TextEdit is that a word consists of a series of characters bounded on either end by a space or by an ASCII character below 0x20 (hexadecimal). In word processing applications, however, this may not be the most useful definition. TextEdit allows the application to use its own word definitions, which can be assigned on the level of individual edit records.

To use a custom word definition the application can store a procedure pointer into the wordBreak field of the appropriate edit record. In the analogy to the ClikLoop function we described earlier, the Toolbox calls the application-defined wordBreak routine directly with its parameters in the registers of the 68000, and the result returned as the Z flag of the 68000 status register. In the box entitled "Custom WordBreak Routines," we have included a glue routine written for Think C. The sample program at the end of the chapter uses such a routine to modify the default definition used by TextEdit.

```
                    Custom WordBreak Routines

WordBreak()                             /* WordBreak() */

/* This routine interfaces the Toolbox to a word breaking
        routine written in Think C. The Toolbox passes
        the following parameters:

                D0 - Pointer to locked contents of edit record
                D1 - Offset to character in question (16-bit)

        and expects the following result

                Z-flag SR (Zero result)

                        - SET if word should not break here
                        - CLEAR if word should break here

        The C routine looks like:

                char CWordBreak(textPtr, charPos)
                        char *textPtr;
                        short charPos;
```

```
        and returns

                - TRUE if the word should break here
                - CLEAR if word should not break here
*/
asm {

        MOVEM.L        D1-D7/A0-A6, -(SP)      ; Save registers
        MOVE.W         D0, D1                  ; put textPtr,
        MOVE.L         A0, D0                  ; charPos into D0, D1
        JSR            CWordBreak              ; Call C routine
                                               ; (return result in D0)
        MOVEM.L        (SP)+, D1-D7/A0-A6      ; Restore registers
        TST.B D0                               ; set Z for no break
        RTS
}

/* Skeleton word-break routine */

char CWordBreak(textPtr, charPos)
        char    *textPtr;
        int      charPos;
{
        char c;

        c = *(textPtr + charPos);

        /* decision based on the character and its neighbors
        - return true to break word at charPos
        - return false otherwise */
}
```

A Sample Program Using TextEdit

This concludes our discussion of TextEdit. When we discuss controls and dialogs in Chapters 9 and 10, we will see that TextEdit forms the basis for several of the ideas presented in these chapters.

With the knowledge we have gained so far of the Toolbox, it is possible to build a fairly sophisticated application. Several features related to material that we have not yet covered, like reading from or writing to the disk, will be added in the upcoming chapters. This chapter's program is lengthy, but we have been leading up to this example throughout this and the previous seven chapters. In fact, a great deal of the program has already been presented in examples outlining the use of various routines in the Toolbox.

The program represents what might be considered a first attempt to write a simple word processor that allows several files to be open at once. The user can change the font, size, and style used in each of the edit records, as well as the justification and word wrap settings. Several advanced features like word break, scrolling while selecting, and window zooming (a double-click in the title bar) are included to demonstrate that, with the ideas from this and previous chapters, you can now build a sophistocated text editor. After studying this example, you should be able to begin to design your own applications, perhaps using this code as a rough framework.

Because this example is so long, we will not attempt to describe the program on a line-by-line basis. We have instead divided the application into a number of procedures and functions that perform specific tasks. This structure should help to clarify the details of how the application works.

From text editing we move ahead to resources, another unique feature of the Toolbox designed specifically to make the job of writing application programs easier.

```
/* This application must be broken into two segments, one for the application
      code and the other for the library code. This can be done from the
      Project box in THINK C.      */


#include    <WindowMgr.h>
#include    <MemoryMgr.h>
#include    <EventMgr.h>
#include    <TextEdit.h>
#include    <FontMgr.h>
#include    <MenuMgr.h>
#include    <ToolboxUtil.h>
#include    <stdio.h>
#include    <strings.h>

/* LSC defines txFace as a char */
#define     teNormal        0x00
#define     teBold 0x01
#define     teItalic        0x02
#define     teUnderline     0x04
#define     teOutline       0x08
#define     teShadow        0x10
#define     teCondense      0x20
#define     teExtend        0x40

#define     Desk_ID     200
#define     File_ID     201
#define     Edit_ID     202
#define     Format_ID   203
#define     Font_ID     204
#define     Style_ID    205
#define     iBeamCursor   1

#define     singleSp       0
#define     oneandhalfSp   1
#define     doubleSp       2

#define     grayRgn            *((RgnHandle *) 0x09EE)

struct _WStuff {
   TEHandle   theTEH;
   Rect       oldSize;
};
#define    WindowStuff   struct _WStuff
typedef    WindowStuff   *WSPtr;
typedef    WSPtr         *WSHandle;

/* Global Variables */

    WindowPtr      theWindow, windPtrA, windPtrB;
```

```
    WindowRecord    *windRecA;
    WindowRecord    *windRecB;
    TEHandle        theText;
    Rect            dragBoundsRect, limitRect, fullSize;
    Rect            windowRectA, windowRectB;
    MenuHandle      deskMenu, fileMenu, editMenu, formatMenu, fontMenu, styleMenu;
    char            *titleA = "\pWindow A";
    char            *titleB = "\pWindow B";
    short           scrapIndex;
    CursHandle      iBeam;

/* External or Non-Integer functions */

    WindowPtr    OpenWindow();
    TEHandle     OpenTE();
    long         GetDblTime();
    short        GetScrapCount();
    char         IsValidWindow();
    void         WordBreak();
    void         ClikLoop();

reStartProc()
{
    ExitToShell();
}


/*        Initialization Routine */

Init()      /* Init() */
{
    InitGraf(&thePort);
    InitFonts();
    InitWindows();
    InitDialogs(reStartProc);
    TEInit();
    PutUpMenus();
    iBeam = GetCursor(iBeamCursor);

    /* initialize dragBoundsRect - limits movement of window
        - for use with Mac & MacXL
        - InitGraf returns QD, pointer to QuickDraw globals
        - QD->screenBits.bounds is bounding Rect for screen */

    SetRect(&dragBoundsRect,
       screenBits.bounds.left +4,
       screenBits.bounds.top +24,
       screenBits.bounds.right -4,
       screenBits.bounds.bottom -4);
```

```
   /* initialize limitRect - limits size of window */
   SetRect(&limitRect, 60, 40,
      screenBits.bounds.right  - screenBits.bounds.left -4,
      screenBits.bounds.bottom - screenBits.bounds.top  -24);

   /* set size of window at full size (for Zoom) */
   SetRect(&fullSize,
      screenBits.bounds.left   +10,
      screenBits.bounds.top    +40,
      screenBits.bounds.right  -10,
      screenBits.bounds.bottom -8);

   /* set up initial size for windows */

   SetRect(&windowRectA ,10, 40, 250, 330);
   SetRect(&windowRectB ,260, 40, 500, 330);

   theWindow = NULL;
   theText = NULL;

   windRecA = (WindowRecord *) NewPtr(sizeof(WindowRecord));
   windRecB = (WindowRecord *) NewPtr(sizeof(WindowRecord));

   windPtrB = OpenWindow(windRecB,&windowRectB,titleB);
   windPtrA = OpenWindow(windRecA,&windowRectA,titleA);
}


/*
 *    Main
 */

main()                       /* main() */
{
   char      c;
   short     windowcode;

   EventRecord        theEvent;
   WindowPtr          mouseWindow;
   WindowPtr          tempWindow;

   Init();

   FlushEvents(everyEvent, 0);
   TEFromScrap();                        /* copy desk scrap to TE scrap */
   scrapIndex = GetScrapCount();         /* get value of desk scrap counter */
   SelectWindow(windPtrA);               /* Generate an activate event for window A */
   SetPort(windPtrA);

   InitCursor();
   while (1)   {
```

```
SystemTask();

if(scrapIndex != GetScrapCount()) { /* if new scrapCount then copy desk scrap */
    TEFromScrap();
    scrapIndex = GetScrapCount();
}

if(theText) {
    TEIdle(theText);
    ChangeMouse(theText);
}


if (GetNextEvent(everyEvent, &theEvent)) {
    switch ( theEvent.what )  {
        case autoKey:
        case keyDown:
            c = theEvent.message & charCodeMask;
            if ((theEvent.modifiers & cmdKey)) {
                DoMenuItem(MenuKey(c));
            } else {
                if(theText) {
                    TEKey(c, theText);
                    ScrollInsertPt(theText);
                }
            }
        break;


    case mouseDown:
        windowcode = FindWindow(theEvent.where, &mouseWindow);

        /* mouseDown occurs in active window */
        if ((FrontWindow() == mouseWindow) && (mouseWindow != NULL)) {
            ActiveWindowEvt(&theEvent,mouseWindow,windowcode);
            break;
        }

        /* mouseDown occurs in inactive window */
        if ((FrontWindow() != mouseWindow) && (mouseWindow != NULL)) {
            InactiveWindowEvt(&theEvent,mouseWindow,windowcode);
            break;
        }

        /* mouseDown does not occur in a window */

if (mouseWindow == NULL) {
  NotaWindowEvt(&theEvent,mouseWindow,windowcode);
  break;
}
```

```
            case updateEvt:
                DoUpdateEvt(&theEvent);
                break;

            case activateEvt:
                DoActivateEvt(&theEvent);
                break;


        }
    }
  }
}


/*
 * mouseDown event handler #1 - Active window                          activeWindowEvt()
 */

ActiveWindowEvt(theEvent,mouseWindow,windowcode)
    EventRecord     *theEvent;
    WindowPtr       mouseWindow;
    short           windowcode;
{
    long            growResult, upTime, clickTime;
    EventRecord     upEvent, downEvent;
    Rect            clickRect;
    short           vert, horiz;

    SetPort(mouseWindow);
    switch ( windowcode ) {
        case inContent:
            GlobalToLocal(&theEvent->where);
            TEClick(theEvent->where,(theEvent->modifiers & shiftKey)? 0xff :0, theText);
            break;

        case inDrag:
            /* Delay to wait for mouse-up */
            upTime = theEvent->when + DoubleTime;
            while( TickCount() < upTime );

            /* has a mouse-up occurred? */
            if( GetNextEvent(mUpMask, &upEvent) ) {

                /* Delay to wait for mouse-down */
                clickTime = upEvent.when + DoubleTime;
                vert  = theEvent->where.v;
                horiz = theEvent->where.h;
                SetRect(&clickRect, horiz-8, vert-8, horiz+8, vert+8);

                while( TickCount() < clickTime );
                if( GetNextEvent(mDownMask, &downEvent) ) {
```

```
                if(PtInRect(downEvent.where, &clickRect)) {
                    /* doubleclick in dragRegion */
                    MyZoomWindow(mouseWindow);
                    break;
                }

            }
        } else {
            /* let user drag the window */
            if(StillDown()) {
                DragWindow(mouseWindow,theEvent->where, &dragBoundsRect);
                UpdateWSSize(mouseWindow);
            }
        }
        break;   /* This break was misplaced in the book - see p260 */

    case inGrow:
        growResult = GrowWindow(mouseWindow, theEvent->where, &limitRect);
        if(growResult) {
            SizeWindow(mouseWindow, LoWord(growResult), HiWord(growResult), TRUE);
            EraseRect(&mouseWindow->portRect);
            InvalRect(&mouseWindow->portRect);
            ReSizeTE(mouseWindow);
            DrawGrowIcon(mouseWindow);
            UpdateWSSize(mouseWindow);
        }
        break;

    case inGoAway:
        if (TrackGoAway(theWindow, theEvent->where))  KillWindow(theWindow);
        break;

    case inSysWindow:
        SystemClick(theEvent,mouseWindow);
        break;
    }
}


/*
 * mouseDown event handler #2 - inactive  window
     InactiveWindowEvt()
 */
InactiveWindowEvt(theEvent,mouseWindow,windowcode)

    EventRecord      *theEvent;
    WindowPtr        mouseWindow;
    short            windowcode;
{
    long             ticks;
    EventRecord      dummyEvent;
```

```
    switch ( windowcode ) {
       case inContent:
           SelectWindow(mouseWindow);
           break;

       case inDrag:
           ticks = theEvent->when + DoubleTime -1;
           while( TickCount() < ticks );
           if(StillDown()) {
               DragWindow(mouseWindow, theEvent->where, &dragBoundsRect);
               UpdateWSSize(mouseWindow);
           } else SelectWindow(mouseWindow);
           break;

        case inSysWindow:
            SystemClick(theEvent,mouseWindow);
            break;
       }
}


/*
 * mouseDown event handler #3 -  no window
      NotaWindowEvt()
 */
NotaWindowEvt(theEvent,mouseWindow,windowcode)
   EventRecord     *theEvent;
   WindowPtr       mouseWindow;
   short           windowcode;
{
   switch ( windowcode ) {
      case inMenuBar:
          DoMenuItem(MenuSelect(theEvent->where));
          break;
      case inDesk:
          SysBeep(1);
          break;
     }
  }


 /*
  * Update event handler
       DoUpdateEvt()
  */
DoUpdateEvt(theEvent)
   EventRecord      *theEvent;
{
   WindowPtr   tempWindow,oldPort;
   TEHandle    tempText;
   WSHandle    tempWS;
```

```
        GetPort(&oldPort);
        SetPort(tempWindow = (WindowPtr)theEvent->message);
        BeginUpdate(tempWindow);
        tempWS = (WSHandle)GetWRefCon(tempWindow);
        tempText = (*tempWS)->theTEH;
        HLock(tempText);
        EraseRect(&(*tempText)->viewRect);
        TEUpdate(&(*tempText)->viewRect, tempText);
        HUnlock(tempText);
        DrawGrowIcon(tempWindow);
        EndUpdate(tempWindow);
        SetPort(oldPort);
        return;
    }


    /*
     * Activate event handler
     *      DoActivateEvt()
     */
    DoActivateEvt(theEvent)
        EventRecord     *theEvent;
    {
        WindowPtr       tempWindow;
        TEHandle        tempText;
        WSHandle        tempWS;

        SetPort(tempWindow = (WindowPtr)theEvent->message);
        if(!IsValidWindow(tempWindow)) SysBeep(0);
        tempWS = (WSHandle)GetWRefCon(tempWindow);
        tempText = (*tempWS)->theTEH;
        if ((theEvent->modifiers & activeFlag)) {
            theWindow = tempWindow;
            TEActivate(theText = tempText);
            SetMenus(tempText);
        } else {
            TEDeactivate(tempText);
            theText = NULL;
            ClearMenus();
        }
        DrawGrowIcon(tempWindow);
        return;
    }

    /*
     * Close Window and remove storage
     */
    KillWindow(tempWindow)
        WindowPtr   tempWindow;
    {
        WSHandle    tempWS;
```

```
    tempWS = (WSHandle) GetWRefCon(tempWindow);
    HLock(tempWS);

    TEDispose((*tempWS)->theTEH);
    theText = NULL;

    if(theWindow == windPtrA) windPtrA = NULL;
    if(theWindow == windPtrB) windPtrB = NULL;

    CloseWindow(theWindow);
    theWindow = NULL;

    HUnlock(tempWS);
    DisposHandle(tempWS);
    ClearMenus();
}


/*
 * Put up a new Window
 */
WindowPtr OpenWindow(wRec,rect,title)                /* OpenWindow() */
    WindowRecord        *wRec;
    Rect                *rect;
    char                *title;
{
    WindowPtr    tempWindow;
    TEHandle     tempText;
    WSHandle     tempWS;

    tempWindow = NewWindow(wRec,rect, title, 0xff, 0, -1, 0xff, 0);
    SetPort(tempWindow);
    TextFont(geneva);
    TextFace(italic);
    TextSize(12);
    tempText = OpenTE(tempWindow);
    HLock(tempText);
    tempWS = (WSHandle) NewHandle(sizeof(WindowStuff));
    (*tempWS)->theTEH = tempText;
    SetWRefCon(tempWindow, tempWS);
    UpdateWSSize(tempWindow);
    (*tempText)->wordBreak = (ProcPtr) WordBreak;     /* try out the wordBreak!! */
    (*tempText)->clikLoop = (ProcPtr) ClikLoop;       /* try out the clickLoop!! */
    (*tempText)->crOnly = 1;
    SetLineHeight(0, tempText);
    TEUpdate(&(*tempText)->viewRect, tempText);
    HUnlock(tempText);
    return tempWindow;
}
```

```
/*
 * Get a New a TEHandle
 */
TEHandle OpenTE(tempWindow)                        /* OpenTE() */
    WindowPtr tempWindow;
{

    Rect   destRect, viewRect;

    LocWindowSize(tempWindow, &viewRect);
         viewRect.right  -= 16;      /* Make room for scroll bar */
         viewRect.bottom -= 16;      /* Make room for scroll bar */
    LocWindowSize(tempWindow, &destRect);
         destRect.right  -= 16;      /* Make room for scroll bar */
         destRect.bottom -= 16;      /* Make room for scroll bar */
         destRect.left   += 4;        /* indent a bit */
    return TENew(&destRect, &viewRect);
}


/*
 * ReSize Suffix Rects
 */
ReSizeTE(tempWindow)
/* ReSizeTE() */
    WindowPtr tempWindow;
{
    Rect         rect;
    TEHandle     tempText;
    WSHandle     tempWS;

    tempWS = (WSHandle)GetWRefCon(tempWindow);
    tempText = (*tempWS)->theTEH;

    LocWindowSize(tempWindow, &rect);
     rect.right  -= 16;        /* Make room for scroll bar */
     rect.bottom -= 16;            /* Make room for scroll bar */
    BlockMove(&rect, &(*tempText)->viewRect, sizeof(Rect));
     rect.left    += 4;          /* indent a bit */
     rect.top     += 4;          /* indent a bit */
     rect.right   -= 4;          /* indent a bit */
     rect.bottom  -= 4;          /* indent a bit */
    BlockMove(&rect, &(*tempText)->destRect, sizeof(Rect));
    TECalText(tempText);
}


LocWindowSize(tempWindow, theSize)                          /* LocWindowSize() */
    WindowPtr    tempWindow;
    Rect         *theSize;
```

```
    /* Procedure to copy size of a window's content region
        in LOCAL coordinates of window */
{
    /* copy window's portRect from its GrafPort */
    *theSize = tempWindow->portRect;
}


GlobWindowSize(tempWindow, theSize)                              /* GlobWindowSize() */
    WindowPtr    tempWindow;
    Rect         *theSize;

    /* Procedure to copy size of a window's content region
        in GLOBAL coordinates */
{
    GrafPtr    theCurrentPort;

    /* change grafPort to tempWindow */

    GetPort(&theCurrentPort);
    SetPort(tempWindow);

    LocWindowSize(tempWindow, theSize);

    /* convert Rect to global coordinates - as two Points */
    LocalToGlobal((Point *) &theSize->top);
    LocalToGlobal((Point *) &theSize->bottom);

    /* restore grafPort */

    SetPort(theCurrentPort);
}

UpdateWSSize(tempWindow)
    WindowPtr    tempWindow;
{
    WSHandle    tempWS;
    tempWS = (WSHandle) GetWRefCon(tempWindow);
    HLock(tempWS);
     GlobWindowSize(tempWindow, &(*tempWS)->oldSize);
    HUnlock(tempWS);
}

MyZoomWindow(tempWindow)
/* MyZoomWindow() */
    WindowPtr    tempWindow;
{
    Rect        theStart, theFinal;
    WSHandle    tempWS;
    RgnHandle   theRgn;
    char        ZoomUp;
```

```
      GlobWindowSize(tempWindow, &theStart);
      if(EqualRect(&theStart, &fullSize)) {
          tempWS = (WSHandle) GetWRefCon(tempWindow);
          BlockMove(&(*tempWS)->oldSize, &theFinal, sizeof(Rect));
          ZoomRect(&theStart, &theFinal);
          /* window getting "smaller" */
          LocWindowSize(tempWindow, &theStart);
          EraseRect(&theStart);
          SizeWindow(tempWindow,
              theFinal.right  - theFinal.left,
              theFinal.bottom - theFinal.top, 0xff);
          MoveWindow(tempWindow, theFinal.left, theFinal.top, 0);
      } else {
          BlockMove(&fullSize, &theFinal, sizeof(Rect));
          ZoomRect(&theStart, &theFinal);
          /* window getting "bigger" */
          LocWindowSize(tempWindow, &theStart);
          EraseRect(&theStart);
          MoveWindow(tempWindow, theFinal.left, theFinal.top, 0);
          SizeWindow(tempWindow,
              theFinal.right  - theFinal.left,
              theFinal.bottom - theFinal.top, 0xff);
      }

      LocWindowSize(tempWindow, &theFinal);
      EraseRect(&theFinal);
      InvalRect(&theFinal);
      ReSizeTE(tempWindow);
      DrawGrowIcon(tempWindow);
}

/*
 * Puts up Menus
 */
PutUpMenus()
{
    short items, i;

    InitMenus();

/* Desk Accessory menu */
deskMenu = NewMenu(Desk_ID,"\p\024");
AppendMenu(deskMenu,"\pAbout This ExampleI;(-");
AddResMenu(deskMenu, 'DRVR');
items = CountMItems(deskMenu);
for(i=3;i<=items;i++) DisableItem(deskMenu, i);
InsertMenu(deskMenu, 0);

/* File menu */
fileMenu = NewMenu(File_ID, "\pFile");
```

```
        AppendMenu(fileMenu, "\pNew/N;(Open/O;Close;(-;Zoom/,;Quit/.");
        InsertMenu(fileMenu, 0);

        /* Edit menu */
        editMenu = NewMenu(Edit_ID, "\pEdit");
        AppendMenu(editMenu, "\p(Undo/Z;(-;Cut/X;Copy/C;Paste/V;Clear;(-;Select All");
        InsertMenu(editMenu, 0);

        /* Format menu */
        formatMenu = NewMenu(Format_ID, "\pFormat");
        AppendMenu(formatMenu,
            "\pLeft/L;Center/M;Right/R;(-;WordWrap;(-;CompactMem;ResrvMem");
        InsertMenu(formatMenu, 0);

        /* Font menu */
        fontMenu = NewMenu(Font_ID, "\pFont");
        AppendMenu(fontMenu, "\pChicago;New York;Geneva;Monaco");
        AppendMenu(fontMenu,"\p(-;9 point;10 point;12 point;14 point");
        InsertMenu(fontMenu, 0);

        /* Style menu */
        styleMenu = NewMenu(Style_ID, "\pStyle");
        AppendMenu(styleMenu,
            "\pNormal;Bold;Italic;Underline;Outlined;Shadow;Condense;Extend");
        InsertMenu(styleMenu, 0);

        DrawMenuBar();
}


/*
 * Do what the menu says...
 */
DoMenuItem(menuresult)
    long  menuresult;
{
    Str255    accessoryName;
    short     menuID, itemNumber;

    menuID = HiWord(menuresult);
    itemNumber = menuresult;

    switch ( menuID ) {
        case Desk_ID:
            if(itemNumber == 1) {        /* item 1 is about window */
                AboutWindow();
            } else {
                GetItem(deskMenu, itemNumber, &accessoryName);

                TEToScrap();             /* copy TE scrap to desk scrap for DA's */
                scrapIndex = GetScrapCount();
```

```
                OpenDeskAcc(&accessoryName);
        }
        break;

    case File_ID:
        switch ( itemNumber ) {
            case 1:              /* item 1 is New */
                if(windPtrA == NULL) windPtrA = OpenWindow(windRecA,

                else if(windPtrB == NULL) windPtrB = OpenWindow(windRecB,

                break;

            case 2:              /* item 2 is Open */
                break;

            case 3:              /* item 3 is Close */
                if((theWindow == FrontWindow()) && (theWindow != NULL))
                    KillWindow(theWindow);
                break;

            case 5:              /* item 5 is Zoom */
                if(theWindow != NULL) MyZoomWindow(theWindow);
                break;

            case 6:                  /* item 6 is quit */
                TEToScrap();         /* copy TE scrap to desk scrap */
                ExitToShell();
                break;
        }
        break;

    case Format_ID:
        if(!theText) break;
        HLock(theText);
        switch(itemNumber) {
            case 1:          /* item 1 is Left Justification */
                TESetJust(teJustLeft,theText);
                break;
            case 2:          /* item 2 is Center Justification */
                TESetJust(teJustCenter,theText);
                break;
            case 3:          /* item 3 is Right Justification */
                TESetJust(teJustRight,theText);
                break;
            case 5:          /* item 5 is WordWrap */
                (*theText)->crOnly *= -1;
                EraseRect(&(*theText)->viewRect);
                break;
```

```
         case 7:        /* case 7 is CompactMem */
            CompactMem(maxSize);
            break;
         case 8:        /* case 8 is ReserveMem */
            ResrvMem(maxSize);
            break;
      }
      TECalText(theText);
      TEUpdate(&(*theText)->viewRect, theText);
      HUnlock(theText);
      SetMenus(theText);
      break;

   case Edit_ID:
      if( SystemEdit(itemNumber-1) ) break;
      if(!theText) break;
      switch(itemNumber) {
         case 3:        /* item 3 is Cut */
            TECut(theText);
            TEToScrap();        /* copy TE scrap to desk scrap for DA's */
            scrapIndex = GetScrapCount();
            break;
         case 4:        /* item 4 is Copy */
            TECopy(theText);
            TEToScrap();        /* copy TE scrap to desk scrap for DA's */
            scrapIndex = GetScrapCount();
            break;
         case 5:        /* item 5 is Paste */
            TEPaste(theText);
            break;
         case 6:        /* item 6 is Clear */
            TEDelete(theText);
            break;
         case 8:        /* item 8 is Select All */
            TESetSelect(0,65000,theText);
            break;
      }
      break;

   case Font_ID:
      if(!theText) break;
      switch(itemNumber) {
         case 1:        /* case 1 is Chicago */
            (*theText)->txFont = systemFont;
            break;
         case 2:        /* case 2 is New York */
            (*theText)->txFont = newYork;
            break;
         case 3:        /* case 3 is Geneva */
            (*theText)->txFont = geneva;
            break;
```

```
          case 4:          /* case 4 is Monaco */
              (*theText)->txFont = monaco;
              break;
          case 6:          /* case 6 is 9 point */
              (*theText)->txSize = 9;
              break;
          case 7:          /* case 7 is 10 point */
              (*theText)->txSize = 10;
              break;
          case 8:          /* case 8 is 12 point */
              (*theText)->txSize = 12;
              break;
          case 9:          /* case 9 is 14 point */
              (*theText)->txSize = 14;
              break;
      }
      HLock(theText);
      EraseRect(&(*theText)->viewRect);
      SetLineHeight(0, theText);
      TECalText(theText);
      TEUpdate(&(*theText)->viewRect, theText);
      HUnlock(theText);
      SetMenus(theText);
      break;

case Style_ID:
      if(!theText) break;
      switch(itemNumber) {
          case 1:          /* case 1 is Normal  */
              (*theText)->txFace = teNormal;
              break;
          case 2:          /* case 2 is Bold    */
              (*theText)->txFace ^= teBold;
              break;
          case 3:          /* case 3 is Italic  */
              (*theText)->txFace ^= teItalic;
              break;
          case 4:          /* case 4 is Underline   */
              (*theText)->txFace ^= teUnderline;
              break;
          case 5:          /* case 5 is Outline */
              (*theText)->txFace ^= teOutline;
              break;
          case 6:          /* case 6 is Shadow  */
              (*theText)->txFace ^= teShadow;
              break;
          case 7:          /* case 7 is Condense    */
              (*theText)->txFace ^= teCondense;
              break;
          case 8:          /* case 8 is Extend */
              (*theText)->txFace ^= teExtend;
              break;
```

```
            }
        HLock(theText);
        EraseRect(&(*theText)->viewRect);
        TECalText(theText);
        TEUpdate(&(*theText)->viewRect, theText);
        HUnlock(theText);
        SetMenus(theText);
        break;

    }
    HiliteMenu(0);
}

/*
 * Clear Menus
 */
ClearMenus()
/* ClearMenus() */
{
    short    i;

    for(i=1;i<6;i++) CheckItem(formatMenu,i,0);
    for(i=1;i<10;i++) CheckItem(fontMenu,i,0);
    for(i=1;i<9;i++) CheckItem(styleMenu,i,0);
}

/*
 * Set up Menus for current TextWindow
 */
SetMenus(tempText)                              /* SetMenus() */
    TEHandle  tempText;
{
    ClearMenus();

    switch((*theText)->just) {
        case teJustLeft:
            CheckItem(formatMenu,1,0xff);
            break;
        case teJustCenter:
            CheckItem(formatMenu,2,0xff);
            break;
        case teJustRight:
            CheckItem(formatMenu,3,0xff);
            break;
    }
    if( (*theText)->crOnly > -1 )  CheckItem(formatMenu,5,0xff);
    switch((*theText)->txFont) {
        case systemFont:
            CheckItem(fontMenu,1,0xff);
            break;
```

```
      case newYork:
          CheckItem(fontMenu,2,0xff);
          break;
      case geneva:
          CheckItem(fontMenu,3,0xff);
          break;
      case monaco:
          CheckItem(fontMenu,4,0xff);
          break;
   }
   switch((*theText)->txSize) {
      case 9:
          CheckItem(fontMenu,6,0xff);
          break;
      case 10:
          CheckItem(fontMenu,7,0xff);
          break;
      case 12:
          CheckItem(fontMenu,8,0xff);
          break;
      case 14:
          CheckItem(fontMenu,9,0xff);
          break;
   }
   if( (*theText)->txFace == teNormal )        CheckItem(styleMenu,1,0xff);
   if( (*theText)->txFace & teBold)            CheckItem(styleMenu,2,0xff);
   if( (*theText)->txFace & teItalic)          CheckItem(styleMenu,3,0xff);
   if( (*theText)->txFace & teUnderline)       CheckItem(styleMenu,4,0xff);
   if( (*theText)->txFace & teOutline)         CheckItem(styleMenu,5,0xff);
   if( (*theText)->txFace & teShadow)          CheckItem(styleMenu,6,0xff);
   if( (*theText)->txFace & teCondense)        CheckItem(styleMenu,7,0xff);
   if( (*theText)->txFace & teExtend)          CheckItem(styleMenu,8,0xff);
}


/*
 * Put up About Window
 */
AboutWindow()
{
   Rect        creditR;
   Rect        lineR;
   GrafPtr     port;
   WindowPtr   creditW;
   EventRecord anEvent;
   long        dummy;
   char        *line1 = "Sample Application from";
   char        *line2 = "Using the Macintosh ToolBox from C";
   char         *line3 = "Fred Huxham, Dave Burnard, Jim Takatsuka";
   char        *line4 = "Published by Sybex, Inc.";
   char        *line5 = "developed using THINK Technologies' LightSpeedC*";
```

```
   GetPort(&port);
   SetRect(&lineR,5,10,345,25);
   SetRect(&creditR,75,110,425,230);
   creditW = NewWindow((WindowPeek) NULL,&creditR,"\1x",0xff,
         dBoxProc,(WindowPtr) -1,0xff,0);
   SetPort(creditW);

   TextSize(12);
   TextFont(systemFont);
   TextBox(line1,strlen(line1),&lineR,teJustCenter);
   OffsetRect(&lineR,0,20);

   TextFace(underline);
   TextBox(line2,strlen(line2),&lineR,teJustCenter);

   TextFace(0);

   OffsetRect(&lineR,0,20);
   TextBox(line3,strlen(line3),&lineR,teJustCenter);
   OffsetRect(&lineR,0,20);
   TextBox(line4,strlen(line4),&lineR,teJustCenter);
   OffsetRect(&lineR,0,20);
   TextBox(line5,strlen(line5),&lineR,teJustCenter);

   do {
      GetNextEvent(everyEvent, &anEvent);
   } while (anEvent.what != mouseDown);

   DisposeWindow(creditW);

   SetPort(port);

   return;
}


/*
 * Change Mouse if over active Text region
 */
ChangeMouse(activeTEH)
   TEHandle    activeTEH;

{
   Point mousePt;
   if( FrontWindow() == (WindowPtr) (*activeTEH)->inPort) {
      GetMouse(&mousePt);
      if( PtInRect(&mousePt,&(*activeTEH)->viewRect) ) SetCursor(*iBeam);
      else SetCursor(&arrow);
   }
}
```

```
void WordBreak()
{
    char    CWordBreak();

    asm {

        MOVEM.L     D1-D7/A0-A6, -(SP)    ; Push D1 to stack
        MOVE.W  D0, -(SP)             ; push charPos onto stack
        MOVE.L  A0, -(SP)             ;   "     textPtr     "
        JSR     CWordBreak            ; Call C routine (returns result in D0)
        ADD     #6,SP                 ; Pop arguments from stack
        MOVEM.L     (SP)+, D1-D7/A0-A6  ; Restore registers from stack
        TST.B   D0                    ; Z code set should'nt break
        RTS

    }
}

char    CWordBreak(textPtr, charPos)
    short       charPos;            /* offset into text of character to test */
    char        *textPtr;           /* pointer to text of Edit Record        */

    /*   returns TRUE if break should occur at the char, or FALSE if not */
{
    char    c;

    c = *(textPtr + charPos);

    if((c >= '\000') && (c <= ' '))        return 0xff;
    if((c >= ' ') && (c <= '/'))           return 0xff;
    if((c >= ':') && (c <= '@'))           return 0xff;
    if((c >= '[') && (c <= '`'))           return 0xff;
    if((c >= '{') && (c <= '~'))           return 0xff;

    return 0;
}

void ClikLoop()
{
    char    CClikLoop();
    asm {
    MOVEM.L     D1-D7/A0-A6, -(SP)   ; Save registers to stack
    JSR     CClikLoop                ; Call C routine
    MOVEM.L     (SP)+, D1-D7/A0-A6   ; Restore registers from stack
    MOVEQ.L  #1,D0                   ; keep ClikLoop enabled
    RTS

    }
}
```

```
char    CClikLoop()
{
    Rect    *viewR, *destR;
    Point   mousePt;
    short   viewWidth, lineHeight, destBottom;
    TEPtr   theTEPtr;

    HLock(theText);
    theTEPtr = *theText;

    viewR = &theTEPtr->viewRect;
    destR = &theTEPtr->destRect;
    lineHeight = theTEPtr->lineHeight;
    viewWidth = viewR->right - viewR->left;

    GetMouse(&mousePt);
    if(!PtInRect(mousePt, viewR)) {

        if(mousePt.v > viewR->bottom) {
          destBottom = destR->top + (theTEPtr->nLines)*lineHeight;
          if(viewR->bottom < destBottom) TEScroll(0, -lineHeight, theText);
        } else if((mousePt.h < viewR->left) && (viewR->left > destR->left)) {
          TEScroll(viewWidth/5, 0, theText);
        } else if((mousePt.h > viewR->right) && (viewR->right < destR->right)) {
          TEScroll(-viewWidth/5, 0, theText);
        } else if((mousePt.v < viewR->top) && (viewR->top > destR->top)) {
          TEScroll(0, lineHeight, theText);
        }

    }
    HUnlock(theText);
}


ScrollInsertPt(hTE)
    TEHandle    hTE;
{
    TEPtr     pTE;
    short     position, line, nLines, linePos, lineHeight, viewTop, viewBot;
    HLock(hTE);
    pTE = *hTE;

    nLines = pTE->nLines;
    position = pTE->selEnd;
    viewTop = (pTE->viewRect).top;
    viewBot = (pTE->viewRect).bottom;
    lineHeight = pTE->lineHeight;

    line = 1;
    while((position > pTE->lineStarts[line]) && (line <= nLines)) line += 1;
```

```
    linePos = (pTE->destRect).top + pTE->lineHeight * (line+1);

    if(linePos < viewTop) {

       do {
         TEScroll(0, lineHeight, hTE);
        linePos += lineHeight;
       } while(linePos < viewTop);

    } else if(linePos > viewBot) {

         do {
          TEScroll(0, -lineHeight, hTE);
        linePos -= lineHeight;
         } while(linePos > viewBot);

    }

    HUnlock(hTE);
}


short    GetScrapCount()
{
    return *((short *) 0x0968);
}

SetLineHeight(spacing, hTE)                    /* SetLineHeight() */

    short     spacing;       /* line spacing */
    TEHandle  hTE;           /* the edit record */

    /* this routine changes the lineHeight and fontAscent of
       the edit record hTE to reflect its font and size. The
       line spacing can be either single 1 1/2 or double     */

{

    GrafPtr    theCurrentPort;
    FontInfo   fontStuff;
    short      extra;

    /* set current port to window containing hTE */

    GetPort(&theCurrentPort);
    SetPort((*hTE)->inPort);
    /* set font and size of grafPort to same as hTE */
    TextFont((*hTE)->txFont);
    TextSize((*hTE)->txSize);
    /* get font information */
```

```
    GetFontInfo(&fontStuff);
    /* set up for single space */
    (*hTE)->fontAscent = fontStuff.ascent;
    (*hTE)->lineHeight = fontStuff.ascent + fontStuff.descent +
                         fontStuff.leading;
    /* modify for other spacings */
    if(spacing == singleSp) return;
    else if(spacing == oneandhalfSp) extra = (*hTE)->lineHeight/2;
    else if(spacing == doubleSp) extra = (*hTE)->lineHeight;
    (*hTE)->lineHeight += extra;
    (*hTE)->fontAscent += extra;
    return;
}


ZoomRect(beginR, endR)
    Rect    *beginR, *endR;
{
    #define    Nsteps    8
    Rect       tempRect[Nsteps];
    short      nn1, i;
    Fixed      fnn1, fdLeft, fdRight, fdTop, fdBottom;
    Fixed      fsLeft, fsRight, fsTop, fsBottom;
    GrafPtr    savePort,deskPort;
    RgnHandle  deskClipRgn;

    deskClipRgn = (RgnHandle) NewHandle(sizeof(Region));

    GetPort(&savePort);
    GetWMgrPort(&deskPort);
    SetPort(deskPort);
    GetClip(deskClipRgn);
    SetClip(grayRgn);

    PenPat(&gray);
    PenMode(patXor);

    nn1 = (Nsteps-1)*Nsteps;

    beginR->top -= 20;  /* correct for standard window title */
    endR->top   -= 20;

    fsLeft   = FixRatio(beginR->left,   1);
    fsRight  = FixRatio(beginR->right,  1);
    fsTop    = FixRatio(beginR->top,    1);
    fsBottom = FixRatio(beginR->bottom, 1);

    fdLeft   = FixRatio(2*(endR->left   - beginR->left),   nn1);
    fdRight  = FixRatio(2*(endR->right  - beginR->right),  nn1);
    fdTop    = FixRatio(2*(endR->top    - beginR->top),    nn1);
    fdBottom = FixRatio(2*(endR->bottom - beginR->bottom), nn1);
```

```
    for(i=1;i<Nsteps;i++) {
        fnn1 = FixRatio(i*(i+1), 1);
        tempRect[i-1].left   = FixRound(fsLeft   + FixMul(fnn1, fdLeft));
        tempRect[i-1].right  = FixRound(fsRight  + FixMul(fnn1, fdRight));
        tempRect[i-1].top    = FixRound(fsTop    + FixMul(fnn1, fdTop));
        tempRect[i-1].bottom = FixRound(fsBottom + FixMul(fnn1, fdBottom));
    }

    FrameRect(beginR);                  /* draw start rectangle */
    FrameRect(&tempRect[0]);            /* draw first rectangle */
    FrameRect(&tempRect[1]);            /* draw second rectangle */

    FrameRect(beginR);                  /* erase start rectangle */

    for(i=2;i<Nsteps-1;i++) {
        FrameRect(&tempRect[i]);        /* draw next rectangle */
        FrameRect(&tempRect[i-2]);      /* erase rectangle two steps back */
    }

    FrameRect(endR);                    /* draw final rectangle */

    FrameRect(&tempRect[Nsteps-3]);     /* erase next to last rectangle */
    FrameRect(&tempRect[Nsteps-2]);     /* erase last rectangle */
    FrameRect(endR);                    /* erase final rectangle */

        beginR->top += 20;  /* correct for standard window title */
        endR->top   += 20;

        SetClip(deskClipRgn);
        DisposHandle(deskClipRgn);
        SetPort(savePort);
}


char   IsValidWindow(tempWindow)
   WindowPtr        tempWindow;
   /* determines if tempWindow is a valid window
      by searching through the window list */
{

   WindowPeek       aWindow, testWindow;

   /* define windowList to be the WindowPeek in system global
      - at location 0x09D6 */
   #define   windowList   *((WindowPeek *)0x09D6)

        /* cast tempWindow to WindowPeek */

        testWindow = (WindowPeek) tempWindow;

   /* start at beginning of list */
```

```
    aWindow = windowList;

    /* if we are not at end of list
        - is this tempWindow ?
        - if not then skip to the next window in list */

    while( aWindow != NULL ) {
        if( aWindow == testWindow)   return 0xff;
        else aWindow = aWindow->nextWindow;
    }
    return 0;  /* can't find tempWindow */
}
```

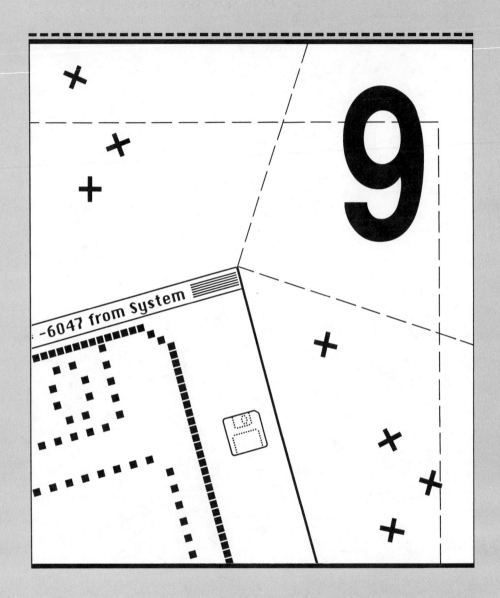

-6047 from System

Resources

Now that we have covered the fundamentals for creating an application, it's a good time to take a look at one of the most powerful features of the Macintosh: the concept of resources. Resources allow the programmer to break an application down into logical segments, so that menus, windows, icons, cursors, pictures, fonts, alert boxes, or any other element of an application can be stored in its own module. This makes it easy to create and modify our applications as they grow increasingly complex. Although resources are used primarily to store data elements, several resource types contain actual code. Window and menu definition procedures, desk accessories, and the code of the application are all contained in resources.

Why would an application want to use resources in the first place? The main reason is flexibility. Because the user interface can be altered independently of an application's code, the programmer can change the cosmetic elements of an application without having to recompile the entire program. This means that the more complex elements of the Macintosh's graphics-oriented interface (icons, cursors, and background patterns) can be easily readjusted.

Organization of Resources

Every Macintosh file is divided into two distinct parts or "forks": the *resource fork* and the *data fork*. The primary distinction between these two forks is the way in which they are accessed. The Resource Manager is responsible for information in the resource fork, whereas information in the data fork is manipulated via the File

Manager. A MacWrite file provides a nice example of the breakdown between resources and data. Creation date, the status of windows and rulers, and a lot of other miscellaneous information is stored in the resource fork, while the actual text of the document is stored in the data fork (see Figure 9.1).

For identification, all resources have associated with them a type, an ID number, and an optional name. A resource type consists of a unique four character string. The system requires that the resource type be exactly four characters long (spaces count as characters) and makes a distinction between uppercase and lowercase letters. By default, the system recognizes a number of reserved resource types and the programmer is free to define his or her own resource types as well (we'll explain shortly why you might want to do that). A list of the reserved resource types is given in Appendix B.

Within each resource fork, more commonly known as a *resource file*, resources are grouped according to their types. For example, all resources of the type 'FONT' would be grouped together. To distinguish among resources of the same type, every resource within a type is identified by its resource ID, a unique integer. The ID must be unique within each resource type, but resources of different types can have the same ID, as we have touched on previously. So, two resources of type 'ICON' cannot both have the ID 2; however, an 'ICON' resource and a 'PICT' resource could share the same ID.

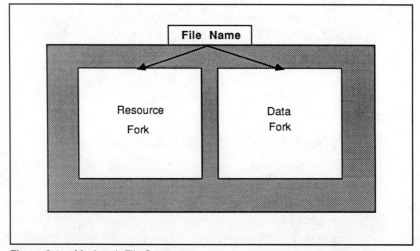

Figure 9.1: Macintosh File Structure

By convention, negative resource IDs and IDs less than 127 are reserved for use by the system. The rest are free to be used in whatever way you wish. If you are working on certain standard system resources, you may be restricted further in the use of ID numbers.

A resource can also have an optional *resource name*. Like the resource ID, the name must be unique within a particular resource type. The types of resources for which names are really useful are those that could potentially appear in menus—specifically fonts and desk accessories. Other types of resources generally don't have names except where names would be a useful reference tool for the programmer.

As far as our treatment of resources goes, it isn't essential to know the exact format of a resource file. However, having a general idea of its format helps in understanding the intricacies of the Resource Manager. Figure 9.2 shows the overall structure of a resource file.

Every resource file begins with a *resource header*, which gives the offsets to and lengths of the *resource data* and *resource map* parts of the file. The directory copy contains information about the file for use by the Finder, and the application data can be used for anything you want.

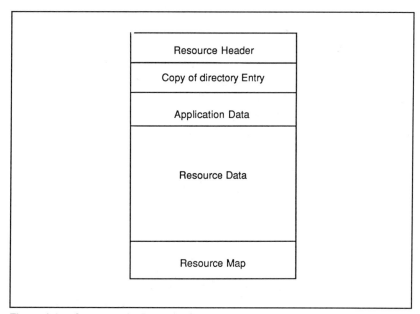

Figure 9.2:   Structure of a Resource File

Next comes the resource data. This is where the meat of the resources is stored: icon bitmaps, procedure definitions for menus, windows, controls, menu item information, and whatever other data elements you want to store.

Finally, the resource map contains the offsets for the resource data. It contains such information as how many resources are stored in the file and what kind of resources they are, as well as information about particular resources, such as length and ID number.

The Role of the Resource Manager

Unlike the other Toolbox managers we have seen so far, the Resource Manager exists primarily for use by other parts of the Toolbox. It's important to realize that the Resource Manager doesn't understand anything about the contents of resource files; it's only responsible for their housekeeping. Actually making use of the information in resource files is up to the particular section of the Toolbox that makes the call. When the Menu Manager processes a **GetMenu** call, for example, it in turn makes calls to Resource Manager routines that access the appropriate information in the resource file.

By default, the Resource Manager searches files for resources in the reverse order to that in which they were opened. For every application, two important resource files are opened automatically by the system. When the computer is first turned on, the system opens the system resource file as part of the initialization of the Resource Manager. The application's resource file is opened when the application starts up. Using the example of a **GetMenu** call again, when the Resource Manager searches for a 'MENU' type resource with the given ID, it will first search the application's resource file. If it doesn't find what it is looking for, it will move on and search the system resource file. (The Resource Manager also allows you to change the search order to begin at any resource file you choose, not just the most recently opened.)

Note that when the Resource Manager searches a resource file, it doesn't search the actual file itself. Rather it searches the resource map that was read into memory when the file was opened. Figure 9.3 shows the order the Resource Manager follows when searching for a particular resource in a file.

As a programmer you can take advantage of the default search sequence whenever you want to modify one of the shared system resources. Say, for example, that you are working in a text editor, writing code for your new program using the Monaco font. The problem is that you keep getting your zeros mixed up with the letter O. One solution would be to put a slash through the zeros, except that, for whatever reason, you don't want the zeros slashed in all the other applications that use the Monaco font. Now that you know the system's search order for resources, however, making the change only in your text editor is easy. You simply make a copy of the Monaco resource from the system resource file with ResEdit, modify it, and paste it into the resource file of your text editor. Then whenever the text editor needs a Monaco font, it will first check its own resource file. Finding your modified font there, it will be satisfied and search no further, using that font for your code.

What else does the Resource Manager do? As mentioned earlier, it is mostly occupied with the housekeeping required by the other sections of the Toolbox that access resources. For advanced applications that create new resource types and modify their contents, the Resource Manager's functions are directly accessible. An application can create,

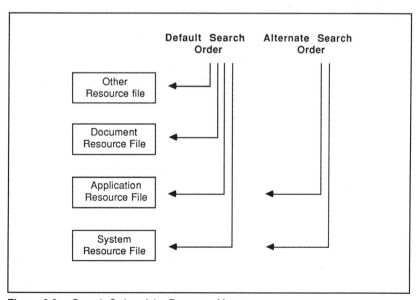

Figure 9.3: Search Order of the Resource Manager

open, and close resource files at its discretion, as well as modify anything about a particular resource other than its type. However, the direct control of resources is a bit beyond the scope of this discussion.

A Look at the System Resource File

The resource file most familiar to Macintosh users is the *system resource file*. The system resource file stores all the standard resources shared by the Finder and all other applications. Studying this file will give us a good feel for what kinds of things can be stored in resource files.

First and foremost, the system resource file serves as the foundation for all the graphics used in the Macintosh's user interface. The resources here can be shared by any application running under a given system file. We can divide the standard resources, as we can all resources, into two general classifications: those that act as a storage space for information and those that direct the computer to carry out a task; in other words, passive and active resources. Passive resources in the system file are of types containing icons, alerts, pictures, dialogs, patterns, fonts and the like.

More crucial to the user interface are the resources of the second type, those that actually carry out a task. If you recall our discussion of menus and windows, you'll remember that the Toolbox allowed us the option of designing our own custom versions of these interface features. Each was defined by something called a "definition procedure" which was pointed to in the feature's data structure by a handle (definition procedures are also used with controls, as we'll see in the next chapter). If we back up a step, it's clear that the system needs to have a definition procedure for the standard features as well. The standard menu and the six predefined windows, as well as the standard button and scroll controls, are all defined in the system resource file. They are identified by the resource types 'MDEF', 'WDEF', and 'CDEF' respectively. These definition procedures are stored as resource data and define not only the appearance of the particular feature but the way it functions as well.

Also in the category of active resources are resources of the type 'DRVR'. In general, these device driver resources handle all the communications between the Macintosh and its external devices (disk drives, hard disks, printers, and so on). The driver for the Imagewriter printer is a good example. Hard disk drives that hook up to the Macintosh's serial port also install their drivers in the system resource file. By far the most popular of the 'DRVR' resources, however, are the desk accessories. Desk accessories are small stand-alone applications that can be run from within other applications and are capable of doing nearly anything an application can do. There are a number of desk accessories provided with the Macintosh system software, and countless thousands of them now exist in both the commercial markets and the public domain.

Another very popular resource type is 'FONT' which defines text fonts. As you know, the Macintosh is capable of displaying many different fonts on the screen at the same time. When fonts are installed into the system, either by Apple's Font/DA Mover or some other utility, they are installed into the system resource file. That's why the system file on a disk seems to grow exponentially whenever you start adding fonts to it.

The system resource file also contains a class of active resources that are essentially extensions to the Toolbox ROM. 'PACK' or *package resources* contain additional functions and data structures for relatively specialized purposes. For example, whenever a program opens or closes a file, it calls a function from the *Standard File package*. The Standard File package (SF package, for short) is automatically read into memory whenever one of its functions is called. It puts up the appropriate dialog box for either opening or closing a file and handles all events until a file is selected and acted upon.

If the user ejects a disk while in the SF package's dialog box and inserts another disk, the SF package will call another 'PACK' resource, the *Disk Initialization package*. This package will inspect the inserted disk and determine if it is an initialized Macintosh diskette. If not, it will put up a dialog box asking the user if the inserted disk is to be initialized or ejected and will carry out the function selected. Both the SF package and Disk Initialization package dialog boxes are probably very familiar to Macintosh users. Nearly every application on the market uses them or a variation of them.

The other packages in the system resource file include one that does binary-to-decimal number conversion, a package for doing floating point arithmetic, and a package to perform transcendental functions (trigonometry, logarithms, and so on).

Using Resources

Since the Resource Manager knows only how to access and manipulate resource files and isn't capable of doing anything with the resource data, how can we make use of resources in our own applications? The answer is that the sections of the Toolbox that we have already discussed are all capable of using information stored as resource data.

As an example, we have seen that the Window Manager allows us to create new windows in two different ways. In the sample program in Chapter 3, we created our window in code using the function **NewWindow**.

```
WindowPtr NewWindow(wStorage, boundsRect, title, visible,
                    procID, behind, goAwayFlag, refCon);
```

You'll recall the many parameters we needed to pass to this function in order to describe the new window we wanted to put up. If it turned out that we didn't like the way the new window looked (say it was the wrong size or the wrong type), we would have to change the parameters of the function and recompile the code in order to change the window.

We also looked at a similar call which used a resource file window definition, **GetNewWindow**.

```
WindowPtr GetNewWindow(windowID, wStorage, behind);
```

The behind and wStorage parameters are the same as in **NewWindow**. The Window ID is the ID of a resource of the type 'WIND' which needs to be in a currently open resource file. It is from this resource that **GetNewWindow** will get information about the new window. The 'WIND' or *window template resources* contain the parameters in **NewWindow** that are missing from **GetNewWindow**. ("Template" means that this resource stores a list of information used to build a Toolbox object.) The bounds-

Rect, procID, visibleFlag, goAwayFlag, refCon, and title data are all stored here in the format shown in Figure 9.4.

We will look at a slightly more formalized way to define these parameters later in this chapter when we deal with RMaker.

GetNewWindow creates a window record for the new window using the information from a resource file and returns a pointer to the window record. The rest of your application cannot tell the difference between **GetNewWindow** and **NewWindow**. The real difference is to the programmer, who now has the flexibility to change the appearance of the new window without having to recompile code or worry too much about disturbing the functionality of the application.

Another example can be found in the Menu Manager. The procedure **GetMenu** works similarly to **GetNewWindow**. Given a resource ID, **GetMenu** searches for the appropriate 'MENU' resource and reads the information required to create a new menu record. Like 'WIND', 'MENU' is a template resource type and contains all the information necessary to fill a menu record, as well as the specifications for each menu item. As we saw in chapter 4, defining a menu in a resource file actually saves us a step in code by replacing both the **NewMenu** and **AppendMenu** functions. The menu template data is stored as shown in Figure 9.5.

Again the flexibility provided by the resource file is clear: all of the menu's characteristics normally specified in code by **New-Menu/AppendMenu** are stored in a resource file where it is easy to change, should the need arise.

The Menu Manager can also store the menu bar as a resource of type 'MBAR'. It simply contains the number of menus in the menu bar and the resource ID of each menu and can be called up by the function **GetNewMBar**.

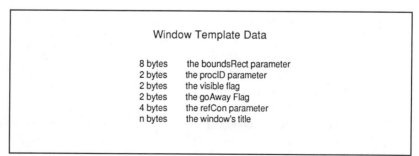

Figure 9.4:   Format of Window Template Data

```
2 bytes          Menu ID
2 bytes          Place holder for menu width
2 bytes          Place holder for menu height
4 bytes          Resource ID of menu defProc
4 bytes          enableFlags field of menu record
1 byte           length of title
n bytes          menu title

For each menu item:
1 byte           byte count for following text
m bytes          text of menu item
1 byte           icon number, or 0 if no icon
1 byte           keyboard equivalent, or 0 if none
1 byte           marking character, or zero if none
1 byte           character style of item's text
1 byte           0, indicating the end of menu items
```

Figure 9.5: Format of Menu Template Data

The convenience of resources really becomes apparent when dealing with the graphic elements of the user interface. Icons, pictures, patterns, cursors, etc. are all bit-mapped entities. Creating these items in code would take a very long time and would probably be very discouraging to new programmers, not to mention very tedious to advanced hackers. What resources allow you to do is create these objects in a resource file and simply read them into memory whenever you need to use them in your program. We'll see in the next section that creating an icon or cursor can be as easy as working in MacPaint.

Creating Resources

In order for resources to truly be a timesaver, there should be a simple way to specify the various data for the different resource types. This could be done by the Resource Manager from within the program, but that would defeat most of the purpose of resources in the first place. Remember, we want to modularize things as much as possible. Fortunately, there are several programs available that make possible the quick and easy creation and modification of resources. With one of these utilities, creating a 'WIND' resource can be as simple as filling in a couple of dialog boxes or typing a couple of lines of text.

The simplest of these is the program Resource Editor, or *Res-Edit*, which allows you to create and modify actual resource files. A more advanced tool, *RMaker* is a compiler which creates resource files from text definitions, much as your C compiler creates executable applications from text source files. Both of these programs are included with Think C in the Utilities 2 folder, although because they are not actually part of Think C itself, they don't integrate easily into its environment. Using RMaker will seem a bit clumsy after you've gotten used to the ease of writing C code in Think C.

In theory, either ResEdit or RMaker can be used to create resources. Once you understand the process of creating resources, you will be able to choose the one that best suits your application. As ResEdit is the simpler of the two to use, we'll begin with it.

In ResEdit, the window template resource appears as shown in Figure 9.6. Since we are familiar with what is required by the Window Manager to create a new window, it is a simple matter to fill in the dialog box shown in the figure. This is the case for all resources. If you are familiar with the resource type you are trying to create or modify, using the Resource Editor, or any other resource utility program, is a very simple matter.

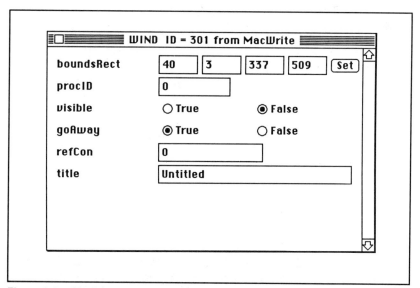

Figure 9.6:   ResEdit Window for Creating a Window Template

Creating bit-mapped resources is where resource utilities really become timesavers. Suppose we wanted to create a new icon for our application to use. Using the Resource Editor, we'd be presented with the dialog box shown in Figure 9.7.

As you can see from the figure, the dialog box looks very much like the fat bits mode in MacPaint and it works the same way. After you create the icon, you'll need to give it a resource ID number. We then close up the file.

It might not be obvious how a resource file on your disk gets to become part of your application. Each development system has its own way of allowing for the compilation of applications which include resource files. Under Think C, if you have a program whose main C language file is called Program.C, the compiler will automatically merge in a resource file called Program.Rsrc. Thus, having your resources included in your program is merely a question of naming the file correctly.

There's a catch to this. Under development systems which force you to explicitly name the resource files you want to include in your application, the compiler will complain if a resource file you've specified doesn't exist. Think C will merely assume that you hadn't intended to have a resource file to begin with, and will create an application which lacks the resources it needs to run properly. As such, it's a good idea not to assume

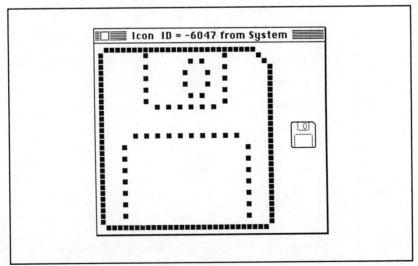

Figure 9.7:   ResEdit Window for Creating an Icon

that all the resources you call for will be there. For example, if you call **GetMenu** to read the resource definition of a menu from your resource file, it's a good idea to check that the handle it returns doesn't point to NULL, which would be the case if the resource wasn't available.

RMaker

We've touched on the syntax for RMaker—short for Resource Maker—in previous chapters. In general, RMaker is preferable if you foresee your application making extensive use of resources. In addition, because it starts with a source code file, you can print out an RMaker resource definition and look at it as hard copy, just as you can a C language source file.

By default, RMaker works with source files having names that end in .R, and you will usually instruct it to create resource files which end in .Rsrc, all ready for Think C to compile into applications. Thus, if your C language source file was Program.C, your RMaker source file would be Program.R.

Figure 9.8 shows a complete RMaker file for the same window definition as ResEdit was creating in Figure 9.6.

To compile this, you would use the Transfer function from the File menu of Think C to transfer to RMaker. RMaker starts with a file

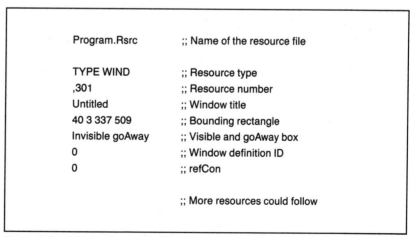

Program.Rsrc	;; Name of the resource file
TYPE WIND	;; Resource type
,301	;; Resource number
Untitled	;; Window title
40 3 337 509	;; Bounding rectangle
Invisible goAway	;; Visible and goAway box
0	;; Window definition ID
0	;; refCon
	;; More resources could follow

Figure 9.8:   RMaker Source for Window

dialog box, and conveniently only shows you file names with the .R ending. Select Program.R. Assuming that there are no syntax errors in your source file, RMaker will compile it and allow you to transfer back to Think C using the "Other" item in the Transfer menu. Program.Rsrc will now exist on your disk for Think C to find.

If you are running under the Multifinder, Think.C will still be loaded. To transfer back select Quit from the File menu, then Think C from the Apple menu.

RMaker recognizes the templates for twelve resource types. These are shown in Figure 9.9.

Complex resource files will have many other resource types as well. RMaker allows you to define your own resource types by building them from these basic types.

There are some things which are not convenient to create in R-Maker. Icons, for example, are much more easily done using ResEdit, as are small custom fonts, and, as we will see in Chapter 11, pictures can be created with MacPaint and included in resource files, such that they become part of your finished application. For this reason, it's often the case that the resource file which RMaker finally writes to your disk is an aggregate of the resources you actually wrote into the initial source file plus several other resource files.

For example, let's say that we used ResEdit to create an icon—for some as yet unspecified purpose—and saved it in a resource file

```
'ALRT' - Alert
'BNDL' - Bundle
'CNTL' - Control
'DITL' - Dialog or alert item list
'DLOG' - Dialog
'FREF' - File reference
'GNRL' - General
'MENU' - Menu
'PROC' - Procedure, that is, code
'STR ' - String
'STR#' - String list
'WIND' - Window
```

Figure 9.9: Recognized Basic Resource Types for RMaker

called ProgramIcon.Rsrc. You can see how this would be done if you glance back at Figure 9.7. This could be made part of Program.Rsrc by adding the following line to Program.R before transferring to RMaker and compiling it.

```
INCLUDE ProgramIcon.Rsrc
```

You can include as many of these little resources as you like, so your final resource file can contain fonts, pictures, code, icons and so on, as well as the windows and menus and such which are easy to do in RMaker.

Resource Power

While having to repeatedly jump from Think C to ResEdit or RMaker and back again may seem tedious at first, becoming proficient at using resources is very important to becoming a fluent Macintosh programmer. Once you understand what you can do with these powerful tools, a number of the things which seem mysterious in commercial applications—the ones that make you wonder how on earth the programmer accomplished that—will start to make sense.

Along these same lines, ResEdit can be a very useful tool to see how other applications use their resources. Take any application which you think is clever and open its resource fork with ResEdit. You can prowl through its workings and, very often, pick up some interesting tricks to apply to your own programs.

Up Region

Thumb

Page Down Region

Down Arrow

10

Controls

Using what we've learned in the previous nine chapters, we could now write a simple word processing program. To make such a program fully functional, we would, however, need to add a few things. The program should contain scroll bars for our text windows, enabling the user to move to different portions of a document. It should also contain alerts, to inform the user of any errors he or she may be making; dialogs, which enable the user to adjust various settings; and finally, disk I/O capabilities so that we can save files to disk. All of these topics are covered in the next three chapters. This chapter deals with controls. We will learn about the various types of controls, what they are used for, and how to use the various Control Manager routines in order to implement controls in our applications.

Controls are another distinctive part of the Macintosh user interface. Just as there were several types of windows, each with a different use, there are a number of different types of controls. The predefined controls, which are pictured in Figure 10.1, consist of buttons, check boxes, radio buttons, and scroll bars.

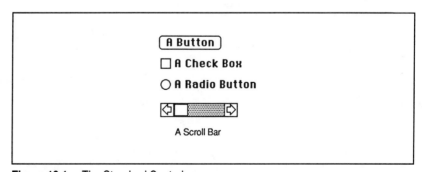

Figure 10.1: The Standard Controls

It is important to note here that although we can put any type of control in a window, it is customary for controls to appear only in alert or dialog boxes. The one exception is scroll bars, which are used with windows to move text or pictures around the content area. We will learn how to implement alerts and dialogs in the next chapter. It is important, however, to read this chapter, in order to learn how controls and the various Control Manager routines work. To effectively use the Dialog Manager, you will need a thorough understanding of controls and the Control Manager routines.

Buttons

Buttons are used to cause an immediate action when the user presses them with the mouse. They are drawn as a rounded-corner rectangle with a title centered inside. The button's title usually indicates the action that will occur when it is pressed. Common button titles are Start, Stop, Resume, Pause, Restart, OK, Cancel, Open, Close, and so on. Buttons may be any size, but it is advisable to make them at least as tall and wide as their title string. Twenty pixels high is sufficient for the tallest character of the system font, and we can find the title's width with the QuickDraw function **StringWidth**. Figure 10.2 shows some sample buttons.

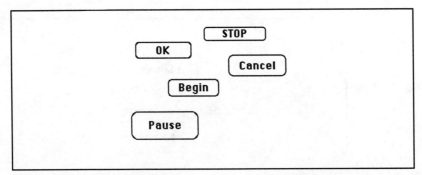

Figure 10.2:   Some Sample Buttons

Check Boxes

Check boxes are used to display the on or off status of a setting. A check box is drawn as a small square box with a title to its right. The title indicates the setting that the user turns on or off by clicking the mouse in the square box. Check boxes do not cause an immediate action; instead they are used to set or unset attributes of a future action. Figure 10.3 shows some sample check boxes for text attributes.

Radio Buttons

Radio buttons are also used to display settings. A radio button is drawn as a small circle with a title to its right. As was the case with check boxes, the radio button's title indicates an attribute that is either on or off. Radio buttons are used instead of check boxes when we have a group of attributes in which only one may be "on" at a time. Between each radio button title we should think of an invisible "or", as in Figure 10.4, where sample radio buttons offer a choice of 300 or 1200 or

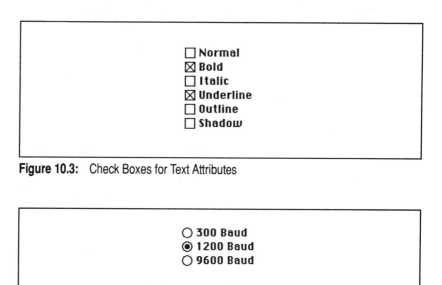

Figure 10.3:   Check Boxes for Text Attributes

Figure 10.4:   Baud Rate Radio Buttons

9600 baud. Only one of the baud rates may be on at any one time, so that clicking in one button causes the others to be turned off.

A radio button is on if it is filled with a small black circle. In Figure 10.4, 1200 baud is on, while 300 and 9600 baud are off. This characteristic—that only one radio button in a group may be on at any one time—is a property of the Macintosh user interface, not of the Control Manager. It is up to the programmer to make sure that when one radio button is selected, all of the others are turned off. Therefore, when the application detects that the user has clicked a button, the application has to turn the other buttons off.

Scroll Bars

The last type of predefined control is the *scroll bar*. Some sample scroll bars are shown in Figure 10.5.

Scroll bars are usually used to move text or pictures around in windows. A window can have both vertical and horizontal scroll bars, but some applications will only use one. As a general rule, if the contents of a window are too tall to be viewed all at one time, the application should provide the user with a vertical scroll bar to scroll through the window's contents. Similarly, if a window's contents are too wide to be viewed, a horizontal scroll bar should be implemented.

Clicking the mouse in the *up* or *down arrows* moves the text one line up or down. Clicking in the *page-up* or *page-down* regions

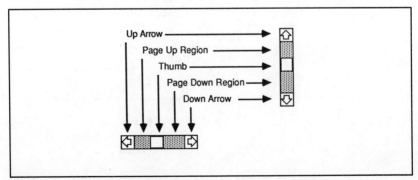

Figure 10.5: Sample Scroll Bars

similarly moves a windowful of text or graphics up or down. (In horizontal scroll bars the up and down arrows and page-up and page-down regions can, of course, be called the left and right arrow and page-left and page-right regions.) When a document is scrolled using the arrows or paging regions, the *thumb*, which indicates the scroll bar's value, follows the document's movement, always displaying the relative position in the file. For example, if page 5 of a 10-page document were displayed in a window—that is, if the middle of a document were displayed—the thumb of the window's scroll bar would likewise be in the middle of the scroll bar. It is also possible for the user to drag the thumb to any position in the scroll bar, causing the application to scroll to the corresponding position in a file.

In addition to scrolling text and pictures, scroll bars can be used as a type of dial, with the thumb always indicating a value relative to its end points. Figure 10.6, which shows how all the standard controls can be combined in a real-life context, includes an example of a scroll bar used as a dial. The value of the thumb may be displayed digitally as well.

Highlighted, Active, and Inactive Controls

While retaining their standard shapes and sizes, controls may have other aspects of their appearance changed by an application when

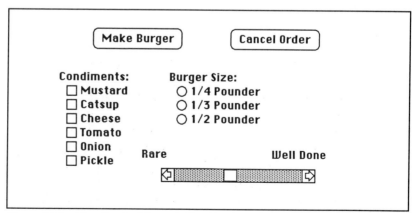

Figure 10.6: The Standard Controls Combined in a Fast-Food Application

they are selected by the user or when their use becomes inappropriate or unavailable. Let's take a look at the conventions for some of these changes in appearance.

Highlighted Controls

When the user clicks the mouse in a control, the control is highlighted. A highlighted control changes its appearance in some manner to indicate that it has been selected with the mouse. Figure 10.7 shows the standard controls in both their normal and highlighted states. The controls in this example follow the "User Interface Guidelines" in displaying highlighted buttons with inverted print (white letters on a dark ground), while the highlighting of check boxes and radio buttons is indicated by a heavier outline around the box or button. Scroll bars are highlighted according to where in the control the user clicks the mouse.

There are also two additional types of highlighting called *254* and *255 highlighting*. Let's take a look at them now.

Active and Inactive Controls

In addition to being either normal or highlighted, controls are also *active* or *inactive*. Active controls are drawn like the normal

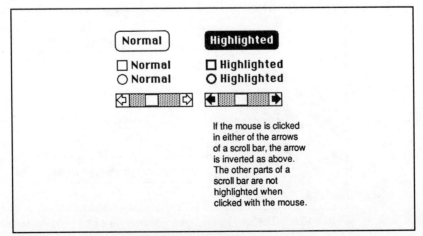

Figure 10.7: Normal and Highlighted Controls

controls in Figure 10.7. They respond to mouse events; that is, they become highlighted when they are clicked. Inactive controls are drawn differently than normal controls. For inactive controls, the titles of buttons, check boxes, and radio buttons are drawn dimmed, in gray instead of black. For inactive scroll bars, the thumb and page regions are not drawn. Figure 10.8 shows the standard controls, in both their active and inactive states.

An application should make a control inactive whenever the operation it performs or controls is inappropriate or unavailable. Consider the following example. Our application puts up a window with three buttons entitled Start, Pause, and Stop (see Figure 10.9). When the control window is initially displayed on the screen, the Start button should be active, with the Pause and Stop buttons displayed as inactive. The Pause and Stop buttons should be inactive because the user can't pause or stop an action that hasn't been started yet. After the user clicks the Start button, thereby starting an operation, the operation can be brought to a pause or stopped. The application should therefore make

Figure 10.8:   Active and Inactive Controls

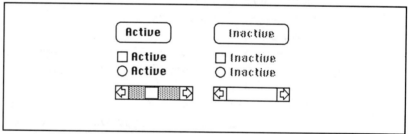

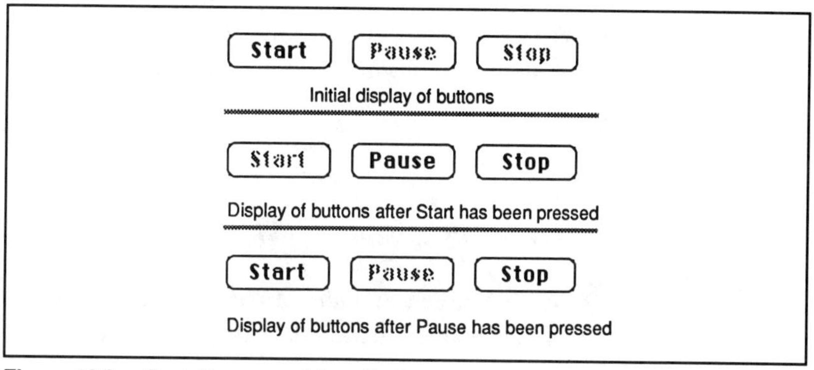

Figure 10.9:   Start, Pause, and Stop Buttons

the Start button inactive and both the Pause and Stop buttons active at this point. Similarly, when the Pause button is pressed, the application should make it inactive, but now starting and stopping is appropriate again, so that the Start and Stop buttons should be made active. The guideline to remember is that as soon as an operation is not possible or becomes inappropriate, the application should make the corresponding control inactive.

Part Codes

Three of the standard controls consist of only one part, while the fourth consists of several parts. Buttons, check boxes, and radio buttons each consist of only one part that encompasses the entire control. In contrast, a scroll bar consists of five parts: the up arrow, down arrow, page-up region, page-down region, and thumb (see Figure 10.5 for an example). Each control part has a corresponding part code that is used by various Control Manager routines.

For example, when an application detects a mouse-down event in a single-part control, knowing which control is pressed is generally enough information for the application to respond accurately. Since single-part controls have only a single action, an application knows exactly what to do when one is pressed. For multiple-part controls, however, the application must also know which part of the control was pressed. In responding to a mouse-down in a scroll bar, for example, the application will need to know whether the mouse was pressed in the up arrow, down arrow, page-up region, page-down region, thumb, or the horizontal equivalents to these in order to respond correctly. The part codes for the standard controls are given in Figure 10.10.

The Control Record Data Structure

As we have seen in many of the previous chapters, each Toolbox Manager has its own internal data structures with which to store its

```
inButton          = 10       [ in a button]
inCheckBox        = 11       [ in a check box or radio button ]
inUpButton        = 20       [ in the up arrow of a scroll bar ]
inDownButton      = 21       [ in the down arrow of a scroll bar ]
inPageUp          = 22       [ in the page-up region of a scroll bar ]
inPageDown        = 23       [ in the page-down region of a scroll bar ]
inThumb           = 129      [ in the thumb of a scroll bar ]
```

Figure 10.10:   Part Codes for Standard Controls

objects. The Control Manager is no different in this respect. Just as events are stored in EventRecords and windows are stored in Window-Records, controls are stored in ControlRecords. The box entitled "Control Manager Data Structures" contains the definition of a ControlRecord as well as the associated types ControlPtr and ControlHandle. These definitions will be found in the header files of Think C.

```
Control Manager Data Structures
struct CR {
        Handle          nextControl;
        WindowPtr       contrlOwner;
        Rect            contrlRect;
        char            contrlVis;
        char            contrlHilite;
        int             contrlValue;
        int             contrlMin;
        int             contrlMax;
        Handle          contrlDefProc;
        Handle          contrlData;
        int             (*contrlAction)();
        long            contrlRfCon;
        Str255          contrlTitle;
        };

#define ControlRecord struct CR

typedef         ControlRecord   *ControlPtr;
typedef         ControlPtr      *ControlHandle;
```

Most of the fields of a ControlRecord are rarely accessed directly by an application; instead the fields are set or changed using Control Manager routines or by the other managers themselves.

The contrlRfCon field of a ControlRecord is very similar to the refCon field of a WindowRecord. An application can store any 32-bit value, typically a pointer or a handle to a related data structure, in the contrlRfCon field of a ControlRecord.

Control Manager Routines

Before calling any of the Control Manager routines, an application must first initialize QuickDraw, the Font Manager, and the Window Manager by calling **InitGraf**, **InitFonts**, and **InitWindows**. An application uses the Control Manager to create its controls and then usually calls the routines **FindControl** and **TrackControl** inside its main event loop to determine if a control has been pressed by the user, and if so, which one has been pressed. When the application determines which control was pressed, it can respond appropriately to the user's actions. The application can also use Control Manager routines to change a control's value, title, or highlighting state.

Defining and Disposing of Controls

There are two routines for defining controls and two routines for disposing of them. The two routines for defining controls, **NewControl** and **GetNewControl**, accomplish exactly the same thing. The difference between the two routines is that **NewControl** takes the control's definition as its arguments while **GetNewControl** takes the control's definition from a resource file.

The NewControl Function

The function **NewControl** creates a control, adds it to theWindow's control list, and returns a handle to the control.

```
ControlHandle NewControl(theWindow, boundsRect, title, visible,
                         value, min, max, procID, refCon)
WindowPtr        theWindow;
```

```
Rect            *boundsRect;
Str255          *title;
char            visible;
int             value,min,max,procID;
long            refCon;
```

The window pointer named theWindow indicates which window the control will belong to. The boundsRect parameter determines the size and location of the control. The boundsRect has to be given in the Windows local coordinate system. As we explained earlier, buttons should be at least 20 pixels high, while check boxes and radio buttons should be made at least 16 pixels high. These heights insure that the control's title isn't truncated on the top or bottom. Scroll bars are typically 16 pixels wide and look best if drawn that size.

Next, the title parameter is the control's title. A control's title should be short but to the point. The visible parameter indicates whether the control should be drawn or not drawn—that is, visible on the screen. If the parameter is true, the control will be drawn.

The min, max, and value arguments are the control's minimum, maximum, and initial value, respectively. For buttons, which have no values or settings, these parameters are not used. For check boxes and radio buttons, an application should set the minimum value to 0 and the maximum value to 1. If the control's initial value is 1, the control will be checked; if it is 0, it will appear unchecked. For scroll bars, the minimum and maximum values can be any integer; the up-end of a scroll bar is set to the minimum value, and the down-end is set to the maximum.

The thumb of the scroll bar is placed at the position indicated by the value parameter. For example, if for a scroll bar the min, max, and value parameters were 0, 10, and 5 respectively, the thumb would be placed in the middle of the scroll bar.

The procID argument indicates the type of control the application is creating: that is, a button, check box, radio button, or scroll bar. The procID numbers are given in Figure 10.11. In addition to defining a control's type, the procID can affect the appearance of a control's title. A control's title is usually drawn with the system font. To draw a control's title in the same font that is used in the window in which the control appears, we simply add the constant useWFont to the control's procID. If, for example, we wanted the title of a button to be displayed in its window's font, we would pass the procID value (pushButProc + useWFont) to the routine that defines the button as a control.

```
pushButProc   = 0    [ Button ]
checkBoxProc  = 1    [ Check Box ]
radioButProc  = 2    [ Radio Button ]
useWFont      = 8    [ use window's font ]
scrollBarProc = 16   [ Scroll Bar ]
```

Figure 10.11: procIDs for Standard Controls

The refCon is an extra field that is reserved for use by the application. As was stated earlier, an application can store any 32-bit value in the refCon field (typically a pointer or a handle to a related data structure). Using the field or not has no effect on the control.

The function **GetNewControl** works the same way as **NewControl**.

```
ControlHandle GetNewControl(controlID, theWindow)
        int           controlID;
        WindowPtr     theWindow;
```

GetNewControl creates a control just as **NewControl** did, but it gets the information for the boundsRect, title, visible, value, max, min, procID, and refCon from the 'CNTL' resource that has an ID of controllD. The 'CNTL' resource can be created with either ResEdit or RMaker, as previously discussed.

The DisposeControl and KillControls Procedures

The two routines for disposing of controls are very simple and straightforward. The procedure **DisposeControl** is used for disposing of individual controls. The application passes to **DisposeControl** the control handle of the control it wants to get rid of. The procedure **KillControls** disposes of all the controls contained in a specified window. First, the application passes a window pointer to **KillControls**, and then **KillControls** calls **DisposeControl** for each control contained in the window.

```
DisposeControl(theControl)
        ControlHandle   theControl;
KillControls(theWindow)
        WindowPtr       theWindow;
```

Displaying and Determining the Appearance of Controls

There are six routines that affect a control's appearance. In the next few pages, we will examine two routines that deal with a control's title, routines to hide and show controls, a routine to draw a window's controls, and a routine to highlight various parts of a control.

Manipulating a Control's Title

The first two routines, **SetCTitle** and **GetCTitle**, set and get a specified control's title.

```
SetCTitle(theControl, title)
      ControlHandle    theControl;
      Str255           *title;
GetCTitle(theControl, title);
      ControlHandle    theControl;
      Str255           *title;
```

The parameter theControl indicates the control whose title is to be set or gotten. For **SetCTitle**, the title parameter is the new title of the control. When an application calls **SetCTitle**, the control's title is changed and the control is redrawn. When an application calls **GetCTitle**, the title parameter is returned to the application with the specified control's title value in it.

Hiding and Showing Controls

To hide and show controls, there are two routines appropriately named **HideControl** and **ShowControl**. **HideControl** makes the specified control invisible by filling its bounding rectangle in with the background pattern of its window's grafPort.

```
HideControl(theControl)
ControlHandle    theControl;
```

To show a control that we have hidden or that was perhaps created invisible, we would call **ShowControl**.

```
ShowControl(theControl)
        ControlHandle   theControl;
```

ShowControl draws theControl in the control's window.

Updating Controls with the DrawControls **Procedure**

The procedure **DrawControls** is used to draw all the visible controls of a specified window. It is generally used to redraw controls in a window whose content region needs to be updated. For example, every time a window with scroll bars is moved or resized, the location and size of its scroll bars have to be recalculated, and then these controls have to be redrawn. The following routine, MoveScrollBars, was taken from the code example at the end of the chapter. It shows one way in which an application can move, resize, and redraw a window's scroll bars.

```
/* hScrollRect and vScrollRect are Global Variables */
MoveScrollBars(whichWindow)
        WindowPtr       whichWindow;
{
        SetRect(&hScrollRect,  (*whichWindow).portRect.left-1,
                               (*whichWindow).portRect.bottom-15,
                               (*whichWindow).portRect.right-14,
                               (*whichWindow).portRect.bottom+1);
        SetRect(&vScrollRect,  (*whichWindow).portRect.right-15,
                               (*whichWindow).portRect.top-1,
                               (*whichWindow).portRect.right+1,
                               (*whichWindow).portRect.bottom-14);

        HLock(hScroll);
        HLock(vScroll);
        (**hScroll).contrlRect = hScrollRect;
        (**vScroll).contrlRect = vScrollRect;
        HUnlock(hScroll);
        HUnlock(vScroll);

        DrawControls(whichWindow);
        DrawGrowIcon(whichWindow);
}
```

The application passes the window that needs updating to Move-ScrollBars. The two calls to **SetRect** calculate the horizontal and vertical scroll bars' new size and location. Space is left for the grow icon of the window. These new sizes and locations are stuffed into the contrlRect fields of their corresponding control records, and then the controls are redrawn along with the window's grow icon.

Highlighting Controls

The last routine that concerns the way controls look on the screen is **HiliteControl**. **HiliteControl** changes the way the specified control is highlighted according to the hiliteState argument.

```
HiliteControl(theControl, hiliteState)
        ControlHandle   theControl;
        int             hiliteState;
```

The hiliteState is an integer between 0 and 255. A value of 0 indicates that the control specified should have no highlighting. Values between 1 and 253 indicate the code for the part of the control that is to be highlighted. (Refer to Figure 10.10 for a list of the part codes and their values.) Values of 254 or 255 indicate that the control is to be highlighted as an inactive control. In effect, if a control has 254 or 255 highlighting, it will be visible but inactive.

The difference between 254 and 255 highlighting is the following: Using the routines **TestControl** or **FindControl**, an application can detect whether the mouse was pressed in a control with 254 highlighting, but it cannot detect a mouse-down event in a control with 255 highlighting. If an application needs to detect mouse-downs in inactive controls, it should use 254 highlighting.

Detecting and Handling Mouse-Downs in Controls

The routines **FindControl** and **TrackControl** are the heart of the Control Manager. When an application detects a mouse-down event, it typically calls the Window Manager routine **FindWindow** to determine what part of the desktop the mouse was pressed in. If the mouse is pressed in the content region of a window that contains controls, the application should then call **FindControl** to determine if the mouse was pressed in a control or not. If it was, **FindControl** will tell the application both which control and which part of the control was pressed.

If a control was pressed, the application should then call the routine **TrackControl**. If the mouse is pressed in a button, check box, or radio button, **TrackControl** highlights and unhighlights the selected control as the mouse is moved in and out of it. If the mouse is pressed in the thumb of a scroll bar, a gray outline of the thumb will follow the mouse until the mouse button is released. When the mouse is released, the thumb is drawn in its new location and its value is changed accordingly.

In contrast, if the mouse is pressed in either of the arrows or paging regions of a scroll bar, **TrackControl** calls an action procedure that defines what should be done as long as the mouse is held down. The action procedure for an up-arrow event might, for example, cause the thumb to slowly move up in the scroll bar, as well as cause the document to scroll up in the window, one line at a time. The action procedure doesn't need to highlight the arrow, however; **TrackControl** takes care of all control highlighting and unhighlighting.

We should now examine the two routines and their arguments. Let's take a look at **FindControl** first:

```
int FindControl(thePoint, theWindow, whichControl)
        Point          thePoint;
        WindowPtr      theWindow;
        ControlHandle  *whichControl;
```

An application passes three arguments to **FindControl**: the point where the mouse was pressed in the window's local coordinates, the window pointer of the window that the mouse was pressed in, and whichControl, a control handle. If the mouse was pressed in a visible, active control or in an inactive control with 254 highlighting, the selected control's handle is placed in whichControl. The function value returned is the part code of the control part that was pressed, or in the case of a mouse-down in a 254-highlighted control, it returns the integer 254. If the mouse was pressed in an invisible control, in an inactive control with 255 highlighting, or in no control at all, whichControl is set to NULL and the value returned by the function is 0.

An application usually calls **TrackControl** right after **FindControl**, so it is appropriate that we take a look at **TrackControl** now.

```
int TrackControl(theControl, startPt, actionProc)
        ControlHandle  theControl;
```

```
Point            startPt;
ProcPtr          actionProc;
```

An application also passes three arguments to **TrackControl**: the control handle of the control that was pressed; the point where the mouse was pressed expressed in the local coordinates of theControl's window; and finally, an optional action procedure that defines any additional actions that need to be performed besides highlighting the control or dragging an indicator. For the standard controls, an application generally only needs an action procedure for the arrow and paging regions of a scroll bar.

An action procedure has the following form:

```
MyAction(theControl, partcode)
        ControlHandle   theControl;
        int             partcode;
```

TrackControl calls the action procedure as long as the mouse button is held down. There is a little problem in getting the action procedure to work with **TrackControl**, however, because **TrackControl** expects the action procedure to be a Pascal routine. If we are programming in C, we must handle this a little differently to make everything work correctly.

Think C allows us to declare functions as being of the type pascal, which means that they will return whatever they return so it looks like it has come from a Pascal function. Here is an example of how this looks.

```
pascal void ScrollAction(theControl, partcode)
        ControlHandle   theControl;
        int             partcode;
```

Moving and Sizing Controls

It is possible for an application to move or resize a control once the control has been defined. To move a control, the application would call the procedure **MoveControl**:

```
MoveControl(theControl, h, v)
        ControlHandle   theControl;
        int             h,v;
```

When an application calls **MoveControl**, the top-left corner of the control specified is moved to the location (h,v) in the window's local coordinate system in the same window. If the control is visible at the time of the call, it will be erased from its previous location and redrawn at its new location. The size of the control is not affected by **MoveControl**.

To resize a control after it has been drawn, an application can call **SizeControl**:

```
SizeControl(theControl,  h,  v)
        ControlHandle    theControl;
        int              h,v;
```

When an application calls **SizeControl**, the control associated with the handle theControl is resized to be v pixels wider and h pixels taller. The top-left corner of the control remains fixed while the bottom-right corner is moved v pixels down and h pixels right. If the control is visible at the time of the call, it is hidden and then redrawn in its new size. The location of the control is not affected by **SizeControl**.

Setting Control Values

Each control has a minimum, maximum, and current setting. An application can get and set each of these values with the six routines **SetCtlValue**, **GetCtlValue**, **SetCtlMin**, **GetCtlMin**, **SetCtlMax**, and **GetCtlMax**.

The first two of these routines, **GetCtlValue** and **SetCtlValue**, allow an application to find out and set a control's current value.

```
int GetCtlValue(theControl)
        ControlHandle    theControl;

SetCtlValue(theControl, theValue)
        ControlHandle    theControl;
        int              theValue;
```

GetCtlValue, given a control handle, will return the current value of the control specified. **SetCtlValue** changes the current setting of theControl to theValue. Using the routine **FindControl** or **TrackControl**, an application will find out which part of which control has been pressed. It is then the responsibility of the application to find out the control's current value and set it to its appropriate new value. For controls like check boxes and radio buttons, which only have two settings, the control should be set to the opposite of its value before it was pressed. For scroll bars, the thumb, which is the scroll bar's current value, is automatically set to its new value whenever it is moved. The application must then use **GetCtl-Value** to obtain the control's new setting and respond appropriately. For example, if the thumb is moved to the middle of its scroll bar, it is up to the application to determine the thumb's new value and then scroll to the appropriate location in the document (in this case, the middle).

The functions **GetCtlMin** and **GetCtlMax** return theControl's minimum and maximum settings, respectively.

```
int GetCtlMin(theControl)
        ControlHandle    theControl;

int GetCtlMax(theControl)
        ControlHandle    theControl;
```

The opposites of these two routines are **SetCtlMin** and **SetCtlMax**. **SetCtlMin** and **SetCtlMax** set the specified control's minimum and maximum settings.

```
SetCtlMin(theControl, minValue)
        ControlHandle    theControl;
        int              minValue;
SetCtlMax(theControl, maxValue)
        ControlHandle    theControl;
        int              maxValue;
```

SetCtlMin sets the minimum value of theControl to the integer minValue. If minValue is greater than the current value of theControl, the current value is also set to minValue. **SetCtlMax** sets the maximum value of theControl to the integer maxValue. If maxValue is less than the current value of theControl, the current value is also set to maxValue.

Miscellaneous Routines

As we saw earlier in the chapter, the contrlRfCon field of a Control-Record is set aside for the application's use. This 32-bit field is often used to store a pointer or a handle to a related data structure. An application can set or get the control's contrlRfCon value with the routines **SetCRefCon** and **GetCRefCon**.

```
SetCRefCon(theControl,data)
        ControlHandle    theControl;
        long             data;


long GetCRefCon(theControl)
        ControlHandle    theControl:
```

With **SetCRefCon**, theControl's contrlRfCon is set to the value indicated by the data parameter. The function **GetCRefCon** returns theControl's contrlRf-Con as its value.

A Sample Program for the Control Manager

As we stated earlier, the standard controls, with the exception of scroll bars, are rarely used outside of alert or dialog boxes. In the sample code at the end of Chapter 11, we will see an implementation of buttons, check boxes, and radio buttons in alert and dialog boxes.

The sample code here shows how scroll bars can be implemented in a window to scroll graphics or text. The program puts up a window that has both horizontal and vertical scroll bars. If the window is moved or resized, the scroll bars are moved and resized in the appropriate manner. The contents of the window contain graphics and text which can be scrolled both horizontally and vertically. The routines in this sample application could easily be integrated with the sample program shown in the previous chapter to give that program the capability to scroll text.

From controls, we move on to the topic of using alerts and dialogs, another important feature of the Macintosh Toolbox, and the place where buttons, check boxes, and radio buttons are used.

```
/****************************************************************/
/*          Sample Application for Chapter 10: Controls         */
/*                                                              */
/*    This application demonstrates how to implement scroll bars */
/*    in a window.  We have tried to demonstrate all possible    */
/*    situations you might have to deal with when implementing   */
/*    scroll bars in your application.                           */
/*                                                              */
/*    This application puts up a window that has both a horizontal */
/*    and a vertical scroll bar.  The contents of the window     */
/*    contains both text and graphics.  The window may be moved  */
/*    or resized.                                                */
/*                                                              */
/*    One thing to note is that this application often uses      */
/*    structure assignment when manipulating rectangles.  If your */
/*    compiler does not support structure assignment, you will   */
/*    have to assign each coordinate of the rectangle separately. */
/*                                                              */
/****************************************************************/

#include <QuickDraw.h>
#include <WindowMgr.h>
#include <MemoryMgr.h>
#include <EventMgr.h>
#include <TextEdit.h>
#include <FontMgr.h>
#include <ControlMgr.h>
#include <MenuMgr.h>
#include <ToolboxUtil.h>
#include <stdio.h>

#define    VISIBLE    1
#define    HORIZ      1
#define    VERT       2

/* Global Variables */
WindowPtr       windPtrA;
TEHandle        theText;
Rect            lowerRect;
Rect            hScrollRect,vScrollRect;
ControlHandle   hScroll,vScroll;
short           startValue,endValue;
short           dhGraf,dvGraf;

/* restart procedure for InitDialogs */
restartProc()
{

  ExitToShell();

}
```

```
/* The main event loop */
main() {
    short         windowcode;
    WindowPtr     whichWindow;
    EventRecord   theEvent;

    InitStuff();

    while (1){
        if (GetNextEvent(everyEvent,&theEvent)){
            switch (theEvent.what){

            case mouseDown:
                windowcode = FindWindow(theEvent.where,&whichWindow);
                DoWindowStuff(&theEvent,whichWindow,windowcode);
                break;

            case updateEvt:
                DoUpdates(&theEvent);
                break;

            case nullEvent:
                break;
            }
        }
    }
} /* end of main()  */


/* InitStuff initializes some toolbox managers, defines
   our window and its scroll bars, and then draws the
   windows text, graphics, and dividing line */
InitStuff() {
    WindowRecord      *windRecordA;
    Rect              windRectA, viewRect, destRect;
    short             i;
    char              *theString = "\pBMUG DEVELOPERS GROUP - CONTROLS";

    InitGraf(&thePort);
    InitFonts();
    InitWindows();
    InitMenus();
    InitDialogs(restartProc);

    FlushEvents(everyEvent, 0);
    SetRect(&windRectA,50,50,450,300);

    windRecordA = (WindowRecord *) NewPtr(sizeof(WindowRecord));
    windPtrA = NewWindow(windRecordA,&windRectA,
    "\pScroll Bar Example",
    0,0,(WindowPtr) -1,0xff,0);
```

```
    SetPort(windPtrA);

    SetRect(&hScrollRect,(*windPtrA).portRect.left-1,
                        (*windPtrA).portRect.bottom-15,
                        (*windPtrA).portRect.right-14,
                        (*windPtrA).portRect.bottom+1);
    SetRect(&vScrollRect,(*windPtrA).portRect.right-15,
                        (*windPtrA).portRect.top-1,
                        (*windPtrA).portRect.right+1,
                        (*windPtrA).portRect.bottom-14);

    hScroll = NewControl(windPtrA,&hScrollRect,"\p",VISIBLE,0,0,100,
                        scrollBarProc,HORIZ);
    vScroll = NewControl(windPtrA,&vScrollRect,"\p",VISIBLE,0,0,100,
                        scrollBarProc,VERT);

    destRect = windPtrA->portRect;
    destRect.right += 200;

    viewRect = windPtrA->portRect;
    viewRect.right -= 15;
    viewRect.bottom = (windPtrA->portRect.bottom)/2 - 12;

    lowerRect = windPtrA->portRect;
    lowerRect.right -= 15;
    lowerRect.top = (windPtrA->portRect.bottom)/2 - 10;
    lowerRect.bottom -= 15;

    theText = TENew(&destRect, &viewRect);
    for(i=1; i<200; ++i) TEInsert(theString, 33, theText);

    DrawGraphics();
    dhGraf = 0;
    dvGraf = 0;
    DrawDivider(windPtrA);

    ShowWindow(windPtrA);
    InitCursor();
}

pascal void ScrollGlue(theControl,partcode)
    ControlHandle    theControl;
    short            partcode;
{
    long            direction;

    startValue = GetCtlValue(theControl);
    direction = GetCRefCon(theControl);
    switch(partcode) {
```

```
        case   inUpButton:
           SetCtlValue(theControl, startValue - 1);
           /* NOTE the bug here which permits scrolling even
               after scroll elevator has reached its limit!! */
           if(direction == VERT) ScrollContents(0, 1);
           else ScrollContents(1, 0);
           break;

        case   inDownButton:
           SetCtlValue(theControl, startValue + 1);
           /* NOTE the bug here which permits scrolling even
               after scroll elevator has reached its limit!! */
           if(direction == VERT) ScrollContents(0, -1);
           else ScrollContents(-1, 0);
           break;

        case    inPageUp:
           SetCtlValue(theControl, startValue - 10);
           if(direction == VERT) ScrollContents(0, 10);
           else ScrollContents(10, 0);
           break;

        case    inPageDown:
           SetCtlValue(theControl, startValue + 10);
            if(direction == VERT) ScrollContents(0, -10);
            else ScrollContents(-10, 0);
            break;
    }
    endValue = GetCtlValue(theControl);
}


/* ScrollContents scrolls the text and graphics that
   are in the content region of the window */
ScrollContents(dh, dv)
   short    dh,dv;
{

   RgnHandle    updateRgn;

   updateRgn = NewRgn();
   TEScroll(dh, dv, theText);
   ScrollRect(&lowerRect, dh, dv, updateRgn);
   UpdateGraphics(dh, dv);
   DisposeRgn(updateRgn);
}


/* DoWindowStuff handles the user's actions when he
   or she clicks in the goAway box or moves or resizes
   the window.  When the scroll bars are clicked in,
   those actions are handled also. */
```

```
DoWindowStuff(theEvent,whichWindow,windowcode)
    EventRecord     *theEvent;
    WindowPtr       whichWindow;
    short           windowcode;
{
    long                growResult;
    long                direction;
    short               partcode,bogus;
    Point               eventPoint;
    ControlHandle       whichControl;
    Rect                screenRect, limitRect;

    SetRect(&screenRect, 4, 24,
            screenBits.bounds.right-4,
            screenBits.bounds.bottom-4);
    SetRect(&limitRect, 80, 80,
            screenBits.bounds.right - screenBits.bounds.left -4,
            screenBits.bounds.bottom - screenBits.bounds.top  -24);

    SetPort(whichWindow);
    switch   (windowcode) {

        case  inDrag:
            DragWindow(whichWindow,theEvent->where,&screenRect);
            break;

        case  inGoAway:
            if(TrackGoAway(whichWindow,theEvent->where)) ExitToShell();
            break;

        case  inGrow:
            growResult = GrowWindow(whichWindow,theEvent->where,&limitRect);
            SizeWindow(whichWindow,LoWord(growResult),HiWord(growResult),0xff);
            EraseRect(&whichWindow->portRect);
            InvalRect(&whichWindow->portRect);
            MoveScrollBars(whichWindow);
            break;

        case  inContent:
            eventPoint = theEvent->where;
            GlobalToLocal(&eventPoint);
              partcode = FindControl(eventPoint,whichWindow,&whichControl);
              if(partcode) direction = GetCRefCon(whichControl);
              if(partcode == inThumb) {
                    startValue = GetCtlValue(whichControl);
                  bogus = TrackControl(whichControl,eventPoint,NULL);
                  endValue = GetCtlValue(whichControl);
                  if(direction == HORIZ) ScrollContents(startValue-endValue,0);
                  else  ScrollContents(0,startValue-endValue);
              } else if(partcode != 0)
                    bogus = TrackControl(whichControl,eventPoint,ScrollGlue);
            break;
```

```
      case    inSysWindow:
         SystemClick(theEvent,whichWindow);
         break;
   }
}


/* MoveScrollBars calculates the new positions of the scroll
   bars, the TextEdit view rect, and the clip rect for the
   graphics.  It also redraws the dividing line of the window */
MoveScrollBars(whichWindow)
   WindowPtr       whichWindow;
{
   SetRect(&hScrollRect, (*whichWindow).portRect.left-1,
                          (*whichWindow).portRect.bottom-15,
                          (*whichWindow).portRect.right-14,
                          (*whichWindow).portRect.bottom+1);
   SetRect(&vScrollRect, (*whichWindow).portRect.right-15,
                          (*whichWindow).portRect.top-1,
                          (*whichWindow).portRect.right+1,
                          (*whichWindow).portRect.bottom-14);

   HLock(hScroll);
   HLock(vScroll);
   (**hScroll).contrlRect = hScrollRect;
   (**vScroll).contrlRect = vScrollRect;
   HUnlock(hScroll);
   HUnlock(vScroll);

   HLock(theText);
   (**theText).viewRect = whichWindow->portRect;
   (**theText).viewRect.right -= 15;
   (**theText).viewRect.bottom = (whichWindow->portRect.bottom)/2 - 12;
   HUnlock(theText);

   lowerRect = whichWindow->portRect;
   lowerRect.right -= 15;
   lowerRect.top = (whichWindow->portRect.bottom)/2 - 10;
   lowerRect.bottom -= 15;

   DrawDivider(whichWindow);
}


/* DoUpdates handles the application's update events */
DoUpdates(theEvent)
   EventRecord *theEvent;

{
   WindowPtr    whichWindow,oldPort;
```

```
    GetPort(&oldPort);
    SetPort(whichWindow = (WindowPtr)theEvent->message);
    BeginUpdate(whichWindow);
    DrawControls(whichWindow);
    DrawGrowIcon(whichWindow);
    UpdateText();
    UpdateGraphics(0, 0);
    DrawDivider(whichWindow);
    EndUpdate(whichWindow);
    SetPort(oldPort);
}


/* UpdateText updates the text in the window */
UpdateText()
{
    HLock(theText);
    TEUpdate(&(**theText).viewRect, theText);
    HUnlock(theText);
}


/* UpdateGraphics updates the area the graphics were
   scrolled out of.  There is a little monkey business
   with the origin in this routine to redraw the
   graphics correctly. */
UpdateGraphics(dh, dv)
    short    dh, dv;
{
    Rect        aBigRect, tempRect;

    dhGraf -= dh;
    dvGraf -= dv;

    tempRect = lowerRect;
    SetRect(&aBigRect,-100,-100,600,600);

    SetOrigin(dhGraf, dvGraf);
    OffsetRect(&tempRect, dhGraf, dvGraf);

    ClipRect(&tempRect);
    DrawGraphics();

    SetOrigin(0, 0);
    ClipRect(&aBigRect);
}

/* DrawDivider draws a line, 2-pixels high,
       through the middle of the window */
    DrawDivider(whichWindow)
        WindowPtr        whichWindow;
```

```
{
    PenSize(1,2);
    MoveTo(whichWindow->portRect.left,
            (whichWindow->portRect.bottom)/2 - 12);
    LineTo((whichWindow->portRect.right)-16,
            (whichWindow->portRect.bottom)/2 - 12);
    PenSize(1,1);

}


/* DrawGraphics draws the graphics of the window */
DrawGraphics()
{
    MoveTo(0,0);
    Line(100,700);
    MoveTo(0,0);
    Line(200,700);
    MoveTo(0,0);
    Line(300,700);
    MoveTo(0,0);
    Line(400,700);
    MoveTo(0,0);
    Line(500,700);
    MoveTo(0,0);
    Line(600,700);
}
```

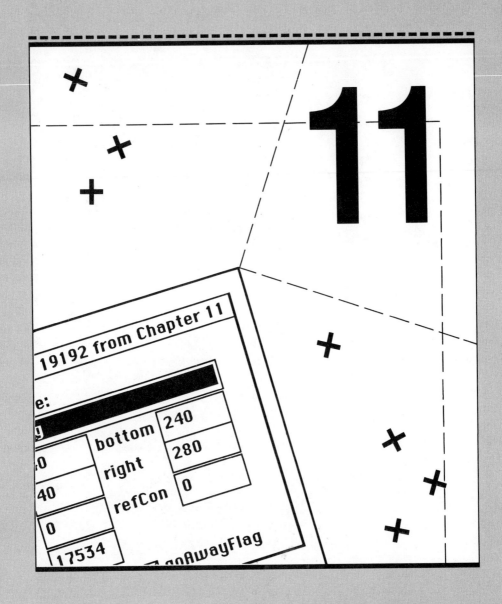

Alerts and Dialogs

As we work our way toward a complete Macintosh application, we need to discuss how to implement alerts and dialogs. Dialog boxes are used whenever an application needs to prompt the user for more input. Alerts are messages from the application to the user, usually announcing errors or warning the user of a potentially dangerous situation. Our discussion of alerts and dialogs has been held off until this point in the book because an understanding of the Event Manager, Window Manager, QuickDraw, TextEdit, and Control Manager is a necessary prerequisite.

Types of Dialogs and Alerts

There are two types of dialog boxes: one that the user must respond to immediately and another that allows the user to proceed with other actions before responding. The first type is referred to as a *modal dialog* since it puts the user in the mode of having to respond, and the second type is called a *modeless dialog* because it doesn't put the user in a particular mode. In addition to the two types of dialogs, the Dialog Manager provides the application with a type of modal dialog called an *alert*. An alert is used to signal an error or give a warning to the user, by displaying a message on the screen, or by emitting an error sound, or both.

▬ ▬ ▬ ▬ ▬ ▬ ▬

Modal Dialogs

A modal dialog is the most commonly used dialog type. The dialog is placed on the screen whenever an application needs more information before it can proceed. A good example is when the user gives the command to print something on the printer. A modal dialog appears because the application needs to know what portion of the document to print, the quality of printing to be used, and how many copies to print. Without this information, the application cannot execute the print command. If the user was to click outside of the dialog window, the Macintosh would emit a loud beep, indicating that all actions must occur in the dialog until it has left the screen.

A modal dialog will typically have one or more buttons, giving the user a number of options. Clicking a button will usually cause the application to proceed, removing the dialog from the screen. One button may be outlined with a heavy line to indicate that it is the preferred or safest choice. Pressing the Return or Enter key will have the same affect as clicking the outlined button. If there is no preferred choice, no button should be outlined, and pressing the Return or Enter key will have no affect. A sample modal dialog is shown in Figure 11.1.

▬ ▬ ▬ ▬ ▬ ▬ ▬

Modeless Dialogs

In contrast to modal dialogs, modeless dialogs do not require the user to respond before doing something else. Modeless dialogs behave just like a normal window; they can be moved, made active or inactive, or closed, all with or without ever being used. Modeless

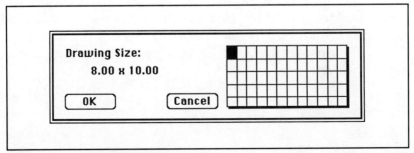

Figure 11.1: Sample Modal Dialog

dialogs also differ in their use of buttons. When the user clicks a button in a modeless dialog, the indicated action will be performed, but the dialog will remain on the screen. To remove a modeless dialog from the screen, the user must click in the dialog window's close box. A sample modeless dialog is shown in Figure 11.2.

Alerts

An alert is a type of dialog that is used to report errors or give warnings to users. Alerts can consist of explanatory messages displayed on the screen, sounds to let the user know he is doing something wrong, or both. A sample alert is shown in Figure 11.3.

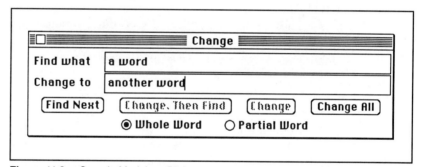

Figure 11.2:   Sample Modeless Dialog

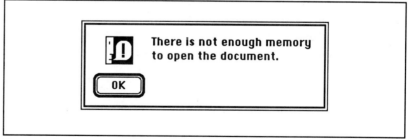

Figure 11.3:   Sample Alert

Alert Stages

An alert can have as many as four stages, with each stage corresponding to the number of times that the user has committed the same error in a row. The first time that an error is committed, the first stage of the alert will take place; if the error is repeated, the second stage will take place; and so on. For errors committed four or more times, the fourth stage alert will be used. Each alert stage, stored in the stage field of the alert's ALRT resource, indicates if the alert will be displayed on the screen, which of the alert's buttons is the default, and which of the four alert sounds should be emitted.

At each alert stage, a sound—numbered 0, 1, 2, or 3—will be emitted. For the standard sound procedure, the sound number indicates the number of beeps that will be emitted. For example, if a stage 1 alert has a sound value of 3, the first time an alert occurs, three beeps will be emitted.

This is done with a sound procedure, which is just a function which accepts an integer argument and produces a sound based on the number passed to it. Declare the function pascal.

Alert Behavior

If an alert is displayed on the screen, it will behave very much like a modal dialog; that is, the alert must be responded to before the user can do anything else. An alert will typically have some text in it that explains the error or warning, along with one or two buttons for the user to click, in order to acknowledge the error or respond to the alert's warning. The alert's default button, which is specified in each of the alert's stages, will have a heavy outline around it to indicate that it is the safe or preferred choice. Pressing the Return or Enter key will have the same affect as clicking the outlined button.

The Contents of Dialog and Alert Boxes

Alerts and dialogs can contain a number of different types of items. They can contain controls, static text (text that cannot be edited by the user), edit text (text that can be edited by the user), icons, or pictures. Each item in an alert or dialog box will have an item number and will be enclosed by a bounding rectangle. In the next few pages, we will learn about the various types of items that can go in an alert or dialog box, about the numbers associated with items, and about the way in which each item is displayed in its bounding rectangle. Once we have this overview of what goes into alert and dialog boxes, we will see how all of these attributes are stored in an item list, or DITL resource.

Controls

Any of the controls that we learned about in the previous chapter—buttons, check boxes, radio buttons, or scroll bars—can be placed in dialogs or alerts. See Figure 11.4 for an example.

Static Text

Static text is text that cannot be edited by the user. It appears in alerts to report errors or give warnings to the user. In dialogs, static text can, for example, explain why the dialog is there or label groups of controls. See Figure 11.4 for an example.

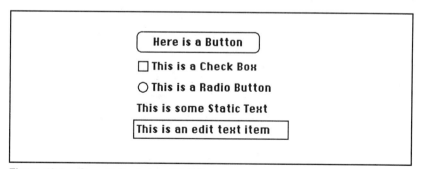

Figure 11.4:   Sample Control and Text Items

Edit Text

Edit text items are used only in dialogs. They allow the user to enter textual information into a dialog. Figure 11.4 shows a sample edit text item.

To handle a user's actions in edit text items, the Dialog Manager calls TextEdit and lets TextEdit take care of the user's actions. TextEdit handles the user's actions in edit text items in the standard manner. When the mouse is clicked in an edit text item, an insertion point will appear, indicating where text typed from the keyboard will be entered. A portion of the text can be selected by dragging the mouse over it, and words can be selected by double-clicking them. Selected text is replaced by anything typed on the keyboard. Backspacing in an edit text item will erase characters to the left of the insertion point, one character per strike of the Backspace key. If a segment of text is selected, backspacing will erase the selected text.

Icons

Icons are 32-by-32 bit images. They are most commonly displayed in alerts to signify the type of alert that has occurred. Figure 11.5 shows the standard alert icons: Stop, Note, and Caution. Icons may also be displayed in dialogs to represent an object, such as a disk or a telephone.

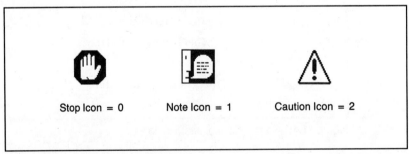

Figure 11.5: The Standard Alert Icons

Pictures

A QuickDraw picture can also be displayed in an alert or dialog box. Many software authors put a digitized picture of themselves in the About... dialog, which informs the user of the software name, version number, author, date written, and so on.

Pictures can be manipulated just like any other resource element. A PICT resource can contain both line primitives and bitmap fragments, so you can easily include part of a MacPaint picture in a resource file. One of the easiest ways to extract part of a MacPaint image into a PICT resource is to copy a fragment of a picture to the ClipBoard, and from there to the Scrapbook. Image fragments stored in the file called Scrapbook in the system folder of your disk are saved as individual PICT resources.

This is one of those cases wherein a little snooping around with ResEdit will turn up something interesting. If you open your Scrapbook file with ResEdit, you will be able to locate the appropriate image fragment, copy it into a new file and change its resource number to something useful, say 128. If you save this resource into a file of its own—let's call it Picture.Rsrc—you can include it in the resource file for your program by adding the line

```
INCLUDE Picture.Rsrc
```

to your RMaker file, as we discussed in Chapter 9.

Item Numbers

Each item in an alert or dialog has a number that corresponds to its position in the item list. By convention, the first item in any item list—whether it's for an alert or a dialog—should be the OK or default button. This is because, when an alert or dialog is the active window on the screen and the user presses the Return or Enter key, the Dialog Manager returns item number one, just as if the user had clicked the first item with the mouse. Also by convention, the second item in the item list for an alert should be the Cancel button. The remaining items can be listed in any order.

How Items Are Displayed

Each item in an alert or dialog has an associated rectangle, called the itmRect, that determines the item's size and location within the alert or dialog window. For control items, the itmRect becomes the contrl-Rect field of the control's control record. For static text and edit text items, the itmRect becomes TextEdit's destination rectangle and view rectangle. In addition, for edit text items, a rectangle is drawn three pixels outside its display rectangle. If pictures or icons are to be drawn in an alert or dialog box, they will be automatically scaled by the Toolbox to fit the itmRect.

DialogRecord Data Type

Although it is rarely used by an application directly, the structure of a DialogRecord is presented in the box below and described in this section.

Dialog Record Data Type

```
struct_DR
        WindowRecord            window;
        Handle                  items;
        TEHandle                textH;
        int                     editField;
        int                     editOpen;
        int                     aDefItem;
};

#define         DialogRecord    structDR
#define         DialogPtr       *DialogRecord
```

The window field of a DialogRecord is the WindowRecord for the dialog's window. The items field is a handle to the item list that is used for this dialog. The next three fields—textH, editField, and editOpen—are used by the Dialog Manager when there are one or more edit text items in the dialog. When there is more than one edit text item in a dialog, the fields correspond to the item that is currently selected or to the one that displays an insertion point. The textH field is a text edit handle to the text in the item. The editField field contains the item number minus 1 of the text edit item. If the dialog has no edit text items, the field will equal -1. The editOpen field is used internally by the Dialog Manager. The aDefItem field contains the item number of a modal dialog's or alert's default button. For modal dialogs, it contains the number 1; for alerts, it contains the number specified in the ALRT resource.

Dialog and Alert Resource Types

There are a few different ways to create dialogs and alerts, but creating them with resources is the easiest, most flexible, fastest, and as a result, it is the best way to do so. In this section, we will discuss the format of dialog and alert resource types as well as how to create them.

DLOG Resource Type

A DLOG resource is used to define various attributes of a dialog window. Many of the fields of a DLOG resource are the same as the arguments that are used by the Window Manager function **NewWindow**. It might be a good idea to refer to Chapter 3 to review the routine **NewWindow** and its arguments. The format of a DLOG resource is given in the box below.

The boundsRect value is the same boundsRect used by the Window Manager function **NewWindow**. It specifies the size and location on the dialog on the screen. The procID value is the same procID value used by **NewWindow**. It specifies the type of window to be used for the dialog. If the visible field is true, the dialog will be drawn; otherwise, it will be invisible. The filler1 field is not used; it simply takes up the lower 8 bits of the word whose top 8 bits are occupied by the visible field.

The goAwayFlag field specifies whether the dialog window should have a close box or not. For modeless dialogs, which have a close box, this value should be true. For modal dialogs, it should be false. The filler2 field is not used; it takes up the lower 8 bits of the word

```
                        DLOG Resource Format

    boundsRect              8 bytes
    procID                  2 bytes
    visible                 1 byte
    filler1                 1 byte
    goAwayFlag              1 byte
    filler2                 1 byte
    refCon                  4 bytes
    itemsID                 2 bytes
    title                   1 count byte followed by the rest
                            of the string
```

whose top 8 bits are occupied by goAwayFlag. **refCon** is the window's reference value, a 32-bit field. It is the same refCon that was discussed in the
chapters about windows, Chapters 3 and 8, and may contain any value
for use by the application. The itemsID field is an integer that specifies the
resource ID of the item list resource DITL, which is to be used with this
dialog window. The title field is the title, if any, of the dialog.

DITL Resource Type

An item list, or DITL resource, is a list or group of items (controls, icons, and so on) that is put into dialog or alert. When an
application creates an alert or dialog using Dialog Manager routines, it
will have to specify a DITL to define the items. The format of a DITL
resource is given in the box below.

```
                        DITL Resource Format

    dlgMaxIndex             2 bytes

    Then, for each item in the item list
    itmHandle               4 bytes
    itmRect                 8 bytes
    itmType                 1 byte
    itmData                 1 byte plus an even number of
                            data bytes for the itmType's data
```

A DITL resource begins with a dlgMaxIndex field, a word that contains the number of items in the item list minus one. Then, for each item (a control, icon, and so on), there are four more fields—itmHandl, itmRect, itmType, and itmData—each containing the information described below:

- The itmHandle field contains a handle to the particular item in the item list.

- The itmRect field is the item's bounding rectangle.

- The itmType field indicates what kind of item this is (for example, an edit text or picture).

- The itmData field is a length byte followed by the item's data.

ALRT Resource Type

Alerts are always created as resources and then invoked by one of the four alert-invoking routines described later in this chapter in the Invoking Alerts section. The box below shows the format of an ALRT resource.

ALRT Resource Format

```
boundsRect        8 bytes
itemsID           2 bytes
stages            2 bytes
```

The boundsRect field is just like the boundsRect field of a DLOG resource. It is a rectangle that determines the size and location of the alert on the screen. The itemsID field contains the resource ID of the DITL resource, which contains all of the alert's items. The stages field is a 16-bit word that contains the information about each of the alert's four stages. The field is broken into four groups of 4-bits each. Each 4-bit group represents one of the alert's stages. The box below shows the format of the stages field.

Stages Format

stg4boldItem	1 bit
stg4boxDrawn	1 bit
stg4sound	2 bits
stg3boldItem	1 bit
stg3boxDrawn	1 bit
stg3sound	2 bits
stg2boldItem	1 bit
stg2boxDrawn	1 bit
stg2sound	2 bits
stg1boldItem	1 bit
stg1boxDrawn	1 bit
stg1sound	2 bits

Each 4-bit stage determines how an alert will behave each time that it is invoked. The first bit of a stage, the stgboldItem, determines whether a heavy line should be drawn around item number 1 or item number 2. If the value of the bit is 0, item 1 will be outlined; if the bit is 1, item 2 will be outlined.

The second bit, the stgboxDrawn, indicates whether or not the alert should be drawn on the screen. A value of 1 indicates yes, and a value of 0 indicates no. The third and fourth bits, the stgsound field, which can represent an integer between 0 and 3, indicate which error sound (0 to 3) should be sounded at this stage of the alert.

Each alert has four stages, for a total of 16 bits. It is important to note that the stages are executed in the reverse order of the way that they are organized. The last 4 bits of the word, the stg1 fields, determine an alert's actions the first time that it occurs while the first 4 bits of the word, the stg4 fields, determine how an alert will behave the fourth and subsequent times that it is invoked.

How to Create a DLOG, DITL, or ALRT Resource

The easiest way to create a DLOG, DITL, or ALRT resource is using ResEdit or RMaker. For each of these resource types, as well as many of the other types, ResEdit has a resource template, which you simply fill in. Under RMaker, the same process is handled by keying in a short text file. Sample resource templates are provided in Appendix D of the Think C User's manual.

Creating a DLOG Resource

Figure 11.6 shows the template for a DLOG resource. Notice that many of the fields of the template have exactly the same name as the fields of a DLOG resource. The top, left, bottom, and right fields specify the boundsRect coordinates for the dialog. The procID, visible, go-AwayFlag, and refCon fields are exactly those same fields of a DLOG resource. We simply need to fill in the values for a particular dialog. The Window title is the title of the dialog window. The resID is the itemsID, the resource ID number of the DITL to be used with this dialog box.

Creating a DITL Resource

To create a DITL resource, we simply need to create each one of the items that we want in the item list. For each item of the item list, we will use the template shown in Figure 11.7. We specify the type of item, whether it is to be enabled or disabled, its bounding rectangle, and its title (if any). From this information, the Resource Editor will fill in the fields of a DITL resource with the appropriate data.

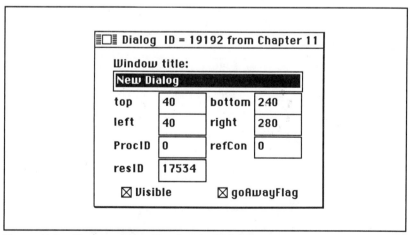

Figure 11.6:   Resource Editor Template for DLOG Resources

Creating an ALRT Resource

To create an ALRT resource, we will use the template shown in Figure 11.8. If we refer back to the description of an ALRT resource format, the template should be fairly self-explanatory. The top, left, bottom,

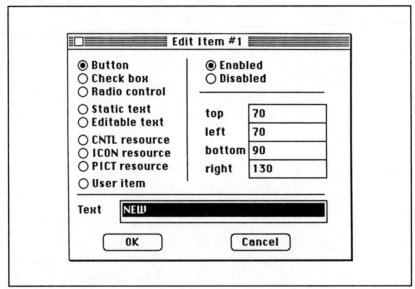

Figure 11.7: Resource Editor Template for DITL Resources

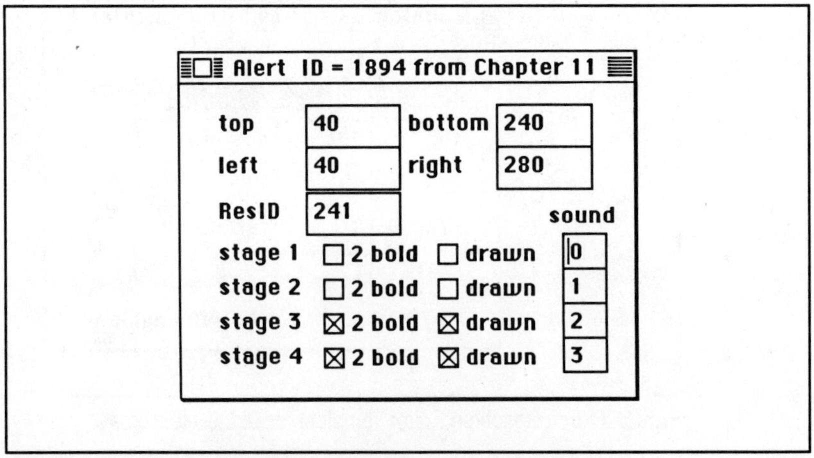

Figure 11.8: Resource Editor Template for ALRT Resources

and right fields of the template indicate the boundsRect and the size and location of the alert on the screen. The resID is the same as the itemsID; it is an integer that specifies the DITL that is to be used with this alert. Finally, for each stage of the alert, the 2 bold field, if checked, means item number 2 of the alert is the default button and should be outlined accordingly. If it is unchecked, item number 1 will be outlined. The drawn field indicates whether or not the alert box is to be drawn on the screen. The sound field contains a number from 0 to 3 that indicates the sound to be emitted at the particular stage of the alert.

Using Alert and Dialog Routines

This section describes the Toolbox routines an application will use to implement alerts and dialogs.

Initialization

There are two routines that have to do with initializing alerts and dialogs. The first of the two, **InitDialogs**, is similar to other Toolbox-initializing routines, such as **InitWindows** and **InitMenus**. It should be called before using any of the other Dialog Manager routines. The procedure initializes the Dialog Manager, sets up the standard sound procedure, and passes empty strings to the routine **ParamText**, a routine which allows an application to substitute text in static text items.

```
InitDialogs(restartProc)
      ProcPtr restartProc;
```

An application can pass a restart procedure to **InitDialogs**, which can be executed whenever a system error occurs (an additional feature of **InitDialogs** that most applications fail to take advantage of). Whenever a system error occurs, the System Error Handler of the Toolbox puts a dialog box on the screen with a message notifying the user of the error that has occurred and two buttons, Resume and Restart. Most of the time, the Resume button is inactive, leaving the Restart button as the user's only choice. If a restart procedure is passed to **InitDialogs**, however, the system error dialog will appear with the Resume button active. Clicking the Resume button will execute the restart procedure.

Depending on which system error occurred, it may or may not be a good idea to actually resume the application that crashed. Pointers and handles may have been jumbled, so restarting the application may lead to even more system errors. In this case, a relatively safe choice for a restart procedure, and also a very useful one, is the Toolbox procedure **ExitToShell**. This will allow the user to get back to the Finder and back up all of his or her files. Being able to get back to the Finder is essential for people using a RAM disk, since restarting the Mac would wipe out all the data that they had stored in that disk, while being able to get back to the Finder would allow them to back up all of their data to a floppy disk. Once all the files had been backed up, the user could then restart the machine to clear memory and start over again. The following piece of code shows how to pass **ExitToShell** to **InitDialogs** as the restart procedure.

```
restartProc()
{
        ExitToShell();
}
InitDialogs(restartProc);
```

The other initialization routine for alerts and dialogs is the procedure **ErrorSound**.

```
ErrorSound(soundProc)
        ProcPtr soundProc;
```

An application passes a sound procedure, which becomes the sound procedure for dialogs and alerts, to **ErrorSound**. If the sound procedure passed is NULL, then alerts and dialogs will have no sound and, in the case that the volume is set to zero, the menu bar will not blink. An application does not have to call **ErrorSound**; if it is not called, the Dialog Manager uses the standard sound procedure.

Format of a Sound Procedure

The format of a sound procedure is shown in the following code:

```
MySound(soundNo)
        int      soundNo;
```

A sound procedure should take integer values from 0 to 3, usually passed from the stages field of an alert, and can emit any sound for each number. The standard sound procedure emits the number of beeps specified by soundNo. For the standard sound procedure, a soundNo of 0 results in no sound, a soundNo of 1 results in 1 beep, and so on. If the user has the volume set to 0, the menu bar will blink in place of each beep. If an application uses its own sound procedure, it's good practice to have sound number 1 be a single beep. When a modal dialog is on the screen and the user clicks outside of it, sound number 1 is emitted. If the current sound procedure does not emit a single beep, it will not be conforming to the Macintosh User Interface Guidelines.

Creating and Disposing of Dialogs

The Dialog Manager provides two routines for creating dialogs, two routines for disposing of them, and two routines for locking or unlocking dialog resources in memory. The first two routines, **NewDialog** and **GetNewDialog**, are analogous to the **New** and **GetNew** routines of other Toolbox Managers.

The NewDialog Routine

The **NewDialog** routine creates a dialog from the arguments that the application passes it, while **GetNewDialog** creates a dialog from a dialog template stored in a resource.

```
DialogPtr NewDialog(dStorage, boundsRect, title, visible,
   procID, behind, goAwayFlag, refCon, items)
        Ptr       dStorage;
        Rect      *boundsRect;
        Str255    *title;
        char      visible;
```

```
int        procID;
WindowPtr  behind;
char       goAwayFlag;
long       refCon;
Handle     items;
```

The first eight arguments of **NewDialog** are the same as the arguments passed to the Window Manager routine **NewWindow**. In fact, **NewDialog** calls **NewWindow** with its first eight parameters to create the dialog window. You might also notice that the arguments of **NewDialog** are the fields of a DLOG resource. We will see why in just a moment when we examine the **GetNewDialog** routine. Finally, **NewDialog** gets the items for the dialog from the items parameter. The items parameter is a handle to a DITL resource. The following code shows how an application, using the Resource Manager routine **GetResource**, can get a handle to a DITL resource with ID number 321.

```
Handle items;
items = GetResource('DITL', 321);
```

The handle items can then be used as an argument to **NewDialog**.

The GetNewDialog **Routine**

The **GetNewDialog** function accomplishes the same thing as **NewDialog** but does it in a different manner.

```
DialogPtr GetNewDialog(dialogID, dStorage, behind)
    int            dialogID;
    WindowRecord   *dStorage;
    WindowPtr      behind;
```

GetNewDialog uses the dStorage and behind parameters just as they were used by **NewDialog**, but it gets the remainder of its dialog definition data—boundsRect, title, visible, procID, goAwayFlag, refCon, and items—from the DLOG resource that has the ID number specified by the argument dialogID.

Disposing of Dialogs

To dispose of a dialog, we have two routines to choose from: **CloseDialog** and **DisposDialog**. If, when a dialog was created with **New-Dialog** or **GetNewDialog**, the dStorage parameter contained a pointer to the dialog storage, we should dispose of it with **CloseDialog**.

```
CloseDialog(theDialog)
        DialogPtr        theDialog;
```

CloseDialog removes the specified dialog from the screen and deletes the dialog's window from the window list. It releases the memory occupied by the dialog window's data structures and by the dialog's items, except for icons and pictures. These data structures include the window record, update region, content region, and control records that may have been allocated for theDialog. **CloseDialog** does not, however, release the memory occupied by the dialog record or the item list. In order to release the memory occupied by the dialog record and the item list, an application will need to use the procedure **DisposDialog**.

```
DisposDialog(theDialog)
        DialogPtr        theDialog;
```

DisposDialog first calls **CloseDialog** and then releases the memory occupied by the dialog record and the item list. Like **CloseDialog**, **Dispos-Dialog** does not release the memory occupied by icons or pictures. **DisposDialog** should also be used to remove dialogs whenever the dialog's storage was allocated on the heap.

Locking and Unlocking Dialog Resources in Memory

To lock or unlock dialog resources in memory, the Dialog Manager provides the routines **CouldDialog** and **FreeDialog**. **CouldDialog** loads the specified DLOG resource, its associated DITL resource, and all their related data structures into memory and marks them as unpurgeable. It's a good idea for an application to lock dialog resources in memory whenever there is a possibility of the application disk not being in the drive (a common situation on a Macintosh with only one disk drive). If an application tries to display a dialog whose data structures aren't in memory and whose resource file is not accessible, the familiar

"Please insert the disk: xxxx" message will appear, and the user will have to do disk swaps until all the necessary dialog data structures are read from disk into memory. Instead of putting the user through the tedious task of disk swapping, an application can simply call **CouldDialog** for each dialog that might be displayed when the resource file is inaccessible.

```
CouldDialog(dialogID)
        int     dialogID;
```

The dialogID parameter is the resource ID for the DLOG resource that needs to be loaded and locked into memory.

An application can undo the work of **CouldDialog** with the procedure **FreeDialog**. **FreeDialog** marks the specified DLOG resource, its associated DITL resource, and all of their related data structures in memory as purgeable. An application should call **FreeDialog** whenever there is no longer a need to have the specified dialog locked in memory.

```
FreeDialog(dialogID)
        int     dialogID;
```

The dialogID parameter is the resource ID of the DLOG resource in memory that can be marked as purgeable.

Responding to Dialog Events

Once a dialog is placed on the screen, the application needs to respond to the user's actions within the dialog window. The Dialog Manager provides four routines for this purpose. It provides us with the mechanism to deal with modal dialogs through a procedure called **ModalDialog**; with two functions for dealing with modeless dialogs, **Is-DialogEvent** and **DialogSelect**; and with a final routine, **DrawDialog**, to handle dialogs that don't need a response.

Handling Modal Dialogs

When a modal dialog is placed on the screen, an application should call **ModalDialog** to handle all of the user's actions. When the user's action occurs in an enabled dialog item, **ModalDialog** returns its item number in the parameter itemHit.

```
ModalDialog(filterProc, itemHit)
        ProcPtr    filterProc;
        int        *itemHit;
```

If **ModalDialog** is passed a NULL value for its filterProc, it will respond to each event that occurs in the following manner:

- If it is a mouse-down event outside of the dialog window, sound number 1 is emitted (usually a single beep), the mouse-down event is thrown out, and the **ModalDialog** responds to the next event.

- If the Return or Enter key is pressed, the procedure returns with itemHit equal to 1.

- If an activate or update event occurs, **ModalDialog** activates or updates the window.

- Mouse-down and key-down events in edit text items are handled in the standard manner, which we discussed earlier in this chapter in the section titled Edit Text. If the event occurred in an enabled edit text item, **ModalDialog** returns with itemHit equal to the edit text's item number. If the event occurs in a disabled item or if a key-down event occurs when there are no edit text items, **Modal-Dialog** returns nothing.

- If a mouse-down event occurs in a control, **ModalDialog** calls the Control Manager routine **TrackControl** (refer to Chapter 10 for more information about **TrackControl**). If the mouse is released in the same control and the control is enabled, **ModalDialog** returns with itemHit equal to the control's item number. If the control is disabled, **ModalDialog** returns nothing.

- If a mouse-down event occurs in any other enabled item, such as an icon or picture, **ModalDialog** returns with its item number in itemHit.

- If a mouse-down event occurs in any other disabled item, in no item, or if any other event takes place, **ModalDialog** returns nothing.

Handling Modeless Dialogs

To handle a user's actions in a modeless dialog, an application should use the routines **IsDialogEvent** and **DialogSelect**. **IsDialogEvent** determines whether or not an event is part of a dialog. If the event is part of a dialog, the application passes it to **DialogSelect** (just as we passed menu events to **MenuSelect** in Chapter 4). Then, **DialogSelect** responds to the user's actions in the same way as **ModalDialog** responds to modal dialog events.

The function **IsDialogEvent** is called inside of a program's main event loop, just after the loop's **GetNextEvent** call.

```
char IsDialogEvent(theEvent)
        EventRecord         *theEvent;
```

An application passes the current event to **IsDialogEvent** to determine whether or not it needs to be handled as part of a modeless dialog. The function returns true whenever there is an update or activate event for a dialog or a mouse-down event in a dialog window, or whenever any other type of event occurs while a dialog window is active. Under any other circumstances, **IsDialogEvent** returns false.

If **IsDialogEvent** returns true, an application should pass theEvent to **DialogSelect**.

```
char DialogSelect(theEvent, theDialog, itemHit)
        EventRecord         *theEvent;
        DialogPtr           *theDialog;
        int                 *itemHit;
```

DialogSelect responds to the same events in modeless dialogs that **ModalDialog** responds to in modal dialogs, in exactly the same manner. If an event takes place in an enabled item, the function returns true, the itemHit parameter is returned containing the item number of the selected item, and theDialog parameter returns a pointer to the dialog. If **DialogSelect** returns true, an application should respond to the dialog event in whatever way is appropriate.

Handling Dialogs That Need No Response

The last dialog-handling routine is **DrawDialog**. **DrawDialog** is used when an application displays a dialog that contains nothing but static text items in order to let the user see what's going on. This type of dialog might appear, for example, when an application is copying a file (see Figure 11.9). Because there is no need for the user to respond to this sort of dialog, an application uses **DrawDialog** instead of any of the other dialog-handling routines.

```
DrawDialog(theDialog)
          DialogPtr         theDialog;
```

DrawDialog draws the items contained in the specified dialog box theDialog.

Invoking Alerts

There are four different routines for invoking alerts. Each of the four functions takes the exact same parameters. The only operational difference between the routines is the icon that the routine draws in the alert window.

The first of the four functions, **Alert**, reads the ALRT resource that has an ID of alertID into memory. Once it's in memory, the ALRT resource are examined, and the appropriate stage's actions are executed. The execution of the alert's stage may include emitting an error sound, drawing an alert on the screen, or both. If an alert is drawn on the screen, **Alert** then calls the routine **ModalDialog**, passing it the filterProc, to handle the user's actions.

```
int Alert(alertID, filterProc)
          int         alertID;
          ProcPtr     filterProc;
```

Once an alert is drawn on the screen, it behaves just as if the application had created it as a modal dialog and then called the routine **ModalDialog**,

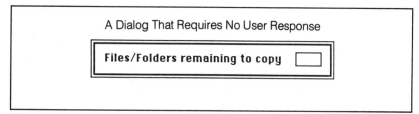

Figure 11.9:   Files Remaining to Copy Dialog

which we discussed earier. The function value returned by **Alert** is –1 if an alert box is not drawn on the screen (because no alert has been defined at this stage); otherwise, it returns the item number of the enabled item that is clicked with the mouse. Just as is the case with modal dialogs, if the user presses the Return or Enter key, a value of 1 is returned. Before returning its function value to the application, **Alert** removes the alert from the screen and releases all the memory allocated to its data structures.

The next three routines, **StopAlert**, **NoteAlert**, and **CautionAlert**, behave in exactly the same manner as **Alert**, except that each draws a different icon in the upper left-hand corner of the alert window. The standard icons for the Stop, Note, and Caution alerts are shown in Figure 11.5. Each of the standard alert icons is in the resource fork of the System file and has a resource ID of 0, 1, and 2, respectively. If an application had ICON resources in its resource fork numbered 0, 1, or 2, these icons would be displayed instead of the standard icons found in the System resources.

Note that the appearance of these "standard" icons has varied with the changing Macintosh system software.

The **StopAlert** routine works exactly like **Alert**, except that it draws the ICON resource that has an ID of 0 in the rectangle (10,20,42,52) within the alert window.

```
int StopAlert(alertID, filterProc)
        int        alertID;
        ProcPtr    filterProc;
```

The **NoteAlert** routine works exactly like **StopAlert**, except that it draws the ICON resource that has an ID of 1.

```
int NoteAlert(alertID, filterProc)
int                alertID;
ProcPtr            filterProc;
```

Finally, the **CautionAlert** routine works exactly like **StopAlert**, except that is draws the ICON resource that has an ID of 2.

```
int CautionAlert(alertID, filterProc)
        int        alertID;
        ProcPtr    filterProc;
```

Locking and Unlocking Alert Resources in Memory

To lock or unlock alert resources in memory, the Dialog Manager provides the routines **CouldAlert** and **FreeAlert**. These two routines do the same things for alerts that **CouldDialog** and **FreeDialog** do for dialogs. An application should use **CouldAlert** to load an alert's resources into memory whenever there is a chance that the alert will be invoked when the disk is not in the drive. When there is no longer a need to have the alert locked in memory, an application should call **FreeAlert** to release the memory occupied by the alert and its associated resources.

CouldAlert loads the specified ALRT resource, its associated DITL resource, and their related data structures in memory and marks them as unpurgeable.

```
CouldAlert (alertID)
        int       alertID;
```

The alertID parameter is the resource ID for the ALRT resource that is to be loaded and locked into memory.

An application can undo the work of **CouldAlert** with the procedure **FreeAlert**. **FreeAlert** marks the specified ALRT resource, its associated DITL resource, and all their related data structures in memory as purgeable.

```
FreeAlert (alertID)
        int       alertID;
```

The alertID parameter is the resource ID of the ALRT resource in memory that can be marked as purgeable.

Manipulating Items in Alerts and Dialogs

An application can manipulate items in alerts and dialogs using the following six Dialog Manager routines: **GetDItem**, **SetDItem**, **GetIText**, **SetIText**, **SelIText**, and **ParamText**. The first two of these routines deal with manipulating any type of dialog or alert item, while the last four, as we might guess from their suffixes, deal with manipulating edit text and static text items.

The GetDItem and SetDItem Procedures

GetDItem and **SetDItem** are two general routines that allow an application to get or set information about any type of item in an item list. When passed a dialog pointer and an item number, **GetDItem** returns to the application a handle to the item specified, the type of item specified (control, icon, and so on), and the item's bounding rectangle.

```
GetDItem(theDialog, itemNo, type, item, box)
        DialogPtr       theDialog;
        int             itemNo;
        int             *type;
        Handle          *item;
        Rect            *box;
```

The item's handle, type, and bounding rectangle are returned in the item, type, and box parameters, respectively. Once an application has a handle to an item, it can change or examine the item by passing the handle to other routines. For example, if an application needed to change or examine the text in a static text or edit text item, it would pass the item's handle to the **SetIText** or **GetIText** routine (we will discuss both of these routines shortly). If the item the application needed to examine or change was a control, the handle would be passed to the appropriate Control Manager routine. For example, the application would pass the handle to **MoveControl** if it needed to move the control, to **GetCtlValue** or **SetCtlValue** if it needed to get or set the control's value, and to **GetCtlTitle** and **SetCtlTitle** if it needed to get and set the control's title.

The **SetDItem** procedure is generally used to add an item to a dialog that was unknown or inaccessible at the time that the item list was defined. To do this, an application could create an item in the item list and set its display rectangle to (0,0,0,0). Once the item became accessible, the application could pass the item's handle and its bounding rectangle to **SetDItem**.

```
SetDItem(theDialog, itemNo, type, item, box)
        DialogPtr       theDialog;
        int             itemNo;
```

```
int          type;
Handle       item;
Rect         *box;
```

The parameters itemNo and theDialog indicate which item of which dialog is to be set. The item, type and box, parameters indicate the new handle, item type, and bounding rectangle that the specified item is to have, respectively. The new item is not drawn by the routine **SetDItem**.

   SetDItem should not be used to change the text of a static text or edit text item or to change a control item in any way. To alter such items, first call the **GetDItem** routine to get a handle to the item, and then pass the item's handle to the appropriate routines, as we outlined in the discussion of **GetDItem**.

Manipulating Text in Alerts and Dialogs

   To examine or change the contents of an edit text or static text item, an application can use the procedures **GetIText** and **SetIText**. **GetIText** takes a handle to an edit text or static text item and returns the contents of the text string in its text parameter.

```
GetIText(item, text)
        Handle       item;
        Str255       *text;
```

The parameter item is typically the handle returned by the Dialog Manager routine **GetDItem**.

   To change the text of an edit text or static text item, the **SetIText** routine can be used.

```
SetIText(item, text)
        Handle       item;
        Str255       *text;
```

SetIText changes the contents of the indicated edit text or static text item to the string specified in the text parameter.

   It is customary for a dialog that contains an edit text item to appear with some selected, default text in it. The text appears selected so that all the user has to do to replace it is to type in the new text from the keyboard. This saves the user from having to manually select the text with the mouse in order to replace it. Anything that the user types will replace the selected text in the edit text item. The Dialog Manager provides us with a means of selecting all or part of an edit text item with the **SellText** routine (Select Item's Text).

```
SelIText(theDialog, itemNo, strtSel, endSel)
        DialogPtr    theDialog;
        int          itemNo;
        int          strtSel;
        int          endSel;
```

Given a pointer to a dialog and the item number of an edit text item, **SellText** selects the portion of text from character position strtSel to the postion endSel. To select all of the text in an edit text item, pass a value of 0 in strtSel and a very large number in endSel. This will ensure that the entire text string is selected.

The ParamText **Routine**

The **ParamText** procedure allows an application to substitute text in static text items. The Pascal strings passed in param0 through param3 will replace the strings "^0" through "^3" in all subsequent static text items that appear in alerts or dialogs.

```
ParamText(param0, param1, param2, param3)
        Str255          *param0, *param1;
        Str255          *param2, *param3;
```

For example, if the static text of an alert was "Completely erase disk entitled ^0," diskName was a Pascal string that contained a disk name, and noString was an empty string, an application could call **ParamText**(diskName, noString, noString, noString).

A Sample Program using Alerts and Dialogs

The sample program following demonstrates almost all of the routines that we have discussed. The program displays a modeless dialog that contains controls that allow the user to put up modal dialogs and alerts.

```
/****************************************************************/
/*      Sample Application for Chapter 11: Alerts and Dialogs   */
/*                                                              */
/*      This application puts up a modeless dialog that         */
/*      contains buttons, check boxes, radio buttons, static    */
/*      text and edit text items.  The buttons allow the user   */
/*      to bring up a modal dialog or any one of 4 alerts.      */
/*                                                              */
/*      The check boxes indicate which of the 4 edit text       */
/*      strings should be passed to the modal dialog, while     */
/*      the radio buttons indicate which of the 4 alerts        */
/*      should be invoked.                                      */
/*                                                              */
/****************************************************************/

#include <QuickDraw.h>
#include <WindowMgr.h>
#include <MemoryMgr.h>
#include <EventMgr.h>
#include <TextEdit.h>
#include <FontMgr.h>
#include <ControlMgr.h>
#include <MenuMgr.h>
#include <DialogMgr.h>
#include <ToolboxUtil.h>
#include <stdio.h>

/* constants for dialog items */
#define modalBut    1
#define edText1     3
#define edText2     4
#define edText3     5
#define edText4     6
#define radBut1     7
#define radBut2     8
#define radBut3     9
#define radBut4     10
#define alertBut    11
#define chkBox1     12
#define chkBox2     13
#define chkBox3     14
#define chkBox4     15

/* constants for alertVal */
#define PlainA      1
#define StopA       2
#define NoteA       3
#define CautionA    4

/* Global variables */
short   alertVal,checkVal;
```

```
/* restart procedure for InitDialogs */
reStartProc()
{
   ExitToShell();
}

/* the main event loop */
main()
{
     EventRecord    theEvent;
     DialogPtr      modeless,whichDialog;
     short          whichItem,windowcode,type;
     WindowPtr      whichWindow;
     Rect           box;
     ControlHandle  radHand1;

     InitGraf(&thePort);
     InitFonts();
     InitWindows();
     InitMenus();
     InitDialogs(reStartProc);
     InitCursor();

   FlushEvents(everyEvent, 0);

     /* put up the modeless dialog with the first
        radio button and edit text item selected */
     modeless = GetNewDialog(331,NULL,(WindowPtr)-1);
     SelIText(modeless,edText1,0,100);
     GetDItem(modeless,radBut1,&type,&radHand1,&box);
     SetCtlValue(radHand1,1);
     alertVal = 1;
     checkVal = 0;
     ShowWindow(modeless);

     while (1)    {

         if (GetNextEvent(everyEvent,&theEvent)) {
             if (IsDialogEvent(&theEvent)) {
                 if (DialogSelect(&theEvent,&whichDialog,&whichItem)) {
                     DoModeless(whichItem,whichDialog);
                 }
             }
             switch (theEvent.what) {

                 case mouseDown:
                     windowcode = FindWindow(theEvent.where,&whichWindow);
                     DoWindowStuff(&theEvent,whichWindow,windowcode);
                     break;
```

```
                }
            }
        }
} /* end of main()  */


/* The procedure DoModeless takes a dialog
   item and a dialog pointer as arguments, and
   responds to the user's actions appropriately */
DoModeless(whichItem,whichDialog)
    short      whichItem;
    DialogPtr  whichDialog;
{
    short           type,result;
    Str255          theText1,theText2,theText3,theText4;
    Handle          item;
    Rect            box;
    ControlHandle   radHand1,radHand2,radHand3,radHand4,chkHand;

    /* Get a handle to each of the radio buttons */
    GetDItem(whichDialog,radBut1,&type,&radHand1,&box);
    GetDItem(whichDialog,radBut2,&type,&radHand2,&box);
    GetDItem(whichDialog,radBut3,&type,&radHand3,&box);
    GetDItem(whichDialog,radBut4,&type,&radHand4,&box);

    switch(whichItem) {

        /* If its the modal button, get the text out of each edit
           text item and pass strings to DoModal */
        case modalBut:
            GetDItem(whichDialog,edText1,&type,&item,&box);
            GetIText(item,&theText1);
            GetDItem(whichDialog,edText2,&type,&item,&box);
            GetIText(item,&theText2);
            GetDItem(whichDialog,edText3,&type,&item,&box);
            GetIText(item,&theText3);
            GetDItem(whichDialog,edText4,&type,&item,&box);
            GetIText(item,&theText4);
            DoModal(&theText1,&theText2,&theText3,&theText4);
            break;
        /* For the next four cases, turn on the radio button that
           was pressed and turn off all the rest.  Also change the
           global variable alertVal which keeps track of the radio
           button that is currently selected */
        case radBut1:
            SetCtlValue(radHand1,1);
            SetCtlValue(radHand2,0);
            SetCtlValue(radHand3,0);
            SetCtlValue(radHand4,0);
            alertVal = 1;
            break;
```

```
            case radBut2:
                SetCtlValue(radHand1,0);
                SetCtlValue(radHand2,1);
                SetCtlValue(radHand3,0);
                SetCtlValue(radHand4,0);
                alertVal = 2;
                break;
            case radBut3:
                SetCtlValue(radHand1,0);
                SetCtlValue(radHand2,0);
                SetCtlValue(radHand3,1);
                SetCtlValue(radHand4,0);
                alertVal = 3;
                break;
            case radBut4:
                SetCtlValue(radHand1,0);
                SetCtlValue(radHand2,0);
                SetCtlValue(radHand3,0);
                SetCtlValue(radHand4,1);
                alertVal = 4;
                break;
        /* When the Alert button is pressed, check alertVal to
           see which alert radio button is selected and invoke
           the appropriate alert routine */
            case alertBut:
                switch(alertVal) {
                    case PlainA:
                        result = Alert(333,NULL);
                        break;
                    case StopA:
                        result = StopAlert(333,NULL);
                        break;
                    case NoteA:
                        result = NoteAlert(333,NULL);
                        break;
                    case CautionA:
                        result = CautionAlert(333,NULL);
                        break;
                }
                break;
        /* For the next four cases, get a handle to the check
           box selected, change its value to the opposite, then
           change the value of the global variable checkVal,
           which keeps track of the check boxes status */
            case chkBox1:
                GetDItem(whichDialog,chkBox1,&type,&chkHand,&box);
                SetCtlValue(chkHand,!GetCtlValue(chkHand));
                checkVal ^= 1;
                break;
```

```
            case chkBox2:
                GetDItem(whichDialog,chkBox2,&type,&chkHand,&box);
                SetCtlValue(chkHand,!GetCtlValue(chkHand));
                checkVal ^= 2;
                break;
            case chkBox3:
                GetDItem(whichDialog,chkBox3,&type,&chkHand,&box);
                SetCtlValue(chkHand,!GetCtlValue(chkHand));
                checkVal ^= 4;
                break;
            case chkBox4:
                GetDItem(whichDialog,chkBox4,&type,&chkHand,&box);
                SetCtlValue(chkHand,!GetCtlValue(chkHand));
                checkVal ^= 8;
                break;
        }
}


/* DoWindowStuff takes care of mouse-downs in the
   drag region and goAway region of the modeless
   dialog */
DoWindowStuff(theEvent,whichWindow,windowcode)
    EventRecord *theEvent;
    WindowPtr    whichWindow;
    short        windowcode;
{
    Rect         screenRect;
    SetRect(&screenRect,10,30,502,332);

    switch(windowcode) {

        case inDrag:
            DragWindow(whichWindow,theEvent->where,&screenRect);
            break;
        case inGoAway:
            if(TrackGoAway(whichWindow,theEvent->where)) ExitToShell();
            break;
    }
}


/* DoModal takes four strings as its arguments,
   and checks the global variable chkVal to
   determine which strings to pass to the
   ParamText routine.  The strings that are
   passed to ParamText are put in the modal
   dialog that is placed on the screen.  */
DoModal(theText1,theText2,theText3,theText4)
    char    *theText1,*theText2,*theText3,*theText4;
```

```
{
    short       itemHit;
    DialogPtr   modal;

    if(!(checkVal & 1)) *theText1 = 0;
    if(!(checkVal & 2)) *theText2 = 0;
    if(!(checkVal & 4)) *theText3 = 0;
    if(!(checkVal & 8)) *theText4 = 0;

    ParamText(theText1,theText2,theText3,theText4);
    modal = GetNewDialog(332,NULL,(WindowPtr)-1);

    while(itemHit != 1) ModalDialog(NULL,&itemHit);
            CloseDialog(modal);
}

*   Source Code for Chapter 11 Sample Application Resources
*
*   Use the Apple Resource Compiler - RMaker

Chapt11.rsrc

Type ALRT

     ,333
100 106 184 368
333
7654


Type DITL

     ,333
2
*   1
BtnItem Enabled
47 152 67 212
OK

*   2
StatText Disabled
15 68 31 228
This is an Alert

     ,332
6
*   1
BtnItem Enabled
152 160 172 220
OK
```

```
*    2
StatText Enabled
9 9 25 369
These are the strings that were passed to ParamText:

*    3
StatText Enabled
40 24 56 384
^0

*    4
StatText Enabled
64 24 80 384
^1

*    5
StatText Enabled
88 24 104 384
^2

*    6
StatText Enabled
112 24 128 384
^3


      ,331
15
*    1
BtnItem Enabled
34 56 74 160
Modal Dialog

*    2
StatText Enabled
96 8 112 200
Text Strings for ParamText:

*    3
EditText Enabled
128 16 144 368
String 1

*    4
EditText Enabled
152 16 168 368
String 2

*    5
EditText Enabled
176 16 192 368
String 3
```

```
*    6
EditText Enabled
200 16 216 368
String 4

*    7
RadioItem Enabled
8 384 32 488
Plain Alert

*    8
RadioItem Enabled
32 384 56 488
Stop Alert

*    9
RadioItem Enabled
56 384 80 488
Note Alert

*    10
RadioItem Enabled
80 384 104 496
Caution Alert

*    11
BtnItem Enabled
32 280 72 368
Alert

*    12
ChkItem Enabled
128 376 144 472
Use String 1

*    13
ChkItem Enabled
152 376 168 472
Use String 2

*    14
ChkItem Enabled
176 376 192 480
Use String 3

*    15
ChkItem Enabled
200 376 216 480
Use String 4
```

```
Type DLOG

      ,332
Modal Dialog
62 72 242 470
Visible  NoGoAway
0
0
332

      ,331
Modeless Dialog
48 6 284 508
Invisible  GoAway
0
0
331
```

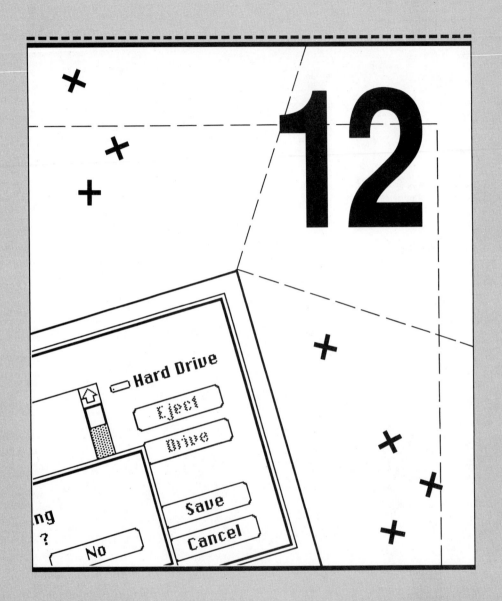

12

The Macintosh File System

The final topic that we need to cover before we can create a truly complete application is the Macintosh file system. In this chapter, we will explain how the Toolbox creates, reads, and writes data files. We will introduce the various elements of the file system, take a closer look at the standard file package that was introduced in Chapter 9, and then discuss the actual Toolbox calls used to manipulate and maintain files.

Volumes

A *volume* can be any piece or segment of storage medium that is capable of containing files. A volume can be the entire medium, as is the case with the 3 1/2-inch Macintosh disks, or it can be a smaller segment or partition of a larger storage device, such as a hard disk. Each volume is, in turn, subdivided into logical blocks of up to 512 bytes, depending on the medium. These blocks are the basic unit of space allocation on a volume. Every file on a volume is made up of an integral number of *allocation blocks*, which contain multiple logical blocks.

Volume Information

Every volume contains some important information about itself for use by the File Manager. This information includes the volume name, a file directory, and a volume allocation block map. The *volume name* consists of a string of up to 27 printing characters. Uppercase and lowercase letters can be used, but the File Manager does not make a distinction between the two. The *file directory* contains an entry for each file on the volume. Each entry contains the file's name, its location on the desktop, and the number of the first allocation block it occupies, as well as all the characteristic information about a file that we will discuss in this chapter. The *volume allocation block map* tells the File Manager which allocation blocks are free and which already belong to a file.

Accessing Volumes

Before a volume can be recognized by the Macintosh, it must first be *mounted* by the File Manager. When mounting a volume, the File Manager reads descriptive information about the volume into memory and assigns the volume a *volume buffer* and *volume reference number*. The volume buffer serves as a temporary storage space on the heap which is used when the File Manager reads and writes information on the volume. The volume reference number is used by many of the File Manager calls to identify the volume. It has an advantage over volume names in that it is always unique. Including the descriptive information and the space allocated for the volume buffer, each mounted volume occupies about 1.5K of memory. The number of volumes that may be mounted at any one time depends on the number of drives present and the amount of available memory.

Once mounted, volumes can be placed *on-line* or *off-line*. A volume is considered on-line as long as all the information in its volume buffer is still present in memory. When placed off-line, the volume buffer is flushed and removed from memory, leaving only essential descriptive information in memory. The File Manager can only access on-line volumes.

One volume is always the *default volume*. If no other volume is specified for an operation, the default volume is accessed. The volume used to start up the system is initially the default volume, but the application can designate which volume it wants to use as the default volume at any time.

Files

A Macintosh *file* consists of a sequential group of bytes identified by a *file name* and *version number*. The file name can be any string of up to 31 printing characters, excluding colons (:). In practice, any file name much longer than about 15 characters may be difficult to read on a crowded desktop. As with volume names, the File Manager allows the use of both uppercase and lowercase letters in the file name, but it doesn't make a distinction between the two. Finally, the file's version number is an integer between 0 and 255 and is used by the File Manager to distinguish between two files with the same name.

Each byte within a file is identified by its position within the sequence. Numbering begins at 0 and can increase to 16,777,216, making the maximum file size on the Macintosh 16 megabytes. Bytes can be read or written either singly or in sequences to or from anywhere within a file.

As mentioned in Chapter 9, a Macintosh file is divided into a resource fork and a data fork. For the most part, all of the data dealt with by the File Manager is contained in the data fork. There are a few occasions, however, when the File Manager needs to access the resource fork. Copying files is a good example. In this chapter, whenever we talk about "files," we are talking about the file's data fork unless stated otherwise.

File Layout

The physical size of a file, that is, the space it occupies on the disk, is indicated by the *physical end of file* (physical EOF). This number is always 1 greater than the sequence number of the last byte in the last allocation block of the file. The file's actual size, in bytes, is indicated by the *logical end of file* (logical EOF). The logical EOF is equal to 1 greater than the sequence number of the last byte in the file and (since the first byte of a file is 0) is equal to the number of bytes in the file. The logical EOF is always less than the physical EOF.

The file's *position marker*, which is often simply called its *mark*, indicates the number of the next byte that will be read or written. Of course, the value of the mark can't exceed the value of the logical

EOF. The mark is moved forward automatically by the File Manager after every read or write operation. If, during a write operation, the mark runs into the logical EOF, the File Manager will automatically advance the logical EOF as it needs to. The same thing happens when the physical EOF is reached. The difference is that, instead of being incremented by 1 (as the logical EOF is), the physical EOF will be incremented by 512 (the number of bytes in an allocation block), as the File Manager assigns another allocation block to the file.

The logical EOF can also be moved by the application to any position between the beginning of the file and the physical EOF. If the logical EOF is moved to a position more than one allocation block less than the physical EOF, the unneeded allocation block(s) will be deleted from the file. Figure 12.1 shows a schematic representation of a Macintosh file.

Accessing Files

Files can be either *open* or *closed*. Many operations can only be performed on files in one state or the other. For instance, only open files can be read from or written to, whereas only closed files can be deleted. When opening a file, the File Manager creates an *access path* to the file. The access path specifies the volume on which the file is located and the file's location on the volume. The File Manager also assigns a unique *path reference number* to each access path. Path reference numbers should always be used instead of names for identifying open files so that files with the same name won't get mixed up.

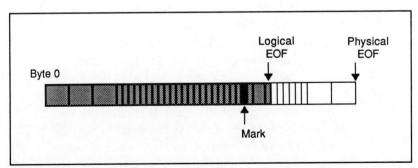

Figure 12.1: Macintosh Data Fork Structure

An access path will allow the File Manager to read from a file, write to it, or do both. Each file can have up to 12 access paths open at a time. However, only one access path can have write permission to a given file; the rest will be only able to read. Each of these access paths keeps track of its own mark within the file, but they will all share common logical and physical EOFs.

Before reading and writing files, the File Manager requires you to have an *application data buffer* from which the application actually gets its data. The File Manager always reads and writes data to files in logical blocks. During a read operation, the File Manager transfers data in logical block sized increments from the file to its application data buffer. If there is any data amounting to less than one logical block, it is read as a logical block anyway, except that the data is stored in a temporary storage space. The file system then determines how much of the data stored in the temporary storage space belongs to the file and reads it into the application.

The situation in writing to a file is very similar. When an application writes data to a file, it actually writes it to the application data buffer. The File Manager then transfers the data to the file in logical blocked sized increments. Any data less than one logical block in size is stored in a temporary storage space until a full logical block has accumulated or until the File Manager is specifically instructed to write the data to the file. Unless specified otherwise, the temporary storage space for read and write operations is in the volume buffer. The application does have the option to create a specific access path buffer to serve as this temporary storage space.

The Standard File Interface

Before we can begin actually manipulating files, we'll need to talk a bit about the Standard File package (SF package). The SF package provides the standard interface for file access on the Macintosh and consists of two dialog boxes: one for selecting a file to open and another for specifying a file to save to.

The SF package is made up of two basic procedures. **SFGetFile** displays the dialog box shown in Figure 12.2 and allows the user to specify which file on which volume and in which folder he or she wishes to select. The other procedure, **SFPutFile**, displays the dialog box shown in Figure 12.3 to let the user name the file to be saved or written to.

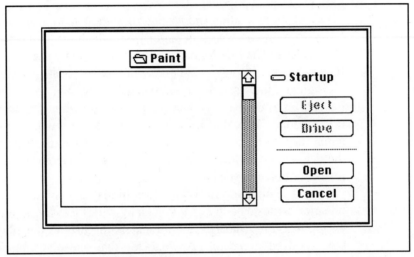

Figure 12.2: The **SFGetFile** Dialog Box

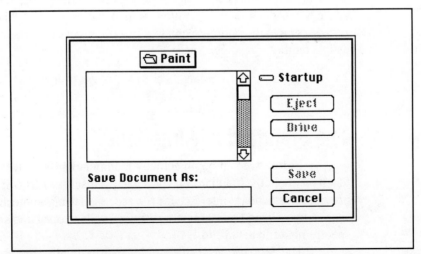

Figure 12.3: The **SFPutFile** Dialog Box

These dialog boxes share a few general characterstics. On the right-hand side of each dialog box, you'll notice the name of the current drive. At the top of the box, you'll find the current volume. In the example, the current volume is named Startup. Below this volume name are four buttons. When the Eject button is pressed, the Macintosh will eject the volume specified by the displayed volume name and display the name of the next mounted volume. If there are no other mounted volumes, the area where the volume name is displayed is left blank.

The Drive button allows the user to switch between mounted volumes, changing the displayed volume name accordingly. If only one volume is on-line, the Drive button is disabled.

The SF package is also prepared to handle disk inserted events. If the user responds to the dialog box by inserting a new disk into the disk drive, the SF package routine makes the newly inserted disk the current volume. If the inserted disk is uninitialized or not a Macintosh disk, the SF package routine will call the Disk Initialization package to prompt the user to initialize or eject the disk.

Both of these dialog boxes, as well as all of their behaviors, are already specified by the system. All the programmer needs to do is call the SF package procedures, as we will describe shortly. First, however, we'll need a little more background information about the SF package calls.

- - - - - - - -
The Reply Record

Both **SFGetFile** and **SFPutFile** use the same data structure, called a *reply record*, to communicate with the application that calls them. When passed a pointer to a reply record, each routine fills the structure with information and returns to the application a pointer to the structure.

The reply record's data type is defined to be SFReply, as shown in the box below.

The Macintosh interprets the first two fields as Pascal Booleans (if true, bit 0 is set; if false, bit 0 is clear). The first field is false when the user clicks the Cancel button and true if it's okay to continue on with the procedure. The copy field is not currently used by the operating system, so the next relevant field is fType. This field is used only by **SFGetFile** to store the selected file's type. Next, the vRefNum field contains the volume reference number associated with the selected file. The version field

---

Reply Record

```
struct SF {
        char            good;
        char            copy;
        long            fType;
        int             vRefNum;
        int             version;
        char[64]        fName;
};
#define SFReply struct SF
```

---

contains the selected file's version number. The last field, fName, contains the file's name. Be careful to note that the fName field is returned as a Pascal string. These three fields—vRefNum, version, and fName—are set up for use by the File Manager calls that we will cover later in this chapter.

Selecting a File

Whenever our application needs to access a file on a volume, it should call **SFGetFile**. It will display the modal dialog box shown in Figure 12.2 and handle all events until a file is selected or the Cancel button is pressed.

```
SFGetFile (where, prompt, fileFilter, numTypes, typeList,
   dlgHook, reply)
        Point           where;
        Str255          *prompt;
        ProcPtr         fileFilter;
        int             numTypes;
        SFTypeList      *typeList;
        ProcPtr         dlgHook;
        SFReply         *reply;
```

The where parameter specifies the location of the upper left-hand corner of the dialog box in global coordinates. The prompt parameter is left over from an older version of the standard file interface and is ignored by the procedure.

The next three parameters—fileFilter, numTypes, and typeList—all help determine which files are displayed in the **SFGetFile** dialog box.

SFGetFile first looks at the numTypes and typeList parameters to determine which files to display. Pass -1 in numTypes if you wish to display all file types; otherwise, pass the number of different file types that you wish to display in numTypes and pass the types themselves in typeList. The SFType-List data structure is defined in the box below.

SFTypeList

```
struct ST {
        long fType[4];
};

#define SFTypeList struct ST
```

Notice that the SFTypeList structure is defined to hold a maximum of four different file types. This is more than enough for most situations. However, if your application needs to specify more file types, you can define your own array type with the necessary number of entries and pass a pointer to it.

Using a File-Filter Routine

If you require more filtering than simply selecting files by file type, you can write a file-filter routine which would do any additional filtering required to specify the files that you wanted to display. For example, RMaker uses this to display only files which end in ".R". A pointer to this function is passed to **SFGetFile** in the fileFilter parameter. **SFGetFile** executes the filter function for each file to determine whether or not that file should be displayed. The filter function is passed a single parameter that we will discuss shortly (a pointer to a parameter block) and returns a Pascal Boolean result.

The general form of the filter function must be as follows:

```
char FileFilter (paramBlock)
      FileParam     *paramBlock;
```

This function is called by **SFGetFile** once for each file on the volume and returns false if the file is to be displayed, or true if it isn't. In determining which files to display, **SFGetFile** first looks at numTypes and SFTypeList and then looks at fileFilter. If you do not have a filter procedure, pass NULL as the fileFilter parameter. We've written an example of a file-filter function and included it in the sample code at the end of this chapter.

The dlgHook parameter is NULL. It is intended to act as a pointer to a control procedure for a custom dialog box, but since custom dialog boxes are beyond the scope of this discussion, we'll just define this parameter as NULL.

Finally, reply is a pointer to the reply record that **SFGetFile** used to identify the selected file. We will use reply when we begin accessing files.

Using SFPutFile

SFPutFile is the reciprocal function of **SFGetFile** and, not surprisingly, it works very similarly. **SFPutFile** requires five parameters, as follows:

```
SFPutFile (where, prompt, origName, dlgHook, reply)
        Point     where;
        Str255    *prompt;
        Str255    *origName;
        ProcPtr   dlgHook;
        SFReply   *reply;
```

The where parameter is the same as in **SFGetFile**. In contrast to **SFGetFile**, however, the prompt parameter here is used to specify a static text item that appears in the dialog box—for example, the message "Save current document as" (see Figure 12.3). The origName parameter is a pointer to a Pascal string that will serve as the default name in the **SFPutFile** dialog box. Quite often, origName is specified as Untitled, but you are free to define it to be anything that you wish. The last two parameters, dlgHook and reply, are the same as in **SFGetFile**.

Once displayed, the **SFPutFile** dialog box will handle all events until either the Save or Cancel button is pressed. **SFPutFile** will write the appropriate information to the reply record pointed to by reply if the Save button is pressed, and it will do nothing but cancel the dialog box if the Cancel button is pressed.

SFPutFile is also smart enough to deal with some of the problems it may encounter while trying to write its reply record. For instance, if the file name the user specifies in the dialog box already exists on the volume, **SFPutFile** will display the alert box shown in Figure 12.4.

Aside from clicking the Drive button, the user can specify a destination volume in **SFPutFile** by preceding the file name with a volume name and a colon. For instance, typing volumeName:folderName:FileName will save onto the volume named volumeName the file named FileName in the folder specified by folderName. If the user specifies a nonexisting volume in this manner or if the destination volume is locked, **SFPutFile** will display the appropriate alert boxes.

We need to make an important point before we move on. The **SFGetFile** and **SFPutFile** procedures only read and write to the specified reply record. They know nothing about the actual file whose identity is specified in the reply record. When calling **SFGetFile**, the application still needs to issue commands to open and read from a file before it can be aware of any information that exists there. Likewise, **SFPutFile** does not write and close a file. That also needs to be done by the application. Remember that **SFGetFile** and **SFPutFile** are only the interface to files and do not access the contents of the file. We'll learn how to do that next.

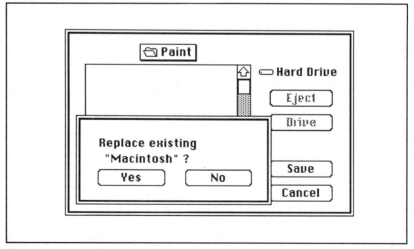

Figure 12.4:   Alert Box for Replacing an Existing File

The File Manager

In contrast with the SF package, which implements a standard user interface for file operations, the File Manager contains the actual Toolbox routines used to manipulate the contents of files. In many disk-related operations (such as copying or renaming a file), the SF package and the File Manager are used one after the other. The application will first call one or more routines from the SF package to allow the user to select the file and volume names to be used in the upcoming operation. After the necessary information has been obtained, the application will carry out the operation with the appropriate routines from the File Manager. In addition to the individual files, the File Manager is responsible for the volume's directory information, which covers every file on the volume.

An Overview of the File Manager

The routines found in the File Manager can be divided into three functional categories. First there are the routines for handling familiar I/O operations: opening a disk file, reading from and writing to a file, closing a file, and creating a new file. Next are the routines for manipulating files as a whole: renaming or deleting a file and obtaining or altering the descriptive information maintained for each file by the File Manager. Finally, there are the routines for manipulating entire volumes: mounting and unmounting volumes, changing the default volume, ejecting volumes, and obtaining descriptive information about a particular volume. To complement the routines that perform the tasks we have just mentioned, we will also discuss additional routines that implement less familiar operations on files and volumes.

Before we move on to describe the routines themselves, we must first briefly discuss the different types of routines that are available to our application.

Most of the capabilities of the File Manager can be accessed by using either of two methods. The Toolbox contains calls for all of the features of the File Manager; these routines are referred to as the *low-level* File Manager routines. Inside Macintosh also describes the *high-level* File Manager routines, which are a set of routines built upon the Toolbox routines.

The major difference between using the high-level and low-level routines from within an application are the calling conventions for the routines themselves. For instance, when referring to a particular volume, the high-level routines expect to be passed a pointer to the string containing the name of the volume. In general, the individual parameters required by the high-level routines must be kept in separate variables.

In contrast, each of the low-level routines has only two calling parameters. The first parameter is a pointer to a File Manager data structure known as a *parameter block* which contains all of the information required by the Toolbox routine. The requirements of all of the low-level routines can be met by just three variations on this basic data structure. Because the low-level routines all use nearly the same parameter block, one such block can be assigned to each file or volume. The same parameter block can then be used over and over again, each time a routine acting on the given file is called. Setting up the parameter blocks for the low-level routines requires some effort on the part of the programmer, but this effort is easily justified by the convenience of keeping track of fewer variables. The low-level routines are also faster, since the high-level routines must essentially recreate the parameter block with every call. Finally, in addition to the difference in speed and ease of use, the low-level routines provide other features not included in the high-level routines.

We have chosen not to discuss the high-level File Manager routines here since they do not provide any real advantage over the low-level routines, and our main purpose in writing this book is to describe and show examples using the routines of the Toolbox itself.

File Manager Data Structures

The File Manager, like the other portions of the Toolbox, uses several internal data structures to store and manipulate information about files and volumes. The first of these data types is used to keep information used exclusively by the Finder. The next three data types are the parameter blocks used by the low-level routines.

Finder Information

The first of these data structures is the FInfo, whose contents are listed in the box below. In this structure, the File Manager stores information used by the Finder for each file on a volume.

File Manager Data Structures: Finder Info

```
typedef long     OSType;

struct FInfo {
        OSType          fdType;         /* type of the file */
        OSType          fdCreator;      /* creator of the file */
        int             fdFlags;        /* file flags */
        Point           fdLocation;     /* position in window */
        int             fdFldr;         /* which folder */
};

#define    FInfo     struct FInfo
```

The type and creator of the file are stored in the fdType and fdCreator fields of the Finder information structure. The type and creator are contained in 32-bit fields and are composed of four ASCII characters, similar to the way resource types are made up, as described in Chapter 9. For example, the file type 'TEXT' is used to designate generic text documents; whereas a file of type 'WORD' and creator 'MACA' is a formatted word-processing document from MacWrite.

The fdFlags field consists of 16 flags (1 bit each) that contain information used by the Finder for every file on a volume. Figure 12.5 lists the locations of the various flags in the fdFlags field, along with several predefined constants that can be used when examining the value of the flags.

We have included a brief description of each flag in the box below, even though it is rarely necessary to use these flags from within an application. These flags are designed to be used by the Finder, and the result of altering any of their values from within an application is unreliable at best. Several applications do exist that allow the values of these flags to be safely changed, however. See, for instance, the file editor FEdit (written by John Mitchell) or the SetFile desk accessory (writ-

Bit Position	Flag Name	Constant Name and Value*	
0 - 7	Unused in Finder 4.1		
8	inited	#define cfInited	0x0100
9	changed	#define cfHasChanged	0x0200
10	busy	#define cfIsBusy	0x0400
11	no-copy or "bozo"	#define cfNoCopy	0x0800
12	system	#define cfSystemFile	0x1000
13	bundle	#define cfHasBundle	0x2000
14	invisible	#define cfInvisible	0x4000
15	locked	#define cfLocked	0x8000

* These are not the same as the predefined constants found in Inside Macintosh. The values in Inside Macintosh are measured relative to bit 8 of the word (the high-order byte). We have added the prefix "c" to the constant names to indicate this difference.

Figure 12.5:   The Finder Information Flags

Finder Flags

The *inited* flag is a signal to the Finder that it has seen this file in the past and has completed the process of initializing the file, which includes assigning it a location on the desktop and determining the icon used to represent the file.

The *changed* flag is used by the Finder to record whether the contents of a file have changed since the last time it was saved to disk.

The *busy* flag is set if the file has been opened by the File Manager so that it will not be destroyed or renamed inside the Finder.

If the *bozo* or *no-copy* flag is set, the Finder will not allow a file to be copied.

The *system* flag is used to indicate that a file is needed by the Macintosh operating system; the Finder posts an alert when the user attempts to throw away such a file.

The *invisible* flag determines whether or not the file's icon will be visible on the desktop.

The *bundle* flag determines if the file has its own icon for use on the desktop (see Chapter 13 for a discussion of assigning an icon to a file).

The *locked* bit can be used to ensure that the contents of a file are not disturbed; a locked file cannot be deleted, renamed, or written to from the Finder.

ten by Sam Roberts).

The final two fields of the Finder information structure, fdFolder and fdLocation, describe the window in which the file's icon will appear on the desktop and the icon's position in the local coordinates of this window. Three predefined constants are used to indicate special windows on the desktop. These constants are listed in Figure 12.6. We will see in the examples at the end of the chapter how the fdFolder field can be used to place a file into the same desktop folder as another file.

Parameter Blocks

In our introduction to the File Manager, we mentioned that parameter blocks are used to pass information back and forth between the application and the low-level routines of the File Manager. The three different forms of a parameter block correspond to the division of the File Manager routines into I/O-, file-, and volume-related routines. Roughly the first third of each type of parameter block is identical, with the latter two-thirds depending on the corresponding type of low-level operation.

Notice that the first eight fields are common to each of the three types of parameter blocks. Of these eight fields, only the last two are of any consequence to most applications; the first four fields are used internally by the File Manager, and the other two are used only during asynchronous operations. Since the final two fields, ioNamePtr and ioVRefNum, are used by almost every low-level routine, it is appropriate that we discuss the significance of these fields before we move on to the routines themselves.

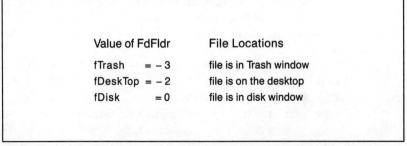

Value of FdFldr	File Locations
fTrash = −3	file is in Trash window
fDeskTop = −2	file is on the desktop
fDisk = 0	file is in disk window

Figure 12.6: Special Values of the fdFolder Field of the Finder Information Structure

File Manager Data Structures: The Parameter Blocks

```
/* file I/O parameter block */

struct IO {
        /* fields common to all parameter blocks */
        struct IO      *qLink;
        int            qType;
        int            ioTrap;
        Ptr            ioCmdAddr;
        ProcPtr        ioCompletion;      /* completion routine */
        OSErr          ioResult;          /* result code */
        char           *ioNamePtr;        /* volume or filename */
        int            ioVRefNum;         /* volume reference number */
        /* fields specific to I/O routines */
        int            ioRefNum;          /* path reference number */
        char           ioVersNum;         /* file version number */
        char           ioPermssn;         /* read/write permission */
        Ptr            ioMisc;            /* misc parameter */
        Ptr            ioBuffer;          /* buffer for read/write */
        long           ioReqCount;        /* requested number of bytes */
        long           ioActCount;        /* actual number of bytes */
        int            ioPosMode;         /* type of file positioning */
        long           ioPosOffset;       /* file position offset */
};

#define    ioParam    struct IO
#define    IOParam    struct IO /* added for consistency */

/* file info parameter block */

struct FP {
        /* fields common to all parameter blocks */
        struct FP      *qLink;
        int            qType;
        int            ioTrap;
        Ptr            ioCmdAddr;
        ProcPtr        ioCompletion;      /* completion routine */
        OSErr          ioResult;          /* result code */
        char           *ioNamePtr;        /* volume or filename */
        int            ioVRefNum;         /* volume reference number */
        /* fields specific to file info routines */
        int            ioFRefNum;         /* path reference number */
        char           ioFVersNum;        /* file version number */
        char           filler1;           /* not used */
        int            ioFDirIndex;       /* file directory index */
        char           ioFlAttrib;        /* file attributes */
        char           ioFlVersNum;       /* file version number */
```

```
        FInfo         ioFlFndrInfo;       /* finder information */
        long          ioFlNum;            /* file number */
        int           ioFlStBlk;          /* first block of data fork */
        long          ioFlLgLen;          /* logical length "" */
        long          ioFlPyLen;          /* physical length "" */
        int           ioFlRStBlk;         /* first block of resource fork */
        long          ioFlRLgLen;         /* logical length "" */
        long          ioFlRPyLen;         /* physical length "" */
        long          ioFlCrDat;          /* date and time of creation */
        long          ioFlMdDat;          /* date and time of modification */
};

#define       FileParam      struct FP


/* volume info parameter block */

struct VP {
/* fields common to all parameter blocks */
        struct VP     *qLink;
        int           qType;
        int           ioTrap;
        Ptr           ioCmdAddr;
        ProcPtr       ioCompletion;       /* completion routine */
        OSErr         ioResult;           /* result code */
        char          *ioNamePtr;         /* volume or filename */
        int           ioVRefNum;          /* volume reference number */
        /* fields specific to file info routines */
        long          filler2;            /* not used */
        int           ioVolIndex;         /* volume index */
        long          ioVCrDate;          /* initialization date/time */
        long          ioVLsBkUp;          /* last backup date/time */
        int           ioVAtrb;            /* volume attributes */
        int           ioVNmFls;           /* number of files */
        int           ioVDirSt;           /* first block of directory */
        int           ioVBlLn;            /* number of blocks in dir */
        int           ioVNmAlBlks;        /* number of alloc blocks */
        long          ioVAlBLkSiz;        /* size of alloc block */
        long          ioVClpSiz;          /* number of bytes to allocate */
        int           ioAlBlSt;           /* first block in block map */
        long          ioVNxtFNum;         /* next free file number */
        int           ioVFrBlk;           /* number of free alloc blocks */
};

#define       VolumeParam        struct VP
```

The application may specify a file on a particular volume in one of the following ways:

- The File Manager assumes the default volume is to be used if ioVRefNum contains the value zero.

- The File Manager interprets the value as a drive number (where 1 is the internal drive and 2 is the external drive) if ioVRefNum is positive.

- The application can use the value obtained from **SFPutFile** or any other routine that returns a volume reference number (here ioVRef-Num will be negative).

- The application can use the name of the volume, if the user included it, in the string pointed to by ioNamePtr, where the file, folder, and volume names are separated by a colon, as in the string volumeName:folderName:fileName. (This method is not recommended, as it may mislead the user into thinking he or she must always remember the names of the different volumes in use.)

Throughout the descriptions of the File Manager routines, we will assume that the reader is familiar with these four methods of specifying a file.

Using the Low-Level File Manager Routines

In this section, we will describe the low-level routines of the File Manager, beginning with a brief overview of how the application calls the routines and a discussion of the distinction between synchronous and asynchronous I/O operations. Next, we will discuss the routines by dividing them into the three categories: I/O, file, and volume routines. Along the way, we will include elementary examples showing how some of the routines may be used. In the final section of this chapter, we present more detailed examples using the Macintosh file system.

The application does not need to initialize the File Manager before calling any of its routines. The File Manager is automatically initialized along with other parts of the operating system when the Macintosh is powered up.

Low-Level Routines and Parameter Blocks

The names of the low-level File Manager routines begin with the letters **PB** to indicate that they require a parameter block. The general form of nearly all of these routines is that of a function consisting of two parameters that returns an error code.

However, the interaction between the low-level routines of the File Manager and the parameter blocks used to pass parameters back and forth complicates the manner in which we have been describing the routines of the Toolbox. It is now necessary to distinguish between the fields of the parameter block that are required by the Toolbox routine on the one hand and the fields that are used to return information to the application on the other. The following example illustrates the way in which we shall present this additional information:

```
OSErr PBSample(paramBlock, asynch)
        IOParam         *paramBlock; /* or
        FileParam       *paramBlock; or
        VolumeParam     *paramBlock; */
        char            asynch;

/*

        Parameter Block fields passed to PBSample:
                ioPassField1
                ioPassField2
                ioPassField3
                ioPassField4
                ioPassField5

        Parameter Block fields returned by PBSample:
                ioRetField1
                ioRetField2

        Possible Result Codes:
                noErr       anErr1      anErr2      anErr3      anErr4
                anErr5      anErr6

*/
```

The first three lines define the Toolbox routine in the same manner as we have used throughout the rest of the book—that is, in terms of the routine's calling arguments and return value. The paramBlock parameter is a pointer to one of the three types of parameter blocks, in particular, the type appropriate for the low-level routine in question. The asynch parameter is explained in the next section, Synchronous and Asynchronous Operations. The comment block following the function definition in the example above lists the fields of the parameter block that should be passed to the File Manager routine and which field will be returned to the application. The significance of each of these parameter block fields will be discussed for the individual File Manager routines.

All of the low-level File Manager routines return a 16-bit error code similar to the error codes returned by some of the routines in the Memory Manager. As a part of the definition of each low-level routine, we have included a listing of the error codes that can be returned from each routine. These error codes are summarized in Figure 12.7. A complete listing of the operating system error codes can be found in Appendix D. The sample application at the end of this chapter illustrates how to incorporate these error codes into an informative dialog box that can be used while debugging.

Synchronous and Asynchronous Operations

The majority of the File Manager's low-level routines can be executed either *synchronously* or *asynchronously*. If the application specifies that a routine be executed synchronously, the application must wait until the File Manager routine has completed before continuing on to the next instruction (this is the case with all other Toolbox routines). However, the application may instead specify that a routine be executed asynchronously, in which case the application is free to perform other tasks during the time the File Manager routine is executing. Requests for asynchronous File Manager operations are posted to the file I/O queue and executed on a first-in-first-out basis. The Boolean parameter asynch, common to nearly all of the low-level routines, specifies whether a particular routine should execute synchronously (asynch = false) or asynchronously (asynch = true).

If the application chooses to execute a File Manager routine asynchronously, then it must monitor two fields of the parameter block that would not otherwise be used. To determine if the routine has been completed, the application can examine the contents of the ioResult field. During the time that the routine is executing, ioResult will contain a positive value. Once the routine has completed, ioResult will contain the result usually returned as the value of the function (a negative error code if an error occurred or noErr if the operation was completed successfully). The application can also specify a routine, known as a *completion routine*, to be called immediately after the asynchronous routine has finished

Event Code			Error Message
badMDBErr	=	-60	bad master directory block - reinitialize volume
badMovErr	=	-122	attempted to move into offspring
dirFulErr	=	-33	file directory full
dirNFErr	=	-120	directory not found
dskFulErr	=	-34	no free allocation blocks on disk
dupFNErr	=	-48	duplicate filename
eofErr	=	-39	logical end-of-file
extFSErr	=	-58	volume in question belongs to an external file system
fBsyErr	=	-47	file is busy doing a delete operation
firstDskErr	=	-84	first of the range of low-level disk errors
fLckdErr	=	-45	file is locked
fnfErr	=	-43	file not found
fnOpnErr	=	-38	file not open
fsDSIntErr	=	-127	internal system file error
fsRnErr	=	-59	error during rename
gfpErr	=	-52	error during GetFPos
ioErr	=	-36	disk I/O error
lastDskErr	=	-64	last of the range of low-level disk errors
memFullErr	=	-108	not enough room in heap zone
mFullErr	=	-41	system heap is full
noErr	=	-0	no error
noMacDskErr	=	-57	not a Macintosh volume
nsDrvErr	=	-56	no such drive (tried to mount a bad drive num)
nsvErr	=	-35	no such volume
paramErr	=	-50	error in user parameter list
permErr	=	-54	permissions error (read/write not allowed)
posErr	=	-40	tried to position to before start of file
rfNumErr	=	-51	nonexistent access path
tmwdoErr	=	-121	Tto many working directories open
tmfoErr	=	-42	too many files open (12 maximum)
vLckdErr	=	-46	volume is locked (software)
volOffLinErr	=	-53	volume is not on line
volOnLinErr	=	-55	volume is already on-line
wrgVolTypErr	=	-123	attempt to do hierarchical operation on nonhierarchical volume
wrPermErr	=	-61	permission doesn't allow writing
wPrErr	=	-44	diskette is write protected (hardware)

Figure 12.7:   The File Manager Error Codes

executing. The application can place a pointer to this routine, or NULL to specify no completion routine, in the ioCompletion field of the parameter block passed to the routine to be executed asynchronously. If a low-level call is executed synchronously by the application, the File Manager will automatically set the ioCompletion field of the parameter block to NULL.

If an error occurs while an application is using asynchronous routines, it should remove the remaining calls from the queue. To flush all pending asynchronous file operations from the file I/O queue, except the one currently executing, the application can call the routine **InitQueue**:

```
InitQueue()
```

The I/O Routines

We begin our description of File Manager Toolbox routines with the familiar file I/O operations of creating, opening, and closing a file. This section also covers the routines for reading from and writing to a file, along with several more advanced routines.

Creating a New File

There are two general situations in which an application will create a new file. The first situation involves a request from the user, as will happen when either the New or Save As... items are chosen from the File menu. The second instance involves creating a file without direction from the user in applications that need to keep a scratch file on a disk for temporary storage.

In the first instance, the application calls **SFPutFile** from the SF package to allow the user to enter a file name and select the volume on which the disk should reside. In the second case, the application itself must determine an appropriate file name and volume. To avoid conflicts with existing files or with the scratch files from your own or other applications running in the Switcher or the MultiFinder, the application should base its scratch file names on the system clock or on a random text string.

After determining the file name and volume for the new file, call the routine **PBCreate**:

```
OSErr PBCreate (paramBlock, asynch)
        IOParam  *paramBlock;
        char     asynch;

/*

        Parameter Block fields passed to PBCreate:
                ioCompletion
                ioNamePtr
                ioVRefNum
                ioVersNum

        Parameter Block fields returned by PBCreate:
                ioResult

        Possible Result Codes:
                noErr    bdNamErr  dupFNErr  dirFulErr extFSErr
                ioErr    nsvErr    vLckdErr  wPrErr
*/
```

This routine will create an empty, unlocked file with the name contained in the Pascal string pointed to by the ioNamePtr field, on the volume specified by ioVRefNum (refer to the discussion earlier in the chapter on specifying a file). The ioVersNum parameter specifies the version number to be assigned to the new file. Your application must always set ioVersNum to 0 since the Resource Manager and the Segment Loader cannot operate on files with nonzero version numbers.

The file created by **PBCreate** will have its creation and modification dates set to the current time on the system clock. The application should call **PBSetFInfo** (which we will describe when we discuss file routines later in the chapter) to complete the information used by the Finder.

The following example shows how to use **SFPutFile** and **PBCreate** to create a new file on a volume. This example uses two routines that are included in the sample application at the end of the chapter. The first is the routine Pstrcpy, which is used to copy a string in Pascal format from one location to another, in analogy with the standard C routine strcpy. The second routine, OSError, can be used while debugging an application to inform the programmer about the occurrence File Manager errors. OSError displays a dialog box containing information about the error code passed as its second parameter; the other two parameters are arbitrary C strings specified by the application.

```
/* Example of creating a file with SFPutFile and PBCreate */

/* define some local variables */
SFReply         reply;
OSErr           theErr;
ioParam         newIOParmBlk;
Point           loc;
Str255          defaultName;

/* specify the upper right hand corner of SFPutFile's dialog */
SetPt(&loc,100,80);

/* set up a default filename */
Pstrcpy(&defaultName, "\pUntitled");

/* have the user enter a file name*/
SFPutFile(loc, "\pName the new file:", &defaultName, NULL,
          &reply);

/* if the user cancelled, abort and return . . . */
if(!reply.good) return;

/* otherwise, create the new file begin by setting up an IOParam
block*/

newIOParmBlk.ioNamePtr = &reply.fName;
newIOParmBlk.ioVRefNum = reply.vRefNum;
newIOParmBlk.ioVersNum = reply.version;

theErr = PBCreate(&newIOParmBlk, 0);

/* if theErr is non-zero, an error has occurred */
if(theErr) OSError("PBCreate", theErr, "creating the new file");
```

Opening a File for Reading or Writing

Before the application can examine or change the contents of a file with a read or write call, the file must first be opened. As we described at the beginning of this chapter, the process of opening a file creates an access path and a unique path reference number that will subsequently be used whenever the application accesses the file through this path. A file can have at most one access path with read and write or write-only permission at a given time; there is no such restriction for read-only paths. To open the data fork of a file, the application should call the routine **PBOpen**:

```
OSErr PBOpen(paramBlock, asynch)
        IOParam    *paramBlock;
        char       asynch;

/*

        Parameter Block fields passed to PBOpen:
                ioCompletion
                ioNamePtr
                ioVRefNum
                ioVersNum
                ioPermssn
                ioMisc

        Parameter Block fields returned by PBOpen:
                ioResult
                ioRefNum

        Possible Result Codes:
            noErrbdNamErr   extFSErr      fnfErr        ioErr
            mFullErr        nsvErr        opWrErr       tmfoErr
*/
```

The volume, name, and version number of the file to be opened should be placed into the parameter block, as always, before calling **PBOpen**. The parameter ioPermssn contains the read and write permission for the new access path. The predefined number values for specifying read and write permissions are listed in Figure 12.8. If the application attempts to open a second access path to a file with write permission, **PBOpen** will return the path reference number of the existing path in ioRefNum and the error code opWrErr as its function value. This same error code will be returned when the application attempts to open an access path with write permission for a locked file. However, **PBOpen** will not return an error if the application attempts to open a file for writing that resides on a locked volume; instead, the File Manager will report the error on the first write operation.

The ioMisc parameter can optionally contain a pointer to a 522-byte data buffer to be used by the access path instead of the volume

Value		Permission
fsCurPerm	= 0	whatever is currently allowed
fsRdPerm	= 1	read only permission
fsWrPerm	= 2	write only permission
fsRdWrPerm	= 3	read and write permission

Figure 12.8:   Constants Used to Set Read and Write Permission

buffer; pass the value NULL to use the volume buffer. If the application specifies such a buffer to be used, then all other access paths must share the same buffer to ensure that any write operations in the buffer are flushed to the disk before a read operation can take place.

An identical function exists to open the resource fork of a file. **PBOpenRF** should not be used to access the contents of a resource file; instead, use the routines of the Resource Manager. An application can use **PBOpenRF** to copy the resource fork of a file.

```
OSErr PBOpenRF (paramBlock, asynch)
        IOParam         *paramBlock;
        char            asynch;

/*

        Parameter Block fields passed to PBOpenRF:
                ioCompletion
                ioNamePtr
                ioVRefNum
                ioVersNum
                ioPermssn
                ioMisc

        Parameter Block fields returned by PBOpenRF:
                ioResult
                ioRefNum

        Possible Result Codes:
                noErr   bdNamErr   extFSErr      fnfErr        ioErr
                mFullErr           nsvErr        opWrErr       tmfoErr

*/
```

The following example shows how the SF package routine **SFGetFile** can be combined with **PBOpen** to open a file specified by the user.

```
/* Example of opening a file with SFGetFile and PBOpen */

/* define some local variables */
SFTypeList  typeList;
short       numTypes;
SFReply     reply;
OSErr       theErr;
ioParam     openIOParmBlk;
Point       loc;

/* location for SFGetFile's dialog box */
SetPt(&loc,100,80);

/* set up the filetypes to be shown in SFGetFile select only
'TEXT' and 'WORD' documents */

numTypes = 2;
typeList.ftype[0] = 'TEXT';
typeList.ftype[1] = 'WORD';

/* have the user select a file name */
SFGetFile(loc, NULL, NULL, numTypes, &typeList, NULL, &reply);

/* if the user cancelled, return to wherever we came from... */
if(!reply.good) return;

/* otherwise open the file's data fork set up the IOParam, choose
read-only permission */

openIOParmBlk.ioNamePtr = &reply.fName;
openIOParmBlk.ioVRefNum = reply.vRefNum;
openIOParmBlk.ioVersNum = reply.version;
openIOParmBlk.ioPermssn = fsRdPerm;
openIOParmBlk.ioMisc = NULL; /* use volume buffer */

theErr = PBOpen(&openIOParmBlk, 0);
if(theErr) {
        /* an error occurred while opening the file */
        OSError("PBOpen", theErr, "can't open this file");
        return;
}
```

Closing a File

To close an access path to a file, the application should call **PBClose** with the appropriate path reference number in the ioRefNum field of the parameter block.

```
OSErr PBClose(paramBlock, asynch)
        IOParam     *paramBlock;
        char        asynch;

        /* Parameter Block fields passed to PBClose:
                ioCompletion
                ioRefNum

        Parameter Block fields returned by PBClose:
                ioResult

        Possible Result Codes:
                noErr     extFSErr  fnfErr    fnOpnErr
                ioErr     nsvErr    rfNumErr  */
```

Each access path for a file must be closed individually before the application finishes; otherwise, the File Manager will not remove the flag indicating that the file is still open from the file's directory entry. The access path's buffer is flushed to complete any pending write operations before the access path is removed.

Reading the Contents of a File

To read from a disk file through an access path with read permission, use the function **PBRead**, as follows:

```
OSErr PBRead(paramBlock, asynch)
        IOParam     *paramBlock;
        char        asynch;

/*      Parameter Block fields passed to PBRead:
                ioCompletion
                ioRefNum
                ioBuffer
                ioReqCount
                ioPosMode
                ioPosOffset
```

```
Parameter Block fields returned by PBRead:
        ioResult
        ioActCount
        ioPosOffset

Possible Result Codes:
    noErr      eofErr          extFSErr          fnOpnErr
    ioErr      paramErr        rfNumErr
*/
```

The parameter ioRefNum specifies the access path to the file. **PBRead** attempts to read ioReqCount bytes from the file and places the data into the buffer pointed to by ioBuffer.

The ioPosMode and ioPosOffset parameters specify where the read operation should begin. Bits 0 and 1 specify whether the data to be read should begin relative to the beginning or end of the file, or from the current location of the file mark of the access path (recall that the file mark simply points to the byte following the last byte read from, or written to, the file). Bit 6 of ioPosMode, the verify flag, indicates that the File Manager should verify the data read into memory against the contents of the disk. When bit 7, the newline flag, is set, the File Manager will terminate **PBRead** at the first newline character, unless ioReqCount bytes have been read or the end of the file is encountered before a newline character can be found. The application specifies the desired newline character by placing it in the upper 8 bits of ioPosMode. Figure 12.9 lists the values used to position a call to **PBRead** and includes some convenient constants for manipulating the value of ioPosMode. Finally, the ioPosOffset parameter contains the offset in bytes, relative to the location indicated by ioPosMode, from which the first byte should be read.

After the **PBRead** routine has been completed, the current location of the file mark for this access path is returned in ioPosOffset. The number of bytes successfully read from the file is returned in ioActCount. If **PBRead** attempts to read past the logical EOF, the file mark for the access path will be placed at the end of the file and the error code eofErr will be returned.

The following short example illustrates how an application can read a section of a file into an arbitrary data buffer allocated by the application, for example, a WindowRecord. We assume that the file has

Value of ioPosMode   File positioning for Read/Write Operations

fsAtMark   = 0   begin at position of current file mark (ignore ioPosOffset)
fsFromStart = 1   use offset relative to start of file (use ioPosOffset)
fsFromLEOF = 2   use offset relative to logical end-of-file (use ioPosOffset)
fsFromMark = 3   use offset relative to current file mark (use ioPosOffset)

Notes:

Verify flag   - Bit 6 of ioPosMode can be set to force all read operations to be verified

Newline flag - Bit 7 of ioPosMode force read operation to terminate at the character
    specified in the upper 8 bits of ioPosMode.

Figure 12.9: Positioning Read and Write Operations with ioPosMode

already been opened with read permission, as in the previous example. This example makes use of the routine ErrDialog, which allows the application to display an error dialog consisting of three arbitrary C strings.

```
/* Example of reading from a file with PBRead
we assume the file has been previously opened
with the IOParam openIOParmBlk */

OSErr           theErr;
ioParam         openIOParmBlk;
Ptr             buffer;
WindowRecord    *aWindow;

/* allocate the WindowRecord on the heap */
aWindow = (WindowRecord *) NewPtr(sizeof(WindowRecord));

/* set up the IOParam for the read call */
openIOParmBlk.ioBuffer = aWindow;
openIOParmBlk.ioReqCount = sizeof(WindowRecord);
openIOParmBlk.ioPosMode = fsAtMark; /* read from the */
openIOParmBlk.ioPosOffset = 0L; /* current file mark */

theErr = PBRead(&openIOParmBlk, 0);
```

```
/* did an error occur? */
if(theErr) OSError("PBRead", theErr, "reading the WindowRecord");

/* check that the correct number of bytes were returned */
if(openIOParmBlk.ioActCount != openIOParmBlk.ioReqCount)
    ErrDialog("PBRead","wrong number of bytes read from file","");

/* close the access path when finished with file */
PBClose(&openIOParmBlk, 0);
```

We will use this method at the end of the chapter to read text from a file into an edit record as part of a text editor.

Writing to a File

Writing data to a file is very similar to reading from a file. The application can simply call the function **PBWrite** with the reference number of a path that has write permission to the file.

```
OSErr PBWrite(paramBlock, asynch)
        IOParam         *paramBlock;
        char            asynch;

        /* Parameter Block fields passed to PBWrite:
                ioCompletion
                ioRefNum
                ioBuffer
                ioReqCount
                ioPosMode
                ioPosOffset

        Parameter Block fields returned by PBWrite:
                ioResult
                ioActCount
                ioPosOffset

        Possible Result Codes:
                noErr      extFSErr  fnfErr     ioErr
                fnOpnErr   nsvErr    rfNumErr
*/
```

PBWrite will attempt to write ioReqCount bytes, from the buffer pointed to by ioBuffer, to the specified file. The parameters ioPosMode and ioPosOffset specify where the first byte from the write operation should be placed relative to the beginning or end of the file or to the current location of the file mark. The positioning methods used for **PBWrite** are identical to the methods used for **PBRead**, which are described in Figure 12.9.

PBWrite returns the number of bytes successfully written in ioActCount and the new position of the file mark in ioPosOffset. **PBWrite** automatically increments the number of allocation blocks assigned to the file if data would otherwise be written past the current end of the file.

The following short example illustrates how an application can write the contents of an arbitrary data structure to file. Notice that this example is nearly identical to the previous example for reading data from a file.

```
/* Example of writing to a file with PBWrite
we assume the file has been previously opened
for writing with the IOParam openIOParmBlk */

OSErr          theErr;
ioParam        openIOParmBlk;
Ptr            buffer;
WindowRecord   *aWindow;

/* assume the data in the WindowRecord is all ready to be written
to the disk */

/* set up the IOParam for the write call */
openIOParmBlk.ioBuffer = aWindow;
openIOParmBlk.ioReqCount = sizeof(WindowRecord);
openIOParmBlk.ioPosMode = fsAtMark; /* write starting at */
openIOParmBlk.ioPosOffset = 0L; /* the current file mark */

theErr = PBWrite(&openIOParmBlk, 0);

/* did an error occur? */
if(theErr)
        OSError("PBWrite", theErr, "writing the WindowRecord ");

/* check that the correct number of bytes were written */
if(openIOParmBlk.ioActCount != openIOParmBlk.ioReqCount)
        ErrDialog("PBRead",
                "wrong number of bytes written to file","");
```

```
/* close the access path when finished with file */
PBClose(&openIOParmBlk, 0);
```

Finding and Changing the Length of a File

To determine the length of a file, the application can call **PBGetEOF** with the reference number of an open access path to the file. The **PBGetEOF** routine returns the current location of the logical EOF in the ioMisc parameter.

```
OSErr PBGetEOF (paramBlock, asynch)
        IOParam          *paramBlock;
        char             asynch;

/*

        Parameter Block fields passed to PBGetEOF:
                ioCompletion
                ioRefNum

        Parameter Block fields returned by PBGetEOF:
                ioResult
                ioMisc

        Possible Result Codes:
                noErr           extFSErr
                fnOpnErr        ioErr
                rfNumErr

*/
```

The application can change the length of a file by changing either the logical or the physical EOF. The functions **PBSetEOF** and **PBAllocate** are designed for this purpose. **PBSetEOF** changes the length of a file by moving the logical EOF (and if necessary the physical EOF). **PBAllocate**, on the other hand, changes the file length by moving only the physical EOF. The access path that is used to specify the file for either **PBSetEOF** or **PBAllocate** must have write permission; otherwise, the error code wrPermErr will be returned. We will see in the examples at the end of the chapter how these routines are used in an application to read or write the contents of a file.

The application should pass **PBSetEOF** the desired location, in bytes, of the new logical EOF as the ioMisc parameter.

```
OSErr PBSetEOF(paramBlock, asynch)
        IOParam         *paramBlock;
        char            asynch;

/*
        Parameter Block fields passed to PBSetEOF:
                ioCompletion
                ioRefNum
                ioMisc

        Parameter Block fields returned by PBSetEOF:
                ioResult

        Possible Result Codes:
            noErr dskFulErr     extFSErr    fLckdErr fnOpnErr
            ioErr rfNumErr      vLckdErr    wPrErr   wrPermErr
*/
```

The new position of the logical EOF may be either beyond the current physical EOF or well short of it. If the logical EOF is more than a full allocation block short of the physical EOF, the extra block will be removed from the file. If the logical EOF is beyond the physical EOF, the File Manager will check to see if the required number of allocation blocks are available on the disk. If the additional space is available, the space will be added to the file and both the logical and physical EOFs will be moved to their appropriate locations. If the additional space is not available, the logical EOF is not moved, no allocation blocks are added to the file, and **PBSetEOF** will return the error code dskFulErr.

Setting the logical EOF to zero releases all disk space from the volume associated with the file, although the file will still exist in the file directory on the volume.

An application should not use **PBSetEOF** to lengthen a file unless it immediately writes into the newly created space and then readjusts the end of the file to the end of the data. Otherwise, the position of the logical EOF may confuse this or other applications, since the space located between the old and new logical EOFs is likely to contain garbage. Given this proviso, however, **PBSetEOF** can be used to find out if an upcoming write operation will overflow the disk.

The correct way for an application to reserve space for a file for the long term is with the routine **PBAllocate**. This routine might be useful, for example, when you wish to reserve space for a scratch file required by the application. The application should pass the reference number of an access path to the file in the ioRefNum parameter and the number of bytes to add to the file in the ioReqCount field of an IOParam.

```
OSErr PBAllocate (paramBlock, asynch)
        IOParam           *paramBlock;
        char              asynch;

/*

        Parameter Block fields passed to PBAllocate:
              ioCompletion
              ioRefNum
              ioReqCount

        Parameter Block fields returned by PBAllocate:
              ioResult
              ioActCount

        Possible Result Codes:
            noErr dskFu'     fLckdErr      fnOpnErr        ioErr
            rfNumErr         vLckdErr      wPrErr          wrPermErr
*/
```

The parameter ioActCount returns the number of bytes actually added to the file. Any difference between ioActCount and ioReqCount is due to the fact that the number of bytes added must be rounded up to the nearest multiple of the volume's allocation block size. Note that **PBAllocate** does not change the position of the logical EOF.

PBAllocate has the strange feature of allocating the remaining space on the volume before returning the error code dskFulErr if the amount of space available on the volume is less than the amount requested.

Miscellaneous I/O Routines

To flush any pending read or write operations from the buffer of an access path and update the file's directory entry on the disk, call **P-BFlshFile**, passing the appropriate path reference number. The application should call **PBFlshFile** (or better still, **PBFlshVol**, which is described in the Volume Routines section later in the chapter) periodically during extended write operations to minimize the amount of information lost in the event of an unexpected system error or power interruption.

```
OSErr PBFlshFile(paramBlock, asynch)
        IOParam          *paramBlock;
        char             asynch;

/*

        Parameter Block fields passed to PBFlshFile:
                ioCompletion
                ioRefNum

        Parameter Block fields returned by PBFlshFile:
                ioResult

        Possible Result Codes:
                noErr    extFSErr        fnfErr      fnOpnErr
                ioErr    nsvErr          rfNumErr
*/
```

The File Manager also contains two routines that allow the application to find or change the location of the file mark of an open access path. The application can call the routine **PBGetFPos** to determine the location of the file mark for the access path specified in the ioRefNum parameter of an IOParam.

```
OSErr PBGetFPos(paramBlock, asynch)
        IOParam     *paramBlock;
        char        asynch;

/*

        Parameter Block fields passed to PBGetFPos:
                ioCompletion
                ioRefNum

        Parameter Block fields returned by PBGetFPos:
                ioResult
                ioReqCount
                ioActCount
                ioPosMode
                ioPosOffset

        Possible Result Codes:
                noErr    extFSErr        fnOpnErr
                ioErr    rfNumErr
*/
```

The file mark is returned in ioPosOffset, while ioReqCount, ioAct-Count, and ioPosMode are all set to zero.

The application can also change the position of the file mark with the routine **PBSetFPos**.

```
OSErr PBSetFPos(paramBlock, asynch)
        IOParam          *paramBlock;
        char             asynch;

/*

        Parameter Block fields passed to PBSetFPos:
                ioCompletion
                ioRefNum
                ioPosMode
                ioPosOffset

            Parameter Block fields returned by PBSetFPos:
                ioResult

        Possible Result Codes:
                noErr       eofErr      extFSErr   fnOpnErr
                ioErr       posErr      rfNumErr
*/
```

The new file mark is specified as an offset in bytes, contained in ioPosOffset, from either the beginning or end of the file or from the current file mark, as specified by ioPosMode (see Figure 12.9). If the application attempts to position the file mark before the beginning of the file (or after the logical EOF) the error code posErr (or eofErr) will be returned by **PBSetFPos**. If one of these errors occurs, **PBSetFPos** will position the file mark at either the first byte of the file or at the logical EOF.

File Routines

The File Manager's file information routines are those routines that obtain or alter information concerning the file as a whole. The routines include familiar features such as renaming and deleting a file and locking (or unlocking) a file as a means of write-protecting its contents. In addition to describing these routines, we will take a look at two other routines that allow the application to access the File Manager's own internal information about each file on a disk. It's important to note that two of the routines we will discuss, **PBRename** and **PBSetFVers**, must use an IOParam as their parameter block. **PBSetFInfo** and **PBGetFInfo** must use a FileParam. The remaining routines in this section can use either a FileParam or an IOParam as their parameter block.

The sample program at the end of this chapter demonstrates many of the routines described in this section. For example, the sample program allows the user to rename or delete a file from within the application. The program also allows the user to view the internal File Manager information for a file with a dialog box.

Deleting a File

To delete a closed file from a volume, the application can call the function **PBDelete**, which expects the name, volume, and version number of the file to be in the ioNamePtr, ioVRefNum, and ioVersNum parameters of its parameter block. These parameters are used in the same way here as they are for the routine **PBCreate**.

```
OSErr PBDelete(paramBlock, asynch)
        IOParam        *paramBlock;
        char           asynch;
/*
        Parameter Block fields passed to PBDelete:
                ioCompletion          ioNamePtr
                ioVRefNum             ioVersNum

        Parameter Block fields returned by PBDelete:
                ioResult

        Possible Result Codes:
        noErr    bdNamErr     extFSErr     fBsyErr    fLckdErr
        fnfErr   ioErrnsvErr  vLckdErr     wPrErr
*/
```

Renaming Files and Volumes

The function **PBRename** can be used to rename either a file or a volume. To rename a file, the application should pass the name, volume, and version number of the file in the ioNamePtr, ioVRefNum, and ioVersNum fields, respectively. To rename a volume, pass either the volume name (ending in a colon) in ioNamePtr or just the volume reference number in ioVRefNum, along with the new volume name. **PBRename** expects to find a pointer to a Pascal string containing the new name in the ioMisc field of an IOParam block.

```
OSErr PBRename (paramBlock, asynch)
        IOParam         *paramBlock;
        char            asynch;

/*

        Parameter Block fields passed to PBRename:
                ioCompletion
                ioNamePtr
                ioVRefNum
                ioVersNum
                ioMisc

        Parameter Block fields returned by PBRename:
                ioResult

        Possible Result Codes:
         noErr      bdNamErr  dirFulErr   extFSErr      fLckdErr
         fnfErr     fsRnErr   ioErrnsvErr paramErr
         vLckdErr   wPrErr
*/
```

It is possible, although not recommended, to rename an open file. Since any existing access paths will not be disturbed, this can lead to the situation where the application will contain two parameter blocks indicating different names for the same file.

Locking and Unlocking a File

As we explained at the beginning of the chapter, the File Manager allows files to be locked or write-protected. A locked file cannot be deleted, renamed, or written to in any way (including changing the File Manager's internal file information). To lock (or unlock) a file, call **PBSetFLock** (or **PBRstFLock**) with the file name, the volume, and the version number in the ioNamePtr, ioVRefNum, and ioVersNum fields, respectively, of either an IOParam or a FileParam parameter block.

```
OSErr PBSetFLock (paramBlock, asynch)
        IOParam          *paramBlock;
        char             asynch;

/*

        Parameter Block fields passed to PBSetFLock:
                ioCompletion
                ioNamePtr
                ioVRefNum
                ioVersNum

        Parameter Block fields returned by PBSetFLock:
                ioResult

        Possible Result Codes:
                noErr       extFSErr  fnfErr    ioErr
                nsvErr      vLckdErr  wPrErr
*/


OSErr PBRstFLock (paramBlock, asynch)
        IOParam          *paramBlock;
        char             asynch;

/*

        Parameter Block fields passed to PBRstFLock:
                ioCompletion
                ioNamePtr
                ioVRefNum
                ioVersNum

        Parameter Block fields returned by PBRstFLock:
                ioResult

        Possible Result Codes:
                noErr       extFSErr  fnfErr    ioErr
                nsvErr      vLckdErr  wPrErr
*/
```

Access paths that are already open at the time the application locks or unlocks a file will not be affected. The application must close and then reopen all of the access paths leading to a file, so that the paths will reflect the new status of the file.

The File Manager also contains a routine for setting the version number of a file. The older versions of the Finder and of the Macintosh ROM handled the file version ambiguously. If you want to ensure backward compatibility for your application, this field should be set to zero. If you must use **PBSetFVers**, the file is specified by its name, volume, and current version number in the usual manner. The new version number for the file should be put into the ioMisc field of an IOParam block.

```
OSErr PBSetFVers(paramBlock, asynch)
        IOParam         *paramBlock;
        char            asynch;

/*
        Parameter Block fields passed to PBSetFVers:
                ioCompletion
                ioNamePtr
                ioVRefNum
                ioVersNum
                ioMisc

        Parameter Block fields returned by PBSetFVers:
                ioResult

        Possible Result Codes:
                noErr       bdNamErr    dupFNErr   fLckdErr   fnfErr
                ioErr       nsvErr      paramErr   vLckdErr   wPrErr
*/
```

PBSetFVers does not affect access paths open at the time it is called by the application.

Copying or Modifying Information About a File

The File Manager maintains a rather long list of information about each file on a volume. The information, which is returned in the form of a FileParam parameter block, includes the following:

- A copy of the Finder information
- A set of attribute flags for the File Manager

- The file creation and modification dates and times
- Information about the location and number of allocation blocks assigned to the resource and data forks of the file

The Finder information is kept in a data structure called a FInfo (described in the File Manager Data Structures section earlier in the chapter) as a part of the FileParam parameter block, and it can be examined or modified by an application through the File Manager. Earlier in the chapter, we pointed out which portions of this information can be altered by the application and which portions cannot.

The File Manager's internal file attribute flags are stored in the ioFlAttrib field of the FileParam. The current version of the Macintosh file system uses 5 bits of the ioFlAttrib to indicate that a file is locked, in use, or not copyable. Figure 12.10 shows how to interpret the value of the ioFlAttrib field. In practice, only the locked flag is normally changed by an application. For more information about this field, consult *Inside Macintosh*, IV-122.

The remaining fields in a FileParam are either self-explanatory (such as the creation and modification dates) or beyond the scope of this book. We will not discuss, for example, the subject of which allocation blocks are assigned to the data and resource forks of a file.

To obtain a copy of the File Manager information for a particular file, call the routine **PBGetFInfo** with the name, volume, and

Bit Position	Flag Name	Constant Name and Value*	
0	locked	#define fsLocked	0x01
2	resource fork open	#define fsResOpen	0x04
3	data fork open	#define fsDataOpen	0x08
4	directory	#define fsDirectory	0x10
7	file open (busy)	#define fsBusy	0x80

*These constants are not found in Inside Macintosh. We have defined them here for use in the examples at the end of the chapter. The prefix "fs" indicates that these are File System flags, as opposed to Finder flags.

Figure 12.10:   File Manager Attribute Flags

version number of the file in the ioNamePtr, ioVRefNum, and ioFVersNum parameters, respectively, of a FileParam block.

The ioFDirIndex field should be set to zero. It can be used in an alternate form of file addressing, which we will not get into here. If you're interested in its application, consult *Inside Macintosh*, IV-148.

```
OSErr PBGetFInfo(paramBlock, asynch)
        FileParam       *paramBlock;
        char            asynch;
/*

        Parameter Block fields passed to PBGetFInfo:
                ioCompletion
                ioNamePtr
                ioVRefNum
                ioFVersNum
                ioFDirIndex

        Parameter Block fields returned by PBGetFInfo:
                ioResult
                ioFRefNum
                ioFlAttrib
                ioFlVersNum
                ioFlFndrInfo
                ioFlNum
                ioFlStBlk
                ioFlLgLen
                ioFlPyLen
                ioFlRStBlk
                ioFlRLgLen
                ioFlRPyLen
                ioFlCrDat
                ioFlMdDat

        Possible Result Codes:
                noErr      bdNamErr       extFSErr       fnfErr
                ioErr      nsvErr         paramErr
*/
```

The File Manager allows the application to modify only the Finder information and creation and modification dates for a file. The remaining fields of the File Manager information are used internally by the File Manager. The application should call the routine **PBSetFInfo** with the name, volume, and version number of the file in the appropriate parameters of a FileParam block. The modified Finder information and new creation and modification dates should be put into the ioFndrInfo, ioFlCrDat, and ioFlMdDat fields, respectively, of the FileParam prior to calling **PBSetFInfo**.

```
OSErr PBSetFInfo (paramBlock, asynch)
        FileParam       *paramBlock;
        char            asynch;

/*

        Parameter Block fields passed to PBSetFInfo:
                ioCompletion
                ioNamePtr
                ioVRefNum
                ioVersNum
                ioFndrInfo
                ioFlCrDat
                ioFlMdDat

        Parameter Block fields returned by PBSetFInfo:
                ioResult

        Possible Result Codes:
                noErr  bdNamErr   extFSErr    fLckdErr  fnfErr
                ioErr  nsvErr     vLckdErr    wPrErr

*/
```

The following example illustrates the combined use of **PBGetFInfo** and **PBSetFInfo** to set the relevant information for a file being copied from another file. This ensures that copy has the same type and creator and creation and modification dates as the original file. In addition, the file is placed into the same folder on the desktop as the original file.

```
/* example using PBGetFInfo and PBSetFInfo during a file copy to
make the new file (file2) look like a copy of file1 */

/* declare the local variables */

OSErr       theErr;
FileParam   f1FParmBlk, f2FParmBlk;

/* we assume the FileParam blocks have already had the ioNamePtr,
ioVRefNum, and ioVersNum fields filled in with information from
SFPutFile and SFGetFile */
```

```
/* Get the information about the existing file, file1 */
theErr = PBGetFInfo(&f1FParmBlk, 0);
if(theErr) OSError("PBGetFInfo", theErr, "for file1");

/* Get the information about the new file, file2 */
theErr = PBGetFInfo(&f2FParmBlk, 0);
if(theErr) OSError("PBGetFInfo", theErr, "for file2");

/* copy the Finder Information to the new file */
f2FParmBlk.ioFlFndrInfo.fdType = f1FParmBlk.ioFlFndrInfo.fdType;
f2FParmBlk.ioFlFndrInfo.fdCreator =
    f1FParmBlk.ioFlFndrInfo.fdCreator;
f2FParmBlk.ioFlFndrInfo.fdFlags =
    f1FParmBlk.ioFlFndrInfo.fdFlags;
f2FParmBlk,ioFlFndrInfo.fdFldr = f1FParmBlk,ioFlFndrInfo.fdFldr;

/* clear the inited flag; the Finder needs to initialize file 2
    */
f2FParmBlk.ioFlFndrInfo.fdFlags &= 0xffff - cfInited;

/* copy the creation and modification dates */
f2FParmBlk.ioFlCrDat = f1FParmBlk.ioFlCrDat;
f2FParmBLk.ioFlMdDat = f1FParmBLk.ioFlMdDat;

/* call PBSetFInfo to set the information for file2 */
theErr = PBSetFInfo(&f2FParmBlk, 0);
if(theErr) OSError("PBSetFInfo", theErr, "for file2");
```

Volume Routines

The File Manager's volume information routines are those routines that deal with information about entire volumes. The tasks performed by the volume routines include flushing I/O buffers, ejecting volumes, and obtaining a copy of the File Manager's private volume information. Many of the volume routines embody concepts that will be unfamiliar to most readers unless they are familiar with low-level file operations from another computer. These routines include mounting and unmounting volumes, placing a volume off-line, and changing the default volume. All of the routines we are about to describe, with the exception of **PBGetVolInfo**, use only the first few fields of a parameter block and can therefore use either an IOParam, a FileParam, or a VolumeParam. **PBGetVolInfo** requires that a VolumeParam be used as its parameter block.

The File Manager's Volume Information

In addition to the information that the File Manager maintains for every file on a volume, it also keeps a list of information about the volume itself. This information, which can be obtained by the application as a VolumeParam block, includes the date that the volume was first initialized and when it was last copied as a whole. Other fields of a VolumeParam contain a set of 16 volume attribute flags, a description of the layout of the volume's file directory, and information about the size of the volume and the number of free allocation blocks on the volume. Bit 15 of the volume attribute flags field will be set if the volume is locked. To obtain a copy of this information, the application can call the routine **PBGetVolInfo**, as follows:

```
OSErr PBGetVolInfo(paramBlock, asynch)
        VolumeParam      *paramBlock;
        char             asynch;

/*
        Parameter Block fields passed to PBGetVolInfo:
                ioCompletion
                ioNamePtr
                ioVRefNum
                ioVolIndex

        Parameter Block fields returned by PBGetVolInfo:
                ioResult
                ioNamePtr
                ioVRefNum
                ioVCrDate
                ioVLsBkUp
                ioVAtrb
                ioVNmFls
                ioVDirSt
                ioVBlLn
                ioVNmAlBlks
                ioVAlBLkSiz
                ioVClpSiz
```

```
                    ioAlBlSt
                    ioVNxtFNum
                    ioVFrBlk

          Possible Result Codes:
                    noErr       nsvErr       paramErr
*/
```

If the application passes a positive value for ioVolIndex, **PBGetVol-Info** will attempt to return information about the volume with the given index. (Volume indices are assigned in the order that volumes are mounted; that is, the first mounted volume is assigned index 1, and so on.) If ioVolIndex is negative, the File Manager assumes that the application has either specified the volume by name in the ioNamePtr field or by its volume reference number or drive number in ioVRefNum. If ioVolIndex is zero, only the ioVRefNum field is used to determine the volume. **PBGet-VolInfo** returns the volume reference number of the volume in ioVRefNum and copies the name of the volume into the string pointed to by ioName-Ptr, unless ioNamePtr is a NULL pointer.

The Default Volume

The File Manager specifies one of the volumes currently mounted as the default volume. If the application does not specify a volume reference number for a File Manager routine that requires one, the default volume will be used instead (an error will occur if a default volume has not been selected). The application can call the routine **P-BGetVol** to obtain the name and reference number of the current default volume.

```
OSErr PBGetVol(paramBlock, asynch)
          VolumeParam       *paramBlock;
          char              asynch;

/*

          Parameter Block fields passed to PBGetVol:
                    ioCompletion

          Parameter Block fields returned by PBGetVol:
                    ioResult
                    ioNamePtr
                    ioVRefNum
```

```
        Possible Result Codes:
                noErrnsvErr
*/
```

PBGetVol returns the name of the default volume in the string pointed to by ioNamePtr, unless ioNamePtr is a NULL pointer.

The application can change the default volume by calling **PBSet-Vol**. The volume that is to become the default is specified by a suitable combination of ioVRefNum and ioNamePtr (recall our earlier discussion of specifying volumes in the section called Creating a New File).

```
OSErr PBSetVol(paramBlock, asynch)
        VolumeParam     *paramBlock;
        char            asynch;

/*
        Parameter Block fields passed to PBSetVol:
                ioCompletion
                ioNamePtr
                ioVRefNum

        Parameter Block fields returned by PBSetVol:
                ioResult

        Possible Result Codes:
                noErr           bdNamErr
                nsvErr          paramErr*/
```

The SF package routines **SFGetFile** and **SFPutFile** will use the default disk when they first put up their respective dialog boxes. Thus, one possible use for these routines is to change the SF package dialog boxes to begin with a particular disk.

Preparing to Eject a Volume

The process of ejecting a volume from an application is usually handled by one of the SF package routines. It is also possible for the application to eject a disk on its own.

Ejecting a volume occurs in three separate stages. First, the volume buffers and access paths for files on the volume are flushed. Next, the volume is placed off-line to release most of the memory space associated with the volume. Finally, the command to eject the volume is sent to the driver controlling the disk drive containing the volume (this allows for disk drives other than the standard 3 1/2-inch floppy drives).

The simplest way for an application to eject a disk is to call the routine **PBEject**.

```
OSErr PBEject(paramBlock, asynch)
        VolumeParam      *paramBlock;
        char             asynch;

/*

        Parameter Block fields passed to PBEject:
                ioCompletion
                ioNamePtr
                ioVRefNum

        Parameter Block fields returned by PBEject:
                ioResult

        Possible Result Codes:
                noErr        bdNamErr        extFSErr   ioErr
                nsDrvErr     nsvErr          paramErr
*/
```

The application specifies the volume to eject with the ioNamePtr and ioVRefNum fields of the parameter block it passes to **PBEject**. Before ejecting the volume, **PBEject** calls the File Manager's routines **PBFlshVol** and **PBOffLine**. Let's take a look at each of these routines.

To flush the volume buffer and the buffers of each access path associated with a file on a volume, the application can call the routine **PBFlshVol**. It is a good idea for the application to call **PBFlshVol** frequently to keep the contents of open files as up-to-date as possible in case of a power failure or any disaster that might interfere with the normal operation of the application.

```
OSErr PBFlshVol(paramBlock, asynch)
        VolumeParam      *paramBlock;
        char             asynch;

/*

        Parameter Block fields passed to PBFlshVol:
                ioCompletion
                ioNamePtr
```

```
                    ioVRefNum

            Parameter Block fields returned by PBFlshVol:
                    ioResult

            Possible Result Codes:
                    noErr        bdNamErr        extFSErr  ioErr
                    nsDrvErr     nsvErr          paramErr
    */
```

In situations where an application is desperately in need of memory space, one possible source of relief is to place unused volumes off-line. Putting unused volumes off-line will release all but 94 bytes of descriptive information about the volume, with a resulting release of between 1 and 1.5K bytes of memory per volume. If the File Manager subsequently needs to access an off-line volume, it will automatically be placed back on-line.

The application can call **PBOffLine** with the name of the volume or the volume reference number in the ioNamePtr or ioVRefNum fields of the parameter block.

```
OSErr PBOffLine(paramBlock, asynch)
        VolumeParam     *paramBlock;
        char            asynch;

/*

        Parameter Block fields passed to PBOffLine:
                ioCompletion
                ioNamePtr
                ioVRefNum

        Parameter Block fields returned by PBOffLine:
                ioResult

        Possible Result Codes:
                noErr        bdNamErr   extFSErr  ioErr
                nsDrvErr     nsvErr     paramErr
    */
```

PBOffLine calls **PBFlshVol** to flush the volume and access path buffers before placing the volume off-line.

Mounting and Unmounting Volumes

As is the case with ejecting volumes, most applications will not ever need to mount or unmount a volume. Volumes are mounted automatically whenever the Event Manager routine **GetNextEvent** detects a disk-inserted event. The routine **PBMountVol** mounts the volume in the drive indicated by the drive number in the ioVRefNum parameter and then returns the volume reference number, again in ioVRefNum. If at the time **PBMountVol** was called there was no default volume, the volume to be mounted will become the default volume. Neither **PBMountVol**, or its counterpart PBUnmountVol, may be executed asynchronously.

```
OSErr PBMountVol(paramBlock)
        VolumeParam      *paramBlock;


/*

        Parameter Block fields passed to PBMountVol:
                ioVRefNum


        Parameter Block fields returned by PBMountVol:
                ioResult        ioVRefNum


        Possible Result Codes:
                noErr           bdNamErr        extFSErr    ioErr mFulErr
                noMacDskErr     nsDrvErr        paramErr    volOnLinErr
*/
```

PBUnmountVol unmounts the volume indicated by the ioNamePtr and ioVRefNum fields. Before releasing all of the memory space associated with the volume, **PBUnmountVol** calls **PBFlshVol** to flush the volume and access path buffers to the volume and then closes all of the open files on the volume. The application must never unmount the start-up volume, since it contains files required by the operating system.

```
OSErr PBUnmountVol(paramBlock)
        VolumeParam      *paramBlock;

 /*

        Parameter Block fields passed to PBUnmountVol:
                ioVRefNum


        Parameter Block fields returned by PBUnmountVol:
                ioResult
```

```
        ioVRefNum

Possible Result Codes:
        noErr     bdNamErr  extFSErr  ioErr
        nsDrvErr  nsvErr    paramErr
*/
```

Programming Examples

In this final section of the chapter, we will present several programming examples built upon routines of the SF package and the File Manager. The first example is a filtering function to be used in conjunction with **SFGetFile** to select only files of a specific type and creator for your application. The example contains three routines to be added to the text-editing application that we presented in Chapter 8. These routines allow the user to open text files and save them back to disk. The final example is a small application that allows the user to copy, rename, delete, and obtain descriptive information about a file.

The final two sections make frequent use of several routines that we have not yet discussed. These include standard routines for manipulating C and Pascal formatted strings. The remaining routines, OSError and ErrDialog, are used to display a generic dialog box containing debugging information as well as information intended for the user. The C sources for the string routines and the dialog routines are included in the sample application at the end of the chapter.

A Filter Procedure for SFGetFile

There will be times in your application when you will need to filter files for selection by **SFGetFile** on a more specific basis than simply by type. You'll recall that when we discussed the SF Package, we mentioned that **SFGetFile** is capable of calling a supplemental filter routine that will determine whether a specific file should be displayed by the **SFGetFile** dialog box. This routine can be as simple or complex as you care to make it.

The sample filter function that follows is for the very simple case of choosing files by creator. The actual filter routine is called File-Filter. It is passed a pointer to a parameter block and must return a Boolean indicating whether or not the file represented by the parameter block should appear in the **SFGetFile** dialog box.

```
pascal Boolean FileFilter(FlParamBlk)   /* The Filter function */
    FileParam     *FlParamBlk;
{   char    show;
    OSType  myCreator;
    myCreator = 'MACA';      /* Created by MacWrite */
    if ((FlParamBlk->ioFlFndrInfo).fdCreator == myCreator)
        show = 0;  /* Show It */
    else
        show = 1;  /* Don't Show It */
    return show;
    /* Tell SFGetFile whether to display it or not */
}
```

To let **SFGetFile** know that we wish to use a filter function, we need to pass a pointer to the function in its filterProc field.

Adding Open and Save Commands to the Text-Editing Application

The major ingredient missing from the text-editing sample application presented in Chapter 8 is the ability to open a file on a disk or to save a file back to a disk. The only major modification to the code of Chapter 8 is the addition of several fields to the WindowStuff data structure that we associated with each open window. We have added fields for a file name, volume, and version number, and a flag to indicate if the file has been changed since it was last saved.

Opening a File for Editing

The procedure DoOpen, described below, allows the user to read the contents of a specified file into the editor. To include DoOpen in the sample text editor, simply add an Open item to the File menu, which when selected calls DoOpen. This routine obtains a file name from the user with **SFGetFile**, creates a new window and edit record, and then proceeds to read the contents of the file into the edit record. Along the way, the application checks to make certain that the file is not too big to fit in an edit record and that sufficient memory space is available.

```
DoOpen()/* DoOpen() */

/* This routine will open any 'TEXT' and if its length does not
exceed 30K, will open a window, create an edit record and copy
the contents of the file into the edit record. This assumes that
in addition to the fields discussed previously, we have added the
following fields to the WindowStuff structure assigned to each
window:

struct WindowStuff {
        Str255     fileName;      - file name for the window
        int        vRefNum;       - volume refNum of file
        char       versNum;       - version number of file
        char       changed;       - file changed since last save

};
*/

{ /* define local variables */
        SFTypeList typeList;
        int        numTypes;
        SFReply    reply;
        OSErr      theErr, anErr;
        ioParam    anIOParmBlk;
        Point      loc;
        Ptr        buffer;
        long       textLength, size;
        WindowPtr  tempWindow;
        TEHandle   temphTE;
        WSHandle   tempWS;
        Handle     textH;
        Ptr        textPtr;
        CursHandle watchH;

        /* select filetypes for SFGetFile: all file of type
    'TEXT' */
        numTypes = 1;
        typeList.ftype[0]='TEXT';
```

```
/* let the user select a file to open */
SetPt(&loc,100,80);
SFGetFile(loc, NULL, NULL, numTypes, &typeList, NULL,
          &reply);

/* did the user hit cancel? */
if(!reply.good) return;

/* open the file's data fork with read-only permission */
anIOParmBlk.ioNamePtr = &reply.fName;
anIOParmBlk.ioVRefNum = reply.vRefNum;
anIOParmBlk.ioVersNum = reply.version;
anIOParmBlk.ioPermssn = fsRdPerm;
anIOParmBlk.ioMisc = NULL;

theErr = PBOpen(&anIOParmBlk, 0);
if(theErr) {
    /* bail out . . . can't open the file */
    OSError("PBOpen", theErr, "error opening the file");
    return;
}

/* how much text is in the file? */
theErr = PBGetEOF(&anIOParmBlk, 0);
if(theErr) {
    /* something is wrong, close file and return */
    OSError("PBGetEOF", theErr, "error determining EOF");
    PBClose(&anIOParmBlk, 0);
    return;
}

/* will the file fit in an edit record? */
if((textLength = anIOParmBlk.ioMisc) >= 30*1024) {
    /* the file is too long, close it and return */
    ErrDialog("The file", PtoCstr(anIOParmBlk.ioNamePtr),
    "exceeds 30K, too long for this editor");

    CtoPstr(anIOParmBlk.ioNamePtr);
    PBClose(&anIOParmBlk, 0);
    return;
}
```

```
/* At this point, we are ready to read the file, first open a
window, and create an edit record for the text. Use the file name
as the title of the window */
```

```
        /* is one of the two windows free?
        - what must be done to add more windows? */
        if(windPtrA != NULL && windPtrB != NNULL) {
                /* Both windows are open, close file and return */
                ErrDialog("Both windows are already occupied",
                "I'm too dumb to open another window", "Fix Me!");

                PBClose(&anIOParmBlk, 0);
                return;
        }

    /* Open a new window, OpenWindow is part of the application in
    Chapter 8 */

        if(windPtrA == NULL) {
                tempWindow =

OpenWindow(windRecA, &windowRectA, anIOParmBlk.ioNamePtr);
                windPtrA = tempWindow;
        }
        else if(windPtrB == NULL) {
                tempWindow =

OpenWindow(windRecB, &windowRectB, anIOParmBlk.ioNamePtr);
                windPtrB = tempWindow;
        }

    /* get a copy of the text handle for the edit record, resize to
    the file size */

        tempWS = (WSHandle)GetWRefCon(tempWindow);
        temphTE = (*tempWS)->theTEH;

        textH = (*temphTE)->hText;
        SetHandleSize(textH, textLength);
        size = GetHandleSize(textH);

        /* was there enough memory available? */
        if(size != textLength) {
                ErrDialog("Insufficient Memory to open the file",
                "or some other memory problem", "");

                PBClose(&anIOParmBlk, 0);
                /* Dispose of the Window and the edit record */
                KillWindow(tempWindow);
                return;
```

```
    }

    /* put up the watch cursor until we're finished */
    watchH = GetCursor(watchCursor);
    SetCursor(*watchH);

    /* lock and dereference the text handle, to use as a
buffer */
    HLock(textH);
    textPtr = *textH;

    /* read the contents of the file into the buffer textPtr
*/
    anIOParmBlk.ioBuffer = textPtr;
    anIOParmBlk.ioReqCount = textLength;
    anIOParmBlk.ioPosMode = fsAtMark;
    anIOParmBlk.ioPosOffset = 0L;

    theErr = PBRead(&anIOParmBlk, 0);
    /* any errors during the read?, EOF's are OK */
    if((theErr) && (theErr!=eofErr))
        OSError("PBRead", theErr, "reading the text file");

    /* did we get the expected number of bytes? */
    if(anIOParmBlk.ioActCount != anIOParmBlk.ioReqCount)
        ErrDialog("PBRead","wrong number of bytes read from
        file","");

    /* close the file, we're finished with it */
    PBClose(&anIOParmBlk, 0);

    /* Unlock the text handle */
    HUnlock(textH);

    /* change the teLength field of the edit record */
    (*temphTE)->teLength = textLength;

    /* set-up the file stuff in the WindowStuff for the
    window */
    HLock(tempWS);

    /* copy the filename, version number and volume
    reference number into the WindowStuff */

    (*tempWS)->vRefNum = anIOParmBlk.ioVRefNum;
    (*tempWS)->versNum = anIOParmBlk.ioVersNum;
```

```
        /* copy the string used by the IOParam, into the
WindowStuff */
        Pstrcpy(&(*tempWS)->fileName, anIOParmBlk.ioNamePtr);

        /* clear the file's dirty bit, we just opened it */
        (*tempWS)->changed = 0;

        HUnlock(tempWS);

        /* calculate line starts draw the text */
        HLock(temphTE);
        TECalText(temphTE);
        TEUpdate(&(*temphTE)->viewRect, temphTE);
        HUnlock(temphTE);

        /* ready to go, fix the cursor and return */
        SetCursor(&QD->arrow);

        return;
}
```

Saving the File Back to Disk

Most text editors and word processors will have both a Save
and a Save As . . . menu item to allow the user to save the text that they
have created in either the same file as the text came from or in another
file. The procedures DoSave and DoSaveAs should be called whenever the
user chooses either the Save or Save As . . . menu items from the File
menu. The first procedure, DoSave, opens the file named in the Window-
Stuff of the active window and writes the contents of the window's edit
record into the open file. If the user has not yet specified a file name to
be used, for example, if the user opens a new window, DoSave calls the
second procedure, DoSaveAs, to get a name from the user. DoSaveAs, in
turn, calls DoSave to complete the task of writing the file to disk.

```
DoSave()      /* DoSave() */
/* This routine will save the contents of the front window to the
file named in its WindowStuff record. It warns the user if the
file cannot be found, or if sufficient space is not available on
the disk. */
```

```
{        /* local variables */
         OSErrtheErr, anErr;
         ioParam        anIOParmBlk;
         Pointloc;
         Ptr  buffer;
         long textLength, size;
         int  kind;
         char changed;
         Str255         str1;
         WindowPtr      tempWindow;
         TEHandle       temphTE;
         WSHandle       tempWS;
         Handle         textH;
         Ptr  textPtr;
         CursHandle     watchH;

         /* Is the front window an editing window?
         - we have added a line to OpenWindow that sets the
         windowKind of each of the applications editing windows
         to the constant myKind
         */

         tempWindow = FrontWindow();
         kind = ((WindowPeek) tempWindow)->windowKind;
         if(kind != myKind) {
            ErrDialog("This window is not an edit window!","","");
            return;
         }

         /* has the text changed since the last save? check the
dirty bit */

         tempWS = (WSHandle) GetWRefCon(tempWindow);
         changed = (*tempWS)->changed;
         if(!changed) {
                 ErrDialog("Text has not changed since",
                 "the last time it was saved","");

                 return;
         }

         /* does the window have a file name? if not, try
         DoSaveAs */
         if((*tempWS)->fileName.count == NULL) {
                 DoSaveAs();
                 return;
```

```
        }

        /* get the text handle and length of the text */
        HLock(tempWS);
        temphTE = (*tempWS)->theTEH;
        textH = (*temphTE)->hText;
        textLength = (*temphTE)->teLength;

        /* set up the IOParam for the file with write permission
and open
        the file */

        anIOParmBlk.ioNamePtr = (char *) &(*tempWS)->fileName;
        anIOParmBlk.ioVRefNum = (*tempWS)->vRefNum;
        anIOParmBlk.ioVersNum = (*tempWS)->versNum;
        anIOParmBlk.ioPermssn = fsWrPerm;
        anIOParmBlk.ioMisc = NULL;

        theErr = PBOpen(&anIOParmBlk, 0);
        if(theErr) {
                OSError("PBOpen", theErr, "can't open the file");
                HUnlock(tempWS);
                return;
        }

        /* set Logical EOF to length of text in edit record */
        /* Caution: ioMisc is a Ptr must cast textLength to
        a Ptr */
        anIOParmBlk.ioMisc = (Ptr) textLength;
        theErr = PBSetEOF(&anIOParmBlk, 0);
        if(theErr) {
                /* an error occurred close file and return */
                OSError("PBSetEOF", theErr, "on output file");
                if(theErr==dskFulErr) ErrDialog("The disk is full",
                "Try saving to another disk",
                PtoCStr(NumToString(textLength, &str1)) );
                PBClose(&anIOParmBlk, 0);
                HUnlock(tempWS);
                return;
        }

        /* set file mark to beginning of file */
        anIOParmBlk.ioMisc = NULL;
        anIOParmBlk.ioPosMode = fsFromStart;
        anIOParmBlk.ioPosOffset = 0L;
```

```
theErr = PBSetFPos(&anIOParmBlk, 0);
if(theErr) {
        OSError("PBSetFPos", theErr,
                "error setting file mark");
        PBClose(&anIOParmBlk, 0);
        HUnlock(tempWS);
        return;
}

/* display the watch cursor until we're finished */
watchH = GetCursor(watchCursor);
SetCursor(*watchH);

/* write text into file - first lock handle to text and
dereference to get a buffer pointer */

HLock(textH);
textPtr = *textH;

/* write the contents of the file into the block
at textH */
anIOParmBlk.ioBuffer = textPtr;
anIOParmBlk.ioReqCount = textLength;
anIOParmBlk.ioPosMode = fsAtMark;
anIOParmBlk.ioPosOffset = 0L;

theErr = PBWrite(&anIOParmBlk, 0);

/* check for errors */
if(theErr)
        OSError("PBWrite", theErr,
                "writing into the file");

/* were the expected number of bytes written? */
if(anIOParmBlk.ioActCount != anIOParmBlk.ioReqCount)
        ErrDialog("PBWrite",
                "wrong number of bytes written to file",
                "");

/* close the file and flush it's volume */
PBClose(&anIOParmBlk, 0);
PBFlshVol(&anIOParmBlk, 0);

HUnlock(textH);

/* clear the file's dirty bit, since we just saved it */
```

```
        (*tempWS)->changed = 0;

        HUnlock(tempWS);

        /* restore cursor and return to the application */
        SetCursor(&QD->arrow);

        return;
}
```

The final procedure, DoSaveAs, allows the user to save the text under a different file name than the window's current title or to assign a file name to an untitled window. One important feature of DoSaveAs is exercised when the user chooses to save a file to a file that already exists. The routine **SFPutFile** warns the user if a file already exists and requires the user to acknowledge this fact before replacing the file. DoSaveAs must then reset the logical EOFs of both the data and resource forks to eliminate the previous contents of the file.

```
DoSaveAs()
/* This routine obtains a new file name from the user and creates
it the specified disk, deleting older versions if necessary. It
then changes the window title, updates the WindowStuff and calls
  DoSave. */

{       /* local variables */
        SFReply         reply;
        OSErr           theErr, anErr;
        ioParam         newIOParmBlk;
        FileParam       newFParmBlk;
        Point           loc;
        int             kind;
        char            *putStr = "Save File as:";
        Str255          defaultName;
        WindowPtr       tempWindow;
        WSHandle        tempWS;

        /* Is the front window an editing window? */
        tempWindow = FrontWindow();
        kind = ((WindowPeek) tempWindow)->windowKind;
        if(kind != myKind) {
                ErrDialog("This window is not an editing window!",
                        "","");
                return;
```

```
    }

    /* make the default title string */
    tempWS = (WSHandle) GetWRefCon(tempWindow);
    HLock(tempWS);
    if((*tempWS)->fileName.count == NULL) {
            Pstrcpy(&defaultName, "\pUntitled");
    }
    else {
            Pstrcpy(&defaultName, "\pCopy of ");
            Pstrcat(&defaultName, &(*tempWS)->fileName);
    }
    HUnlock(tempWS);

    /* select the destination file */
    SetPt(&loc,100,80);
    SFPutFile(loc, CtoPstr(putStr), &defaultName, NULL,
            &reply);
    PtoCstr(putStr);

    /* did the user choose cancel? */
    if(!reply.good) return;

    /* create the new file */
    newIOParmBlk.ioNamePtr = &reply.fName;
    newIOParmBlk.ioVRefNum = reply.vRefNum;
    newIOParmBlk.ioVersNum = reply.version;

    if(theErr = PBCreate(&newIOParmBlk, 0)) {

            /* for all errors except file exists, return */
            if(theErr != dupFNErr) {
                    OSError("PBCreate", theErr,
                            "Creating the new file");
                    return;
            }

            /* if the new file name exists
               - set EOF's to zero */
            if(theErr == dupFNErr) {
                newIOParmBlk.ioPermssn = fsWrPerm;
                newIOParmBlk.ioMisc = NULL;
                theErr = PBOpen(&newIOParmBlk, 0);
                newIOParmBlk.ioMisc = (Ptr) 1;
                /* well, not quite zero */
                theErr |= PBSetEOF(&newIOParmBlk, 0);
```

```
                    PBClose(&newIOParmBlk, 0);
                    newIOParmBlk.ioMisc = NULL;
                    theErr |= PBOpenRF(&newIOParmBlk, 0);
                    theErr |= PBSetEOF(&newIOParmBlk, 0);
                    PBClose(&newIOParmBlk, 0);
                    if(theErr) {
                      ErrDialog("Problems setting EOF's to NULL",
                                "on an existing file",
                                "during Save As");

                                return;
                            }
                    }
            }

        /* set file and creator of the file to our own type */
        newFParmBlk.ioCompletion = NULL;
        newFParmBlk.ioNamePtr = newIOParmBlk.ioNamePtr;
        newFParmBlk.ioVRefNum = newIOParmBlk.ioVRefNum;
        newFParmBlk.ioFVersNum = newIOParmBlk.ioVersNum;
        newFParmBlk.ioFDirIndex = 0;

        theErr = PBGetFInfo(&newFParmBlk, 0);
        if(theErr) OSError("PBGetFInfo", theErr, "getting info
for file");

        /* set creator, type, creation and mod date, attributes
*/
        newFParmBlk.ioFlFndrInfo.fdType = 'TEXT';
        newFParmBlk.ioFlFndrInfo.fdCreator = 'FD&J';
        newFParmBlk.ioFlFndrInfo.fdFlags = NULL;

        theErr = PBSetFInfo(&newFParmBlk, FALSE);
        if(theErr) OSError("PBSetFInfo", theErr,
                        "setting info file");

                /* flush volume buffers to the disk */
                PBFlshVol(&newIOParmBlk, 0);

        /* change the window title and update the WindowStuff */
        HLock(tempWS);

        Pstrcpy(&(*tempWS)->fileName, newIOParmBlk.ioNamePtr);
        (*tempWS)->vRefNum = newIOParmBlk.ioVRefNum;
```

```
(*tempWS)->versNum = newIOParmBlk.ioVersNum;
(*tempWS)->changed = 0xff;
/* true - go ahead and save it */

SetWTitle(tempWindow, newIOParmBlk.ioNamePtr);

HUnlock(tempWS);

/* call DoSave to write text to the disk */
DoSave();
return;
}
```

There are still a few remaining items that need to be added to
the text-editing application to make it complete. The most obvious ones
are scroll bars for the text windows and features for handling desk accessories. Other minor additions include changing the Close menu item
so that a window's contents will be saved if its dirty bit is set, fixing the
Font menu so that it shows the available fonts and sizes, and adding
more informative dialog boxes and alerts. In the next chapter, we will
discuss the topic of desk accessories. The remaining features are left up
to the interested reader.

▬ ▬ ▬ ▬ ▬

A Sample Program Illustrating the Macintosh File System

This sample application is a relatively simple program that allows
the user to rename, delete, or copy a file. We have also included a menu
item that displays a dialog box containing useful information about a file,
including the Finder information, and the File Manager attribute flags. At
the end of the program listing, we have included the source code to several
string-manipulation routines that we have used throughout the examples in
this chapter. Also included are two routines for displaying generic dialog
boxes during the debugging phase of writing an application.

```
/* This application must be broken into two segments, one for the application
      code and the other for the library code. This can be done from
      Project box in THINK C.     */


/* include Mac header files */
#include <WindowMgr.h>
#include <MemoryMgr.h>
#include <EventMgr.h>
#include <TextEdit.h>
#include <FontMgr.h>
#include <MenuMgr.h>
#include <ToolboxUtil.h>
#include <DialogMgr.h>
#include <PackageMgr.h>
#include <StdFilePkg.h>
#include <IntlPkg.h>
#include <FileMgr.h>
#include <Strings.h>
#include <stdio.h>


extern    char      *Pstrcpy();
extern    char      *Pstrcat();

/* add Complete Finder attributes flags */
#define    cfInited        0x0100
#define    cfHasChanged    0x0200
#define    cfIsBusy        0x0400
#define    cfNoCopy        0x0800
#define    cfSystemFile    0x1000
#define    cfHasBundle     0x2000
#define    cfInvisible     0x4000
#define    cfLocked        0x8000
/* add File System attribute flags */
#define    fsLocked        0x01
#define    fsNoCopy        0x40
#define    fsBusy          0x80


/* size of disk buffer for file copies */
#define BUFFERSIZE  4096

/* constants for menus and menuitems */
#define    Desk_ID   100

#define    Edit_ID     102
#define    undoItem    1
#define    cutItem     3
#define    copyItem    4
```

```
#define    pasteItem      5
#define    clearItem      6

#define    File_ID        101
#define    fcopyItem      1
#define    frenameItem    2
#define    fdeleteItem    3
#define    finfoItem      4
#define    quitItem       6

/* constants for dialogs kept in the resource file prog12.res
    (Resource Compiler source code listed at end of application code) */
#define errDialogID       9999
#define finfoDialogID     10000

#define    fnameDItem           7
#define    vnameDItem           8
#define    typeDItem            9
#define    createDItem          10
#define    sizeDItem            11
#define    fLockedDItem         25
#define    fInvisibleDItem      26
#define    fBundleDItem         27
#define    fSystemDItem         28
#define    fNoCopyDItem         29
#define    fBusyDItem           30
#define    fChangedDItem        31
#define    fInitedDItem         32
#define    fsBusyDItem          33
#define    fsNoCopyDItem        34
#define    fsLockedDItem        35
#define    creationDItem        38
#define    modifiedDItem        39

#define    SFName2ROM(x)        (x)

/* External and non-integer functions */

char       *ErrMessage();
Str255     *Num2String();
long       String2Num();

/* Global Variables */
MenuHandle  DeskMenu;
MenuHandle  FileMenu;
MenuHandle  EditMenu;

/* begin code */

reStartProc()
{
```

```
   ExitToShell();
}


SetUpMenus()                                              /* SetUpMenus() */
{
   long    items, i;

   InitMenus();

   DeskMenu=NewMenu(Desk_ID, "\p\24");
   AppendMenu(DeskMenu,"\pAbout...;(-");
   AddResMenu(DeskMenu,'DRVR');
   items = CountMItems(DeskMenu);
       for(i=3;i<=items;i++) DisableItem(DeskMenu, i); /* disable desk accessories */
   InsertMenu(DeskMenu,0);                                    /* until Chapter 13 */

   FileMenu=NewMenu(File_ID,"\pFile");
   AppendMenu(FileMenu,
      "\pCopy File;Rename File;Delete File;File Info;(-;Quit/Q");
   InsertMenu(FileMenu,0);

   EditMenu=NewMenu(Edit_ID,"\pEdit");
   AppendMenu(EditMenu, "\pUndo;(-;Cut/X;Copy/C;Paste/V;Clear");
   DisableItem(EditMenu,0);                             /* disable Edit menu until */
   InsertMenu(EditMenu,0);                              /* a desk accessory is opened */

   DrawMenuBar();
}


Init()                                                    /* Init() */
{
   InitGraf(&thePort);
   InitFonts();
   InitWindows();
   InitDialogs(reStartProc);
   TEInit();
   SetUpMenus();
   InitCursor();

   FlushEvents(everyEvent, 0);
}

/* the main event loop */
main()                                                    /* main() */
{
   short          windowcode,stillInGoAway;
   char           c;
   long           newSize;
   EventRecord    theEvent;
```

```
    WindowPtr      whichWindow;

    Init();

    while(0xff) {

        if(GetNextEvent(everyEvent,&theEvent)) {
            switch (theEvent.what) {

                case keyDown:
                    c=theEvent.message & keyCodeMask;
                    if (theEvent.modifiers & cmdKey) {
                        DoMenu(MenuKey(c));
                        HiliteMenu(0);
                    }
                    break;

                case mouseDown:
                    windowcode=FindWindow(theEvent.where,&whichWindow);
                    switch(windowcode) {
                        case inDesk:
                            break;

                        case inMenuBar:
                            DoMenu(MenuSelect(theEvent.where));
                            break;

                        case inSysWindow:
                            break;

                    }
                    break;

                default:
                    break;
            }
        }
    }
}

/* respond to menu selections */
DoMenu(menuResult)                                        /* DoMenu() */
    long    menuResult;
{
    short    menuID,itemNumber;

    menuID=HiWord(menuResult);
    itemNumber=LoWord(menuResult);

    switch(menuID) {
```

```
        case Desk_ID:
           if(itemNumber==1)  AboutWindow();
           else {
               /* Desk accessory was selected - see Chapter 13 */
           }
           break;

        case File_ID:
           switch (itemNumber) {
              case fcopyItem:
                 DoFileCopy();
                 break;

              case frenameItem:
                 DoFileRename();
                 break;

              case fdeleteItem:
                 DoFileDelete();
                 break;

              case finfoItem:
                 DoFileInfo();
                 break;

               case quitItem:
                 ExitToShell();
                 break;
           }
        break;

        case Edit_ID:                     /* ignore Edit menu for now */
           switch(itemNumber) {           /* -only used here for DA's */
              case undoItem:
                 break;
              case cutItem:
                 break;
              case copyItem:
                 break;
              case pasteItem:
                 break;
              case clearItem:
                 break;
           }
      }
   HiliteMenu(0);
}

/* Rename a file */
DoFileRename()                                          /* DoFileRename() */
{
```

```
SFTypeList    typeList;
short         numTypes;
SFReply       reply, Preply;
OSErr         theErr, anErr;
IOParam       theIOParmBlk, dupIOParmBlk;
Point         loc;
char          *putStr = "\pRename File to:";
Str255        defaultName;

/* select filetypes for SFGet */
numTypes = -1;

/* select the file to rename */
SetPt(&loc,100,80);
SFGetFile(loc, "\p", (Ptr) NULL, numTypes, &typeList, NULL, &reply);

/* exit if user hit cancel button */
if(!reply.good) return;
   /* set up default name for rename: Not-... */
   strcpy(&defaultName, "Not-");
   strcat(&defaultName, PtoCstr((char *) &reply.fName));
   CtoPstr((char *) &reply.fName);
   CtoPstr((char *) &defaultName);

/* let user select the new file name (must be same disk!) */
do {
   SFPutFile(loc, putStr, &defaultName, NULL, &Preply);
   if(!Preply.good) return;                   /* user cancelled operation */
   if(reply.vRefNum != Preply.vRefNum)
     ErrDialog("You cannot rename a file across disks","Please try again","");
} while(reply.vRefNum != Preply.vRefNum);

/* set up an IOParam */
theIOParmBlk.ioNamePtr    = SFName2ROM(reply.fName);
theIOParmBlk.ioVRefNum    = reply.vRefNum;
theIOParmBlk.ioVersNum    = reply.version;
theIOParmBlk.ioMisc       = (Ptr) SFName2ROM(Preply.fName);  /* new file name */

theErr = PBRename(&theIOParmBlk, 0);
if(theErr==dupFNErr) {          /* file with new name exists - delete it first */
   dupIOParmBlk.ioNamePtr    = SFName2ROM(Preply.fName);
   dupIOParmBlk.ioVRefNum    = reply.vRefNum;
   dupIOParmBlk.ioVersNum    = reply.version;
   PBDelete(&dupIOParmBlk, 0);

   /* try renaming again */
   theErr = PBRename(&theIOParmBlk, 0);
   if(theErr) OSError("PBRename", theErr, "Couldn't rename after delete");
} else {
   if(theErr) OSError("PBRename", theErr, "Error during Rename");
}
```

```
    PBFlshVol(&theIOParmBlk, 0);
}

/* delete a file */
DoFileDelete()                                    /* DoFileDelete() */
{
    SFTypeList   typeList;
    short        numTypes;
    SFReply      reply, Preply;
    OSErr        theErr, anErr;
    IOParam      theIOParmBlk;
    Point        loc;

    /* select filetypes for SFGet */
    numTypes = -1;

    /* select the file to delete */
    SetPt(&loc,100,80);
    SFGetFile(loc, "\p", (Ptr) NULL, numTypes, &typeList, NULL, &reply);

    /* quit of user hit cancel button */
    if(!reply.good) return;

    /* set up an IOParam */
    theIOParmBlk.ioNamePtr    = SFName2ROM(reply.fName);
    theIOParmBlk.ioVRefNum    = reply.vRefNum;
    theIOParmBlk.ioVersNum    = reply.version;

    theErr = PBDelete(&theIOParmBlk, 0);
    if(theErr) OSError("PBDelete", theErr, "could not delete the file");

    PBFlshVol(&theIOParmBlk, 0);
}

/* Put up dialog with Finder Info, etc... */
DoFileInfo()                                              /* DoFileInfo() */
{
    SFTypeList   typeList;
    short        numTypes, shr;
    SFReply      reply, Preply;
    OSErr        theErr, anErr;
    FileParam    anFParmBlk;
    VolumeParam  aVolParmBlk;
    Point        loc;
    Str255       sizeStr, volStr, str1, str2;
    char         *p;
    DialogPtr    theDialog;
    short        itemHit;
    short        itemType;
    Handle       itemHandle;
```

```
    Rect          itemRect;

    /* select filetypes for SFGet (all) */
    numTypes = -1;

    /* select the file to delete */
    SetPt(&loc,100,80);
    SFGetFile(loc, "\p", (Ptr) NULL, numTypes, &typeList, (Ptr) NULL, &reply);
    if(!reply.good) return;                  /*user cancelled operation */

    /* prepare FileParam for PBGetFInfo */
    anFParmBlk.ioNamePtr    = SFName2ROM(reply.fName);
    anFParmBlk.ioVRefNum    = reply.vRefNum;
    anFParmBlk.ioFVersNum   = reply.version;
    anFParmBlk.ioFDirIndex  = 0;

    /* prepare VolumeParam for PBGetVolInfo */
    aVolParmBlk.ioVRefNum   = reply.vRefNum;
    aVolParmBlk.ioVolIndex  = 0;
    aVolParmBlk.ioNamePtr   = (unsigned char *) &volStr;

    /* get file information */
    theErr = PBGetFInfo(&anFParmBlk, 0);
    if(theErr) {
       OSError("PBGetFInfo", theErr, "the requested file for info");
       return;
    }

    /* get volume information */
    theErr = PBGetVolInfo(&aVolParmBlk, 0);
    if(theErr) {
       OSError("PBGetVolInfo", theErr, "the file's volume info");
       return;
    }

    /* Start setting up the dialog */
    theDialog = GetNewDialog(finfoDialogID, NULL, (WindowPtr) -1L);


    /* File Name */
    GetDItem(theDialog, fnameDItem, &itemType, &itemHandle, &itemRect);
    SetIText(itemHandle, anFParmBlk.ioNamePtr);

    /* Volume Name */
    GetDItem(theDialog, vnameDItem, &itemType, &itemHandle, &itemRect);
    SetIText(itemHandle, aVolParmBlk.ioNamePtr);

    /* File Type */
    GetDItem(theDialog, typeDItem, &itemType, &itemHandle, &itemRect);
/* In general strncpy does NOT put the NULL at the end of the string */
    p = strncpy(&str1, &anFParmBlk.ioFlFndrInfo.fdType, 4);
```

```
      *(p+4) = '\0';
      SetIText(itemHandle, CtoPstr((char *) &str1));

      /* File Creator */
      GetDItem(theDialog, createDItem, &itemType, &itemHandle, &itemRect);
/* In general strncpy does NOT put the NULL at the end of the string */
      p = strncpy(&str1, &anFParmBlk.ioFlFndrInfo.fdCreator, 4);
      *(p+4) = '\0';
      SetIText(itemHandle, CtoPstr((char *) &str1));

      /* File Size - first the logical size */
      GetDItem(theDialog, sizeDItem, &itemType, &itemHandle, &itemRect);
      strcat(PtoCstr((char *) Num2String(anFParmBlk.ioFlLgLen + anFParmBlk.ioFlRLgLen,
            &sizeStr)), " bytes; accounts for ");
      /* - then the physical size */
      strcat(PtoCstr((char *) Num2String((anFParmBlk.ioFlPyLen
            + anFParmBlk.ioFlRPyLen + 10)/1024, &str1)), "K on the volume");
      /* put strings together and display */
      SetIText(itemHandle, CtoPstr(strcat(&sizeStr, &str1)));

      /* put up finder flags */
      for(shr=0;shr<8;shr++) {
         GetDItem(theDialog, fLockedDItem +shr, &itemType, &itemHandle, &itemRect);
         if(anFParmBlk.ioFlFndrInfo.fdFlags & ((cfLocked) >> shr)) {
            SetIText(itemHandle, "\p *");
         } else {
            SetIText(itemHandle, "\p  ");
         }
      }

      /* put up file system flags */
      GetDItem(theDialog, fsBusyDItem, &itemType, &itemHandle, &itemRect);
      if(anFParmBlk.ioFlAttrib & fsBusy) {
         SetIText(itemHandle, "\p *");
      } else {
         SetIText(itemHandle, "\p  ");
      }
      GetDItem(theDialog, fsNoCopyDItem, &itemType, &itemHandle, &itemRect);
      if(anFParmBlk.ioFlAttrib & fsNoCopy) {
         SetIText(itemHandle, "\p *");
      } else {
         SetIText(itemHandle, "\p  ");
      }
      GetDItem(theDialog, fsLockedDItem, &itemType, &itemHandle, &itemRect);
      if(anFParmBlk.ioFlAttrib & fsLocked) {
         SetIText(itemHandle, "\p *");
      } else {
         SetIText(itemHandle, "\p  ");
      }

      /* set up file creation and modification dates
```

```
        use IUDateString and IUTimeString from International Utilities
        Package in IM...glue routines are at the end of the code */
    GetDItem(theDialog, creationDItem, &itemType, &itemHandle, &itemRect);
    IUDateString(anFParmBlk.ioFlCrDat, abbrevDate, &str2);
    Pstrcat(&str2, "\p at ");
    IUTimeString(anFParmBlk.ioFlCrDat, 0xff, &str1);
    Pstrcat(&str2, &str1);
    SetIText(itemHandle, &str2);

    GetDItem(theDialog, modifiedDItem, &itemType, &itemHandle, &itemRect);
    IUDateString(anFParmBlk.ioFlMdDat, abbrevDate, &str2);
    Pstrcat(&str2, "\p at ");
    IUTimeString(anFParmBlk.ioFlMdDat, 0xff, &str1);
    Pstrcat(&str2, &str1);
    SetIText(itemHandle, &str2);

    ShowWindow(theDialog);    /* display the dialog */

    /* wait until the user clicks mouse in button */
    do {
        ModalDialog((ProcPtr) NULL, &itemHit);
    } while(itemHit != 1);

    DisposDialog(theDialog);

}

/* Copy a file */
DoFileCopy()                                           /* DoFileCopy() */
{
    SFTypeList   typeList;
    short        numTypes;
    SFReply      reply, Preply;
    OSErr        theErr, anErr;
    IOParam      openIOParmBlk, newIOParmBlk;
    FileParam    newFParmBlk, oldFParmBlk;
    Point        loc, offset;
    Ptr          buffer;
    char         *putStr = "Destination file:";
    Str255       defaultName;

    /* select filetypes for SFGet */
    numTypes = -1;

    /* select the file to copy */
    SetPt(&loc,100,80);
    SFGetFile(loc, "\p", (Ptr) NULL, numTypes, &typeList, NULL, &reply);
    if(!reply.good) return;                    /*user cancelled operation */

        /* default destination name is Copy of... */
        strcpy(&defaultName, "Copy of ");
```

```
    strcat(&defaultName, PtoCstr((char *) SFName2ROM(reply.fName)));
    CtoPstr((char *) &reply.fName);

/* select the destination file */
SFPutFile(loc, CtoPstr((char *) putStr), CtoPstr((char *) &defaultName),
    NULL, &Preply);
PtoCstr(putStr);
/* quit if user hit cancel button */
if(!Preply.good) return;

/* create the new file */
newIOParmBlk.ioNamePtr   = SFName2ROM(Preply.fName);
newIOParmBlk.ioVRefNum   = Preply.vRefNum;
newIOParmBlk.ioVersNum   = Preply.version;
theErr = PBCreate(&newIOParmBlk, 0);
if(theErr) {                                    /* an error occurred */

    /* for all errors except file exists, return */
    if(theErr != dupFNErr) {
        OSError("PBCreate", theErr, "Creating the new file");
        return;
    }

    /* if the new file name exists - set logical EOF's to zero */
    if(theErr == dupFNErr) {
        newIOParmBlk.ioPermssn = fsWrPerm;
        newIOParmBlk.ioMisc   = (Ptr) NULL;
        theErr   = PBOpen(&newIOParmBlk, 0);
        theErr  |= PBSetEOF(&newIOParmBlk, 0);
        PBClose(&newIOParmBlk, 0);

        newIOParmBlk.ioMisc   = (Ptr) NULL;
        theErr  |= PBOpenRF(&newIOParmBlk, 0);
        theErr  |= PBSetEOF(&newIOParmBlk, 0);
        PBClose(&newIOParmBlk, 0);
        if(theErr) {
            ErrDialog("Problems setting EOF's to 0",
              "on existing destination file","during file copy");
            return;
        }
    }
}

/* set file and creator of new file to same as existing file */

/* get info for existing file */
oldFParmBlk.ioNamePtr    = SFName2ROM(reply.fName);
oldFParmBlk.ioVRefNum    = reply.vRefNum;
oldFParmBlk.ioFVersNum   = reply.version;
oldFParmBlk.ioFDirIndex  = 0;
theErr = PBGetFInfo(&oldFParmBlk, 0);
```

```
   if(theErr) OSError("PBGetFInfo", theErr, "existing file");

/* get info for existing file */
newFParmBlk.ioNamePtr    = newIOParmBlk.ioNamePtr;
newFParmBlk.ioVRefNum    = newIOParmBlk.ioVRefNum;
newFParmBlk.ioFVersNum   = newIOParmBlk.ioVersNum;
newFParmBlk.ioFDirIndex  = 0;
theErr = PBGetFInfo(&newFParmBlk, 0);
   if(theErr) OSError("PBGetFInfo", theErr, "new file");

/* set creator, type, creation and mod date, and attributes */
newFParmBlk.ioFlFndrInfo.fdType    = oldFParmBlk.ioFlFndrInfo.fdType;
newFParmBlk.ioFlFndrInfo.fdCreator = oldFParmBlk.ioFlFndrInfo.fdCreator;
newFParmBlk.ioFlFndrInfo.fdFlags   = (oldFParmBlk.ioFlFndrInfo.fdFlags &
        (0xFFFF-cfInited));
newFParmBlk.ioFlFndrInfo.fdFldr    = oldFParmBlk.ioFlFndrInfo.fdFldr;

newFParmBlk.ioFlCrDat   = oldFParmBlk.ioFlCrDat;
newFParmBlk.ioFlMdDat   = oldFParmBlk.ioFlMdDat;

theErr = PBSetFInfo(&newFParmBlk, 0);
   if(theErr) OSError("PBSetFInfo", theErr, "new file");

/* create buffer for read/write */
buffer = NewPtr(BUFFERSIZE);

/* set up an IOParam for the existing file */
openIOParmBlk.ioNamePtr    = SFName2ROM(reply.fName);
openIOParmBlk.ioVRefNum    = reply.vRefNum;
openIOParmBlk.ioVersNum    = reply.version;
openIOParmBlk.ioPermssn    = fsRdPerm;
openIOParmBlk.ioMisc       = (Ptr) NULL;

/* set up an IOParam for the new file */
newIOParmBlk.ioNamePtr     = SFName2ROM(Preply.fName);
newIOParmBlk.ioVRefNum     = Preply.vRefNum;
newIOParmBlk.ioVersNum     = Preply.version;
newIOParmBlk.ioPermssn     = fsWrPerm;
newIOParmBlk.ioMisc        = (Ptr) NULL;

/* copy the resource fork if it is Non-empty */

if(oldFParmBlk.ioFlRStBlk) {
   theErr = PBOpenRF(&openIOParmBlk, 0);
   if(theErr) {                          /* error opening existing file */
      OSError("PBOpenRF", theErr, "existing file resource fork");
      return;
   }

   /* open the new file's resource fork */
   newIOParmBlk.ioPermssn    = fsWrPerm;
```

```
   newIOParmBlk.ioMisc      = (Ptr) NULL;
   theErr = PBOpenRF(&newIOParmBlk, 0);
   if(theErr) {                       /* error opening new file */
      OSError("PBOpenRF", theErr,"new file resource fork");
        /* close open file and quit */
      theErr = PBClose(&openIOParmBlk, 0);
      return;
   }

   /* by this point both the resource forks of the old and new files are open */

   /* copy data fork */
   openIOParmBlk.ioBuffer    = buffer;
   openIOParmBlk.ioReqCount  = BUFFERSIZE;
   openIOParmBlk.ioPosMode   = fsAtMark;
   openIOParmBlk.ioPosOffset = 0L;

   newIOParmBlk.ioBuffer     = buffer;
   newIOParmBlk.ioPosMode    = fsAtMark;
   newIOParmBlk.ioPosOffset = 0L;

   do {
      theErr = PBRead(&openIOParmBlk, 0);
      if((theErr) && (theErr!=eofErr))
         OSError("PBRead", theErr, "resource fork");

      newIOParmBlk.ioReqCount  = openIOParmBlk.ioActCount;
      anErr = PBWrite(&newIOParmBlk, 0);
         if(anErr) OSError("PBWrite", theErr, "resource fork");
   } while (theErr>=noErr);

   /* flush file buffers and close the files' resource forks */
   theErr = PBFlshFile(&newIOParmBlk, 0);
    if(theErr) OSError("PBFlshFile", theErr, "New file");
   theErr = PBClose(&newIOParmBlk, 0);
    if(theErr) OSError("PBClose", theErr, "New File");
   theErr = PBClose(&openIOParmBlk, 0);
    if(theErr) OSError("PBClose", theErr, "Old File");
}

/* copy the data fork if it is Non-empty */
if(oldFParmBlk.ioFlStBlk) {

   theErr = PBOpen(&openIOParmBlk, 0);
   if(theErr) {                                /* error opening existing file */
      OSError("PBOpen", theErr, "existing file");
      return;
   }

   /* open the new file's data fork */
   newIOParmBlk.ioPermssn    = fsWrPerm;
```

```
        newIOParmBlk.ioMisc      = (Ptr) NULL;
        theErr = PBOpen(&newIOParmBlk, 0);
        if(theErr) {                              /* error opening new file */
           OSError("PBOpen", theErr,"new file");
            /* close open file and quit */
           theErr = PBClose(&openIOParmBlk, 0);
           return;
        }

        /* by this point both the data forks of the old and new files are open */

        /* copy data fork */
        openIOParmBlk.ioBuffer    = buffer;
        openIOParmBlk.ioReqCount  = BUFFERSIZE;
        openIOParmBlk.ioPosMode   = fsAtMark;
        openIOParmBlk.ioPosOffset = 0L;

        newIOParmBlk.ioBuffer    = buffer;
        newIOParmBlk.ioPosMode   = fsAtMark;
        newIOParmBlk.ioPosOffset = 0L;

        do {
            theErr = PBRead(&openIOParmBlk, 0);
            if((theErr) && (theErr!=eofErr))
               OSError("PBRead", theErr, "data fork");

            newIOParmBlk.ioReqCount  = openIOParmBlk.ioActCount;
            anErr = PBWrite(&newIOParmBlk, 0);
                if(anErr) OSError("PBWrite", theErr, "data fork");
        } while (theErr>=noErr);

        /* flush file buffers and close the files' data forks */
        theErr = PBFlshFile(&newIOParmBlk, 0);
         if(theErr) OSError("PBFlshFile", theErr, "New file");
        theErr = PBClose(&newIOParmBlk, 0);
         if(theErr) OSError("PBClose", theErr, "New File");
        theErr = PBClose(&openIOParmBlk, 0);
         if(theErr) OSError("PBClose", theErr, "Old File");
    }

    /* flush the volume of the new file */
    theErr = PBFlshVol(&newIOParmBlk, 0);
     if(theErr) OSError("PBFlshVol", theErr, "the new file's volume");

    DisposPtr(buffer);

    return;
}

/* Put up the AboutI window */
AboutWindow()                                    /* AboutWindow() */
```

```
{
   long        dummy;
   Rect        creditR;
   Rect        lineR;
   GrafPtr         port;
   WindowPtr   creditW;
   EventRecord anEvent;
   char   *line1="Sample Application for the Mac File System";
   char   *line2="Toolbox from C - from Sybex Books";
   char   *line3="written by DB & JT";
   char   *line4="Portions Copyright 1986 )THINK Technologies, Inc.";

   GetPort(&port);
   SetRect(&lineR,5,5,345,20);
   SetRect(&creditR,75,120,425,220);
   creditW=NewWindow((WindowPeek) NULL, &creditR, "\1x", 0xff, dBoxProc,
      (WindowPtr)-1L,0xff,0);
   SetPort(creditW);

   TextSize(12);
   TextFont(0);
   TextBox(line1,strlen(line1),&lineR,1);
   OffsetRect(&lineR,0,20);
   TextBox(line2,strlen(line2),&lineR,1);
   OffsetRect(&lineR,0,20);
   TextBox(line3,strlen(line3),&lineR,1);
   OffsetRect(&lineR,0,20);
   TextBox(line4,strlen(line4),&lineR,1);

   do {
      GetNextEvent(everyEvent,&anEvent);
   } while (anEvent.what != mouseDown);

   DisposeWindow(creditW);

   SetPort(port);
   return;
}

/* display a dialog for a system error */
OSError(procName, errNum, msg)                              /* OSError() */
   char   *procName, *msg;
   short  errNum;
{
   Str255  errMsg, trapMsg;

   /* paste together trap message */
   strcpy(&trapMsg, procName);

   /* paste together errorNum message */
   strcat(PtoCstr((char *) Num2String((long) errNum, &errMsg)), " = ");
```

```
    ErrDialog(strcat(&trapMsg, " reports an error"),
        strcat(&errMsg, ErrMessage(errNum)), msg);
}

/* Generic Error dialog with 3 definable messages */
ErrDialog(str1, str2, str3)                                      /* ErrDialog() */
    char    *str1;
    char    *str2;
    char    *str3;
{
    EventRecord     anEvent;
    DialogPtr       theDialog;
    short           itemHit;
    char            *err = "An Error has occurred...";

    ParamText(CtoPstr(err), CtoPstr(str1), CtoPstr(str2), CtoPstr(str3));

    theDialog = GetNewDialog(errDialogID, NULL, (WindowPtr) -1L);

    ShowWindow(theDialog);
    PtoCstr(err);
    PtoCstr(str1);
    PtoCstr(str2);
    PtoCstr(str3);

    do {
        ModalDialog((ProcPtr) NULL, &itemHit);
    } while( itemHit != 1);

    DisposDialog(theDialog);
}


/* Get a message corresponding to an OSErr  code */
char    *ErrMessage(anOSErr)                                     /* ErrMessage() */
    OSErr    anOSErr;

    /* this routine would be much more space efficient if the
       strings were kept in a single 'STR#' resource... */
{
static char *str;

    switch(anOSErr) {

        case noErr:
            str = "No Error";
            break;

        /* File System Error Messages */
        case badMDBErr:
```

```
              str = "Bad master directory block";
              break;
         case bdNamErr:
              str = "Bad file/volume name";
              break;
         case dirFulErr:
              str = "Directory full";
              break;
         case dskFulErr:
              str = "Disk full";
              break;
         case dupFNErr:
              str = "Duplicate file name";
              break;
         case eofErr:
              str = "Logical EOF reached";
              break;
         case extFSErr:
              str = "External file system";
              break;
         case fBsyErr:
              str = "File busy";
              break;
         case fLckdErr:
              str = "File locked";
              break;
         case fnfErr:
              str = "File not found";
              break;
         case fnOpnErr:
              str = "File not open";
              break;
         case fsRnErr:
              str = "Error during PBRename";
              break;
         case ioErr:
              str = "Disk I/O error";
              break;
         case mFulErr:
              str = "Memory full";
              break;
         case noMacDskErr:
              str = "Not a Macintosh Disk";
              break;
         case nsDrvErr:
              str = "No such drive";
              break;
         case nsvErr:
              str = "No such volume";
              break;
         case opWrErr:
```

```
                str = "File already open for writing";
                break;
            case paramErr:
                str = "No default volume";
                break;
            case permErr:
                str = "File not open for writing";
                break;
            case posErr:
                str = "Attempt to position before file start";
                break;
            case rfNumErr:
                str = "Bad reference number";
                break;
            case tmfoErr:
                str = "Too many files open";
                break;
            case volOffLinErr:
                str = "Volume not on-line";
                break;
            case volOnLinErr:
                str = "Volume already on-line";
                break;
            case vLckdErr:
                str = "Software volume lock";
                break;
            case wPrErr:
                str = "Hardware volume lock";
                break;
            default:
                str = "No message for this error";
                break;
        }
        return str;
}


Str255   *Num2String(theNum, theStr)
   long        theNum;
   Str255    *theStr;
/*     This is a minor variation on the Binary-Decimal Conversion
        Package of the same name. Here we have made the procedure
        into a function returning a pointer to the string.
  */
{
   NumToString(theNum, theStr);
   return(theStr);
}


long    String2Num(theStr)
   Str255    *theStr;
/*     This is a minor variation on the Binary-Decimal Conversion
```

```
        Package of the same name. Here we have made the procedure
        into a function returning the long number.
*/
{
        long        theNum;

        StringToNum(theStr, &theNum);
        return (theNum);
}

/* strlib.c -- DJB 10/18/85 */

/* USE STRINGS LIBRARY FOR MOST FUNCTIONS */
#include <MacTypes.h>

char    *Pstrcpy(s, t)
    char    *s, *t;
{
        int     i, length;
        char    *p;

        length = *t;
        p = s;

        for (i=0;i<=length;i++) *p++ = *t++;
        return s;
}


char    *Pstrcat(s, t)
    char    *s, *t;
{
        int     i, length;
        char    *p;

        length = *t;
        p = s + *s +1;
        t++;

        for (i=0;i<length;i++) *p++ = *t++;
        *s += length;
        return s;
}


*    Source code for Chapter 12 Sample Application Resources
*      Use the Apple Resource Compiler - RMaker
*

Chapt12.rsrc

Type DITL
```

```
      ,10000
39
*    1
BtnItem Enabled
266 177 286 237
Thanks

*    2
StatText Enabled
6 8 23 107
All About File:

*    3
StatText Enabled
22 25 40 107
On Volume:

*    4
StatText Enabled
46 72 65 140
File Type:

*    5
StatText Enabled
46 203 65 264
Creator:

*    6
StatText Enabled
71 30 90 95
File Size:

*    7
StatText Enabled
6 111 23 330
File Name

*    8
StatText Enabled
22 111 40 330
Volume Name

*    9
StatText Enabled
46 139 65 179
????

*    10
StatText Enabled
46 263 65 303
????
```

```
*    11
StatText Enabled
71 94 90 380

*    12
StatText Enabled
96 30 115 131
Finder Flags:

*    13
StatText Enabled
121 71 141 131
Locked

*    14
StatText Enabled
140 71 160 137
Invisible

*    15
StatText Enabled
159 71 179 131
Bundle

*    16
StatText Enabled
178 71 198 131
System

*    17
StatText Enabled
197 71 217 138
No-Copy

*    18
StatText Enabled
216 71 236 131
Busy

*    19
StatText Enabled
235 71 255 139
Changed

*    20
StatText Enabled
254 71 274 131
Inited
```

```
*    21
StatText Enabled
96 248 116 391
File System Flags:

*    22
StatText Enabled
119 292 139 352
Busy

*    23
StatText Enabled
138 292 158 359
No-Copy

*    24
StatText Enabled
157 292 177 359
Locked

*    25
StatText Enabled
121 52 141 72
%

*    26
StatText Enabled
140 52 160 72
%

*    27
StatText Enabled
159 52 179 72
%

*    28
StatText Enabled
178 52 198 72
%

*    29
StatText Enabled
197 52 217 72
%

*    30
StatText Enabled
216 52 236 72
%
```

```
*   31
StatText Enabled
235 52 255 72
%


*   32
StatText Enabled
254 52 274 72
%


*   33
StatText Enabled
119 273 139 293
%


*   34
StatText Enabled
138 273 158 293
%


*   35
StatText Enabled
157 273 177 293
%


*   36
StatText Enabled
186 186 206 246
Created:


*   37
StatText Enabled
228 176 248 246
Modified:


*   38
StatText Enabled
186 251 223 377


*   39
StatText Enabled
228 251 264 377


     ,9999 (4)

6
*    1
BtnItem Enabled
117 121 141 177
OK
```

```
*    2
StatText Enabled
40 8 56 288
^1

*    3
StatText Enabled
64 8 80 288
^2

*    4
StatText Enabled
88 8 104 288
^3

*    5
StatText Enabled
11 47 28 288
^0

*    6 - ARRRGH! Can't put icons into dialogs this way. Thats what I get
*        for trying to be nice and use RMaker. Use Resource Editor like
*        I did, or just use an Alert! <<IconItem is undefined here!>>
IconItem Enabled
3 9 35 41
0


Type DLOG

       ,10000
File Info
31 24 323 477
Invisible NoGoAway
1
0
10000


       ,9999
A Message...
87 67 235 378
Invisible NoGoAway
1
0
9999
```

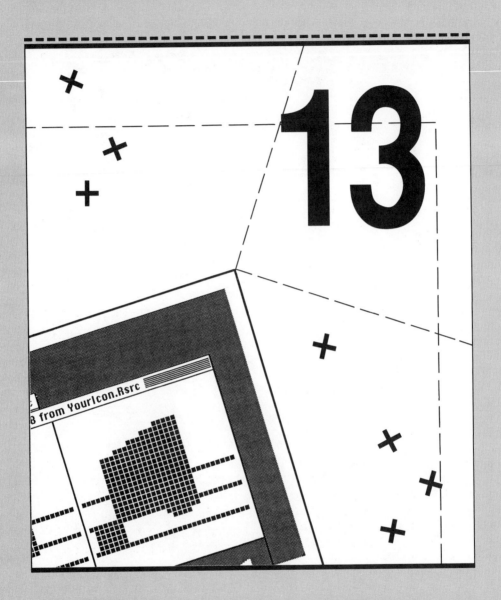

Finishing Touches

This chapter is a small grab bag of miscellaneous topics that we decided to put in a little chapter of their own. We will cover three subjects here: how to create and design an icon for your application, how to let your application handle desk accessories, and how to add icons to menus.

Creating Your Own Icon

Half the fun of writing your own application is creating and assigning its desktop icon. For an application to have a custom icon, it must have a unique signature, and, in its resource fork, a number of Finder-related resources. In this section we will examine file signatures and all the Finder-related resources an application needs in order to have a custom desktop icon. Using ResEdit and RMaker, we will also create all the resources necessary to assign a custom icon to a sample application named YourProgram. The application YourProgram is shown in Figure 13.1 with its generic application icon.

Note: In order to have a custom icon appear in the finder, your application must have its bundle bit set. This is one of the Finder flags, as described in Chapter 12. When you set the project type to Application under Think C, the compiler automatically creates an application with its bundle bit set. As such, you need not explicitly set this bit. However, if you change any of the Finder flags externally (such as with Fedit or miniDos), make sure you leave this bit set.

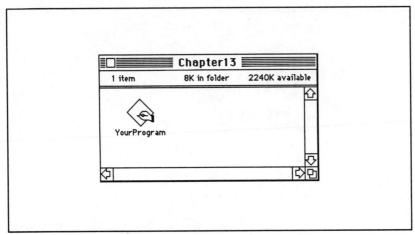

Figure 13.1: Your Program with Generic Icon

File Signatures and Bundle Bits

In order to have a custom icon, a Macintosh application must have a unique signature that the Finder can identify it by. An application's signature, often referred to as its creator or creator ID, is a unique four-character sequence. The creator must be unique in that no other application on a currently mounted disk may have the same four-character signature. In this example, we'll set the creator of our application Your-Progam to be the four-character sequence FRED.

When an application's bundle bit is set, the Finder copies the application's ICN#, FREF, and BNDL resources into the Desktop file along with the version data resources, if they have been created. The version data, ICN#, FREF, and BNDL resources are the Finder-related resources we will shortly learn how to create. The Desktop file is the invisible file on each disk that keeps track of all the custom icons for files and programs on the disk. Once an application has a unique signature and its finder-related resources have been copied to the desktop file, its custom icon will appear.

Now let's move onto the four Finder-related resources.

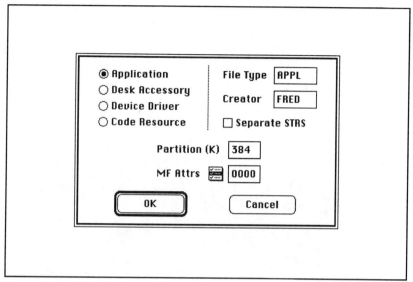

Figure 13.2:   Think C's Set Application Type Box

The Icon

The first thing we'll do is create a custom icon. This is, as we've mentioned before, easiest to manage in ResEdit. Double click on Res-Edit and select New from the file menu. This creates a new resource file. You will see a dialog box like the one in Figure 13.3. Type in the name YourIcon.Rsrc.

Next, we must add a new ICN# resource to the file. Select New from the file menu again to bring up the resource type selector. Select the type ICN#, as shown in Figure 13.4.

Now, use the Get Info function as shown in figure 13.5 from the file menu to change the resource number of the icon to 128. It will usually be assigned an arbitrary number by ResEdit when you initially create it.

Finally, use the icon editor as shown in figure 13.6 to create your icon. It behaves pretty much as does MacPaint's fatbits mode. When you're done, copy the icon to the mask area and close Your-Icon.Rsrc to save the icon to your resource file.

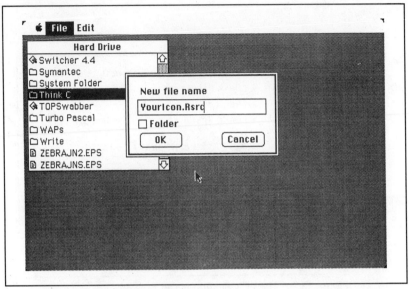

Figure 13.3: Creating a New Resource File

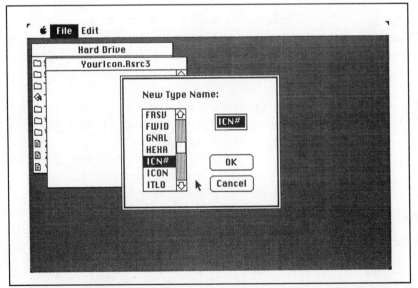

Figure 13.4: Selecting an ICN# Resource

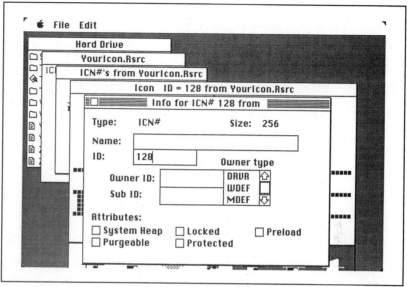

Figure 13.5:   The Get Info Box

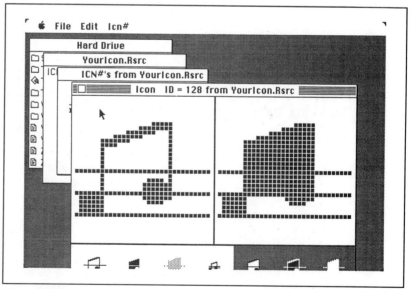

Figure 13.6:   The Icon Editor

The Finder Related Resources

The other three resources related to your custom icon will be handled as an RMaker source file. Here is the complete file. The last line is used to tell RMaker to include the icon you just created with ResEdit.

```
YourProgram.Rsrc

Type FRED = STR
,0    ;; 'STR'
Your program vers 1.0     ;; Get Info text

Type FREF        ;; Finder reference
  ,128
APPL 0           ;; Local icon number 0

Type BNDL        ;; Bundle
  ,128
FRED 0           ;; Version data
ICN#             ;; Icon
0 128            ;; Local number / resource number
FREF             ;; Finder reference
0 128            ;; Local number / resource number

INCLUDE YourIcon.Rsrc
```

Let's see what these resources do.

Version Data Resource

Each application must have a version data resource, a special resource that has the application's creator as its resource type. Thus, our application, YourProgram, will have a version data resource type of FRED. The data of this resource constitutes a Pascal string which will appear as the Get Info comments for our application.

FREF Resources

A FREF or file reference resource needs to know only what type of file the custom icon is being assigned to and the local ID of the custom icon. The file type for YourProgram, and for any application program, is APPL. Thus we enter the type APPL into the FREF resource. The icon local ID, which we have entered as zero, can be any number so long as it is consistent with the local ID that we specify in the BNDL resource, which we will do next.

BNDL Resources

The last resource type an application needs for a custom icon is a BNDL, a resource that serves to bundle everything together. You might want to look at the above RMaker listing as we go over the fields of this resource.

The first line under the BNDL type declaration is the number of the resource, for which we'll use 128. The next field, the owner's name, has to be set to the file's creator and local reference number. For Your-Program, of course, the creator is FRED. FRED's local resource number is 0.

Following this is a list of the items we want to bundle together. The first one is ICN# number 128, which actually lives in the included file YourIcon.Rsrc. The BNDL assigns this a local resource number of 0. The second is the FREF resource we've just created, which is also assigned a local resource number of 0.

This list has assigned the mapping between the local IDs and the resource IDs. These IDs can be set to whatever we want so long as we are consistent throughout all of the Finder-related resources.

With this short file typed in, run RMaker to compile it. One common error occurs in the declaration of the version type resource, FRED. If there is not a space after STR, RMaker will complain.

Wrapping Things Up

Once YourProgram's Finder-related resources are created, your new custom icon should appear as in Figure 13.7.

If you follow the general directions we have just given for creating a new icon and the new icon does not appear, it may be that the file or application for which you are creating the icon already had a custom icon assigned to it. To force the new icon to appear, double-click the mouse on the Finder while holding down the Command and Option keys. This throws out the old desktop file and creates a new one, with your custom icon in place.

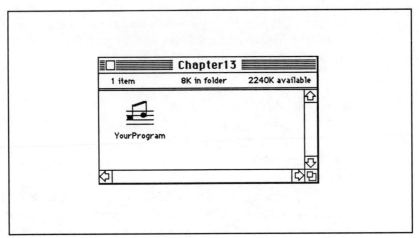

Figure 13.7: YourProgram with Its New Custom Icon

Supporting Desk Accessories from Your Application

As your application nears completion you will undoubtedly want to include the necessary code to support desk accessories. Desk accessories have evolved quite a bit since the original set that was provided with the Macintosh. The simplest desk accessories are truly as they were originally called, desk ornaments. These include the Alarm Clock, the Puzzle, the Control Panel, and the Calculator. Another type of desk accessory consists of utility programs designed to be used during an application. These desk accessories include features like renaming, copying or deleting a file, transferring to another application, and blanking the screen when the machine is idle. A third category consists of desk accessories that are actually miniature applications which can be active along with the main application. These mini-applications include text editors, terminal emulators, spreadsheets, and even graphics programs.

As you can see, there is quite a bit of variety and versatility in desk accessories as a group. What makes desk accessories even more powerful as a tool is that they are available to the user at any time within almost any application. By including desk accessories in your application, you can make it possible for the user to virtually tailor the Macintosh to her or his needs.

How Desk Accessories Work

Desk accessories operate by borrowing (or stealing, depending on how you look at it) control of the Macintosh's processor from time to time from the current application. Periodically the application will ask the operating system to check on the active desk accessories to see if any of them are ready to borrow some time.

When the user opens a desk accessory, it will inform the operating system how often it needs to take control of the processor. Exactly how often a desk accessory needs to borrow time from the application, and how much time it will use each time, depends, of course, on the nature of the desk accessory's function. The alarm clock, for instance, needs to update its display once every second. On the other hand, a desk accessory using one of the Macintosh's serial ports for terminal emulation must empty its buffers much more frequently to avoid losing any characters, perhaps as often as once every one or two ticks of the system clock (recall that a tick equals 1/60 of a second). In addition, desk accessories must respond to different types of events just like an application program. They must be able to respond to mouse and keyboard-related events as well as to activate and update events. Some types of events are automatically passed to the desk accessory by the Event Manager function GetNextEvent, while others must be forwarded by the application.

This section of the chapter describes what an application must do to support desk accessories. We will first discuss how to open a desk accessory when the user chooses one from the Apple menu, and how to close a desk accessory when the user has finished with it. We will then move on to the task, shared by the application and the Toolbox, of making sure that a desk accessory receives the events and menu selections that are intended for it.

- - - - - - -

Opening and Closing Desk Accessories

When the user selects an item from the Apple menu, the application must check to see whether the item selected is a desk accessory or another item instead. The standard layout for the Apple menu has the "About. . ." item first, followed by a dotted line, followed by the names of the desk accessories. The application can call **OpenDeskAcc** to open the desk accessory whose name is contained in the string pointed to by the parameter theAcc:

```
int OpenDeskAcc(theAcc)
        Str255  *theAcc;
```

The value returned by **OpenDeskAcc** is the reference number of the desk accessory; this value can be safely ignored by the application. According to *Inside Macintosh*, the desk accessory itself is responsible for informing the user if for some reason, such as lack of available memory, it cannot be opened. Many applications also check the available memory to avert the potential paradox that results when a desk accessory that will not fit into memory is required to inform the user of this fact.

To obtain the name of the desk accessory, the application can call the Menu Manager procedure **GetItem**, which copies the text of a given menu item into the string variable passed from the application. The following example is an excerpt from the menu selection section of almost any application:

```
/* global MenuHandle for apple menu */
extern      MenuHandle      appleMenu;

/* define local variables */
int         menuID, itemNumber; /* see Chapter 4: Menus */
Str255      daName;
GrafPtr     theCurrentPort;

switch(menuID) {
        case AppleID:
                if(itemNumber == 1) {
                        /* put the applications About . . . window */
                        AboutWindow();
                }
```

```
        else {
                /* which DA to open */
                GetItem(appleMenu, itemNumber, &daName);

                /* local check for memory space */
                /* copy private scrap(s) to Clipboard
                   if application window at the front */

                /* save the current grafPort in case the
                   DA doesn't restore it to the previous
                   value */
                GetPort(&theCurrentPort);

                /* open the DA if sufficient memory
                   space exists and restore the current
                   grafPort */
                OpenDeskAcc(&daName);
                SetPort(theCurrentPort);

                break;
        }
        /* cases for other menus, . . . */
}
```

The user can close a desk accessory in one of several ways. Both methods involve desk accessories with windows. In the first case if the window has a close box, the user can close the desk accessory with a mouse-down in the close box of the window. This method involves mouse events, which we will discuss in a moment. The second method uses the Close item found in the File menu of most applications. If the user selects the Close item while a desk accessory window is at the front, the application should call **CloseDeskAcc** with the reference number of the desk accessory.

```
CloseDeskAcc(refNum)
        int     refNum;
```

The reference number of the desk accessory can be found in the windowKind field of the WindowRecord defining its window. The following example shows how to close a desk accessory with this method.

```
/* define local variables */
int  menuID, itemNumber;        /* see Chapter 4: Menus */
```

```
int   refNum;

switch(menuID) {
        case EditID:
                /* get the windowKind of the active window */
                refNum = ((WindowPeek)
   FrontWindow())->windowKind;

                if(refNum <= 0) {
                        /* close the desk accessory with refNum */
                        CloseDeskAcc(refNum);
                }
                else {
                        /* handle the Close item for an
                           application window */
                }
                break;
        /* cases for other menus, . . . */
}
```

Lending Time to a Desk Accessory

In order to allow desk accessories to carry out periodic operations, such as updating clock or flashing a TextEdit insertion point, the
application must call the procedure **SystemTask** in the main event loop.

```
SystemTask()
```

SystemTask checks each active desk accessory to see if it has requested time on a periodic basis. If the elapsed time since it was last
given control is longer than the time interval it requested when it was
installed, control is passed to the desk accessory.

Forwarding Mouse-Down Events to a Desk Accessory

In our discussions of the Window Manager in Chapters 3 and 7,
we learned that the routine **FindWindow** will return the constant inSys-
Window when a mouse-down occurs in a desk accessory window. In

order to pass the event on to the desk accessory, the application must call the routine **SystemClick**, passing a pointer to the EventRecord and the WindowPtr of the window in the parameters theEvent and theWindow.

```
SystemClick(theEvent ,theWindow)
        EventRecord     *theEvent;
        WindowPtr       theWindow;
```

   SystemClick first determines if it can handle the event itself. If the mouse-down occurs in the content region and the window is inactive, **SystemClick** will activate the window. If the event occurs in the title bar, **SystemClick** calls **DragWindow** to allow the user to drag window. Afterwards, if the window was inactive, it will be activated unless the Command key was held down. If the mouse-down occurs in the close box, **SystemClick** calls **TrackGoAway** and if appropriate, signals the desk accessory to close itself. Finally, if none of these scenarios apply, the mouse-down event is forwarded to the desk accessory.

Events Forwarded or Handled by the Toolbox

   The Event Manager routine **GetNextEvent** automatically intercepts activate, update, key-down, and auto-key events intended for desk accessories. **GetNextEvent** calls the function **SystemEvent** to determine if a given event should be handled by the operating system instead of the application.

```
char SystemEvent(theEvent)
        EventRecord     *theEvent;
```

   If **SystemEvent** determines that the operating system should handle the event, it will call the appropriate system routines and return true, otherwise, if the application should handle the event **SystemEvent** returns false. Note that **SystemEvent** does not attempt to filter mouse-down events. It is the responsibility of the application to call **SystemClick** for mouse-down events. An application should not attempt to call **SystemEvent** directly.

Selecting an Item from a Desk Accessory Menu

Many desk accessories install their own menus into the menu bar. The Menu Manager routines **MenuSelect** and **MenuKey** are responsible for intercepting menu selections belonging to desk accessories. Both **MenuSelect** and **MenuKey** call the procedure **SystemMenu** if the menu item chosen by the user belongs to a desk accessory menu.

```
SystemMenu(menuResult)
      long    menuResult;
```

The menuResult parameter has the same value as the value usually returned to the application by either **MenuSelect** or **MenuKey** (see Chapter 4).

Desk Accessories and the Edit Menu

Many desk accessories will respond to the standard items contained in the Edit menu (namely Undo, Cut, Copy, Paste, and Clear). Whenever the user selects an item from the Edit menu, the application should call **SystemEdit** with the appropriate value of the editCmd parameter (see Figure 13.7 for a listing of the values of editCmd corresponding to the standard editing commands).

```
char SystemEdit(editCmd)
      int    editCmd;
```

Value	Editing Command
0	Undo
1	-None-
2	Cut
3	Copy
4	Paste
5	Clear
>6	-None-

Figure 13.8: Command Numbers for SystemEdit

SystemEdit returns true if the menu selection was forwarded to the desk accessory and false if the menu selection applies to the application. If the items in the application's Edit menu are in the order suggested by the User Interface Guidelines, the application can simply subtract 1 from the value of the menu item to obtain the appropriate value for editCmd, as illustrated in the following example.

```
/* define local variables */
int     menuID, itemNumber;      /* see Chapter 4: Menus */
Str255  daName;

switch(menuID) {
        case EditID:

                /* if command intended for a DA,
                   forward it and exit */
                if(SystemEdit(itemNumber - 1)) break;

                /* command intended for the
                   application do whatever is necessary */

                switch(editItem) {
                        case . . .
                }
                break;

        /* cases for other menus, ... */
}
```

Supporting Desk Accessories: A Final Word

We have seen that the Macintosh operating system handles many of the chores involved in supporting desk accessories. As a result, the amount of extra code necessary to support desk accessories in an application is quite small.

In this discussion we have learned how to open and close desk accessories, and how to forward the remaining types of events and commands not automatically intercepted by the Toolbox. This information, combined with the discussion of the TextEdit scrap and the Clipboard in Chapter 8, should enable you to include desk accessories in your application.

Menu Icons

You'll recall from Chapter 4 that the one menu-item enhancement we didn't talk about was adding icons to our menus. Now that we are familiar with resources, we can go ahead and cover the coding methods for adding an icon to a menu item.

Adding an icon to a menu item is not difficult and can be coded in two different ways. The first method is through the use of the procedure **SetItemIcon**.

```
SetItemIcon(theMenu, item, icon)
        MenuHandle      theMenu;
        int             item;
        int             icon;
```

You pass this procedure a menu handle, the item number of the menu item you wish to modify, and the icon number of the icon you wish to use. The Menu Manager will add 256 to this icon number to get the resource ID of the icon it will use in the menu. Since icon resource IDs 257 through 511 are reserved for menu icons, the icon number can be any number from 1 to 255.

The other way to add an icon to a menu item is through the caret (^) metacharacter in the **AppendMenu** data string.

```
AppendMenu (myMenu, "\pFirst Item;^2Icon Item");
```

In the **AppendMenu** data string, the caret precedes the icon number of the icon that is going to be associated with a particular menu item. The same rules apply to the item number in **AppendMenu** as in the **SetItemIcon** procedure.

If you have created your menu as an RMaker source file initially, you can simply write the caret metacharacter into the initial menu definition, like this:

```
Type MENU
        ,130
First Item
^2Icon Item
```

Of course, you will have to create an 'ICON' resource with the appropriate resource ID and add it to the resource fork of your application. If either of these procedures cannot find the icon designated by the icon number, they will simply display a white space where the icon would normally appear (to the left of the menu item).

C Calling Conventions

This appendix contains the C calling conventions of the Tool-box routines discussed in this book.

Chapter 2: Using the Event Manager

```
/* declare some variables */
char          TrueOrFalse;
int           eventMask, eventCode, OSErr, stopMask, noOfTicks;
long          eventMsg, eventandstopMask;
Point         mouseLoc;
EventRecord   theEvent;
```

Manipulating Event Records

```
TrueOrFalse = GetNextEvent(eventMask, &theEvent);

TrueOrFalse = EventAvail(eventMask, &theEvent);

OSErr = PostEvent(eventCode, eventMsg);

FlushEvents(eventMask, stopMask);
```

or

```
FlushEvents(eventandstopMask);
```

Mouse Routines

```
GetMouse(&mouseLoc);

TrueOrFalse = Button();

TrueOrFalse = StillDown();
```

Time Routines

```
noOfTicks = TickCount();
```

Chapter 3: Introduction to the Window Manager

```
/* declare some variables */
char         goAwayFlag, inGoAway, front, fUpdate;
int          procID, partCode, h, v, hi, lo;
int          width, height;
long         refCon, newSize;
Point        thePt, startPt;
Rect         boundsRect;
GrafPtr      gp;
Str255       aPString;
WindowPtr    theWindow, behindWindow;
WindowRecord aWindowRec;
```

Initialization

```
InitWindows();
```

Changing GrafPorts

```
SetPort(gp);

GetPort(&gp);
```

Creating and Disposing of Windows

```
theWindow = NewWindow(&aWindowRec, &boundsRect, &aString,
                      visible, procID, behindWindow, goAwayFlag,
                      refCon);

DisposeWindow(theWindow);

CloseWindow(theWindow);
```

The Front-to-Back Order on the Desktop

```
SelectWindow(theWindow);

ShowWindow(theWindow);

HideWindow(theWindow);

theWindow = FrontWindow();
```

Window Titles

```
SetWTitle(theWindow, &aPString);

GetWTitle(theWindow, &aPString);
```

The Size Box

```
DrawGrowIcon(theWindow);
```

Locating Mouse-Down Events

```
partCode = FindWindow(thePt, &whichWindow);

inGoAway = TrackGoAway(theWindow, thePt);
```

Moving and Resizing Windows

```
DragWindow(theWindow, startPt, &boundsRect);
```

```
MoveWindow(theWindow, h, v, front);

newSize = GrowWindow(theWindow, startPt, &boundsRect);

SizeWindow(theWindow, width, height, fUpdate);
```

Miscellaneous

```
hi = HiWord(newSize);

lo = LoWord(newSize);
```

Chapter 4: An Introduction to Menus

```
/* declare some variables */
MenuHandle    theMenu;
int           menuID, afterItem, item, beforeID, resourceID;
Str255        menuTitle, itemString, data;
ResType       theType;
char          checked, markChar, keyChar;
Style         chStyle;
Point         startPt;
```

Initialization

```
InitMenus();
```

Creating a New Menu

```
theMenu = NewMenu(menuID, &menuTitle);

AppendMenu(theMenu, &data);

AddResMenu(theMenu, theType);

InsertResMenu(theMenu, theType, afterItem);
```

Modifying Menu Items

```
GetItem(theMenu, item, &itemString);

SetItem(theMenu, item, &itemString);
```

Enabling/Disabling Menu Items

```
EnableItem(theMenu, item);

DisableItem(theMenu, item);
```

Marking Menu Items

```
CheckItem(theMenu, item, checked);

SetItemMark(theMenu, item, markChar);

GetItemMark(theMenu, item, &markChar);
```

Changing Text Syles in Menu Items

```
SetItemStyle(theMenu, item, chStyle);
```

Working with the Menu List

```
InsertMenu(theMenu, beforeID);

DisposeMenu(theMenu);

DeleteMenu(menuID);

DrawMenuBar();
```

Selecting from a Menu

```
menuResult = MenuSelect(startPt);

menuResult = MenuKey(keyChar);
```

Hilighting the Menu Bar

```
HiliteMenu(menuID);
```

Reading Menus in from Resources

```
GetNewMenu(resourceID);
```

Chapter 5: Drawing with QuickDraw

```
/* declare some variables */
char        TrueOrFalse, aCharacter;
char        *textBuf, *globalPtr;
int         horiz, vert, left, top, right, bottom;
int         mode, width, height, font, face, size, extra;
int         firstByte, byteCount, ovalWidth, ovalHeight;
int         angle, startAngle, arcAngle, cursorID;
Point       point1, point2, location;
Rect        rect1, rect2, srcRectA, srcRectB, destRect, picFrame;
Pattern     *yourPattern, *aPattern;
PenState    thePenState;
Str255      *aHexString, *aString;
FontInfo    info;
GrafPtr     aGrafPointer;
BitMap      srcBits, dstBits;
Cursor      aCursor;
RgnHandle   region, sourceRgnA, sourceRgnB, destRgn;
PolyHandle  aPolygon;
PicHandle   aPictureHand;
CursHandle  aCursorHand;
```

Defining Points

```
SetPt(&Point1, horiz, vert);
```

Manipulating Points

```
EqualPt(point1, point2);
```

```
AddPt(point1, &point2);

SubPt(point1, &point2);
```

Changing a Point's Coordinate System

```
LocalToGlobal(&point1);

GlobalToLocal(&point1);
```

Defining Rectangles

```
SetRect(&rect1, left, top, right, bottom);

TrueOrFalse = SectRect(&srcRectA, &srcRectB, &destRect);

UnionRect(&srcRectA, &srcRectB, &destRect);

Pt2Rect(point1, point2, &destRect);
```

Moving Rectangles

```
OffsetRect(&rect1, horiz, vert);
```

Resizing Rectangles

```
InsetRect(&rect1, horiz, vert);
```

Determining if Points are enclosed in Rectangles

```
TrueOrFalse = PtInRect(point1, &rect1);
```

Comparing Rectangles

```
TrueOrFalse = EqualRect(&rect1, &rect2);

TrueOrFalse = EmptyRect(&rect1);
```

Pattern Defining Routines

```
StuffHex(yourPattern, aHexString);
```

Pen Field Manipulating Routines

```
GetPen(&location);

PenSize(width, height);

PenMode(mode);

PenPat(aPattern);

HidePen();

ShowPen();
```

Restoring the Pen's Default Fields

```
PenNormal();
```

Moving the Pen

```
MoveTo(horiz, vert);

Move(horiz, vert);
```

Drawing Lines with the Pen

```
LineTo(horiz, vert);

Line(horiz, vert);
```

Preserving a Pen's Characteristics

```
GetPenState(&thePenState);

SetPenState(&thePenState);
```

Text Field Manipulating Routines

```
TextFont(font);

TextFace(face);

TextMode(mode);

TextSize(size);

SpaceExtra(extra);
```

Drawing Characters, Strings, and Text Buffers

```
DrawChar(aCharacter);

DrawString(aString);

DrawText(textBuf, firstByte, byteCount);
```

Determining the Width of a Character, String, or Text in a Buffer

```
width = CharWidth(aCharacter);

width = StringWidth(aString);

width = TextWidth(textBuf, firstByte, byteCount);
```

Determining a Font's Ascent, Descent, Width, and Leading

```
GetFontInfo(&info);
```

GrafPort Routines

```
InitGraf(&globalPtr);
```

Creating and Disposing of GrafPorts

```
OpenPort(aGrafPointer);
```

```
InitPort(aGrafPointer);
```

```
ClosePort(aGrafPointer);
```

Keeping Track of GrafPorts

```
SetPort(aGrafPointer);
```

```
GetPort(&aGrafPointer);
```

Moving a GrafPort's Coordinate System

```
SetOrigin(horiz, vert);
```

Manipulating a GrafPort's clipRect

```
GetClip(region);
```

```
SetClip(region);
```

```
ClipRect(&rect1);
```

Changing a GrafPort's Background Pattern

```
BackPat(aPattern);
```

Drawing Rectangles

```
FrameRect(&rect1);
```

```
PaintRect(&rect1);
```

```
EraseRect(&rect1);
```

```
InvertRect(&rect1);
```

```
FillRect(&rect1, aPattern);
```

Drawing Ovals

```
FrameOval(&rect1);

PaintOval(&rect1);

EraseOval(&rect1);

InvertOval(&rect1);

FillOval(&rect1, aPattern);
```

Drawing Rounded-Corner Rectangles

```
FrameRoundRect(&rect1, ovalWidth, ovalHeight);

PaintRoundRect(&rect1, ovalWidth, ovalHeight);

EraseRoundRect(&rect1, ovalWidth, ovalHeight);

InvertRoundRect(&rect1, ovalWidth, ovalHeight);

FillRoundRect(&rect1, ovalWidth, ovalHeight, aPattern);
```

Defining an Angle

```
PtToAngle(&rect1, &point1, &angle);
```

Drawing Angles

```
FrameArc(&rect1, startAngle, arcAngle);

PaintArc(&rect1, startAngle, arcAngle);

EraseArc(&rect1, startAngle, arcAngle);

InvertArc(&rect1, startAngle, arcAngle);

FillArc(&rect1, startAngle, arcAngle, aPattern);
```

Defining and Disposing Polygons

```
aPolygon = OpenPoly();

ClosePoly();

KillPoly(aPolygon);
```

Moving Polygons

```
OffsetPoly(aPolygon, horiz, vert);
```

Drawing Polygons

```
FramePoly(aPolygon);

PaintPoly(aPolygon);

ErasePoly(aPolygon);

InvertPoly(aPolygon);

FillPoly(aPolygon, aPattern);
```

Defining Regions

```
region = NewRgn();

OpenRgn();

CloseRgn(region);
```

Manipulating Regions

```
OffsetRgn(region, horiz, vert);

InsetRgn(region, horiz, vert);

SectRgn(sourceRgnA, sourceRgnB, destRgn);
```

```
UnionRgn (sourceRgnA, sourceRgnB, destRgn);

DiffRgn (sourceRgnA, sourceRgnB, destRgn);

XorRgn (sourceRgnA, sourceRgnB, destRgn);

TrueOrFalse = PtInRgn (&point1, region);

TrueOrFalse = RectInRgn (&rect1, region);

TrueOrFalse = EqualRgn (sourceRgnA, sourceRgnB);

TrueOrFalse = EmptyRgn (region);
```

Drawing Regions

```
FrameRgn (region);

PaintRgn (region);

EraseRgn (region);

InvertRgn (region);

FillRgn (region);
```

Defining Pictures

```
aPictureHand = OpenPicture (&picFrame);

ClosePicture ();
```

Disposing of Pictures

```
KillPicture (aPictureHand);
```

Drawing Pictures

```
DrawPicture (aPictureHand, &picFrame);
```

Bit-Transfer Operations

```
ScrollRect(&rect1, horiz, vert, region);

CopyBits(srcBits, dstBits, &srcRect, &destRect, mode, region);
```

Cursor Routines

```
InitCursor();

SetCursor(aCursor);

aCursorHand = GetCursor(cursorID);

HideCursor();

ShowCursor();

ObscureCursor();
```

Chapter 6: An Introduction to Memory Management

```
/* declare some variables */
long      howBig, howMuch;
Ptr       aPtr, sourcePtr, destPtr;
Handle    aHandle;
```

Non-Relocatable Blocks

```
aPtr = NewPtr(howBig);

DisposPtr(aPtr);

howBig = GetPtrSize(aPtr);

SetPtrSize(aPtr, howBig);
```

Relocatable Blocks

```
aHandle = NewHandle(howBig);

DisposHandle(aHandle);

howBig = GetHandleSize(aHandle);

SetHandleSize(aHandle, howBig);

HLock(aHandle);

HUnlock(aHandle);

HPurge(aHandle);

HNoPurge(aHandle);

ReallocHandle(aHandle, howBig);
```

Heap Routines

```
howMuch = FreeMem();

howMuch = CompactMem(howBig);

ReservMem(howBig);
```

Miscellaneous Memory Routines

```
BlockMove(sourcePtr, destPtr, howMuch);
```

Chapter 7: Using Multiple Windows

```
/* declare some variables */
long       theRefCon, time;
WindowPtr  theWindow;
Rect       goodRect, badRect;
RgnHandle  goodRgn, badRgn;
PicHandle  thePic;
```

Update Events and the Update Region

```
BeginUpdate(theWindow);

EndUpdate(theWindow);

InvalRect(&badRect);

InvalRgn(badRgn);

ValidRect(&goodRect);

ValidRgn(goodRgn);
```

The Window RefCon

```
SetWRefCon(theWindow, theRefCon);

theRefCon = GetWRefCon(theWindow);
```

Windows and QuickDraw Pictures

```
SetWindowPic(theWindow, thePic);

thePic = GetWindowPic(theWindow);
```

The Double-Click Time

```
time = GetDblTime();
```

Chapter 8: Text Editing with the Toolbox

```
/* declare some variables */
char      c, extend;
int       whichJust, dh, dv;
OSErr     theErr;
long      length, selStart, selEnd;
Point     thePt;
Ptr       textPtr;
```

```
Handle    textHndl;
Rect      destRect, viewRect, rUpdate, box;
TEHandle  theText;
```

Initializing TextEdit

```
TEInit();
```

Creating and Disposing of Edit Records

```
theText = TENew(&destRect, &viewRect);
```

```
TEDispose(theText);
```

The Text of an Edit Record

```
TESetText(text, length, theText);
```

```
textHndl = TEGetText(theText);
```

Activating an Edit Record

```
TEActivate(theText);
```

```
TEDeactivate(theText);
```

Blinking the Insertion Point

```
TEIdle(theText);
```

Entering Text from the Keyboard

```
TEKey(c, theText);
```

Editing Routines

```
TECut(theText);
```

```
TECopy(theText);

TEPaste(theText);

TEDelete(theText);

TEInsert(textPtr, length, theText);
```

Responding to Mouse-Down Events

```
TEClick(&thePt, extend, theText);
```

Changing the Selection Range

```
TESetSelect(selStart, selEnd, theText);
```

Redrawing the Text

```
TEUpdate(&rUpdate, theText);

TECalText(theText);

TESetJust(whichJust, theText);
```

Scrolling an Edit Record

```
TEScroll(dh, dv, theText);
```

Drawing Text in Boxes

```
TextBox(textPtr, length, &box, whichJust);
```

The TextEdit Scrap Routines

```
theErr = TEToScrap();

theErr = TEFromScrap();
```

```
textHndl = TEScrapHandle();

length = TEGetScrapLen();

TESetScrapLen(length);
```

Chapter 10: Controls

```
/* declare some variables */
char           visible;
int            value, min, max, procID, controlID, hiliteState;
int            partcode, horiz, vert, theValue;
long           refCon, refConData;
Point          thePoint, startPoint;
Rect           boundsRect;
Str255         *title;
ProcPtr        actionProc;
WindowPtr      theWindow;
ControlHandle  aControlHand, theControl, whichControl;
```

Defining and Disposing of Controls

```
aControlHand = NewControl(theWindow, &boundsRect, title, visible,
                          value, min, max, procID, refCon);

aControlHand = GetNewControl(controlID, theWindow);

DisposeControl(theControl);

KillControls(theWindow);
```

Displaying and Determining the Appearance of Controls

```
SetCTitle(theControl, title);

GetCTitle(theControl, title);

HideControl(theControl);
```

```
ShowControl(theControl);

DrawControls(theWindow);

HiliteControl(theControl, hiliteState);
```

Detecting and Handling Mouse-Downs in Controls

```
partcode = FindControl(thePoint, theWindow, &whichControl);

partcode = TrackControl(theControl, startPoint, actionProc);
```

Moving and Sizing Controls

```
MoveControl(theControl, horiz, vert);

SizeControl(theControl, horiz, vert);
```

Setting Control Values

```
theValue = GetCtlValue(theControl);

SetCtlValue(theControl, theValue);

theValue = GetCtlMin(theControl);

theValue = GetCtlMax(theControl);

SetCtlMin(theControl, theValue);

SetCtlMax(theControl, theValue);
```

Miscellaneous Routines

```
SetCRefCon(theControl, refConData);

refConData = GetCRefCon(theControl);
```

Chapter 11: Alerts and Dialogs

```
/* declare some variables */
char          visible, goAwayFlag, TrueOrFalse;
int           procID, dialogID, itemHit, alertID, itemNo, type;
int           startSel, endSel;
long          refCon;
Rect          boundsRect, box;
Str255        *title, *theText, *param0;
Str255        *param1, *param2, *param3;
WindowRecord  dStorage;
Handle        items, item;
DialogPtr     theDialog, aDialogPtr;
WindowPtr     behind;
ProcPtr       restartProc, soundProc, filterProc;
```

Initialization

```
InitDialogs(restartProc);

ErrorSound(soundProc);
```

Creating and Disposing of Dialogs

```
aDialogPtr = NewDialog(&dStorage, &boundsRect, title, visible,
                       procID, behind, goAwayFlag, refCon,
                       items);

aDialogPtr = GetNewDialog(dialogID, &dStorage, behind);

CloseDialog(aDialogPtr);

DisposDialog(aDialogPtr);

CouldDialog(dialogID);

FreeDialog(dialogID);
```

Responding to Dialog Events

```
ModalDialog(filterProc, &itemHit);
```

```
TrueOrFalse = IsDialogEvent(&theEvent);

TrueOrFalse = DialogSelect(&theEvent, &theDialog, &itemHit);

DrawDialog(theDialog);
```

Invoking Alerts

```
itemHit = Alert(alertID, filterProc);

itemHit = StopAlert(alertID, filterProc);

itemHit = NoteAlert(alertID, filterProc);

itemHit = CautionAlert(alertID, filterProc);
```

Locking and Unlocking Alert Resources in Memory

```
CouldAlert(alertID);

FreeAlert(alertID);
```

Manipulating Items in Alerts and Dialogs

```
GetDItem(theDialog, itemNo, &type, &item, &box);

SetDItem(theDialog, itemNo, type, item, &box);

GetIText(item, theText);

SetIText(item, theText);

SelIText(theDialog, itemNo, startSel, endSel);

ParamText(param0, param1, param2, param3);
```

Chapter 12: The Macintosh File System

```
/* declare some variables */
Point         loc;
Str255        defaultName, promptStr;
ProcPtr       FilterGlue;
int           numTypes;
SFTypeList    typeList;
ProcPtr       dlgHook;
SFReply       reply;

char          asynch;
OSErr         anErr;
IOParam       anIOParam;
FileParam     anFParam;
VolumeParam   aVParam;
```

The Standard File Package

```
SFGetFile(loc, &PromptStr, FilterGlue, numTypes, &typeList,
        dlgHook, &reply);

SFPutFile(loc, &PromptStr, &defaultName, dlgHook, &reply);
```

Emptying the I/O Queue

```
InitQueue();
```

I/O Calls

```
anErr = PBCreate(&anIOParam, asynch);

anErr = PBOpen(&anIOParam, asynch);

anErr = PBOpenRF(&anIOParam, asynch);

anErr = PBClose(&anIOParam, asynch);

anErr = PBRead(&anIOParam, asynch);

anErr = PBWrite(&anIOParam, asynch);
```

```
anErr = PBGetEOF(&anIOParam, asynch);

anErr = PBSetEOF(&anIOParam, asynch);

anErr = PBAllocate(&anIOParam, asynch);

anErr = PBFlshFile(&anIOParam, asynch);

anErr = PBGetFPos(&anIOParam, asynch);

anErr = PBSetFPos(&anIOParam, asynch);
```

File Routines

```
anErr = PBDelete(&anIOParam, asynch);

anErr = PBRename(&anIOParam, asynch);

anErr = PBSetFLock(&anIOParam, asynch);

anErr = PBRstFLock(&anIOParam, asynch);

anErr = PBSetFVers(&anIOParam, asynch);

anErr = PBGetFInfo(&anFPram, asynch);

anErr = PBSetFInfo (&anFParam, asynch);
```

Volume Routines

```
anErr = PBGetVolInfo(&aVParam, asynch);

anErr = PBGetVol(&anIOParam, asynch);

anErr = PBSetVol(&anIOParam, asynch);

anErr = PBEject(&anIOParam, asynch);

anErr = PBFlshVol(&anIOParam, asynch);

anErr = PBOffLine(&anIOParam, asynch);
```

```
anErr = PBMountVol(&anIOParam);

anErr = PBUnmountVol(&anIOParam);
```

Chapter 13: The Finishing Touches

```
/* declare some variables */
char            aFlag;
int             refNum, editCmd, item, iconNumber;
long            menuResult;
Str255          theName;
WindowPtr       theWindow;
EventRecord     theEvent;
MenuHandle      theMenu;
```

Opening and Closing Desk Accessories

```
refNum = OpenDeskAcc(&theName);

CloseDeskAcc(refNum);
```

Desk Accessories and Events

```
SystemTask();

SystemClick(&theEvent ,theWindow);

aFlag = SystemEvent(&theEvent);

SystemMenu(menuResult);

aFlag = SystemEdit(editCmd);
```

Icons in Menus

```
SetItemIcon(theMenu, item, iconNumber);
```

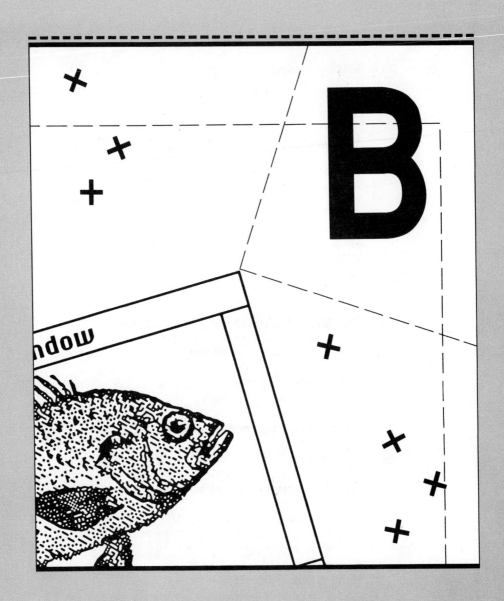

Error Codes and Reserved Resource Types

The following is a list of the Macintosh Operating System Error Codes and Reserved Resource Types.

Macintosh Operating System Error Codes

Null Error

noErr	=	0	no Error

General System Errors (Vertical Retrace Mgr, Queuing, Etc.)

qErr	=	-1	queue element not found during deletion
vTypErr	=	-2	invalid queue element
corErr	=	-3	core routine number out of range
unimpErr	=	-4	unimplemented core routine

I/O System Error Codes

controlErr	=	-17	driver can't respond to the Control call
statusErr	=	-18	driver can't respond to the Status call
readErr	=	-19	driver can't respond to the Read call
writErr	=	-20	driver can't respond to the Write call
badUnitErr	=	-21	reference number doesn't match unit table
unitEmptyErr	=	-22	Reference number specifies NIL handle in unit table
openErr	=	-23	driver can't respond to the Open call
closErr	=	-24	driver can't respond to the Close call
dRemoveErr	=	-25	tried to remove an open driver
dInstErr	=	-26	DrvrInstall couldn't find driver in resources
abortErr	=	-27	I/O call aborted by KillIO
notOpenErr	=	-28	Couldn't rd/wr/ctl/sts because driver not opened

File System Error Codes

dirFulErr	=	-33	file directory full
dskFulErr	=	-34	all allocation blocks on the disk are full
nsvErr	=	-35	no such volume
ioErr	=	-36	disk I/O error

bdNamErr	=	-37	bad file or volume name (zero length?)
fnOpnErr	=	-38	file not currently open
eofErr	=	-39	logical EOF reached during a read operation
posErr	=	-40	tried to position mark before start of file (r/w)
mFulErr	=	-41	system heap is full
tmfoErr	=	-42	too many files open (12 maximum)
fnfErr	=	-43	file not found
wPrErr	=	-44	diskette is write protected (hardware)
fLckdErr	=	-45	file is locked (one of the File System flags)
vLckdErr	=	-46	volume is locked in software
fBsyErr	=	-47	file is busy (one of the File System flags)
dupFNErr	=	-48	a file with the specified name already exists
opWrErr	=	-49	file already open with write permission
paramErr	=	-50	error in user parameter list: bad volume and no default
rfNumErr	=	-51	reference number specifies non-existent access path
gfpErr	=	-52	error during GetFPos
volOffLinErr	=	-53	volume not on-line (was Ejected?)
permErr	=	-54	read/write permission doesn't allow writing
volOnLinErr	=	-55	drive volume already on-line at MountVol
nsDrvErr	=	-56	no such drive number, not in drive queue

noMacDskErr	=	-57	not a Mac diskette, wrong or bad directoryfile format
extFSErr	=	-58	volume in question belongs to an external file system
fsRnErr	=	-59	problem occurred during rename
badMDBErr	=	-60	bad master directory block, volume must be reinitialized
wrPermErr	=	-61	read/write or open permission does not allow writing
lastDskErr	=	-64	last of the range of low-level disk errors
dirNFErr	=	-120	directory not found
tmwdoErr	=	-121	too many working directories open
badMovErr	=	-122	attempted to move into offspring
wrgVolTypErr	=	-123	attempt to do hierarchical operation on nonhierarchical volume
fsDSIntErr	=	-127	internal file system error

Disk Driver, Serial Ports, & Clock Error Codes

noDriveErr	=	-64	drive not installed
noNybErr	=	-66	couldn't find 5 nybbles in 200 tries
noAdrMkErr	=	-67	couldn't find valid addr mark
dataVerErr	=	-68	read verify compare failed
badCkSmErr	=	-69	addr mark checksum didn't check
badBtSlpErr	=	-70	bad addr mark bit slip nibbles
noDtaMkErr	=	-71	couldn't find a data mark header
badDCkSum	=	-72	bad data mark checksum
badDBtSlp	=	-73	bad data mark bit slip nibbles

wrUnderRun	=	-74	write underrun occurred
cantStepErr	=	-75	step handshake failed
tk0BadErr	=	-76	track 0 detect doesn't change
initIWMErr	=	-77	unable to initialize IWM
twoSideErr	=	-78	ried to read 2nd side on a 1-sided drive
spdAdjErr	=	-79	unable to correctly adjust disk speed
SeekErr	=	-80	track number wrong on address mark
sectNFErr	=	-81	sector number never found on a track
firstDskErr	=	-84	first of the range of low-level disk errors
clkRdErr	=	-85	unable to read same clock value twice
clkWrErr	=	-86	time written did not verify
pRWrErr	=	-87	parameter RAM written didn't read-verify
pRInitErr	=	-88	InitUtil found the parameter RAM uninitialized
rcvrErr	=	-89	SCC receiver error (framing, parity, OR)
breakRecd	=	-90	Break received (SCC)

Scrap Manager Error Codes

noScrapErr	=	-100	No scrap exists error
noTypeErr	=	-102	No object of that type in scrap

Memory Manager Error Codes

memROZErr	=	-99	operation on a read only zone
memFullErr	=	-108	not enough room in heap zone
nilHandleErr	=	-109	Master Pointer was NIL
memAdrErr	=	-110	specified address is odd or out of range
memWZErr	=	-111	attempt to operate on a free block
memPurErr	=	-112	trying to purge a locked or non-purgeable block
memAZErr	=	-113	address in zone check failed
memPCErr	=	-114	pointer check failed
memBCErr	=	-115	block check failed
memSCErr	=	-116	size check failed

Resource Manager Error Codes (other than I/O errors)

resNotFound	=	-192	Resource not found
resFNotFound	=	-193	Resource file not found
addResFailed	=	-194	AddResource failed
addRefFailed	=	-195	AddReference failed
rmvResFailed	=	-196	RmveResource failed
rmvRefFailed	=	-197	RmveReference failed
resAttrErr	=	-198	Attribute inconsistent with operation
mapReadErr	=	-199	Map inconsistent with operation

System Startup Alerts

=	-10	MacsBug installed

=	-11	Disassembler installed
=	-12	RAM-based Operating System installed
=	40	"Welcome to Macintosh" box
=	42	Can't mount system startup

volume: Couldn't mount disk in internal drive or couldn't read system resource file into memory

=	43	"Warning—this startup disk is not usable" box

"Desperate Situation" Alerts

dsBusErr	=	1	Bus Error: Never happens on a Macintosh
dsAddressErr	=	2	Address Error: Word or long-word reference made to an odd address
dsIllInstErr	=	3	Illegal 68000 instruction
dsZeroDivErr	=	4	Zero Divide: DIVS or DIVU instruction with a divisor of 0 was executed
dsChkErr	=	5	Check Exception: CHK instruction was executed and failed
dsOvflowErr	=	6	TrapV Exception: TRAPV instruction was executed and failed
dsPrivErr	=	7	Privilege Violation: Perhaps an erroneous RTE instruction was executed
dsTraceErr	=	8	Trace Exception: The trace bit in the staus register is set
dsLineAErr	=	9	Line 1010 Exception: The 1010 trap dispatcher is broken

dsLineFErr	=	10	Line 1111 Exception: Usually a breakpoint
dsMiscErr	=	11	Miscellaneous Exception: All other 68000 exceptions
dsCoreErr	=	12	Unimplemented Core routine: An unimplemented trap number was encountered
dsIrqErr	=	13	Spurious Interrupt: usually occurs with level 4, 5, 6, or 7 interrupts
dsIOCoreErr	=	14	I/O System Error
dsLoadErr	=	15	Segment Loader Error: A GetResource call to read a segment into memory failed
dsFPErr	=	16	Floating Point Error: The halt bit in the floating-point environment word was set
dsNoPackErr	=	17	Can't load package 0
dsNoPk1	=	18	Can't load package 1
dsNoPk2	=	19	Can't load package 2
dsNoPk3	=	20	Can't load package 3
dsNoPk4	=	21	Can't load package 4
dsNoPk5	=	22	Can't load package 5
dsNoPk6	=	23	Can't load package 6
dsNoPk7	=	24	Can't load package 7
dsMemFullErr	=	25	Out of memory
dsBadLaunch	=	26	Segment Loader Error: usually indicates a nonexecutable file
dsFSErr	=	27	File Map trashed: Bad logical block number is found
dsStkNHeap	=	28	Stack Overflow error: The stack and heap have collided
dsReinsert	=	30	"Please insert the disk:": File Manager alert

dsNotThe1	=	31	This is not the correct disk
memTrbBase	=	32	Memory Manager failed
neg2cbFreeErr	=	33	2cbFree is negative
	=	41	The file named "Finder" can't be found on the disk
menuPrgErr	=	84	A menu was purged
	=	100	Couldn't read the system resource file into memory
	=	32767	System Error

Reserved System Resource Types

'ALRT'	Alert Template
'ADBS'	Apple desktop bus service routine
'BNDL'	Bundle
'CACH'	RAM cache code
'CDEF'	Control Definition
'CNTL'	Control Template
'CODE'	Application Code Segment
'CURS'	Cursor
'DITL'	Dialog item list for alerts and dialogs
'DLOG'	Dialog Template
'DRVR'	Device Driver (desk accessories, printer drivers, etc.)
'DSAT'	System startup alert table
'FCMT'	"Get Info" Comment—used by the Finder
'FKEY'	Command-Shift-number key routine
'FMTR'	3 ½ inch disk formatting code

'FOBJ'	Folder Names—used by the Desk-Top File
'FOND'	Font family record
'FONT'	Font
'FREF'	File Reference
'FRSV'	Font reserved for system use
'FWID'	Font widths
'ICN#'	Icon list
'ICON'	Icon
'INIT'	Initialization Resource
'INTL'	International Resource
'INT#'	List of integers owned by Find File
'KCAP'	Physical layout of keyboard
'KCHR'	ASCII mapping
'KMAP'	Keyboard mapping
'KSWP'	Keyboard script table
'LDEF'	List definition procedure
'MACS'	Mac Software Creator
'MBAR'	Menu Bar
'MDEF'	Menu Definition
'MENU'	Menu
'MMAP'	Mouse tracking code
'MINI'	MiniFinder Creator
'NBPC'	Name Binding Protocol
'NFNT'	128K ROM font
'PACK'	Package
'PAPA'	Current selection of the Choose Printer Desk Accessory
'PAT '	Pattern (the space is required)
'PAT#'	Pattern List
'PDEF'	Printer Definition
'PICT'	Picture

'PREC'	Print Record
'PRER'	Device type for Chooser
'PRES'	Device type for Chooser
'PTCH'	ROM patch code
'RDEV'	Device type for Chooser
'ROvr'	Code for overriding ROM resources
'ROv#'	List of ROM resources to override
'SERD'	Serial Driver
'STR '	String (the space is required)
'STR#'	String List
'WDEF'	Window Definition
'WIND'	Window

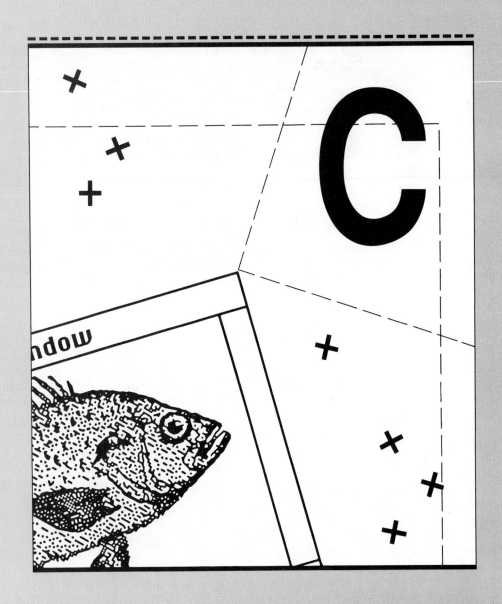

ASCII Chart of the
Macintosh System Font

This appendix contains an ASCII chart of the system font (Chicago). The first four characters are exclusive to the system font and are often used in creating menus. The chart was from a program written by Dave Richey.

The characters in $00, $09, $0d, $20, $7f, and $ca denote the effect of the ASCII code, rather than illustrating what is printed by it.

ASCII Chart of the Macintosh System Font

	0	1	2	3	4	5	6	7	8	9	a	b	c	d	e	f
0	NUL	□	Space	0	@	P	`	p	Ä	ê	†	∞	¿	–	□	□
1	□	⌘	!	1	A	Q	a	q	Â	ë	°	±	¡	—	□	□
2	□	✓	"	2	B	R	b	r	Ç	í	¢	≤	¬	"	□	□
3	□	◆	#	3	C	S	c	s	É	ì	£	≥	√	"	□	□
4	□		$	4	D	T	d	t	Ñ	î	§	¥	ƒ	'	□	□
5	□	□	%	5	E	U	e	u	Ö	ï	•	µ	≠	'	□	□
6	□	□	&	6	F	V	f	v	Ü	ñ	¶	∂	Δ	÷	□	□
7	□	□	'	7	G	W	g	w	á	ó	ß	Σ	«	◇	□	□
8	□	□	(	8	H	X	h	x	à	ò	®	∏	»	ÿ	□	□
9	TAB	□	)	9	I	Y	i	y	â	ô	©	π	...	□	□	□
a	□	□	*	:	J	Z	j	z	ä	ö	™	∫	non-break space	□	□	□
b	□	□	+	;	K	[	k	{	ã	õ	´	ª	À	□	□	□
c	□	□	,	<	L	\	l	|	å	ú	¨	º	Ã	□	□	□
d	CR	□	-	=	M	]	m	}	ç	ù	≠	Ω	Õ	□	□	□
e	□	□	.	>	N	^	n	~	é	û	Æ	æ	Œ	□	□	□
f	□	□	/	?	O	_	o	DEL	è	ü	Ø	ø	œ	□	□	□

Index

Selections from The SYBEX Library

LANGUAGES

Mastering Turbo Pascal 5
Douglas Hergert
595pp. Ref. 529-8

This in-depth treatment of Turbo Pascal Versions 4 and 5 offers separate sections on the Turbo environment, the new debugger, the extensive capabilities of the language itself, and special techniques for graphics, date arithmetic, and recursion. Assumes some programming knowledge.

Advanced Techniques in Turbo Pascal
Charles C. Edwards
309pp. Ref. 350-3

This collection of system-oriented techniques and sample programs shows how to make the most of IBM PC capabilities using Turbo Pascal. Topics include screens, windows, directory management, the mouse interface, and communications.

Turbo BASIC Instant Reference SYBEX Prompter Series
Douglas Hergert
393pp. Ref. 485-2

This quick reference for programmers offers concise, alphabetical entries on every command--statement, metastatement, function, and operation--in the Turbo BASIC language with descriptions, syntax, and examples cross-referenced to related commands.

Introduction to Turbo BASIC
Douglas Hergert
523pp. Ref. 441-0

A complete tutorial and guide to this now highly professional language: Turbo BASIC, including important Turbo extras such as parameter passing, structured loops, long integers, recursion, and 8087 compatibility for high-speed numerical operation.

Advanced Techniques in Turbo Prolog
Carl Townsend
398pp. Ref. 428-3

A goldmine of techniques and predicates for control procedures, string operations, list processing, database operations, BIOS-level support, program development, expert systems, natural language processing, and much more.

Introduction to Turbo Prolog
Carl Townsend
315pp. Ref. 359-7

This comprehensive tutorial includes sample applications for expert systems, natural language interfaces, and simulation. Covers every aspect of Prolog: facts, objects and predicates, rules, recursion, databases, and much more.

Turbo Pascal Toolbox (Second Edition)
Frank Dutton
425pp. Ref. 602-2

This collection of tested, efficient Turbo Pascal building blocks gives a boost to intermediate-level programmers, while teaching effective programming by example. Topics include accessing DOS, menus, bit maps, screen handling, and much more.

Introduction to Pascal: Including Turbo Pascal (Second Edition)
Rodnay Zaks
464pp. Ref. 533-6

This best-selling tutorial builds complete mastery of Pascal--from basic structured programming concepts, to advanced I/O, data structures, file operations, sets, pointers and lists, and more. Both ISO Standard and Turbo Pascal.

Introduction to Pascal
(Including UCSD Pascal)
Rodnay Zaks

420pp. Ref. 066-0

This edition of our best-selling tutorial on Pascal programming gives special attention to the UCSD Pascal implementation for small computers. Covers everything from basic concepts to advanced data structures and more.

Celestial BASIC: Astronomy on Your Computer
Eric Burgess

300pp. Ref. 087-3

A complete home planetarium. This collection of BASIC programs for astronomical calculations enables armchair astronomers to observe and identify on screen the configurations and motions of sun, moon, planets and stars.

Mastering Turbo C
Stan Kelly-Bootle

578pp. Ref. 462-3

No prior knowledge of C or structured programming is required for this introductory course on the Turbo C language and development environment by this well-known author. A logical progression of tutorials and useful sample programs build a thorough understanding of Turbo C.

Systems Programming in Turbo C
Michael J. Young

365pp. Ref. 467-4

An introduction to advanced programming with Borland's Turbo C, and a goldmine of ready-made routines for the system programmer's library: DOS and BIOS interfacing, interrupt handling, windows, graphics, expanded memory, UNIX utilities, and more.

Understanding C
Bruce H. Hunter

320pp. Ref. 123-3

A programmer's introduction to C, with special attention to implementations for

microcomputers--both CP/M and MS-DOS. Topics include data types, storage management, pointers, random I/O, function libraries, compilers and more.

Mastering C
Craig Bolon

437pp. Ref. 326-0

This in-depth guide stresses planning, testing, efficiency and portability in C applications. Topics include data types, storage classes, arrays, pointers, data structures, control statements, I/O and the C function library.

Data Handling Utilities
in Microsoft C
Robert A. Radcliffe/Thomas J. Raab

519pp. Ref. 444-5

A C library for commercial programmers, with techniques and utilities for data entry, validation, display and storage. Focuses on creating and manipulating custom logical data types: dates, dollars, phone numbers, much more.

ASSEMBLY LANGUAGE

Programming the 8086/8088
James W. Coffron

311pp. Ref. 120-9

A concise introduction to assembly-language programming for 8086/8088-based systems, including the IBM PC. Topics include architecture, memory organization, the complete instruction set, interrupts, I/O, and IBM PC BIOS routines.

Programming the 80286
C. Vieillefond

487pp. Ref. 277-9

In-depth treatment of assembly-level programming for the IBM PC/AT's 80286 processor. Topics include system architecture, memory management, address modes, multitasking and more; plus a complete reference guide to the instruction set.

Programming the 80386
John H. Crawford/
Patrick P. Geisinger
775pp. Ref. 381-3
A detailed tour of the 80386 for assembly-language programmers. Topics include registers, data types and instruction classes, memory management, protection models, multitasking, interrupts, the numerics coprocessor, and more.

DOS Assembly Language Programming
Alan R. Miller
365pp. Ref. 487-9
This book covers PC-DOS through 3.3 and gives clear explanations of how to assemble, link, and debug 8086, 8088, 80286, and 80386 programs. The example assembly language routines are valuable for students and programmers alike.

Programming the 68000
Steve Williams
539pp. Ref. 133-0
This tutorial introduction to assembly-language programming covers the complete 68000 architecture and instruction set, as well as advanced topics such as interrupts, I/O programming, and interfacing with high-level languages.

Programming the 6809
Rodnay Zaks/William Labiak
362pp. Ref. 078-4
A step-by-step course in assembly-language programming for 6809-based home computers. Covers hardware organization, the instruction set, addressing, I/O, data structures, program development and complete sample applications.

Programming the 6502
Rodnay Zaks
408pp. Ref. 135-7
The best-selling, step-by-step course in assembly-language programming for the 6502 chip used in Apple, Atari and Commodore computers. From basic concepts to architecture, instruction set, addressing, I/O, sample applications and more.

Programming the Z80 (Third Edition)
Rodnay Zaks
624pp. Ref. 069-5
A self-teaching guide to assembly-language programming for the wide range of Z80-based microcomputers. Includes the Z80 architecture and instruction set, addressing, I/O techniques and devices, data structures and sample programs.

Z80 Applications
James W. Coffron
295pp. Ref. 094-6
A handbook for assembly-language programmers on the principles of Z80 hardware operations. Topics include using ROM, static and dynamic RAM, I/O, interrupts, serial communication and several specific LSI peripheral devices.

APPLE/MACINTOSH

Mastering ProDOS
Timothy Rice/Karen Rice
260pp. Ref. 315-5
An in-depth look at the inner workings of ProDOS, for advanced users and programmers--with discussion of system programming techniques, sample programs in BASIC and assembler, and scores of ready-made ProDOS utility routines.

Mastering Adobe Illustrator
David A. Holzgang
330pp. Ref. 463-1
This text provides a complete introduction to Adobe Illustrator, bringing new sophistication to artists using computer-aided graphics and page design technology. Includes a look at PostScript, the page composition language used by Illustrator.

Desktop Publishing with Microsoft WORD On the Macintosh
Tim Erickson/William Finzer
517pp. Ref. 447-X

The authors have woven a murder mystery through the text, using the sample publications as clues. Explanations of page layout, headings, fonts and styles, columnar text, and graphics are interwoven with the mystery theme of this exciting teaching method.

Mastering WordPerfect on the Macintosh
Kay Yarborough Nelson
462pp. Ref. 515-8

The graphics-oriented Macintosh version of WordPerfect is discussed from startup to mastery in this excellent tutorial. Detailed treatment of software features, plus sample layouts and design tips especially for the Mac. Includes Fast Track speed notes.

Understanding HyperCard
Greg Harvey
580pp. Ref. 506-9

The enormous potential of this major software development is clarified and explained in this extensive hands-on tutorial which covers all aspects of the Hyper-Card and HyperText world, using step-by-step discussions, examples, and insights. The best way to construct, fill, and use stacks efficiently is covered in detail.

HyperTalk Instant Reference
Greg Harvey
316pp. Ref. 530-1

For serious HyperCard users, this finger-tip reference offers complete, cross-referenced summaries of HyperTalk commands, functions, properties, and constants. Examples of usage and an introduction to Scripting are provided.

Mastering AppleWorks (Second Edition)
Elna Tymes
479pp. Ref. 398-8

New chapters on business applications, data sharing DIF and Applesoft BASIC make this practical, in-depth tutorial even better. Full details on AppleWorks desktop, word processing, spreadsheet and database functions.

AppleWorks Tips and Techniques (Second Edition)
Robert Ericson
462pp. Ref. 480-1

An indispensible collection of timesaving techniques, practical solutions, and tips on undocumented problems for every AppleWorks user. This expanded new edition covers all versions through 2.0, and includes in-depth treatment of macros.

The ABC's of Excel on the Macintosh
Douglas Hergert
314pp. Ref. 562-X

This title is written for users who want a quick way to get started with this highly-acclaimed spreadsheet program. The ABC's offers a rich collection of hands-on examples and step-by-step instructions for working with worksheets, charts, databases, and macros. Covers Excel through Version 1.5.

Mastering Excel on the Macintosh (Second Edition)
Carl Townsend
607pp. Ref. 439-9

A new edition of our popular hands-on guide to using Excel's extensive worksheet, database, and graphics capabilities. With in-depth coverage of special features and techniques, sample applications, and detailed treatment of macros.

Programming the Macintosh in Assembly Language
Steve Williams
779pp. Ref. 263-9

A comprehensive tutorial and reference covering assembly-language basics, the 68000 architecture and instruction set, the Macintosh Toolbox, linking with high-level languages and more; plus an extensive macro library and sample programs.

Programming the Macintosh in C
Bryan J. Cummings/Lawrence J. Pollack
294pp. Ref. 328-7

A comprehensive introduction to C programming, especially for Macintosh users. Covers the design philosophy and special advantages of C, as well as every feature of the language. With extensive reference material.

COMMUNICATIONS

Mastering Crosstalk XVI
Peter W. Gofton
187pp. Ref. 388-0

Recoup the cost of this book in a matter of hours with ready-made routines that speed up and automate your on-line database sessions. Tutorials cover every aspect of installing, running and customizing Crosstalk XVI.

HARDWARE

The RS-232 Solution
Joe Campbell
194pp. Ref. 140-3

A complete how-to guide to trouble-free RS-232-C interfacing from scratch. In-depth coverage of concepts, techniques and testing devices, and case studies deriving cables for a variety of common computers, printers and modems.

Mastering Serial Communications
Peter W. Gofton
289pp. Ref. 180-2

The software side of communications, with details on the IBM PC's serial programming, the XMODEM and Kermit protocols, non-ASCII data transfer, interrupt-level programming and more.

Sample programs in C, assembly language and BASIC.

Microprocessor Interfacing Techniques (Third Edition)
Austin Lesea/Rodnay Zaks
456pp. Ref. 029-6

This handbook is for engineers and hobbyists alike, covering every aspect of interfacing microprocessors with peripheral devices. Topics include assembling a CPU, basic I/O, analog circuitry, and bus standards.

From Chips to Systems: An Introduction to Microcomputers (Second Edition)
Rodnay Zaks/Alexander Wolfe
580pp. Ref. 377-5

The best-selling introduction to microcomputer hardware--now fully updated, revised, and illustrated. Such recent advances as 32-bit processors and RISC architecture are introduced and explained for the first time in a beginning text.

Mastering Digital Device Control
William G. Houghton
366pp. Ref. 346-5

Complete principles of system design using single-chip microcontrollers, with numerous examples. Topics include expanding memory and I/O, interfacing with multi-chip CPUs, clocks, display devices, analog measurements, and much more.

HOME COMPUTERS

Amiga Programmer's Handbook, Volume I (Second Edition)
Eugene P. Mortimore
624pp. Ref. 367-8

The complete reference for Amiga graphics programming. System commands and function calls are presented in detail, organized by funcitonal class: Exec, Graphics, Animation, Layers, Intuition and the Workbench. Includes AmigaDOS version 1.2.

Amiga Programmer's Handbook, Volume II
Eugene P. Mortimore
365pp. Ref. 384-8
In-depth discussion of Amiga device I/O programming--including programming with sound and speech--with complete details on the twelve Amiga devices and their associated commands and function calls. Inclues AmigaDOS version 1.2.

Programmer's Guide to the Amiga
Robert A. Peck
352pp. Ref. 310-4
A programmer's hands-on tour through the Amiga system--AmigaDOS, Exec, Graphics, Intuition, Devices, Sound, Animation, and more--packed with in-depth information and sample programs (in Amiga C) showing proper use of system routines.

OTHER OPERATING SYSTEMS AND ENVIRONMENTS

Essential OS/2
Judd Robbins
367pp. Ref. 478-X
This introduction to OS/2 for new and prospective users offers clear explanations of multitasking, details key OS/2 commands and functions, and updates current DOS users to the new OS/2 world. Details are also given for users to run existing DOS programs under OS/2.

Programmer's Guide to OS/2
Michael J. Young
625pp. Ref. 464-X
This concise introduction gives a complete overview of program development

under OS/2, with careful attention to new tools and features. Topics include MS-DOS compatibility, device drivers, services, graphics, windows, the LAN manager, and more.

Programmer's Guide to GEM
Phillip Balma/William Fitler
504pp. Ref. 297-3
GEM programming from the ground up, including the Resource Construction Set, ICON Editor, and Virtual Device Interface. Build a complete graphics application with objects, events, menus, windows, alerts and dialogs.

Understanding Hard Disk Management
Jonathan Kamin
500pp. Ref. 561-1
Put your work, your office or your entire business literally at your fingertips, in a customized, automated MS-DOS work environment. Topics include RAM disks, extended and expanded memory, and more.

Programmer's Guide to Windows (Second Edition)
David Durant/Geta Carlson/Paul Yao
704pp. Ref. 496-8
The first edition of this programmer's guide was hailed as a classic. This new edition covers Windows 2 and Windows/386 in depth. Special emphasis is given to over fifty new routines to the Windows interface, and to preparation for OS/2 Presentation Manager compatibility.

Graphics Programming Under Windows
Brian Myers/Chris Doner
646pp. Ref. 448-8
Straightforward discussion, abundant examples, and a concise reference guide to graphics commands make this book a must for Windows programmers. Topics range from how Windows works to programming for business, animation, CAD, and desktop publishing. For Version 2.

An authoritative guide to PC-DOS, including version 3.2. Designed to make experts out of beginners, it explores everything from disk management to batch file programming. Includes an 85-page command summary.

The IBM PC-DOS Handbook
(Third Edition)
Richard Allen King
359pp. Ref. 512-3

A guide to the inner workings of PC-DOS 3.2, for intermediate to advanced users and programmers of the IBM PC series. Topics include disk, screen and port control, batch files, networks, compatibility, and more.

DOS Instant Reference
SYBEX Prompter Series
Greg Harvey/Kay Yarborough Nelson
220pp. Ref. 477-1; 4 3/4x8

A complete fingertip reference for fast, easy on-line help:command summaries, syntax, usage and error messages. Organized by function--system commands, file commands, disk management, directories, batch files, I/O, networking, programming, and more.

SPREADSHEETS AND INTEGRATED SOFTWARE

The ABC's of 1-2-3
(Second Edition)
Chris Gilbert/Laurie Williams
245pp. Ref. 355-4

Online Today recommends it as "an easy and comfortable way to get started with the program." An essential tutorial for novices, it will remain on your desk as a valuable source of ongoing reference and support. For Release 2.

Mastering 1-2-3
(Second Edition)
Carolyn Jorgensen
702pp. Ref. 528-X

Get the most from 1-2-3 Release 2 with this step-by-step guide emphasizing advanced features and practical uses. Topics include data sharing, macros, spreadsheet security, expanded memory, and graphics enhancements.

Lotus 1-2-3 Desktop Companion
(SYBEX Ready Reference Series)
Greg Harvey
976pp. Ref. 501-8

A full-time consultant, right on your desk. Hundreds of self-contained entries cover every 1-2-3 feature, organized by topic, indexed and cross-referenced, and supplemented by tips, macros and working examples. For Release 2.

Advanced Techniques
in Lotus 1-2-3
Peter Antoniak/E. Michael Lunsford
367pp. Ref. 556-5

This guide for experienced users focuses on advanced functions, and techniques for designing menu-driven applications using macros and the Release 2 command language. Interfacing techniques and add-on products are also considered.

Lotus 1-2-3 Tips and Tricks
Gene Weisskopf
396pp. Ref. 454-2

A rare collection of timesavers and tricks for longtime Lotus users. Topics include macros, range names, spreadsheet design, hardware considerations, DOS operations, efficient data analysis, printing, data interchange, applications development, and more.

Lotus 1-2-3 Instant Reference
SYBEX Prompter Series
Greg Harvey/Kay Yarborough Nelson
296pp. Ref. 475-5; 4 3/4x8

Organized information at a glance. When

DOS

The ABC's of DOS 4
Alan R. Miller
250pp. Ref. 583-2

This step-by-step introduction to using DOS 4 is written especially for beginners. Filled with simple examples, *The ABC's of DOS 4* covers the basics of hardware, software, disks, the system editor EDLIN, DOS commands, and more.

ABC's of MS-DOS
(Second Edition)
Alan R. Miller
233pp. Ref. 493-3

This handy guide to MS-DOS is all many PC users need to manage their computer files, organize floppy and hard disks, use EDLIN, and keep their computers organized. Additional information is given about utilities like Sidekick, and there is a DOS command and program summary. The second edition is fully updated for Version 3.3.

Mastering DOS
(Second Edition)
Judd Robbins
700pp. Ref. 555-7

"The most useful DOS book." This seven-part, in-depth tutorial addresses the needs of users at all levels. Topics range from running applications, to managing files and directories, configuring the system, batch file programming, and techniques for system developers.

MS-DOS Handbook
(Third Edition)
Richard Allen King
362pp. Ref. 492-5

This classic has been fully expanded and revised to include the latest features of MS-DOS Version 3.3. Two reference books in one, this title has separate sections for programmer and user. Multi-DOS partitons, 3 1/2disk format, batch file call and return feature, and comprehensive coverage of MS-DOS commands are included.

MS-DOS Power User's Guide, Volume I
(Second Edition)
Jonathan Kamin
482pp. Ref. 473-9

A fully revised, expanded edition of our best-selling guide to high-performance DOS techniques and utilities--with details on Version 3.3. Configuration, I/O, directory structures, hard disks, RAM disks, batch file programming, the ANSI.SYS device driver, more.

MS-DOS Power User's Guide, Volume II
Martin Waterhouse/Jonathan Kamin
418pp, Ref. 411-9

A second volume of high-performance techniques and utilities, with expanded coverage of DOS 3.3, and new material on video modes, Token-Ring and PC Network support, micro-mainframe links, extended and expanded memory, multitasking systems, and more.

DOS User's Desktop Companion
Judd Robbins
969 pp. Ref. 505-0 Softcover

This comprehensive reference covers DOS commands, batch files, memory enhancements, printing, communications and more information on optimizing each user's DOS environment. Written with step-by-step instructions and plenty of examples, this volume covers all versions through 3.3.

MS-DOS Advanced Programming
Michael J. Young
490pp. Ref. 578-6

Practical techniques for maximizing performance in MS-DOS software by making best use of system resources. Topics include functions, interrupts, devices, multitasking, memory residency and more, with examples in C and assembler.

Essential PC-DOS
(Second Edition)
**Myril Clement Shaw/
Susan Soltis Shaw**
332pp. Ref. 413-5

you don't have time to hunt through hundreds of pages of manuals, turn here for a quick reminder: the right key sequence, a brief explanation of a command, or the correct syntax for a specialized function.

Mastering Lotus HAL
Mary V. Campbell
342pp. Ref. 422-4
A complete guide to using HAL "natural language" requests to communicate with 1-2-3—for new and experienced users. Covers all the basics, plus advanced HAL features such as worksheet linking and auditing, macro recording, and more.

Mastering Symphony (Fourth Edition)
Douglas Cobb
857pp. Ref. 494-1
Thoroughly revised to cover all aspects of the major upgrade of Symphony Version 2, this Fourth Edition of Doug Cobb's classic is still "the Symphony bible" to this complex but even more powerful package. All the new features are discussed and placed in context with prior versions so that both new and previous users will benefit from Cobb's insights.

The ABC's of Quattro
Alan Simpson/Douglas J. Wolf
286pp. Ref. 560-3
Especially for users new to spreadsheets, this is an introduction to the basic concepts and a guide to instant productivity through editing and using spreadsheet formulas and functions. Includes how to print out graphs and data for presentation. For Quattro 1.1.

Mastering Quattro
Alan Simpson
576pp. Ref. 514-X
This tutorial covers not only all of Quattro's classic spreadsheet features, but also its added capabilities including extended graphing, modifiable menus, and the macro debugging environment. Simpson brings out how to use all of Quattro's new-generation-spreadsheet capabilities.

Mastering Framework II
Douglas Hergert/Jonathan Kamin
509pp. Ref. 390-2
This business-minded tutorial includes a complete introduction to idea processing, "frames," and software integration, along with its comprehensive treatment of word processing, spreadsheet, and database management with Framework.

The ABC's of Excel on the IBM PC
Douglas Hergert
326pp. Ref. 567-0
This book is a brisk and friendly introduction to the most important features of Microsoft Excel for PC's. This beginner's book discusses worksheets, charts, database operations, and macros, all with hands-on examples. Written for all versions through Version 2.

Mastering Excel on the IBM PC
Carl Townsend
628pp. Ref. 403-8
A complete Excel handbook with step-by-step tutorials, sample applications and an extensive reference section. Topics include worksheet fundamentals, formulas and windows, graphics, database techniques, special features, macros and more.

Mastering Enable
Keith D. Bishop
517pp. Ref. 440-2
A comprehensive, practical, hands-on guide to Enable 2.0—integrated word processing, spreadsheet, database management, graphics, and communications—from basic concepts to custom menus, macros and the Enable Procedural Language.

Mastering Q & A (Second Edition)
Greg Harvey
540pp. Ref. 452-6
This hands-on tutorial explores the Q & A Write, File, and Report modules, and the Intelligent Assistant. English-language command processor, macro creation,

interfacing with other software, and more, using practical business examples.

Mastering SuperCalc 4
Greg Harvey
311pp. Ref. 419-4

A guided tour of this spreadsheet, database and graphics package shows how and why it adds up to a powerful business planning tool. Step-by-step lessons and real-life examples cover every aspect of the program.

Understanding Javelin PLUS
John R. Levine
Margaret Levine Young
Jordan M. Young
558pp. Ref. 358-9

This detailed guide to Javelin's latest release includes a concise introduction to business modeling, from profit-and-loss analysis to manufacturing studies. Readers build sample models and produce multiple reports and graphs, to master Javelin's unique features.

DATABASE MANAGEMENT

Mastering Paradox
(Third Edition)
Alan Simpson
663pp. Ref. 490-9

Paradox is given authoritative, comprehensive explanation in Simpson's up-to-date new edition which goes from database basics to command-file programming with PAL. Topics include multiuser networking, the Personal Programmer Application Generator, the Data-Entry Toolkit, and more.

The ABC's of dBASE IV
Robert Cowart
300pp. Ref. 531-X

This superb tutorial introduces beginners to the concept of databases and practical dBASE IV applications featuring the new menu-driven interface, the new report writer, and Query by Example.

Understanding dBASE IV
(Special Edition)
Alan Simpson
880pp. Ref. 509-3

This Special Edition is the best introduction to dBASE IV, written by 1 million-reader-strong dBASE expert Alan Simpson. First it gives basic skills for creating and manipulating efficient databases. Then the author explains how to make reports, manage multiple databases, and build applications. Includes Fast Track speed notes.

dBASE III PLUS Programmer's Reference Guide
(SYBEX Ready Reference Series)
Alan Simpson
1056pp. Ref. 508-5

Programmers will save untold hours and effort using this comprehensive, well-organized dBASE encyclopedia. Complete technical details on commands and functions, plus scores of often-needed algorithms.

The ABC's of dBASE III PLUS
Robert Cowart
264pp. Ref. 379-1

The most efficient way to get beginners up and running with dBASE. Every 'how' and 'why' of database management is demonstrated through tutorials and practical dBASE III PLUS applications.

Mastering dBASE III PLUS:
A Structured Approach
Carl Townsend
342pp. Ref. 372-4

In-depth treatment of structured programming for custom dBASE solutions. An ideal study and reference guide for applications developers, new and experienced users with an interest in efficient programming.

Also:
Mastering dBASE III: A Structured Approach
Carl Townsend
338pp. Ref. 301-5

Understanding dBASE III PLUS
Alan Simpson
415pp. Ref. 349-X
A solid sourcebook of training and ongoing support. Everything from creating a first database to command file programming is presented in working examples, with tips and techniques you won't find anywhere else.

Also:
Understanding dBASE III
Alan Simpson
300pp. Ref. 267-1

Understanding dBASE II
Alan Simpson
260pp. Ref. 147-0

Advanced Techniques in dBASE III PLUS
Alan Simpson
454pp. Ref. 369-4
A full course in database design and structured programming, with routines for inventory control, accounts receivable, system management, and integrated databases.

Simpson's dBASE Tips and Tricks (For dBASE III PLUS)
Alan Simpson
420pp. Ref. 383-X
A unique library of techniques and programs shows how creative use of built-in features can solve all your needs--without expensive add-on products or external languages. Spreadsheet functions, graphics, and much more.

Expert dBASE III PLUS
Judd Robbins/Ken Braly
423pp. Ref. 404-6
Experienced dBASE programmers learn scores of advanced techniques for maximizing performance and efficiency in program design, development and testing, database design, indexing, input and output, using compilers, and much more.

dBASE Instant Reference SYBEX Prompter Series
Alan Simpson
471pp. Ref. 484-4; 4 3/4x8
Comprehensive information at a glance: a brief explanation of syntax and usage for every dBASE command, with step-by-step instructions and exact keystroke sequences. Commands are grouped by function in twenty precise categories.

Understanding R:BASE
Alan Simpson/Karen Watterson
609pp. Ref.503-4
This is the definitive R:BASE tutorial, for use with either OS/2 or DOS. Hands-on lessons cover every aspect of the software, from creating and using a database, to custom systems. Includes Fast Track speed notes.

Also:
Understanding R:BASE 5000
Alan Simpson
413pp. Ref. 302-3

Understanding Oracle
James T. Perry/Joseph G. Lateer
634pp. Ref. 534-4
A comprehensive guide to the Oracle database management system for administrators, users, and applications developers. Covers everything in Version 5 from database basics to multi-user systems, performance, and development tools including SQL*Forms, SQL*Report, and SQL*Calc. Includes Fast Track speed notes.

GENERAL UTILITIES

The ABC's of the IBM PC (Second Edition)
Joan Lasselle/Carol Ramsay
167pp. Ref. 370-8
Hands-on experience—without technical detail—for first-time users. Step-by-step

tutorials show how to use essential commands, handle disks, use applications programs, and harness the PC's special capabilities.

COMPUTER-AIDED DESIGN AND DRAFTING

The ABC's of AutoCAD (Second Edition)
Alan R. Miller
375pp. Ref. 584-0

This brief but effective introduction to AutoCAD quickly gets users drafting and designing with this complex CADD package. The essential operations and capabilities of AutoCAD are neatly detailed, using a proven, step-by-step method that is tailored to the results-oriented beginner.

Mastering AutoCAD (Third Edition)
George Omura
825pp. Ref. 574-3

Now in its third edition, this tutorial guide to computer-aided design and drafting with AutoCAD is perfect for newcomers to CADD, as well as AutoCAD users seeking greater proficiency. An architectural project serves as an example throughout.

Advanced Techniques in AutoCAD (Second Edition)
Robert M. Thomas
425pp. Ref. 593-X

Develop custom applications using screen menus, command macros, and AutoLISP programming--no prior programming experience required. Topics include customizing the AutoCAD environment, advanced data extraction techniques, and much more.

FOR SCIENTISTS AND ENGINEERS

1-2-3 for Scientists and Engineers
William J. Orvis
341pp. Ref. 407-0

Fast, elegant solutions to common problems in science and engineering, using Lotus 1-2-3. Tables and plotting, curve fitting, statistics, derivatives, integrals and differentials, solving systems of equations, and more.

BASIC Programs for Scientists and Engineers
Alan R. Miller
318pp. Ref. 073-3

The algorithms presented in this book are programmed in standard BASIC code which should be usable with almost any implementation of BASIC. Includes statistical calculations, matrix algebra, curve fitting, integration, and more.

Turbo BASIC Programs for Scientists and Engineers
Alan R. Miller
276pp. Ref. 429-1

This practical text develops commonly-needed algorithms for scientific and engineering applications, and programs them in Turbo BASIC. Simultaneous solution, curve fitting, nonlinear equations, numerical integration and more.

Turbo Pascal Programs for Scientists and Engineers
Alan R. Miller
332pp. Ref. 424-0

The author develops commonly-needed algorithms for science and engineering, then programs them in Turbo Pascal. Includes algorithms for statistics, simultaneous solutions, curve fitting, integration, and nonlinear equations.

FORTRAN Programs for Scientists and Engineers (Second Edition)
Alan R. Miller
280pp. Ref. 571-9

In this collection of widely used scientific algorithms--for statistics, vector and matrix operations, curve fitting, and more--the author stresses effective use of little-known and powerful features of FORTRAN.

WORD PROCESSING

The ABC's of WordPerfect 5
Alan R. Neibauer
283pp. Ref. 504-2

This introduction explains the basics of desktop publishing with WordPerfect 5: editing, layout, formatting, printing, sorting, merging, and more. Readers are shown how to use WordPerfect 5's new features to produce great-looking reports.

The ABC's of WordPerfect
Alan R. Neibauer
239pp. Ref. 425-9

This basic introduction to WordPefect consists of short, step-by-step lessons— for new users who want to get going fast. Topics range from simple editing and formatting, to merging, sorting, macros, and more. Includes version 4.2

Mastering WordPerfect 5
Susan Baake Kelly
709pp. Ref. 500-X

The revised and expanded version of this definitive guide is now on WordPerfect 5 and covers wordprocessing and basic desktop publishing. As more than 200,000 readers of the original edition can attest, no tutorial approaches it for clarity and depth of treatment. Sorting, line drawing, and laser printing included.

Mastering WordPerfect
Susan Baake Kelly
435pp. Ref. 332-5

Step-by-step training from startup to mastery, featuring practical uses (form letters, newsletters and more), plus advanced topics such as document security and macro creation, sorting and columnar math. Includes Version 4.2.

Advanced Techniques in WordPerfect 5
Kay Yarborough Nelson
586pp. Ref. 511-5

Now updated for Version 5, this invaluable guide to the advanced features of Word-Perfect provides step-by-step instructions and practical examples covering those specialized techniques which have most perplexed users--indexing, outlining, foreign-language typing, mathematical functions, and more.

WordPerfect Desktop Companion
SYBEX Ready Reference Series
Greg Harvey/Kay Yarbourough Nelson
663pp. Ref. 507-7

This compact encyclopedia offers detailed, cross-referenced entries on every software feature, organized for fast, convenient on-the-job help. Includes self-contained enrichment material with tips, techniques and macros. Special information is included about laser printing using WordPerfect that is not available elsewhere. For Version 4.2.

WordPerfect 5 Desktop Companion
SYBEX Ready Reference Series
Greg Harvey/Kay Yarborough Nelson
1000pp. Ref. 522-0

Desktop publishing features have been added to this compact encyclopedia. This title offers more detailed, cross-referenced entries on every software features including page formatting and layout, laser printing and word processing macros. New users of WordPerfect, and those new to Version 5 and desktop publishing will find this easy to use for on-the-job help. For Version 5.

WordPerfect Tips and Tricks (Third Edition)
Alan R. Neibauer
650pp. Ref. 520-4

This new edition is a real timesaver. For on-the-job guidance and creative new uses, this title covers all versions of Word-Perfect up to and including 5.0—covers streamlining documents, automating with macros, new print enhancements, and more.

WordPerfect 5 Instant Reference
Greg Harvey/Kay Yarborough Nelson
316pp. Ref. 535-2

This pocket-sized reference has all the program commands for the powerful WordPerfect 5 organized alphabetically for quick access. Each command entry has the exact key sequence, any reveal codes, a list of available options, and option-by-option discussions.

WordPerfect Instant Reference SYBEX Prompter Series
Greg Harvey/Kay Yarborough Nelson
254pp. Ref. 476-3

When you don't have time to go digging through the manuals, this fingertip guide offers clear, concise answers: command summaries, correct usage, and exact keystroke sequences for on-the-job tasks. Convenient organization reflects the structure of WordPerfect.

Mastering SAMNA
Ann McFarland Draper
503pp. Ref. 376-7

Word-processing professionals learn not just how, but also when and why to use SAMNA's many powerful features. Master the basics, gain power-user skills, return again and again for reference and expert tips.

The ABC's of Microsoft WORD
Alan R. Neibauer
321pp. Ref. 497-6

Users who want to wordprocess straight-forward documents and print elegant reports without wading through reams of documentation will find all they need to know about MicroSoft WORD in this basic guide. Simple editing, formatting, merging, sorting, macros and style sheets are detailed.

Mastering Microsoft WORD (Third Edition)
Matthew Holtz
638pp. Ref. 524-7

This comprehensive, step-by-step guide includes Version 4.0. Hands-on tutorials treat everything from word processing basics to the fundamentals of desktop publishing, stressing business applications throughout.

Advanced Techinques in Microsoft WORD
Alan R. Neibauer
537pp. Ref. 416-X

The book starts with a brief overview, but the main focus is on practical applications using advanced features. Topics include customization, forms, style sheets, columns, tables, financial documents, graphics and data management.

Mastering DisplayWrite 4
Michael E. McCarthy
447pp. Ref. 510-7

Total training, reference and support for users at all levels--in plain, non-technical language. Novices will be up and running in an hour's time; everyone will gain complete word-processing and document-management skills.

Mastering MultiMate Advantage II
Charles Ackerman
407pp. Ref. 482-8

This comprehensive tutorial covers all the capabilities of MultiMate, and highlights the differences between MultiMate Advantage II and previous versions--in pathway support, sorting, math, DOS access, using dBASE III, and more. With many practical examples, and a chapter on the On-File database.

The Complete Guide to MultiMate
Carol Holcomb Dreger
208pp. Ref. 229-9

This step-by-step tutorial is also an excellent reference guide to MultiMate features and uses. Topics include search/replace, library and merge functions, repagination, document defaults and more.

Advanced Techniques in MultiMate
Chris Gilbert
275pp. Ref. 412-7
A textbook on efficient use of MultiMate for business applications, in a series of self-contained lessons on such topics as multiple columns, high-speed merging, mailing-list printing and Key Procedures.

Introduction to WordStar
Arthur Naiman
208pp. Ref. 134-9
This all time bestseller is an engaging first-time introduction to word processing as well as a complete guide to using WordStar--from basic editing to blocks, global searches, formatting, dot commands, SpellStar and MailMerge.

Mastering Wordstar on the IBM PC (Second Edition)
Arthur Naiman
200pp. Ref. 392-9
A specially revised and expanded introduction to Wordstar with SpellStar and MailMerge. Reviewers call it "clearly written, conveniently organized, generously illustrated and definitely designed from the user's point of view."

Practical WordStar Uses
Julie Anne Arca
303pp. Ref. 107-1
A hands-on guide to WordStar and MailMerge applications, with solutions to comon problems and "recipes" for day-to-day tasks. Formatting, merge-printing and much more; plus a quick-reference command chart and notes on CP/M and PC-DOS.

Practical Techniques in WordStar Release 4
Julie Anne Arca
334pp. Ref. 465-8

A task oriented approach to WordStar Release 4 and the DOS operating system. Special applications are covered in detail with summaries of important commands and step-by-step instructions.

Mastering WordStar Release 4
Greg Harvey
413pp. Ref. 399-6
Practical training and reference for the latest WordStar release--from startup to advanced featues. Experienced users will find new features highlighted and illustrated with hands-on examples. Covers math, macros, laser printers and more.

WordStar Instant Reference
David J. Clark
314pp. Ref. 543-3
This quick reference provides reminders on the use of the editing, formatting, mailmerge, and document processing commands available through WordStar 4 and 5. Operations are organized alphabetically for easy access. The text includes a survey of the menu system and instructions for installing and customizing WordStar.

Understanding WordStar 2000
David Kolodney/Thomas Blackadar
275pp. Ref. 554-9
This engaging, fast-paced series of tutorials covers everything from moving the cursor to print enhancements, format files, key glossaries, windows and MailMerge. With practical examples, and notes for former WordStar users.

Advanced Techniques in WordStar 2000
John Donovan
350pp. Ref. 418-6
This task-oriented guide to Release 2 builds advanced skills by developing practical applications. Tutorials cover everything from simple printing to macro creation and complex merging. With MailList, StarIndex and TelMerge.

DESKTOP PUBLISHING

Mastering Ventura
(Second Edition)
Matthew Holtz
600pp. Ref. 581-6

A complete, step-by-step guide to IBM PC desktop publishing with Xerox Ventura Publisher. Practical examples show how to use style sheets, format pages, cut and paste, enhance layouts, import material from other programs, and more.

Ventura Tips and Techniques
Carl Townsend/Sandy Townsend
424pp. Ref. 559-X

Packed with an experienced Ventura user's tips and tricks, this volume is a time saver and design booster. From crop marks to file management to using special fonts, this book is for serious Ventura users. Covers Ventura 2.

Ventura Instant Reference
Matthew Holtz
320pp. Ref. 544-1

This compact volume offers easy access to the complex details of Ventura modes and options, commands, side-bars, file management, output device configuration, and control. Written for versions through Ventura 2, it also includes standard procedures for project and job control.

Mastering PageMaker
on the IBM PC
(Second Edition)
Antonia Stacy Jolles
400pp. Ref. 521-2

A guide to every aspect of desktop publishing with PageMaker: the vocabulary and basics of page design, layout, graphics and typography, plus instructions for creating finished typeset publications of all kinds.

Mastering Ready, Set, Go!
David A. Kater
482pp. Ref. 536-0

This hands-on introduction to the popular desktop publishing package for the Macintosh allows readers to produce professional-looking reports, brochures, and flyers. Written for Version 4, this title has been endorsed by Letraset, the Ready, Set, Go! software publisher.

Understanding PostScript
Programming
(Second Edition)
David A. Holzgang
472pp. Ref. 566-2

In-depth treatment of PostScript for programmers and advanced users working on custom desktop publishing tasks. Hands-on development of programs for font creation, integrating graphics, printer implementations and more.

SYBEX®

TO JOIN THE SYBEX MAILING LIST OR ORDER BOOKS
PLEASE COMPLETE THIS FORM

NAME _____ COMPANY _____

STREET _____ CITY _____

STATE _____ ZIP _____

☐ PLEASE MAIL ME MORE INFORMATION ABOUT **SYBEX** TITLES

ORDER FORM (There is no obligation to order)

PLEASE SEND ME THE FOLLOWING:

TITLE	QTY	PRICE
_____	___	___
_____	___	___
_____	___	___
_____	___	___

TOTAL BOOK ORDER   ___ $___

CUSTOMER SIGNATURE _____

SHIPPING AND HANDLING PLEASE ADD $2.00 PER BOOK VIA UPS   ___

FOR OVERSEAS SURFACE ADD $5.25 PER BOOK PLUS $4.40 REGISTRATION FEE   ___

FOR OVERSEAS AIRMAIL ADD $18.25 PER BOOK PLUS $4.40 REGISTRATION FEE   ___

CALIFORNIA RESIDENTS PLEASE ADD APPLICABLE SALES TAX   ___

TOTAL AMOUNT PAYABLE   ___

☐ CHECK ENCLOSED   ☐ VISA
☐ MASTERCARD   ☐ AMERICAN EXPRESS

ACCOUNT NUMBER _____

EXPIR. DATE _____   DAYTIME PHONE _____

CHECK AREA OF COMPUTER INTEREST:

☐ BUSINESS SOFTWARE

☐ TECHNICAL PROGRAMMING

☐ OTHER: _____

THE FACTOR THAT WAS MOST IMPORTANT IN YOUR SELECTION:

☐ THE SYBEX NAME

☐ QUALITY

☐ PRICE

☐ EXTRA FEATURES

☐ COMPREHENSIVENESS

☐ CLEAR WRITING

☐ OTHER _____

OTHER COMPUTER TITLES YOU WOULD LIKE TO SEE IN PRINT:

_____

_____

OCCUPATION

☐ PROGRAMMER   ☐ TEACHER

☐ SENIOR EXECUTIVE   ☐ HOMEMAKER

☐ COMPUTER CONSULTANT   ☐ RETIRED

☐ SUPERVISOR   ☐ STUDENT

☐ MIDDLE MANAGEMENT   ☐ OTHER:

☐ ENGINEER/TECHNICAL   _____

☐ CLERICAL/SERVICE

☐ BUSINESS OWNER/SELF EMPLOYED

CHECK YOUR LEVEL OF COMPUTER USE

☐ NEW TO COMPUTERS

☐ INFREQUENT COMPUTER USER

☐ FREQUENT USER OF ONE SOFTWARE

   PACKAGE:

   NAME _____

☐ FREQUENT USER OF MANY SOFTWARE

   PACKAGES

☐ PROFESSIONAL PROGRAMMER

OTHER COMMENTS:

_____

_____

_____

_____

_____

_____

_____

_____

PLEASE FOLD, SEAL, AND MAIL TO SYBEX

SYBEX, INC.
2021 CHALLENGER DR. #100
ALAMEDA, CALIFORNIA USA
        94501

SEAL

SYBEX Computer Books are different.

Here is why . . .

At SYBEX, each book is designed with you in mind. Every manuscript is carefully selected and supervised by our editors, who are themselves computer experts. We publish the best authors, whose technical expertise is matched by an ability to write clearly and to communicate effectively. Programs are thoroughly tested for accuracy by our technical staff. Our computerized production department goes to great lengths to make sure that each book is well-designed.

In the pursuit of timeliness, SYBEX has achieved many publishing firsts. SYBEX was among the first to integrate personal computers used by authors and staff into the publishing process. SYBEX was the first to publish books on the CP/M operating system, microprocessor interfacing techniques, word processing, and many more topics.

Expertise in computers and dedication to the highest quality product have made SYBEX a world leader in computer book publishing. Translated into fourteen languages, SYBEX books have helped millions of people around the world to get the most from their computers. We hope we have helped you, too.

For a complete catalog of our publications:

SYBEX, Inc. 2021 Challenger Drive, #100, Alameda, CA 94501
Tel: (415) 523-8233/(800) 227-2346   Telex: 336311
Fax: (415) 523-2373

Window Manager

Initializations and Allocation

```
void InitWindows();
void GetWMgrPort(GrafPtr *wPort);
WindowPtr NewWindow(Ptr wStorage; Rect
    *boundsRect; Str255 *title; char
    visible; int procID; WindowPtr behind;
    char goAwayFlag; long refCon);
WindowPtr GetNewWindow(int windowID; Ptr
    wStorage; WindowPtr behind);
void CloseWindow(WindowPtr theWindow);
void DisposeWindow(WindowPtr theWindow);
```

Window Display

```
void SetWTitle(WindowPtr theWindow; Str255
    *title);
void GetWTitle(WindowPtr theWindow; Str255
    *title);
void SelectWindow(WindowPtr theWindow);
void HideWindow(WindowPtr theWindow);
void ShowWindow(WindowPtr theWindow);
void ShowHide(WindowPtr theWindow; char
    showFlag);
void HiliteWindow(WindowPtr theWindow; char
    fHilite);
void BringToFront(WindowPtr
    theWindow,behindWindow);
WindowPtr FrontWindow();
void DrawGrowIcon(WindowPtr theWindow);
```

Mouse Location

```
int FindWindow(Point pt; WindowPtr
    *whichWindow);
char TrackGoAway(WindowPtr theWindow;
    Point pt);
```

Window Movement and Sizing

```
void MoveWindow(WindowPtr theWindow; int
    hGlobal,vGlobal);
void DragWindow(WindowPtr theWindow; Point
    startPt; Rect *boundsRect);
long GrowWindow(WindowPtr theWindow; Point
    startPt; Rect *sizeRect);
void SizeWindow(WindowPtr theWindow; int w,h;
    char fUpdate);
```

Update Region Maintenance

```
void InvalRect(Rect *badRect);
void InvalRgn(RgnHandle badRgn);
```

```
void ValidRect(Rect *goodRect);
void ValidRgn(RgnHandle goodRgn);
void BeginUpdate(WindowPtr theWindow);
void EndUpdate(WindowPtr theWindow);
```

Miscellaneous Routines

```
void SetWRefCon(WindowPtr theWindow; long
    data);
long GetWRefCon(WindowPtr theWindow);
void SetWindowPic(WindowPtr theWindow;
    PicHandle pic);
PicHandle GetWindowPic(WindowPtr theWindow);
long PinRect(Rect *theRect; Point thePt);
long DragGrayRgn(RgnHandle rgn; Point
    startPt; Rect limitRect,slopRect; int
    axis; ProcPtr actionProc);
```

Control Manager

Initializations and Allocation

```
ControlHandle NewControl(WindowPtr theWindow;
    Rect *boundsRect; Str255 *title; char
    visible; int value,min,max,procID; long
    refCon);
ControlHandle GetNewControl(int controlID;
    WindowPtr theWindow);
void DisposeControl(ControlHandle theControl);
void KillControls(WindowPtr theWindow);
```

Control Display

```
void SetCTitle(ControlHandle theControl;
    Str255 *title);
void GetCTitle(ControlHandle theControl;
    Str255 *title);
void HideControl(ControlHandle theControl);
void ShowControl(ControlHandle theControl);
void DrawControls(WindowPtr theWindow);
void HiliteControl(ControlHandle theControl;
    int hiliteState);
```

Mouse Location

```
int FindControl(Point thePoint; WindowPtr
    theWindow; ControlHandle *whichControl);
int TrackControl(ControlHandle theControl;
    Point startPt; ProcPtr actionProc);
int TestControl(ControlHandle theControl;
    Point thePoint);
```